Speaking for Buddhas

SPEAKING *for* BUDDHAS

Scriptural Commentary in Indian Buddhism

RICHARD F. NANCE

COLUMBIA UNIVERSITY PRESS *NEW YORK*

Columbia University Press
Publishers Since 1893
New York Chichester, West Sussex

Library of Congress Cataloging-in-Publication Data
Nance, Richard F.
Speaking for Buddhas: scriptural commentary in Indian Buddhism / Richard F. Nance.
p. cm.
Includes bibliographical references and index.
ISBN 978-0-231-15230-3 (cloth: alk. paper)—
ISBN 978-0-231-52667-8 (e-book)
1. Buddhist literature—India—History and criticism. 2. Buddhism—India—History.
I. Title.
BQ1029.I42N36 2011
294.3′85—dc22
2011015986
Casebound editions of Columbia University Press books are printed on permanent and durable acid-free paper.
Printed in the United States of America
c 10 9 8 7 6 5 4 3 2 1

Contents

Acknowledgments

This book has been in preparation for many years. Over the course of writing it, I have received feedback and encouragement from many people. Thanks are due first to my parents, Richard E. Nance and Ann M. Nance, who have been unfailing in their support. At the University of Chicago, I had the good fortune to be taught by a remarkable group of scholars, each of whom contributed in different ways to the work represented here. The members of my dissertation committee—Matthew Kapstein, Paul J. Griffiths, and Sheldon Pollock—provided invaluable guidance on issues both philological and philosophical. While at Chicago, I also learned a great deal from other faculty members inside and outside Swift Hall, among them Yigal Bronner, Steven Collins, James Conant, Arnold Davidson, Wendy Doniger, Franklin Gamwell, Ngawang Jorden, Bruce Lincoln, Leonard Linsky, Shirō Matsumoto, Lawrence McCrea, H. V. N. Rao, and Michael Silverstein. For financial support during my years of graduate study, I am grateful to the University of Chicago Divinity School, the Henry Luce Foundation, and the University of Chicago Committee on Southern Asian Studies. Since 2007, the Department of Religious Studies at Indiana University has provided me with a wonderfully supportive institutional home, and I am indebted to its faculty for a very stimulating—and ongoing—conversation about the ideas developed here. I also wish to thank the faculty of Indiana University's Department of Central Eurasian Studies, most especially Christopher Atwood, Christopher Beckwith, and Elliot Sperling.

For comments on earlier drafts of, or thoughts on, material that ended up working its way into this book, I wish to thank Dan Arnold, Jeremy Biles, Heather Blair, David Brakke, Candy Gunther Brown, José Cabezón, Kate Lawn Chouta, Lance Cousins, Collett Cox, Mario D'Amato, Ronald Davidson, John Dunne, Constance Furey, Geoffrey Goble, Jonathan Gold, David Haberman, Charles Hallisey, J. Albert Harrill, Richard Hayes, R. Kevin Jaques, Sylvester Johnson, Ethan Kroll, Nancy Levene, Dan Lusthaus, Shaul Magid, Rebecca Manring, Sara McClintock, Karin Meyers, Richard Miller, Parimal Patil, Lisa Sideris, Aaron Stalnaker, Blake Wentworth, two anonymous readers for Columbia University Press, and the participants in the 2002 Luce Seminar at the University of Chicago Divinity School. Thanks are also due to my editors at Columbia University Press, Wendy Lochner and Christine Mortlock, for their faith in this project and for their help in bringing it to fruition.

My work in Ulan-Ude, Republic of Buryatia, Russian Federation, was aided by Andrey Bazarov and Nikolai Tsyrempilov. I wish to thank them both for their extraordinary hospitality and their generosity in allowing me to inspect a xylograph edition of the *Vyākhyāyukti* housed in the Institute of Mongolian, Buddhist, and Tibetan Studies of the Siberian Branch of the Russian Academy of Sciences. Thanks also to Peter Skilling, Stephen Hodge, and the late E. Gene Smith for providing additional feedback, manuscripts, and publications that I would not otherwise have been able to obtain.

Portions of chapter 2 have previously appeared in "Indian Buddhist Preachers Inside and Outside the Sūtras," *Blackwell Religion Compass* 2, no. 2 (2008): 134–159, doi: 10.1111/j.1749-8171.2007.00057.x. Permission to reprint these passages is gratefully acknowledged.

Finally, I wish to thank Kathryn Graber, who has made both this book and its author much better than they otherwise would have been. For her warmth, intelligence, humor, enthusiasm, and keen editorial eye—and for much else—I am profoundly grateful.

Speaking for Buddhas

Introduction

CLASSICAL INDIAN śāstras (treatises) regularly enjoin aspiring authors to announce at least two things at the outset of their works, so as to secure the interest of judicious readers. The first of these is what in Sanskrit is termed the *abhidheya*, or, roughly, the work's topic: what it's about. According to Sanskrit commentators, authors should state this explicitly so that their audiences do not presume their texts to be meaningless or incoherent. Additionally, authors are told to make explicit their work's *prayojana*: its point. Unless a point is specified up front, a prospective audience is likely to ignore a text, presuming that the text has no point, or that the point it does have is so recondite (or trivial) as to be practically useless. This is good advice, even today. In tribute to the authors whose texts are addressed here, and in the hope of securing the interest of today's judicious readers, this introduction aims to delineate the *abhidheya* and the *prayojana* of the book to follow: what the work is about, and why it matters to the study of Buddhism.

In brief, the work to follow explores some of the ways in which successive generations of Buddhists—more specifically, Indian Buddhists—have transmitted Buddhist teachings through time. For more than a thousand years, over the course of the first millennium C.E., Buddhism flourished in India. The forms this flourishing assumed were, of course, varied; Robert Sharf is correct to note that from the perspective of a modern historian, "the term 'Buddhism' turns out to be a site of unremitting contestation, as a cacophony of voices—each averring privileged access to the essence of the tradition—lays claim to its authority."[1] Yet even in this cacophony, one finds a measure of consonance, for the cacophony itself testifies to a generalized need to appropriate authority via acts of speech. These attempts to speak authoritatively were complex discursive events through which Buddhists aimed to speak not only for themselves, but also for Buddhism more generally—and thus to speak for Buddhas.

This book explores what Indian Buddhist scholastic authors held such speaking to involve. In speaking for Buddhas, Buddhist scholastics were recapitulating an activity of the very Buddhas whose authority they assumed. Indian Buddhist literature portrays Buddhas as speakers par excellence, ceaselessly and patiently consenting to instruct others in the means by which they might be liberated from saṃsāra. As speakers, Buddhas generate—or at least appear to generate—texts; in this respect, they are no different from Buddhist scholastic authors.[2] The words and sentences of these texts may subsequently be memorized, repeated, chanted, inscribed, collected, categorized, elaborated, debated, and paraphrased. Insofar as they are understood to instantiate "the speech of a Buddha" (*buddhavacana*), they are also held to manifest the characteristics of what the tradition terms "right speech" (*samyagvāc*). In the *Brahmajālasutta*, the characteristics of right speech are explicitly and succinctly laid down by (and with reference to) the Buddha Gotama himself:

> Abandoning false speech, refraining from false speech, the ascetic Gotama dwells—a truth speaker, one to be relied on, trustworthy, dependable, not a deceiver of the world. Abandoning malicious speech, refraining from malicious speech, he does not repeat what he has heard here to the detriment of these, or repeat what he has heard there to the detriment of those. Thus, he is one who reconciles those at variance and one who encourages those in concord. Rejoicing in peace, loving it, delighting in it, he is one who speaks up for peace. Abandoning harsh speech, he refrains from it. He speaks whatever is blameless, pleasing to the ear, agreeable—that which reaches the heart, is urbane, pleasing, and attractive to the multitude. Abandoning idle chatter, he speaks at the right time, correctly, and to the point; he is a speaker of the teaching (*dhamma*), a speaker of the discipline (*vinaya*), a speaker whose words are to be treasured, [whose words are] relevant, reasoned, well-defined, and connected with the goal.[3]

Here as elsewhere, Buddhist āgama portrays a Buddha as one who, having attained perfect awakening, has abandoned four ways of speaking: a Buddha no longer engages in false speech (*musāvāda*), malicious speech (*pisunavācā*), harsh speech (*pharusavācā*), and idle chatter (*samphappalāpa*).[4] His speech is thus seen to be pure; it is true, promotes concord, is pleasing, and is concerned with matters of import.[5]

If "right speech" is to be a component of the Buddhist path, it must describe more than the purified utterances of a Buddha; those who aspire to awakening must likewise be capable—at least in principle—of engaging in it. The āgamic literature recognizes this imperative. In the *Sāmaññaphalasutta*, for example, the previously quoted passage from the *Brahmajālasutta* is repeated, but the figure of Gotama has vanished. In his place stands an idealized Buddhist monk whose moral conduct has been perfected. Such a monk speaks as a Buddha does.[6] From the intersection of these two passages, a normative conception of the Buddhist monk as speaker begins to take shape. A monk's rhetoric is to be viewed as authoritative precisely insofar as it recapitulates (what is taken to be) the rhetoric of Buddhas. Like a Buddha, then, an ideal monk is a speaker of the teaching and of the discipline. He speaks in a manner that is timely, correct, and to the point; he knows when (and to whom) to speak, what to say, and how to say it. His discourse is, moreover, true, conciliatory, and pleasing.

As Buddhist literature acknowledges, any speech that stands a chance of being counted as true, conciliatory, and pleasing must accord with particular conventions—whether social, institutional, or linguistic. These conventions are held to apply even to Buddhas, insofar as Buddhas are seen to communicate effectively: Buddhist texts repeatedly emphasize the unfailing ability of awakened beings to employ the language and idiom appropriate to the particular circumstances under which they are called upon to teach.[7] According to a tale preserved in the Mūlasarvāstivāda *Vinayavastu*, for example, the Buddha Gautama was once approached by four great kings—Dhṛtarāṣṭra, Virūḍaka, Virūpākṣa, and Vaiśravaṇa—each hailing from a different region. Two—Dhṛtarāṣṭra and Virūḍaka—are identified as *āryan*, while the other two are identified as *dasyu*. The two groups are unable to comprehend one another, which prompts the Buddha to reflect: "Were I to teach the dharma using *āryan* language, two would understand, two would not. Were I to teach the dharma using *dasyu* language, again, two would understand, two would not. So I should teach the dharma to two using *āryan* language, and to two using *dasyu* language."[8] Opting to address the kings separately, the Buddha then teaches each using the particular language appropriate for him.[9]

Comparable assumptions regarding right speech and its proper deployment affected—and were at times explicitly acknowledged by—subsequent Buddhist scholastic authors. These authors consciously endeavored to compose their works in terms appropriate to the audience(s) they sought to address. Such terms were not confined to the broad matter of language choice, but extended also to matters of style: Indian Buddhist scholastics were concerned to address their audience(s) in ways that would be seen as timely, correct, and to the point—ways informed by a network of normative presuppositions concerning what one should rightly say, how one should rightly say it, and when and where such speech is appropriate.

This book excavates some of the nodes in this network. It explores a set of normative protocols and the impact of those protocols on a number of authors who labored during the latter part of the first millennium and worked in or around the great monastic complexes (*mahāvihāra*) of north India.[10] The book focuses principally on Buddhist texts and practices, though it should be kept in mind that such texts and practices did not appear in a vacuum: Indian Buddhism was not simply *Buddhist*; it was also *Indian*, and Buddhist authors of the late first millennium clearly drew on their understanding of non-Buddhist texts and practices when they composed their own works. A sustained exploration of these non-Buddhist sources and their impacts is a desideratum, but it is a project for another time. The ambition of the present work is more limited: I aim to sketch a preliminary map of the territory, in order to call attention to normative aspects of Indian Buddhist textual production that have, as yet, been largely ignored, and also to a huge and neglected corpus of Indian Buddhist literature: commentaries on Buddhist sūtra texts.[11]

1. Indian Buddhist Sūtra Commentaries

Commentary has long been recognized as the preeminent vehicle for the dispensation of knowledge in India.[12] Throughout the first millennium C.E., learned Indian Buddhists appear to have held the study of scriptural commentaries to be an important resource for understanding the speech of

Buddhas, and the composition of sūtra commentaries to be a fitting means for the communication of their understanding.[13]

The extent to which scriptural commentaries were valued by Indian Buddhist intellectuals of the late first millennium is evidenced by the extant Tibetan imperial-period textual catalogues (*dkar chag*)—texts that afford us a window into Buddhist learning as it was transmitted to Tibet during the so-called early propagation period (i.e., the *snga 'dar*, usually dated from the seventh through the early ninth centuries).[14] Two such catalogues are extant. The earliest and best known of these is the *Catalogue of Lhankar* (*Lhan kar ma dkar chag*; hereafter *Catalogue*).[15] Compiled early in the ninth century following the reign of the Tibetan king Khri srong lde'u btsan, the *Catalogue* inventories a collection of texts housed at the palace of Ldan/Lhan (d)kar.[16] It counts and categorizes more than seven hundred texts translated from Indian and Chinese sources. These translations were typically collaborative undertakings in which Tibetan translators were assisted by learned representatives of Indian and Central Asian Buddhist traditions. The texts inventoried in the *Catalogue* were clearly valorized by those who translated them, and it is not unreasonable to assume that this valorization was learned from non-Tibetan Buddhist scholastics. If this assumption is correct, then the *Catalogue* can be seen as casting light—albeit indirect light—on Indian and Central Asian Buddhist scholastic presuppositions current during the eighth century.

With very few exceptions, the *Catalogue* inventories each of its texts as follows. The text is categorized under one of thirty textual categories; its title—and sometimes its author—is noted; and its length is then given (this length is measured in terms of *śloka*s—here referring to a textual unit of sixteen syllables of verse or prose—and Tibetan *bam po*; the latter is an unstable unit of measurement but typically approximates 300 *śloka*s). Some of the information contained in the *Catalogue* is summarized in table 0.1. The left-hand column lists the thirty categories in the order in which they are given in Herrmann-Pfandt's edition of the *Catalogue*.[17] The central column gives the number of discrete texts categorized under each heading, and the right-hand column provides an approximate total aggregated length (in *bam po*) for the texts attested in each category.

The categories that structure the *Catalogue*'s inventory are somewhat Borgesian, and they sometimes make it difficult to judge the nature of the particular texts that they include and exclude. What seems clear, however, is that not all categories commanded equal attention. To judge from the

TABLE 0.1 Text Categories of the *Catalogue*

Category	*Number of Texts*	*Length in bam po*
1. Mahāyāna sūtras: *Prajñāpāramitā*	16	515
2. Mahāyāna sūtras: *Vaipulya (Avataṃsaka)*	8	194
3. Mahāyāna sūtras: *Mahāratnakūṭa*	48	150
4. Mahāyāna sūtras from 11 to 26 *bam po*	12	191
5. [Mahāyāna sūtras from 1] to 10 *bam po*	90	316
6. [Mahāyāna sūtras from 105 verses] to 1 *bam po*	28	16
7. [Mahāyāna sūtras from 10 verses] to 100 verses	37	7
8. *Mahāsūtra*	9	6
9. Mahāyāna sūtras translated from Chinese	22	115
10. Hīnayāna sūtras	38	152
11. Treatises (*śāstra*)	7	6
12. Tantras of secret mantra	13	108
13. *Pañcarakṣā*	5	7
14. Various long and short *dhāraṇī*	103	25
15. One hundred and eight names	108	4
16. Various praise poems (*stotra*)	18	5
17. Various prayers (*pranidhāna*)	12	3
18. Benedictory discourses (*maṅgalagāthā*)	7	< 1
19. *Vinayapiṭaka*	31	766
20. Commentaries on Mahāyāna sūtras	51	345
21. Sūtra commentaries translated from Chinese	8	157
22. Treatises on Madhyamaka	33	157
23. Texts on meditation (*dhyāna*)	8	9
24. Treatises on consciousness[-only] (*vijñāna*)	41	316
25. Various Mahāyāna treatises	31	68
26. Hīnayāna treatises	9	145
27. [Texts on] speculative argument (*tarka*)	28	38
28. Works of Khri srong lde'u btsan	7	14
29. Texts not subjected to revision	1 (in two parts)	No information given
30. Treatises in the course of translation	6	30

sheer bulk of the translated material (see the third column of table 0.1), the translation teams of this period appear to have devoted most of their energies to translating what they marked as three kinds of text: Buddhist sūtras—particularly those identified as Mahāyāna; disciplinary literature (*vinaya*); and commentaries on Mahāyāna sūtras.[18]

The attention lavished on sūtra and vinaya texts is hardly surprising. Sūtra texts were held to constitute the speech of a Buddha—utterances of paramount authority—and the translation of Buddhist vinaya literature was likely to have been seen as a sine qua non for the establishment of Buddhist monasticism in Tibet. The considerable attention that the translation teams granted to Mahāyāna sūtra commentaries may, however, come as a bit of a shock. Modern scholars who study Indian Buddhism have generally ignored this corpus of texts, despite the fact that Indian Buddhist scholastics appear to have put them in a privileged position.

If we hope to gain a more nuanced understanding of the complexity of Indian Buddhist tradition, and the impacts on doctrine wrought by successive contributions to that tradition, we would do well to investigate these works.[19] We are, however, ill-equipped to read them, and approaching them for the first time can be a disorienting and frustrating experience. Buddhist sūtra commentaries were composed according to rhetorical protocols that we do not share. In contrast to the smooth narrative flow of a sūtra text, the commentaries contain a jumble of statements, phrases, and single terms, accompanied by lengthy digressions on issues that may appear only peripherally related to the sūtra under discussion. If we are to begin to understand Buddhist scriptural commentaries, we need to ask what normative conventions shaped—and were shaped by—their production. The present work charts these conventions, at least in part, and aims thereby to encourage further study of this neglected body of literature.[20]

2. Normativity and Positivist Presuppositions in the Study of Indian Buddhism

Normative conventions are not confined to the authors whose texts this book will discuss—and, in fact, the concern with the normative evident throughout this book may well be seen to violate a normative convention that characterizes much of current Buddhist Studies scholarship. According to this convention, to concern oneself with the normative dimensions of texts is to capitulate to a model of scholarship whose problems have been extensively charted over the past two decades, a model that privileges doctrine over practice, the ideal over the actual, and what one finds in texts over what one finds on (or under) the ground. Gregory Schopen, Todd Lewis, Donald Lopez, and others have repeatedly reminded us of the scholarly confusion this model has generated. The present work neither represents nor recommends a return to it.

The terms in which the model has been critiqued were largely set by Schopen's probing and seminal 1991 paper titled "Archaeology and Protestant Presuppositions in the Study of Indian Buddhism."[21] This paper has attained the status of a classic. It manifests exceptional philological acumen, and its argument is presented with tremendous rhetorical skill. Yet the argument is flawed, and flawed in instructive ways.

Schopen begins by distinguishing between two bodies of data: archaeological/epigraphic material (hereafter "inscriptions"), on the one hand, and texts, on the other. Unlike the corpus of texts, the corpus of inscriptions "records or reflects at least a part of what Buddhists—both lay people and monks—actually practiced and believed."[22] Inscriptions, in other words, are typically descriptive as opposed to normative. The distinction between the descriptive and the normative can be thought of as a distinction that marks how particular accounts are used and understood by those who make use of them. *Descriptive* accounts are those that concern (or are taken to concern) what has been, what is, or what will be so. To the extent that an account fails to do this, it will have failed as a descriptive account. On the other hand, *normative* accounts are those that concern (or are taken to concern) what *should* be so. Normative accounts are used prescriptively and proscriptively; their value lies in presenting idealized paradigms—models—to guide belief and action, regardless of whether those models ever conform to what is so.

We need not draw a hard and fast line between the descriptive and the normative. It is true that every successful descriptive account instantiates—even if it does not itself describe—certain norms. Likewise, every normative account is, insofar as it is an *account*, descriptive in at least some sense. But even if the line between the normative and descriptive is not always perfectly clear, it is clear enough to allow us to apprehend a crucial point: the normative and the descriptive rarely coincide perfectly. What happens "on the ground" can diverge considerably from what is held to be worth happening.

Schopen proceeds, then, by delineating two dichotomies—inscriptions vs. texts, on the one hand, and the descriptive vs. the normative, on the other. He then collapses the two dichotomies into one another: inscriptions describe, whereas texts enshrine norms. This collapse enables Schopen to leverage a claim against antecedent Buddhist Studies scholarship: scholars of Buddhism, relying almost exclusively on texts, have failed to recognize the normative nature of their sources. As a result, they—we—have too often unwittingly constructed normative accounts, rather than descriptive accounts, of what Indian Buddhism was. We have propounded doctrine and called it history.

Having diagnosed this scholarly malaise, Schopen proceeds to trace its etiology: we have proceeded in this way because we have inherited a certain set of unquestioned "Protestant presuppositions" about where "real religion" is to be found. This, in Schopen's view, is a mistake. But it is important to be clear about the nature of this mistake: when Schopen tells us that "there is a remarkable similarity between the value assigned literary sources in modern historical and archeological studies and the argument of Protestant reformers concerning the location of true religion,"[23] he is not thereby questioning the idea that something called "true religion" may exist. Rather, he's implying that if it does exist, we will not find it by looking at texts. To think otherwise is to embrace a Protestant presupposition. The solution is simple: we should stop relying exclusively on texts and start looking carefully at inscriptions. Only then will we begin to discover "what actual Buddhists did and believed," and hence, in his view, only then will we recover what Indian Buddhism truly was.

"Archaeology and Protestant Presuppositions in the Study of Indian Buddhism" can be (and should be) taken as a corrective to a one-sided model of Buddhist Studies that opts to focus exclusively on texts while ignoring other available data. Read in this way, Schopen is encouraging us to broaden the body of data from which we draw our conclusions—a suggestion that is eminently reasonable. However, the paper can also be read as implying that if one happens to be interested in what Buddhism *was*, as opposed to what certain Buddhists have thought Buddhism *ought to be*, one need not bother with the investigation of texts. This was almost certainly not Schopen's intention in composing the essay; indeed, to judge from his subsequent extensive—and superb—work on the Mūlasarvāstivāda *Vinayavastu*, it is not a reading that he would endorse. But it is not difficult to find traces of such a reading in recent Buddhist Studies scholarship. Consider, for example, the following programmatic passage, drawn from the preface to Martin Mills's 2003 volume on Gelukpa monasticism in Tibet:

> I have attempted to build a picture of Tibetan Buddhist life that begins by asking what it itself *is*, rather than what it *should be*. In particular, I have attempted to move away from a logocentric approach which either sees Tibetan Buddhism as

> defined by explicit written teachings, or as centered around them. Rather . . . I have sought to examine the practice of Tibetan Buddhism in a particular context . . . in order to see what it can tell us about how we should interpret the intellectual content of Tibetan Buddhist texts.[24]

Here, again, two dichotomies are delineated. The normative is opposed to the descriptive, and texts (and scholarly studies that focus principally on texts) are opposed to practices (and scholarly studies that focus principally on practices). Once delineated, the dichotomies are again collapsed: if we want to know what Tibetan Buddhism *is*, then we should focus on *practices*. Mills elsewhere notes that he sees a text-based approach to be inadequate because such an approach derives from "a thinly-veiled post-Reformation bias against ritual and clericalism that is arguably inappropriate to the study of non-theistic religious traditions."[25] Like Schopen, then, Mills sees Protestant biases at work in Buddhist Studies. Moreover, like Schopen, Mills has not discounted the heuristic utility of postulating (or the possibility of locating) "true Buddhism": he has simply shifted its location from texts to practices.

I have emphasized the way in which both Schopen and Mills attempt to read the distinction between the normative and the descriptive as tracking the distinction between bodies of data in order to encourage further reflection on whether the collapse of such dichotomies is legitimate. We might ask, for example, whether it is true that inscriptions do not express, inculcate, or both express and inculcate normative ideals. This seems a problematic assumption, given that inscriptions are typically formulaic (a fact pointed out by Gérard Fussman in an article that Schopen himself cites approvingly): i.e., they are influenced by and reinforce normative assumptions as to proper form and content.[26] Moreover, there are well-known inscriptions (e.g., Aśoka's fourth pillar edict) that are clearly prescriptive in nature.[27] We might also ask whether it is true that Buddhist texts do not generally express what Buddhists really practiced or believed. This is surely true in some cases, yet it seems to me a mistake to draw from these cases the sweeping conclusion that Buddhist texts are *constitutively* normative (though they undoubtedly contain many claims that do function normatively). The Buddhist textual corpus is more heterogeneous than Schopen suggests; some of the ideas he associates with the "inscriptional story"—

a story he reads as descriptive—can also be found articulated in Buddhist sūtra texts.[28] The upshot is clear: it is a mistake to think that these two dichotomies—inscriptions vs. texts and descriptive data vs. normative data—can be cleanly collapsed. We should not assume that Buddhist inscriptions are constitutively descriptive, nor should we assume that Buddhist texts are constitutively normative.

It may still be true, of course, that in looking principally at *texts* to figure out what Buddhism has been, scholars have been gazing through a lens of presuppositions that is serving to distort our picture of where pertinent information for "true religion"—in this case, "true Buddhism"—is rightly to be found. If we assume that the notion of "true religion" is not itself a manifestation of the very presuppositions that Schopen aims to critique, we might wonder where we should look for a more appropriate heuristic.

Schopen notes that "our picture of Indian Buddhism may reflect more of our own religious history and values than the history and values of Indian Buddhism."[29] This suggests that he would hold Buddhist presuppositions regarding the location of "true Indian Buddhism" to be an improvement over the Protestant presuppositions he excoriates. When we turn to Buddhist sources in search of these presuppositions, however, we find that the sources routinely direct us to *texts and textual practices*: practices of memorization, reflection, discussion, debate, teaching, preaching, and so on. The Chinese pilgrim Xuanzang (600?–664 C.E.), who visited many Buddhist monasteries during his lengthy sojourn to India, explicitly notes a range of material benefits to be gained as a consequence of demonstrating familiarity with the content of Buddhist texts.[30] Although the sources that direct us to texts are often textual themselves, they are not always so: the Nālandā stone inscription of Yaśovarm(m)adeva, for example, describes the residents of Nālandā as "scholars well known for their [knowledge of the] sacred texts and arts" (*sadāgamakalāvikhyātavidvajjanā*).[31]

These data suggest that although Schopen and Mills may well be correct in tracing the origins of many of the presuppositions that inform Buddhist Studies scholarship to Protestantism, similar presuppositions were held by at least some Indian Buddhists. The whole issue of "Protestantism" may, in this specific context, turn out to be something of a red herring.[32] To dismiss the careful study of Buddhist texts as evidence that one is in the grip of a "Protestant presupposition" is to do a disservice to the complexity of the Indian Buddhist tradition—a tradition in which practices aimed at the meticulous exegesis and analysis of claims existed alongside (and, at times, were thoroughly interwoven with) practices of devotion, sorcery, and ritual.

3. The Structure of the Book

I have organized this study so as to facilitate its use by scholars interested in issues that extend beyond the relatively narrow domain of Indian Buddhist sūtra commentary. The book's final chapters trace normative assumptions that pertain specifically to commentarial texts, but this point is reached only after an extended exploration of the wider normative context within which these works—and many others—were composed. The book thus commences by taking a wide-angle approach to context; as it proceeds, this context narrows.

Buddhist commentaries on scripture were—and were seen by their authors to be—paradigmatically (though not exclusively) linguistic utterances. These utterances were also pedagogical: like the texts on which they commented, commentarial texts constituted, and were taken to constitute, teachings. We may thus hypothesize that commentaries were informed by specific (if sometimes implicit) normative assumptions concerning *correct speaking* and *correct teaching*. These assumptions are explored in the first two chapters of the book.

Chapter 1 begins by investigating the notion of "right speech" articulated in Buddhist texts. Two normative models are discussed. The first is prescriptive (it provides a guide to how, what, when, and where one should speak); the second, proscriptive (it provides a guide to how, what, when, and where one should *not* speak). The two models are developed via close reading of portions of texts likely to have been well known to Buddhist commentators working in large Indian monastic complexes during the mid-to-late first millennium C.E.: Mātṛceṭa's *Śatapañcāśatka* and *Catuḥśataka*, and the (Mūlasarvāstivāda) *Prātimokṣasūtra*. These texts appear to have been among the first memorized by Buddhist monastic novices, and they likely served as resources from which monks consciously or unconsciously drew many of their assumptions regarding proper modes of speech.

Chapter 2 focuses on the activity of teaching as it has been portrayed in Buddhist texts and as it has been undertaken by those who have aimed to transmit those texts authoritatively. The chapter is principally concerned with investigating the normative and historical dimensions of a figure regularly associated with the transmission of Buddhist teaching from generation to generation: the Buddhist preacher. In the first of two sections, I examine portraits of this figure sketched in Buddhist sūtras and śāstras. These portraits regularly explain the preacher's pedagogical skill in terms of four discriminations, which I investigate in some detail. The second section of the chapter aims to show the ways in which idealized portraits of teachers painted *in* texts may have conformed—and sometimes failed to conform—to the practices of those *outside* those texts who would shape and be shaped by them.

In chapters 3 and 4, I turn to investigate issues of textual interpretation and composition. What specific resources were acknowledged by Indian Buddhists of the mid-to-late first millennium C.E. to be tools by which the meaning of sūtra texts could be comprehended and communicated? Chapter 3 investigates epistemological discourse and asks whether and how the formalized tools for argument that this discourse provided were presumed to aid in interpretive work. Chapter 4 looks specifically at protocols guiding the composition of scriptural commentary, as set down explicitly in what I term "commentarial guides." These guides provide explicit guidelines for how one should undertake to comment on scriptural texts. The chapter focuses especially on Vasubandhu's *Vyākhyāyukti*, comparing it to other extant guides, including the **Vivaraṇasaṃgrahaṇī*, attributed to Asaṅga, and a short section of the *Abhidharmasamuccayabhāṣya*, sometimes attributed to Sthiramati. To facilitate further study of these texts, reference translations are provided in the book's three appendixes.

The conclusion of the volume begins by recapitulating the findings of the preceding chapters. These findings are then further elaborated and deepened by briefly examining a final exemplary commentary. Through this examination, and through the work as a whole, I hope to illuminate traditional responses to a question that I would argue is crucial for anyone who endeavors to understand Indian Buddhist commentaries and those who composed them: what is it to speak for Buddhas?

ONE

Models of Speaking

Buddhas and Monks

THE CHINESE PILGRIM Yijing (635–713 C.E.), in his seventh-century account of Buddhist monastic life in India, records that during his stay at the great Indian monastery of Nālandā, he was particularly impressed by two hymns and the formal ceremonies in which they were chanted.[1] Yijing refers to these hymns as the *Śatapañcāśatka* (Hymn in one hundred and fifty verses) and the *Catuḥśataka* (Hymn in four hundred verses).[2] Both, he tells us, are by the Buddhist poet Mātṛceṭa (second–third century C.E.), and both are regularly taught to novices shortly after their admission to the monastic community: "In all five parts of India, those who become monks are first taught these two compositions as soon as they can recite the five and ten precepts, this being the rule for all monks regardless of whether they belong to the Mahāyāna or the Hīnayāna schools. . . . After having studied these hymns, one proceeds to learn other scriptural texts."[3] In exploring the normative presuppositions that informed Indian Buddhist notions of right speech, I want to begin with these texts and thus begin as monastic novices themselves may well have begun. If Yijing's testimony is accurate, the *Śatapañcāśatka* and *Catuḥśataka* appear to have been used as something like primers for the introduction of Buddhist doctrine to aspiring monks.

The texts do not immediately seem well suited to this purpose; neither looks to have been composed with novices in mind, and both display a mastery of Sanskrit poetic conventions that would surely have been unfamiliar to the average novice. As a novice tried to memorize these works, he would likely have understood very little of their content. But the process of memorization does not require that one understand content—and, in fact, precise recall of a text's form can actually be impeded if one also comprehends its content, since such comprehension invites paraphrase.[4] Although monastic novices may first have learned the *Śatapañcāśatka* and the *Catuḥśataka* as little more than a string of ordered sounds, their experience of these sounds would undoubtedly have changed as their learning and comprehension increased. Over time, the sounds would have begun to coalesce into words bearing determinate content: content grounded in texts that had already become, through repetition, unforgettable.

These two texts, despite the widespread popularity asserted for them by Yijing, have received very little attention. They are largely ignored by modern scholars who study Indian Buddhism, and they are rarely cited by Indian Buddhist authors. The absence of citations in the canonical literature can perhaps be explained, at least in part, by the use of these works as primers. Primers are rarely explicitly cited in scholarly—or scholastic—discussion; they are, rather, silently presumed to constitute the building blocks of a body of shared knowledge, or "what goes without saying." Yijing's account of monastic practices at Nālandā suggests, however, that what goes without saying is not always left unsaid—and that one place to find it is, ironically, in texts that are regularly and communally recited.

In this chapter, we will examine portions of the *Śatapañcāśatka* and *Catuḥśataka*, supplementing these with passages drawn from another communally recited text, the Mūlasarvāstivāda *Prātimokṣasūtra*. Whereas the *Śatapañcāśatka* and *Catuḥśataka* are largely prescriptive—providing an idealized model of a Buddha's perfected speech—the *Prātimokṣasūtra* is largely proscriptive: it stipulates a range of offenses against which a properly observant monk vows to guard himself. Many of these offenses pertain to speech. Taken together, these sources render explicit a framework of prescriptions and proscriptions that informed the transmission of authoritative speech in north Indian Buddhist monasteries during the first millennium C.E. They articulate ideals in reference to which the speech of Buddhist monks could be (and, evidence suggests, was) assessed. Indian Buddhist monks who wished to speak for Buddhas were expected to internalize these ideals and to use them as cynosures.

1. Speaking as a Buddha: In Praise of Perfection

The *Śatapañcāśatka* and *Catuḥśataka* are praise poems (Skt. *stotra*, *stava*) addressed to the (or a) Buddha. Both are divided into shorter sections, each of which focuses largely on a specific aspect of an awakened being. The *Śatapañcāśatka* ranges over thirteen aspects; the *Catuḥśataka*, twelve.[5] Both poems feature a section devoted to a Buddha's speech.

The section of the *Śatapañcāśatka* devoted to speech contains fifteen verses and is titled simply "Vacanastava" (Praise of speech):

1. Well-worded, of great meaning, true and sweet;
Profound, plain, or both; succinct or detailed;

2. Having heard such utterances from you,
Who would not be certain that you are omniscient?
Even one hostile to you!

3. Most often, your speech is entirely sweet;
As a last resort, some is otherwise;
But all your speech is well-spoken, due to the accomplishment of aims.[6]

4. When pondered, *all* your speech—
Whether gentle, severe, or both—
Has a single flavor.[7]

5. O! The skill of the well-purified actions
By which such a vessel of precious utterances is crafted!

6. From your mouth, beautiful to the eye,
Pours that which is pleasing to the ear;
Your speech is like nectar, dripping from the moon.

7. Your speech is like a rain cloud, settling the dust of desire;
Like a *garuḍa*, slaying the serpent of hatred;

8. Like the sun, dispelling the darkness of delusion;
Like Śakra's scepter, cleaving the mountains of pride.

9. Your speech is auspicious in three ways:
Because it concerns that which [you] have seen, it is not false;
Because it is without defilement, it is not confused;
Because it is well suited [to circumstance], it is convincing.

10. At first, your statements carry away
The minds of those who listen [to them];
Then, upon reflection,
[Those statements] carry away [their] passions and delusions.

11. Suited [to all], your speech
Consoles those who struggle,
Frightens the negligent, and agitates the complacent.

12. It delights the wise,
Strengthens the minds of those who are middling,
And dispels the darkness of the dull.
It is speech for everyone.

13. Your speech draws [one] away from [false] views,
Draws [one] toward nirvāṇa,
Draws out [one's] faults,
And rains down virtuous qualities.

14. Your thought is unobstructed with respect to everything,
Your mindfulness ever present.
Thus, all you reveal is everywhere fruitful.

15. You act neither at the wrong place, nor at the wrong time,
Nor toward one who is unworthy.

Therefore, like effort correctly applied,
Your speech is not in vain.[8]

The corresponding section of the *Catuḥśataka* echoes many of the themes raised in the *Śatapañcāśatka.* It is somewhat longer and praises a Buddha's purity of speech (*vāgviśuddhi*):

1–2. O sage, although worldly beings, clad in the armor of ignorance,
Are scorched by the fire of saṃsāra's fearful sufferings,
They are not discouraged,
Having heard your statements concerning the dangers [of saṃsāra].
Therefore, the meaning of [your] speech, O lord,
Exceeds what they perceive directly in its clarity.

3. Because reality, profound and vastly deep
Is clarified by [your] explanations,
Your speech works miracles even for the perverse.

4. Your words are limitless;
[The] depth of their meaning is fathomless;
Yet they accord with each other.
What is more wonderful than that?

5. O best of speakers,
Your speech has many modes,
Yet it is not repetitive;
And [its] system of connections is reasonable.

6. O best of speakers,
Although your speech has the virtue of four positions
And relies on four responses,
It is unambiguous in meaning.

7. In granting and denying,
Your speech is at times determinate, at times indeterminate,
But it has no inconsistency.

8. [Your speech is] a site of indisputable words,
Because [it] declares the true nature of things.
All those who speak falsely are refuted
By [its] excellent qualities of reasoning and argument.

9. Though aiming solely at the ultimate meaning,
It is faultless with respect to the conventional;
Because it does not contradict the two truths,
Your speech has propriety.

10. Gentle only among those who are not quarrelsome,
And severe only among those who are quarrelsome,
Your speech is free of the faults of gentleness or severity.

11. Your speech favors purification
But is unbiased;
It opposes the afflictions
But is not impatient.

12. Filled with chastisements by the hundreds,
Yet lacking the fault of malice;
Abounding in words of praise,
Yet taking refuge in no one;

13. Free from insertion and omission,
Furnished with brevity and detail,
Pleasant to examine and not inauspicious,
Even on a first hearing.

14. This speech is musical, and uninterrupted;
It is bountiful and significant;
It is varied and unconfused in meaning.
Many are its wonders!

15. O lord of speech, your speech is charming,
Yet one does not become attached to it;

It is blazing, yet it does not harm;
It is clear, yet it is incomprehensible to those who are evil.

16. It makes one's hairs stand on end,
Causes one to sweat,
Stiffens the limbs, and makes one tremble.

17. [Your] resounding voice shakes the world of the immortals,
Causing even the earth, naturally stable, to quake in six ways.

18. It turns back the nature of embodied beings, beginninglessly afflicted,
And it establishes another unfamiliar nature in the heart.

19. For those who do not renounce their own faults,
It is like a torment to the mind;
For learned ones who act with propriety,
It is like a shower of nectar.

20. Your speech is virtuous at the beginning, middle, and end.
In hearing, reflection, and cultivation,
It becomes nectar for one who is accomplished.

21–22. When many [listeners], possessed of many inclinations, gather around
And from the utterance of a single statement
It seems as though many [statements] occur,
And everyone understands "this teaching is for me alone,"
What is more amazing than this?
What is more wonderful than this?

23. [Your speech] accords with worldly convention
But does not forsake reality;
Even as [you] effect proclamations [in accord with the former],
[You] effect contemplation of the latter.

24. Your speech [declares that] affliction and purity exist,
[And that] action and the consequence of action exist,
[But that] a possessor of those—an agent or creator—does not exist.

25. Having heard this speech of yours previously,
All the worlds with their gods and men
Were separately shaken—
As the moon trembles upon the water.

26–27. "If various occurrences, both good and bad,
Depend upon conditions,
How could there be a creator?
If something were independent, it could be a creator—but this is not reasonable."
You spoke this principle regarding the absence of a creator among all dharmas.

28. This is the dharma [you] established:
A drum resounding with the lion's roar of emptiness,
Stilling the advance [of affliction].

29. When it illuminates the world, it is like the sun's light;
All forms of speech other than this bring complete misfortune.[9]

Each of the verses translated here deserves extended exegesis. To survey them all would, however, result in a very unwieldy volume. In what follows, then, I will begin by offering a few general remarks on the section of the *Śatapañcāśatka* translated here—the "Vacanastava"—and then endeavor to unpack its opening verse in detail. My hope is that close attention to the terms used in this first verse will illuminate much of what is at stake in the remaining verses translated here, insofar as these terms thematize issues that resound through both praise poems.

Mātṛceṭa begins the "Vacanastava" by characterizing a Buddha's utterances as indubitable testimony to a quality of mind possessed by their speaker: omniscience (*sarvajña*). The speech of an omniscient Buddha is inevitably well-spoken (*subhāṣita*) and is well-spoken insofar as it is *effective* in accomplishing aims. A Buddha's speech can take many forms: at times, it may be sweet (*madhura*) or gentle (*ślakṣṇa*); at other times, it may be severe (*paruṣa*).[10] But all these forms, varied though they may appear to be, possess a single flavor (*ekarasatā*), insofar as they aim toward liberation.[11] Mātṛceṭa, perhaps concerned that his readers will misunderstand this to imply that a Buddha's speech has only one form, or can be characterized in only one way, then offers a dense volley of similes in rapid succession. The speech of a Buddha is—or is like—jewels, nectar, a rain cloud, a *garuḍa*, the sun, and Śakra's scepter. Although Mātṛceṭa admits that it is impossible to definitively determine all the good qualities possessed by a Buddha and his speech, he clearly presumes that illuminating comparisons can be drawn.[12]

After offering these similes, Mātṛceṭa returns to themes raised in his opening verses. Describing the speech of a Buddha as auspicious, unconfused, and convincing, he notes once again that the Buddha's speech benefits everyone, regardless of disposition or intellect. By acknowledging that audiences are different in these respects, Mātṛceṭa lays the groundwork for resoundingly affirming the Buddha's speech as responsive to a limitless diversity of sensibilities. In the penultimate verse of the "Vacanastava," the theme of universality is hammered home. Universal quantifiers occur no less than four times: *all* that a Buddha reveals is fruitful *everywhere*, insofar as his thought is unobstructed with respect to *everything* and his mindfulness is *ever present*.

One should not, however, be misled by the language of universality here: Mātṛceṭa is not claiming that whatever the Buddha says on a specific occasion will suit the needs of any audience on any other occasion. Rather, his claim is that whatever the Buddha says on any specific occasion is perfectly suited to the demands *of that occasion*, and to the dispositions and capacities of the audience addressed at that time. The model of a Buddha's perfected speech offered here thus points in two directions at once. Perfected speech is *generally*—always and everywhere—well suited to the *particularity* of local context(s)—contexts that may differ as to time, place, language, speaker, and audience. Just as Gautama's teaching to the four kings was expressed in terms that each king could understand, a Buddha is able to move effortlessly among contexts and to suit his words unfailingly to the demands of each. What is it, then, to be well suited to a context? In the opening verse of the "Vacanastava," Mātṛceṭa provides the seeds of a traditional Buddhist answer to this question.

1.1. "Vacanastava," Verse 1

In verse 1, Mātṛceṭa lists attributes that he holds to characterize a Buddha's utterances (*vākya*). These attributes can be grouped into four sets. A Buddha's utterances, Mātṛceṭa tells us, are (1) well-worded and of great meaning; (2) true and sweet; (3) profound, plain, or both; and (4) succinct or detailed. To understand how a well-trained Indian Buddhist monk might have understood these attributes, we will need to look beyond the *Śatapañcāśatka* to the corpus of texts that he would have taken them to describe: texts understood to contain the speech of a Buddha (*buddhavacana*).

The status of *buddhavacana* was accorded to different texts by different communities of Indian Buddhists. Most likely presumed the term to apply to the texts of Buddhist āgama. The Buddhist āgamas that were likely to have been in use at larger north Indian monastic complexes—e.g., Nālandā—are, for the most part, extant only in Chinese translation.[13] The material contained in these āgamas is, however, largely—though not exhaustively—the same as that contained in the first four nikāyas (*Dīgha*, *Majjhima*, *Saṃyutta*, and *Aṅguttara*) of the Pali *Suttapiṭaka*. Étienne Lamotte has outlined some notable differences, which, for my purposes here, are mostly minor. They concern discrepancies in setting and, at times, differences in structure.[14] As Lamotte stresses, however, "the doctrinal basis common to the āgamas and nikāyas is remarkably uniform."[15] In light of this assessment, the careful use of passages in the Pali *Suttapiṭaka* to elucidate doctrinal assumptions held by those versed in Sanskrit āgamic texts is less problematic than it might initially seem.[16]

Textual and epigraphical evidence suggests that at least some of the monks who lived in the great north Indian monasteries during the latter part of the first millennium accorded the status of *buddhavacana* to certain Mahāyāna sūtras.[17] Those who composed texts during this time cite Mahāyāna sūtras by name much more often than they cite individual texts of the āgamic corpus. We should not, however, conclude from this that such authors were unfamiliar with Buddhist āgama; there would, after all, be little reason for an author to cite by name a sūtra that he could reasonably expect his audience to know well. In attempting to determine the specific sources known to specific Indian Buddhist authors, some degree of speculation seems to me to be unavoidable. To take a positivist line here—i.e., to presume that we may presume no familiarity with any text that is not explicitly cited by name—is one way of guarding against uncertainty, but such an approach robs the tradition of its intertextual richness. We are, I think, entitled to presume that Buddhist authors of the late first millennium drew not only from the Mahāyāna texts they cite by name, but also from a common stock of āgamic sources. In elucidating the normative ideal that Mātṛceṭa enshrines in a Buddha's speech, I will do likewise.[18]

1.1.1. WELL-WORDED, OF GREAT MEANING . . . (*SUPADĀNI MAHĀRTHĀNI* . . .)

Mātṛceṭa begins by alluding to a trope often repeated in the āgamic literature, according to which a teaching's phrasing (*vyañjana*) is properly to be distinguished from its meaning (*artha*).[19] The distinction is articulated in a stock description, repeated throughout the āgamic texts: "He [i.e. the Buddha Gotama] teaches the *dhamma*—good in the beginning, good in the middle, and good in the end, with [excellent] meaning and [excellent] phrasing, and he reveals a holy life that is utterly perfect and pure."[20] As this passage makes explicit, the term "dharma" (Pali: *dhamma*), when used to characterize the teaching of a Buddha, is ambiguous. It may be used to refer either to that which is expressed in or by a teaching (that is, its *artha*) or to the phrasing of that teaching (its *vyañjana*).[21] Both are valorized. A Buddha is a being who not only has perfected his insight into what his teaching expresses, but also has perfected his facility in expressing that content. Having understood things just as they are (*yathābhūta*), he is able to expound this understanding in ways that are precisely suited to circumstances.

In Buddhist āgamic literature, these forms of perfection are presented as inculcated by learning or training (*śikṣā*). A student who undertakes this training must direct his efforts in multiple directions. He must endeavor to accurately preserve the phrasing of a teaching in memory, and he must also endeavor to understand its meaning.[22] Both forms of work are interpersonal, as the texts themselves routinely stress:

> And thus you must train yourselves, being assembled in harmony and without dissension. If a fellow in the holy life quotes the *dhamma* in the assembly, and if you think he has either misunderstood the sense or used the wrong phrasing, you should neither applaud nor reject it, but should say to him: "Friend, if you mean such-and-such, you should put it either like this or like that: which is the more appropriate?" or "If you say such and such, you mean either this or that: which is the more appropriate?" If he replies: "This meaning is better expressed like this rather than that," then his words should be neither rejected

> nor disparaged, but you should explain to him carefully the correct meaning and expression.
>
> Again . . . if a fellow in the holy life quotes the *dhamma* in the assembly, and if you think he has misunderstood the sense though his phrases are correct, you should neither applaud nor reject it, but should say to him: "Friend, these words can mean either this or that: which sense is the more appropriate?" And if he replies: "They mean this," then his words should be neither rejected nor disparaged, but you should explain to him carefully the correct meaning.
>
> And similarly . . . if you think he has got the right meaning but his phrases are incorrect . . . you should explain to him carefully the correct phrasing.
>
> But . . . if you think he has got the right meaning and his phrasing is correct . . . you should say: "Excellent!" and should applaud and congratulate him, saying: "We are lucky, we are fortunate to find in you, friend, a companion in the holy life who is so well versed in both the meaning and the phrasing!"[23]

This passage—drawn from the *Pāsādikasutta*—does not portray an isolated monk, alone in his monastic cell, privately subjecting his understanding of a text to critical scrutiny. Instead, we are given a scene of pedagogical give-and-take in which monks work with each other to fix a text's meaning and phrasing precisely.

According to the āgamic literature, this pedagogical give-and-take is to be arbitrated by wise monks (*viyattā bhikkhū*); it is they who judge what is to count as a correct understanding of a teaching's meaning and phrasing. The āgamic texts insist on the necessity of this authority, asserting that without it the community—like the dharma that it inherits, enshrines, and propagates—would decline.[24] A monk's position in the monastic hierarchy is to be determined, at least in part, by the perceived extent of his learning. Senior disciples are presented as those who can proclaim and explicate the dharma and refute opposing doctrines if called upon to do so.[25]

In practice, the benefits accorded to the learned appear to have been material as well as symbolic. Regarding the protocols observed in Indian Buddhist monasteries during the seventh century, Xuanzang writes:

> All books, whether belonging to the Vinaya (discipline), the Abhidharma (treatises) or the sūtras (discourses), are scriptures of the Buddha. A monk who can expound one of the books is exempted from routine monastic duties. One who

> can expound two books is supplied with additional good rooms and daily requisites. One who can expound three is to be served by attendants. One who can expound four is provided with lay servants at his service. One who can expound five is entitled to ride an elephant when going out. One who can expound six has a retinue protecting him.[26]

Having offered this account of the benefits conferred upon the learned, Xuanzang immediately goes on to describe the considerable power these figures wielded in monastic assemblies—and the consequences that a junior monk could expect as a result of their praise and approbation:

> Assemblies for discussion are often held to test the intellectual capacity of the monks, in order to distinguish the superior from the inferior, and to reject the dull and promote the bright. Those who can deliberate on the subtle sayings, and glorify the wonderful theories with refined diction and quick eloquence, may ride richly caparisoned elephants with hosts of attendants preceding and following behind them. But those to whom the theories are taught in vain, or who have been defeated in a debate, explaining few principles in a verbose way, or distorting the teachings with language that is merely pleasant to the ear, are daubed with ocher or chalk in the face, while dust is scattered over the body, and are expelled into the wilderness, or discarded into ditches. In this way the good and the evil are distinguished, and the wise and the ignorant disclosed.[27]

Xuanzang's account here is startling and instructive, revealing as it does the extent to which monastic practices could and did deviate from the normative portrayals offered in the āgamic texts. His description of the treatment meted out to a monk whose knowledge is lacking is obviously far from the guidelines for constructive criticism laid out in the *Pāsādikasutta*, and it reminds us once again to be wary of attempts to use canonical sources as windows for facts on the ground.[28] Yet in spite of these divergences, Xuanzang's passage also suggests that aspects of the normative āgamic picture were operative within the great monastic complexes of India during the seventh century. Monks were lauded or lambasted based on the form their speech took (i.e., its *vyañjana*) and the depth of understanding it evinced (i.e., its *artha*). A monk might employ refined diction and quick eloquence to debate the teaching effectively and succinctly, or he might use coy, inflated, or verbose rhetoric in an attempt to mask his lack of understanding. Those whose speech manifested well-worded phrases that evinced great (understanding of) meaning were likely presumed to approximate the speech of Buddhas.

What sorts of utterances did wise Indian Buddhist monks of this period count as well-worded and of great meaning? It is, of course, risky to speculate (and on criteria internal to the normative picture presented here, especially so; I am hardly a wise monk), but perhaps extant Indian commentaries might usefully be seen as exemplary. They appear to have been held in very high regard by learned Indian Buddhists, and they manifest what could reasonably be called "subtle investigation" and "deep penetration" in their considered and nuanced approach to their root texts.

Moreover, the extant commentaries show a good command of Sanskrit grammar, suggesting that one criterion for counting an utterance as "well-worded" may well have been its correspondence to formal strictures set down in Sanskrit grammatical literature. This may seem surprising, given the common image of Indian Buddhists as manifesting a rather irenic attitude toward linguistic pluralism, and as concerned less with grammatical protocols than with communicative efficacy.[29] This image may, however, need some adjustment, as it does not fit particularly well with the evidence we have—evidence that is augmented by Yijing's testimony regarding the prestige granted to Sanskrit among learned Indian Buddhists.[30] Yijing devotes several pages of his travelogue to enumerating the various grammatical treatises he encountered in India. He emphasizes that these texts were highly prized at Nālandā and suggests that familiarity with Sanskrit may well have been a precondition for acceptance to the institution.[31] Did the scholars of Nālandā view with skepticism (or simply ignore) the apparently pluralist leanings of texts such as the *Vinayavastu* or the *Bhadacaripraṇidhānarāja*? Or, did they accept the pluralism voiced in these texts but nonetheless aim to address (or debate with) Sanskritized audiences?[32] Yijing's remarks regarding the trajectory of an exemplary scholarly career are revealing here: "Those who are praised by wise authorities as excellent scholars become famous for their ability far and near. They may believe that their sword of wisdom is sharp enough for them to go as competent persons to serve at the court of a king, making suggestions and displaying their knowledge, in hopes of being employed."[33] Yijing suggests that scholars who were successful in their appeals at times achieved considerable renown: "Their fame resounds through the five mountains and their repute spreads within the four quarters. They receive feudal estates and are promoted to higher rank, with their names written in white high up on the gates of their houses."[34] Passages such as these suggest that the prestige accorded to Sanskrit learning at Nālandā may well have been motivated by the desire to secure continuing relations with royal power and commensurate economic support for these institutions and their alumni.[35] Risking tautology, then, we may say that a monk's speech would have been held to be praiseworthy at these monasteries if he were to speak as one worthy of praise is described by Mātṛceṭa as speaking: with well-worded phrases of great meaning. By the seventh century C.E., however, the criteria for adjudicating the relative excellence of a monk's utterances in such contexts may well have been determined not only by senior monks, but also by those who granted them patronage.

1.1.2. . . . TRUE . . . (. . . *TATHYĀNI* . . .)

The next quality that Mātṛceṭa attributes to the Buddha's utterances is truth (*tathya*[*tā*]). A Buddha's utterances accord with the way things are; they are offered subsequent to a direct and unimpeded awareness of any matter on which a Buddha may discourse. A stock passage—one that we have already encountered in altered form—has Gotama himself informing his interlocutors that "between the night in which the Tathāgata gains supreme awakening . . . and the night in which he attains nirvāṇa without remainder, whatever he proclaims, says, or explains is so and not otherwise."[36] The truth of the Buddha's speech is further emphasized in many sūtras, among them the *Mahāsakuludāyisutta*, where we find Gotama stating:

> My disciples esteem me for my excellent knowledge and vision thus: "When the recluse Gotama says 'I know,' he truly knows; when he says 'I see,' he truly sees. The recluse Gotama teaches the *dhamma* through direct knowledge (*abhiññā*), not without direct knowledge; he teaches the *dhamma* with a sound basis (*sanidāna*), not without a sound basis; he teaches the *dhamma* in a convincing manner (*sappāṭihāriya*), not in an unconvincing manner."[37]

True speech is elsewhere described as verbal conduct to be cultivated, insofar as it causes nonvirtuous states to decrease and virtuous states to increase.[38]

Yet the texts also emphasize that speaking truly does not entail speaking virtuously.[39] In a passage preserved in the *Aṅguttaranikāya*, purporting to record a conversation between Gotama and the brahman Vassakāra, the Buddha acknowledges that the truth can hurt—and hurt in ways that impede the practice of the path. Though he does not specify whether this harm accrues to speakers, audiences, or both, Gotama is nevertheless clear that saying nothing is sometimes preferable to speaking truly:

> I, for my part, brahman, do not say that all that one has seen should be spoken of. Yet I do not say, brahman, that all that one has seen should not be spoken of. And I say the same of what has been heard . . . sensed . . . understood. Now, brahman, insofar as speaking of what one has seen causes nonvirtuous states to increase and virtuous states to decrease, I say that one should not speak of what one has seen. Insofar as speaking of what one has heard . . . sensed . . . understood causes nonvirtuous states to increase and virtuous states to decrease, I say that one should not speak of what has been heard . . . sensed . . . understood. But in the case where nonvirtuous states decrease and virtuous states increase, I say that one should speak of what one has heard . . . sensed . . . understood.[40]

On a first reading, the view expressed here appears to be similar to one voiced in the non-Buddhist *Mānavadharmaśāstra*, in verse 4.138—a verse that stipulates protocols for brahmanical speech. A brahman, the text tells us, "Shall say what is true (*satya*), and he shall say what is agreeable (*priya*). He shall not say what is true, but disagreeable; nor shall he say what is agreeable, but wrong. This dharma is eternal."[41] As in the *Aṅguttaranikāya* passage, two speech attributes are introduced and combined in various ways. One combination is accepted; the others are rejected. If an utterance is true, the verse tells us, it should be uttered only in the event that it is also agreeable. If an utterance is agreeable, on the contrary, it should be uttered only in the event that it is also true. Thus, of the four possible combinations of attributes, only one (+true, +agreeable) is seen as appropriate to brahmanical speech.[42]

However, the formal similarity between these two passages masks an important difference between them. What is at stake in the passage from the *Aṅguttaranikāya* is not the *agreeability* of an utterance, but the *benefit* it confers.[43] These two things are not the same, as Gotama notes in the *Abhayarājakumārasutta*:

> Such speech as the Tathāgata knows to be untrue, incorrect, and unbeneficial, and which is also disagreeable and unwelcome to others: such speech the Tathāgata does not utter. Such speech as the Tathāgata knows to be true and correct but unbeneficial, and which is also disagreeable and unwelcome to others: such speech the Tathāgata does not utter. Such speech as the Tathāgata knows to be true, correct, and beneficial, but which is also disagreeable and unwelcome to others: the Tathāgata knows the time to use such speech. Such speech as the Tathāgata knows to be untrue, incorrect, and unbeneficial, but which is agreeable and welcome to others: such speech the Tathāgata does not utter. Such speech as the Tathāgata knows to be true and correct but unbeneficial, and which is agreeable and welcome to others: such speech the Tathāgata does not utter. Such speech as the Tathāgata knows to be true, correct, and beneficial, and which is agreeable and welcome to others: the Tathāgata knows the time to use such speech. Why is that? Because the Tathāgata has compassion for beings.[44]

This passage defines three axes, each bounded by a set of complementary attributes, along which Gotama will endeavor to "plot" his own utterances. The three sets of complementary attributes, some of which are designated via multiple terms, are the following: (1) true (*bhūta*)/correct (*taccha*) vs. false (*abhūta*)/incorrect (*ataccha*); (2) beneficial (*atthasaṃhita*) vs. unbeneficial (*anatthasaṃhita*); and (3) agreeable (*piyā*)/welcome (*manāpā*) vs. disagreeable (*appiyā*)/unwelcome (*amanāpā*). Thus, in addition to truth and agreeability, the passage stipulates another attribute: that of benefit. Utterances may benefit, or fail to benefit, those who hear them.[45]

Gotama considers six combinations of attributes; of these, four are rejected and two retained. Table 1.1 elucidates the combinations considered in the passage and Gotama's assessment regarding each. Each row represents one combination of attributes explicitly considered in the text. Across the top of the table, individual attributes are listed: true (T) and untrue (~T), beneficial (B) and unbeneficial (~B), agreeable (A) and disagreeable (~A). A plus sign (+) in a particular cell indicates that the attribute figures in the particular combination (1–6) that Gotama is considering. The right column records Gotama's assessment of a given combination; ∅ marks a combination that he rejects, while √ marks a combination that he finds tenable.

Table 1.1 makes it easy to see that Gotama's account diverges from that of the *Mānavadharmaśāstra* in several important respects. Both truth and

TABLE 1.1 Assessing the Speech of a Buddha in the *Abhayarājakumārasutta*

	T	*~T*	*B*	*~B*	*A*	*~A*	*Final*
1	−	+	−	+	−	+	∅
2	+	−	−	+	−	+	∅
3	+	−	+	−	−	+	√
4	−	+	−	+	+	−	∅
5	+	−	−	+	+	−	∅
6	+	−	+	−	+	−	√

agreeability are here subordinate to benefit: neither exerts any determinative effect on whether an utterance is found appropriate. (Note especially the fifth combination, which rejects utterances that are admissible according to the *Mānavadharmaśāstra*.) In addition, certain characteristics are clearly presented as autonomous—i.e., the presence of one implies nothing about the presence of another. So, for example, the fact that an utterance is agreeable implies nothing about its benefit or truth (see combinations 4 and 6), and the fact that an utterance is true implies nothing about its agreeability (see combinations 2 and 5).

The passage also suggests that the fact that an utterance is true does not imply that it will be beneficial (see combinations 2 and 5). Yet in the end, the conceptual relation between benefit and truth is left somewhat murky. There would seem to be four possibilities. First, an utterance might be untrue and unbeneficial (explicitly rejected in combinations 1 and 4). Second, an utterance might be true and unbeneficial (explicitly rejected in combinations 2 and 5). Third, an utterance might be true and beneficial (explicitly retained in combinations 3 and 6). Finally, an utterance might be untrue and beneficial. This combination, however, is conspicuously absent from the text.

Why is this possibility ignored? The passage from the *Mānavadharmaśāstra* quoted previously—in which only three of the four possible combinations of truth and agreeability are considered explicitly—suggests one possible rationale: the combination was viewed to be so obviously untenable that it could safely be passed over in silence. If we apply this assumption to the omission in the *Abhayarājakumārasutta*, then Gotama's account takes shape as one in which benefit and truth are distinct but not wholly autonomous: truth does not imply benefit, but benefit does imply truth. When considering whether an utterance is appropriate for a Buddha, therefore, all one needs to ask is whether the utterance benefits others; if it does, it is ipso facto true.[46]

However, as we have seen, sometimes a Buddha's overriding concern with benefit will necessitate that he keep silent, withholding true utterances that, if spoken, would fail to benefit their hearers. The notion that a Buddha may keep silent about certain things that he has seen, heard, and experienced is consonant with the traditional view that "the speech of the Buddha embodie[s] the dharma, yet the dharma [goes] beyond the speech of the Buddha."[47] According to this idea, the speech of a Buddha may be supplemented, although a Buddha's knowledge, by definition, cannot be. In Indian Buddhist traditions, the task of supplementation falls to scriptural commentators: those for whom Buddhist sūtras function as occasions for, and formal exemplars of, right speech.

1.1.3. . . . AND SWEET (*MADHURĀṆI CA*)

If what a Buddha says may at times be disagreeable, the same cannot be said of his voice (*svara*), which the āgamic texts repeatedly describe as delightful (*manojña*), beautiful (*valgu*), and sweet (*madhura*). Mātṛceṭa's invocation of sweetness here thus points to a quality traditionally associated with the Buddha's voice—one that is linked to a particular vocal attribute that is counted among the thirty-two "marks of a great man" (*mahāpuruṣalakṣan āni*).[48] The Buddha is said to possess a "voice like that of Brahmā, sounding as delightful as a *kalaviṅka* bird" (*brahmasvaraḥ kalaviṅkamanojñābhāṇī*).[49] In the *Mahāpadānasutta*, the ancient Buddha Vipassī is described in this way: "The youth Vipassī had a delightful voice, a voice beautiful and sweet. Just as in the Himālayan mountains the *kalaviṅka* has a delightful voice, a voice beautiful, sweet, and touching, so, too, was the youth Vipassī's voice delightful, beautiful, sweet, and touching."[50]

Certain Mahāyāna sūtras also have much to say about "sweet speech" and the practices through which it is to be cultivated. Like their āgamic counterparts, these texts often associate the characteristic of sweetness with that of rhetorical force: the capacity to exhilarate, and to persuade, an audience. At times they go much further, identifying these "virtues of the tongue" (*jihvaguṇa*) as means by which certain representatives of Buddhist tradition may assume the discursive authority of fully realized Buddhas. This is possible insofar as the vocal qualities of a Buddha—qualities such as sweetness, beauty, and so on—are also understood to characterize one who is "learned" (*vicakṣaṇa*, *paṇdita*). Among the learned are, as we have seen, those who teach and comment on the dharma as it is presented in particular Mahāyāna texts. More will be said about such figures in chapter 2.

1.1.4. PROFOUND, PLAIN, OR BOTH (*GŪḌHOTTĀNOBHAYĀRTHĀNI*)

As noted previously, traditional accounts of a Buddha's pedagogical activity often rely on notions of phrasing (*vyañjana*) and meaning (*artha*). When teaching, a Buddha makes use of specific turns of phrase in order to communicate particular meanings to his audience. These meanings may be profound (*gūḍha*), plain (*uttāna*), or both. A Buddha's teaching is traditionally presumed to be informed by his perfect insight into all aspects of the speech situation that might be relevant to orienting his hearers to (or cultivating them in) practice on the path. As the interests and capacities of a Buddha's audience shift, so too does his teaching. The audience thus is seen to determine, to a great degree, the meaning to be communicated and the phrasing best suited to communicate it.

Those fortunate enough to hear a Buddha teach are often dazzled by the power of his message; their responses, employing similes of reorientation and illumination, echo throughout the āgamic texts: "Excellent, sir, excellent! It is as if someone were to set up what has been knocked down, or to point the way to one who had got lost, or to bring an oil lamp into a dark place, so that those with eyes could see what was there. Just so, sir, has the Blessed One expounded the *dhamma* in various ways!"[51] A Buddha's immediate audience is, however, not his only one. The audience portrayed within the text of a sūtra may differ considerably from one that later encounters the sūtra and attempts to make sense of it, and a message that strikes one audience as plain might strike another as profound.

Considerations such as these can tempt us into thinking that Mātṛceṭa may be using words such as "profound" and "plain" in order to mark the ways in which various audiences might respond to a given teaching. On this reading, a profound teaching is one that happens to strike its listeners as profound. Yet Mātṛceṭa's commentator *Nandipriya reads the text differently.[52] According to *Nandipriya, Mātṛceṭa should be understood to be claiming that some teachings *just are* profound (or plain, or both), *regardless* of the way in which an audience—of whatever capacity—may assess them.

Whether a teaching is profound or plain depends on whether its meaning is profound or plain—and what a teaching means is not a matter to be determined by assessing a given audience's reaction to it. *Nandipriya offers examples of both kinds of teaching. A profound teaching is that of dependent arising (Tib. *rten cing 'brel bar 'byung ba*, Skt. *pratītyasamutpāda*); a plain teaching is that of giving (Tib. *sbyin pa*, Skt. *dāna*).

In marking dependent arising as profound, *Nandipriya is in good company:

> And the venerable Ānanda came to the Blessed One, saluted him, sat down to one side, and said to him, "It is wonderful, sir, it is marvelous how profound this dependent arising is, and how profound it appears! And yet, it appears to me as plain as plain [can be]!"
>
> "Do not say that, Ānanda, do not say that! This dependent arising is profound and seems profound. It is through not understanding, not penetrating this doctrine that this generation has become like a tangled ball of string, covered as with a blight, tangled like coarse grass, unable to pass beyond states of woe, the ill destiny, ruin, and the round of birth and death."[53]

As this passage—drawn from the *Mahānidānasutta*—makes clear, a profound teaching can falsely appear plain to one who has yet to achieve perfect insight. Ānanda is here invited to reevaluate his assessment of dependent arising—a concept that is (and hence rightly appears) profound—and so to recognize his inadequate understanding of the concept. Ānanda's failure to understand dependent arising masquerades as clarity, and much of the remainder of the *Mahānidānasutta* consists of the Buddha's attempts to rectify this situation, by offering an extended teaching on the conditional nature of existence. If his goal is to facilitate Ānanda's grasp of the profundity of dependent arising, he works to achieve it by leading Ānanda step-by-step through an elaboration of the constitutive conditions of saṃsāra. In keeping with the semantic connotations of plainness, the Buddha unpacks dependent arising by "opening it up" or "stretching it out"; clarity is achieved via an elaborated account that renders explicit the complexities of the concept.

The task of elaborating concepts in this way is not restricted to Buddhas. It is also held to be an activity proper for learned monks, as we learn from a passage in the *Dasuttarasutta* that summarizes "eight things that should be repeatedly practiced" (*aṭṭha dhammā bahukārā*). Among them is the following directive for action:

> One lives close to a teacher or to some other authoritative person of noble conduct . . . [and] goes to him from time to time, asking and interrogating him, "How is that, sir? What does this mean?" Thus one's venerable teachers can reveal what is unrevealed and make plain that which is not plain (*anuttānikatañ ca uttānīkaronti*), removing one's doubts about the numerous things that give rise to doubt.[51]

In "making plain that which is not plain," a person held to be authoritative elucidates in detail what has been previously expressed in an unclear or elliptical manner: he engages in interpretive commentary.

1.1.5. SUCCINCT OR DETAILED (*SAMĀSAVYĀSAVANTI*)

Unlike the previous pair of qualities, which pertained to meaning, these two qualities pertain to a teaching's phrasing—to its terseness or prolixity. The pair of attributes alludes to various āgamic passages in which the Tathāgata is described as teaching the dharma in two ways: concisely (*saṃkṣiptena/saṅkhittena*) and in an elaborated fashion (*vistareṇa/vistāreṇa/vitthāreṇa*).[55]

If utterances that express a "profound meaning" cry out for commentary, no less do utterances that are "concise." In the āgamic texts, the term *saṅkhitta* is routinely used to describe a teaching that listeners find *overly* terse, hence difficult to understand and in need of commentarial elaboration.[56] This elaboration is sometimes provided by Gotama himself. If he is unavailable, it may be provided by a senior disciple and subsequently ratified by the Buddha. In the *Uddesavibhaṅgasutta*, for example, a group of monks are faced with a teaching that they find too terse for ready comprehension. They approach the eminent figure Mahākaccāna—elsewhere identified as "chief among those who elaborate on the meaning of that which is stated concisely" (*saṅkhittena bhāsitassa vitthāreṇa atthaṃ vibhajantānam*)—for a more elaborated account.[57] Mahākaccāna duly expounds on the text, and when the monks next encounter the Buddha, they report all that has unfolded in his absence. Gotama responds: "Mahākaccāna is learned, monks; Mahākaccāna has great wisdom. If you had asked me the meaning of this, I would have explained it to you in the same way that Mahākaccāna has explained it. Such is its meaning, and so you should remember it."[58] Mahākaccāna is not the only figure in the āgamic literature whose commentaries are ratified by Gotama in this way; the tradition clearly allows that certain non-Buddhas may be able to teach, on occasion, just as a Buddha does.[59] The practice of commenting on a Buddha's utterances is thus granted a twofold imprimatur: to comment is not only to speak as a Buddha does, but also to speak as a Buddha explicitly recommends speaking.

2. Speaking as a Monk: Speech Protocols in the *Prātimokṣasūtra*

Although a Buddha's perfected speech was seen to embody an ideal toward which monastic commentators should aspire, this ideal was certainly not the only source from which they drew their assumptions regarding speech protocols. As monks, they would also have been familiar with vinaya texts, which present—among other things—rules and regulations for monastic life.[60] Among these texts, one in particular probably exerted a disproportionate impact: the *Prātimokṣasūtra*, a text that was learned by heart and communally recited every fortnight.[61]

The *Prātimokṣasūtra* inventories offenses against which a properly observant monk vows to guard.[62] Two hundred fifty-eight such offenses are discussed in the Mūlasarvāstivāda rescension of the text. They pertain to an enormous range of practical matters, from improper mealtime decorum to improper care of monastic robes. The vows against committing these offenses are arranged in seven sections, each of which addresses offenses deemed less grave than those of the preceding section. The list commences with offenses that necessitate permanent expulsion from the (local) monastic community or comparable punishment.[63] A monk who transgresses the vows listed in the second section is to be ostracized from the community for a probationary period and forced to undergo penance, whereas a monk who transgresses vows listed in the fifth and sixth sections is to be absolved after confessing the offense.[64] Finally, monks who transgress the vows laid down in the text's seventh section are not subjected to any formal sanction or punishment; this section pertains to what we might think of as rules of etiquette.

More than one-fifth of the vows are concerned with speech protocols; the precise number is, on my count, fifty-nine.[65] The relevant offenses, in the order in which they are specified in the Sanskrit text, are:

I. *Pārājika*

I.4: intentionally and falsely representing oneself as one who has seen or known things that are seeable and knowable only by persons of consummate attainment [C][66]

II. *Saṃghāvaśeṣa*

II.3: addressing a woman lewdly [C]

II.4: attempting to convince a woman to have intercourse [C]

II.5: acting as a go-between between a man and a woman to facilitate a liaison or marriage [C]

II.8: groundlessly accusing another monk of a *pārājika* offense [C]

II.9: groundlessly accusing another monk of an offense involving defeat and doing so by knowingly introducing putative "evidence" against the monk that is irrelevant to the charge one is making [C]

II.10: sowing discord in the community [C]

II.11: failing to admonish a monk who is sowing discord [F]

V. *Pātayantika*

V.1: lying [C]

V.2: using abusive language [C]

V.3: slandering another monk [C]

V.4: attempting to reintroduce discussion on a matter already settled by the community [C]

V.5: teaching the dharma—in more than five or six phrases—to women, unless an intelligent person is present [A]

V.6: teaching dharma verses to those who have not received ordination [A]

V.7: spreading, among those who have not received ordination, reports of a monk's known offenses [A]

V.8: representing oneself to those who have not received ordination as one who has seen or known things that are seeable and knowable only by persons of consummate attainment, even if such claims are true [A]

V.10: disparaging the *prātimokṣa* rules [C]

V.12: deriding or abusing others [C]

V.21: admonishing nuns (*bhikṣuṇī*) without being deputized to do so [A]

V.22: admonishing nuns in the evening [A]

V.23: stating that monks instruct nuns because they [i.e., the monks] desire worldly gain [C]

V.35: causing the annoyance of fellow monks by entreating them to eat after a meal has been completed [C]

V.50: concealing another's offence [F]

V.53: gainsaying previous consent to a community proceeding [C]

V.55: misreporting the dharma [C]

V.56: allying oneself with one who has misreported the dharma [C]

V.62: purposefully arousing suspicion so as to vex another monk [C]

V.69: falsely charging another monk with a *saṃghāvaśeṣa* offense [C]

V.75: deferring the learning of a particular *prātimokṣa* vow until one has been able to question experts about it [F]

V.78: disrespecting other monks [C]

V.83: claiming ignorance of the *Prātimokṣasūtra* and thereby disrespecting it [C]

VI. *Pratideśanīya*

VI.2: failing to admonish a lapse in the conduct of a nun at meals [F]

VII. *Śaikṣadharma*

VII.53: talking with food in the mouth

VII.79: teaching dharma while standing to someone who is seated [A]

VII.80: teaching dharma while sitting to someone who is lying down—unless that person is ill [A]

VII.81: teaching dharma from a low seat to someone on a higher seat—unless that person is ill [A]

VII.82: teaching dharma to one in front of, yet facing away from, oneself—unless that person is ill [A]

VII.83: teaching dharma from the side of a road to one who is on the road—unless that person is ill [A]

VII.84: teaching dharma to someone who has his [or her] head covered—unless that person is ill [A]

VII.85: teaching dharma to someone who has tucked up his garment (*utkṛṣṭikākṛtāya*)—unless that person is ill [A]

VII.86: teaching dharma to a person whose hands are on his shoulder(s) (*utsaktikākṛtāya*)—unless that person is ill [A]

VII.87: teaching dharma to a person whose hands are on his neck (*udvyastikākṛtāya*)—unless that person is ill [A]

VII.88: teaching dharma to a person who folds his arms (*paryastikākṛṭāya*) [A]

VII.89: teaching dharma to a person wearing a turban (*uṣṇīṣa*)—unless that person is ill [A]

VII.90: teaching dharma to a person wearing a hat—unless that person is ill [A]

VII.91: teaching dharma to a person wearing a topknot—unless that person is ill [A]

VII.92: teaching dharma to a person wearing a crown—unless that person is ill [A]

VII.93: teaching dharma to a person wearing a headband—unless that person is ill [A]

VII.94: teaching dharma to a person riding an elephant—unless that person is ill [A]

VII.95: teaching dharma to a person riding a horse—unless that person is ill [A]

VII.96: teaching dharma to a person riding in a palanquin (*śivikā*)—unless that person is ill [A]

VII.97: teaching dharma to a person riding a chariot (*yāna*)—unless that person is ill [A]

VII.98: teaching dharma to a person wearing high shoes (*pādukā*)—unless that person is ill [A]

VII.99: teaching dharma to a person carrying a staff—unless that person is ill [A]

VII.100: teaching dharma to a person carrying a parasol—unless that person is ill [A]

VII.101: teaching dharma to a person carrying a sword—unless that person is ill [A]

VII.102: teaching dharma to a person carrying a dagger—unless that person is ill [A]

VII.103: teaching dharma to a person carrying a weapon (*āyudha*)—unless that person is ill [A]

VII.104: teaching dharma to a person clad in armor (*saṃnadhāya*)—unless that person is ill [A]

Clearly, we have come some distance from the simplicity of the fourfold account of right speech with which we began (i.e., the avoidance of false speech, malicious speech, harsh speech, and idle chatter). Offenses that would be indistinguishable according to that account are here differentiated into ranked categories, acknowledging competing obligations within and beyond the community. So, for example, although the fourfold account emphasizes that one should speak truly, this imperative is at times clearly subordinated to social protocols. For example, rule V.7 stipulates that a monk should speak truth but should not offer reports of another monk's offenses to those who have not received ordination, even if such reports are true. The *Prātimokṣasūtra*, echoing the view voiced in the sūtra texts already examined here, suggests that not every truth is a truth worth uttering. It also suggests that not every lie is equally deserving of censure.[67] Lies are classified into ranked types. All violate the injunction to speak truly, but all do not merit the same degree of punishment. Most are considered *pātayantika* offenses, but one is deemed unforgivable: if a monk intentionally misrepresents his level of attainment, he has committed a *pārājika* offense—on a par with killing, stealing, and sexual intercourse.

The *Prātimokṣasūtra*'s speech protocols pertain both to what a monk may say and to the circumstances in which he may say it. We may therefore group the offenses listed earlier into two broad categories, according to the particular component of the speech situation that each emphasizes. Twenty-two vows seem to be principally—although not always exclusively—concerned with the *content or form* of an utterance; in transgressing these vows, a monk incurs fault because *what he says* is improper. In the list, I have marked these [C]. Thirty-two vows are principally (although, again, not always exclusively) concerned with issues of *context*—and more specifically with a monk's *audience*. In transgressing such vows, the monk incurs fault because he speaks to someone who is, for one reason or another, inappropriate as a listener. The fault is incurred despite the fact that what the monk says may, in other circumstances, be perfectly permissible—even praiseworthy. These I have marked [A]. Four additional vows stipulate fault incurred as a result of failing to speak when speech is called for; these are coded [F].[68]Although a great number of vows concern issues of audience, most of these are classed as *śaikṣadharma*, and their violation is not presented as a particularly grave matter. In general, then, it would seem that *saying the wrong thing* is a matter of greater concern than either *saying the right thing to the wrong person* or *failing to speak*.

Saying the wrong thing can take many forms, and not all such forms are equally egregious. As noted previously, the gravest speech offense is the intentional misrepresentation of oneself as one who perceives and knows things that are properly perceived and known only by Buddhas (and by those who have advanced to a significant degree along the path). The gravity accorded to this offense is understandable, since claims to possess such qualities serve to authorize the actions and speech of those making them. If the claims are true, they effectively render the actions of their claimants immune from criticism by those who are (or who take themselves to be) less advanced. If they are false, however, they make a mockery of the Buddha's own claims to knowledge and threaten the unity of a community founded in part upon the assumption that such claims can—at least in certain instances—be trusted.

Far less egregious, but crucial to a discussion of Buddhist monastic commentarial practice, is the offense of "misreporting the dharma," addressed by vow V.55:

> Any monk who should speak thus: "As I understand [it], the Blessed One taught dharma in this way: those things stated by the Blessed One to be obstructions do not suffice to obstruct one who practices them," should be instructed by the monks. They should say to him, "Friend, do not say, 'As I understand [it], the Blessed One taught dharma in this way: those things stated by the Blessed One to be obstructions do not suffice to obstruct one who practices them.' Do not misrepresent the Blessed One; it is not good! Moreover, the Blessed One did not speak in that way. Friend, on many occasions, the Blessed One said, 'Obstructive things are precisely obstructions, since they obstruct one who serves them.' Friend, you should abandon this pernicious view."
>
> If, upon being instructed in this way by the [other] monks, that monk abandons [his previously stated] position, that is good. If he does not abandon [it], then he should be correctly instructed again—queried a second and third time—so that he might abandon [his] position. If, upon being correctly instructed for a second and third time [and] having been correctly taught, he should abandon his position, that is good. If not, [he thereby incurs] a *pātayantika* [offense].[69]

For the modern reader, this vow manages to be both exceedingly specific and disarmingly vague. The offense recorded here is drawn in terms that are far more detailed than "misreporting the dharma" might initially suggest, but it is this very wealth of specificity that makes generalization difficult. It is unclear, for example, whether the vow aims to censure the monk for expressing only this *particular* view—a view pertaining to the nature of "obstructive things" (*antarāyikā dharmā*)—or whether the offense committed here may be generalized to any view (or to the inappropriate attribution of any view [to Buddhas? to any teacher in the community?]) that authoritative monks deem pernicious.

The combination of particularity and vagueness that we see here is not uncommon among *prātimokṣa* vows; it results, in part, from the manner in which the vows were codified. This vow, like the others, decontextualizes—and thereby aims to generalize the normative implications of—a particular āgamic story, appropriating these implications as guidelines for monastic conduct. Traces of these source narratives, in all their specificity, sometimes remain embedded in the final form of the vow.[70] The story that serves as a source text for V.55 may be found in the opening section of the Pali *Alagaddūpamasutta*.[71] In a passage that contextualizes and reiterates much of the text of the vow, we read:

> Thus have I heard: on one occasion the Blessed One was living at Sāvatthī in Jeta's Grove, Anāthapiṇḍika's Park. Now, on that occasion a pernicious view had arisen in a monk named Ariṭṭha (Skt. *ariṣṭa*; "ill omen"), formerly of the vulture killers, thus: "I understand the dharma taught by the Blessed One in this way: those dharmas stated by the Blessed One to be obstructions do not suffice to obstruct one practicing them." Hearing this, several monks went to the monk Ariṭṭha and asked him, "Friend Ariṭṭha, is it true that such a pernicious view has arisen in you?"
>
> "Just so, friends. As I understand [it], the Blessed One taught the dharma in this way: those dharmas stated by the Blessed One to be obstructions do not suffice to obstruct one who practices them."
>
> Then these monks, desiring to detach him from that pernicious view, pressed and questioned and cross-questioned him thus: "Friend Ariṭṭha, do not say, 'As I understand [it], the Blessed One taught dharma in this way: those dharmas stated by the Blessed One to be obstructions do not suffice to obstruct one who practices them.' Do not misrepresent the Blessed One; it is not

> good to misrepresent the Blessed One. The Blessed One would not speak in that way. Ariṭṭha, in many discourses the Blessed One said that obstructive dharmas are obstructions, and they are sufficient to obstruct one who practices them."[72]

Following this scene, the monks go on to inform the Buddha Gotama of Ariṭṭha's pronouncement, and Ariṭṭha is subsequently called to his presence. Gotama informs him that he is foolish (*mogha*) and that, as a consequence of his delusion, he injures himself. The Buddha then adds that the demerit Ariṭṭha has accrued will lead him to experience prolonged suffering in the future (*bhavaissati dīgharattaṃ ahitāya dukkhāya*). This is the last we hear of Ariṭṭha; the text does not specify whether the Buddha's admonishments had any effect on the monk's views. However, the overall point of the story is clear: the demerit that Ariṭṭha incurs derives from his failure to issue an accurate report of the teaching of the Buddha. Ariṭṭha's erroneous report is held up as a paradigm of incorrect speech in the *Prātimokṣasūtra*, and the offense is generalized: it is explicitly stipulated to be applicable to "any monk who speaks thus."

In both the original narrative and its generalization in the *Prātimokṣasūtra*, the "pernicious view" at issue may appear to be the following: *those dharmas identified by the Buddha as obstructions are not properly to be thought of in that way.* However, to phrase the view in this way makes it look as though we are faced with a simple difference of opinion—Ariṭṭha holding one view about the way things are, Gotama holding another. This should give us pause. Monks are not, as a rule, perfectly awakened beings, nor do they claim to be; in light of this, a difference of opinion between an awakened being and a being that is not awakened would be neither surprising nor rare. The offense that Ariṭṭha incurs is more complex. He is held to be worthy of reprimand because he has attributed to Gotama a position that amounts only to his own misguided assessment (or recall) of the Buddha's teaching. The "pernicious view" is thus not simply a view about obstructions—a view that assesses them in a way that is notably distinct from, and discordant with, Gotama's own view. Rather, a constitutive feature of Ariṭṭha's pernicious view is that *his assessment is Gotama's assessment.* Were this to be true, it would imply that Gotama, insofar as he speaks of obstructive things as obstructions, knowingly engages in false speech—and hence violates the very protocols that he is presumed to endorse.

3. Concluding Remarks

The foregoing reflections on vow V.55 suggest that the practice of commentary was held by Indian Buddhist monks to carry with it a measure of risk. Monastic commentators who endeavored to follow the speech protocols laid down in the *Prātimokṣasūtra* were forced to walk a rhetorical tightrope. They had to interpret the words of a Buddha in an authoritative way—a way sanctioned by wise monks as accurately representing a Buddha's intentions—while avoiding any explicit claim to know the nature of those intentions, lest they incur the fault of Ariṭṭha. Commentators had to speak persuasively for—but not as—Buddhas. This is not to say that qualities of speech and insight associated with Buddhahood could not subsequently be associated with a given author. However, those who proclaimed their own understanding of the dharma to be that of a Buddha ran the risk of running afoul of V.55. Commentarial authority was thus not to be claimed for oneself; it was to be granted by others. Among those to whom it was granted were Buddhist teachers and preachers, and it is to these figures that we now turn.

TWO

Models of Instruction

Preachers Perfect and Imperfect

IN THE PREVIOUS chapter, two models of and for "right speech" were sketched. In sketching the first model, which portrays Buddhas as right speakers par excellence, I drew principally from the corpus of Buddhist sūtra literature. In sketching the second model, which portrays Buddhist monks as speakers normatively (if not always actually) constrained by formalized monastic regulations, I drew principally from the *Prātimokṣasūtra*—a work classified by the tradition under the broad heading of vinaya. These models do not embody all the lessons that a monk might learn from sūtra or vinaya texts regarding how to speak and how not to speak (Buddhist sūtra texts are not simply prescriptive, and the monumental Mūlasarvāstivāda vinaya literature is undoubtedly much more than proscriptive). But they do, I hope, serve to illuminate elements of the complex web of assumptions that informed the work of Indian Buddhist commentators. The present chapter examines another normative resource from which Indian Buddhist intellectuals drew in thinking about commentary and commentators: the shifting portrayals, in Buddhist sūtras and śāstras, of what we might call the "aims of education" of Buddhist monasticism, and the articulation of these aims in, and by, a figure of doctrinal authority: the preacher of dharma.

Dharma preachers have historically served as voices for the dharma, giving successive generations of Buddhists an opportunity to hear, remember, and understand Buddhist sūtra texts. They have also been voiced by the dharma, articulated in the very sūtra texts that they are charged to preserve and protect. In these texts, preachers are portrayed in rather ambivalent terms; though not (simply) students of the dharma, they are also not usually perfected Buddhas. Preachers are thus seen to occupy a middle ground between the perfected authority normatively accorded to Buddhas and the relative lack of authority normatively accorded to most lay and monastic Buddhists. As figures of pedagogical authority, preachers are held to possess some of the skills associated with Buddhas, but they need not possess all such skills.

What, then, is normatively demanded of those who would become dharma preachers? What capacities are they presumed to possess? What is presumed to follow from these capacities? This chapter endeavors to explore these questions. After a brief background discussion (section 1), a portrait of an idealized dharma preacher is sketched. This portrait draws from Buddhist texts that were known to—and cited by—Buddhist scholastic commentators (section 2). In section 3, we will observe these commentators refracting the idealized image of the dharma preacher. The conclusion of the chapter (section 4) reflects on the implications of these findings for our understanding of (traditional understandings of) idealized and realized dharma preachers.

1. The "*Bhāṇaka* System"

To date, much of the scholarship on Buddhist preachers has focused on their role as transmitters of early, oral Buddhist tradition.[1] It is generally accepted that early Buddhist teachings were transmitted without the use of writing, probably in a number of related dialects spoken in north India during the fourth century B.C.E. During this period, the transmission of Buddhist texts appears to have been entrusted to figures known as *bhāṇakas*. These *bhāṇakas* were monks whose job it was to preserve, in memory, the words in which Buddhist teachings were spoken and to transmit these words to others.[2] Different *bhāṇakas* seem to have been responsible for handling different sections of the Buddhist textual corpus: one finds reference to *Dīghabhāṇakas*, *Majjhimabhāṇakas*, *Saṃyuttabhāṇakas*, *Aṅguttarabhāṇakas*, *Jātakabhāṇakas*, *Dhammapadabhāṇakas*, and so on.[3]

Recent scholars—among them K. R. Norman, Sodo Mori, and Steven Collins—have hypothesized that with the introduction of writing as a means for the preservation and transmission of Buddhist canonical texts, the "*bhāṇaka* system" underwent certain changes.[4] The emphasis placed on memorizing the *whole* of a particular textual collection appears to have been gradually reduced. One of Buddhaghosa's two commentaries on the Pali vinaya bears this out, noting that *bhāṇaka*s who specialize in particular textual collections need learn only certain sections of those collections.[5] Collins has concluded from this that at the time the commentary was composed—in the late fourth or early fifth century C.E.—"the different *bhāṇaka*s represent a division of labor not so much in textual transmission as among specialists in public recitation."[6] Whether or not an increased reliance on writing accentuated the *bhāṇaka*s' duties as reciters, it likely brought with it a certain measure of freedom from the time-consuming task of rote memorization.[7] As Mori has emphasized, Buddhist *bhāṇaka*s appear to have put this newfound freedom to use by investigating more closely the doctrinal content of their texts and then comparing their understanding of those texts with that advocated by other *bhāṇaka*s. As a consequence, various groups of *bhāṇaka*s began to notice differences in the material they had memorized and in how they understood this material. One might expect a compensatory parochialism to ensue, with specialist *bhāṇaka*s claiming privileged status for themselves and for the texts in which they specialized. Instead, however, what seems to have happened is that the specializations themselves—*Dīghabhāṇaka*, *Majjhimabhāṇaka*, and the like—gradually weakened and disappeared. References to these specializations are virtually nonexistent in the corpus of Indian Buddhist texts not composed in Pali (with the exception of the *Milindapañha*, a text that today survives in Pali but which may have been composed in Sanskrit or Prakrit).[8] Although such references are occasionally found in Prakrit donative inscriptions (roughly datable to a period between the second century B.C.E. and the first century C.E.), these are largely confined to Sri Lanka.[9] This is not to say that preachers are rarely referenced in Indian inscriptions; the pillar inscriptions at Bhārhut and Sāñcī (c. second century B.C.E.) make several references to them. In each case, however, the term used is simply the unqualified *bhāṇaka* (or the variants *bhānaka*/*bhanaka*).[10]

By the time that the Sanskrit *Prajñāpāramitā* (Perfection of wisdom) texts began to be disseminated widely (in roughly the first century C.E.), the practice of categorizing *bhāṇaka*s by textual specialty appears to have fallen largely out of favor. Whereas we typically find the unqualified term *bhāṇaka* in the Indian inscriptions, the *Prajñāpāramitā* texts tend to rely on another general term—or, more precisely, compound—to designate preachers: *dharmabhāṇaka*.[11] This is not, however, the only term so used. The terms *dharmakathika* and *dharmavādin* are also found in the extant Sanskrit texts; it is not clear whether the latter terms were understood to be interchangeable with each other or with the term *dharmabhāṇaka*.[12] The *Mahāvyutpatti*, a seminal ninth-century Sanskrit-Tibetan lexicon, notes that *dharmabhāṇaka* is properly to be translated as *chos smra ba*, while the term *dharmakathika* is to be translated as *chos sgrogs pa*. This suggests that some distinction between the two terms was held to be worth preserving in translation, even as late as the ninth century. When we turn to inspect the way in which the relevant Tibetan terms were actually employed in translations of Sanskrit texts, however, irregularities surface. The term *chos smra ba* was sometimes used to render *dharmavādin*, the term *chos sgrogs pa* to render *dharmabhāṇaka*, and, on at least one occasion, the terms *chos sgrogs pa* and *chos smra ba* were both used to translate what appears to have been a single underlying Sanskrit term.[13]

These observations suggest that our picture of the Indian Buddhist preacher is one that may well be fated to a measure of indeterminacy and vagueness. If the terms *dharmabhāṇaka*, *dharmakathika*, and *dharmavādin* were viewed as interchangeable by the Tibetan translation teams working during the eighth and early ninth centuries C.E., this may be because none of these terms was presumed to denote a distinct institutional title or exclusive occupation. The terms were likely used more loosely to refer to a person who regularly propounded Buddhist teachings, whether or not this person was an acknowledged member of a monastic community or held any additional title. If so, then when a text calls a person a *dharmabhāṇaka*, *dharmakathika*, or *dharmavādin*, we cannot conclude from this that the person is, or is not, a teacher (*ācārya*), a monastic preceptor (*upādhyāya*), or a monk (*bhikṣu*). Indeed, we cannot even assume that dharma preachers were presumed to uphold lay Buddhist precepts as these precepts have traditionally been understood. An intriguing passage in the *Kāraṇḍavyūhasūtra* refers to a *dharmabhāṇaka* who possesses profound insight, but who "neglects moral precepts and proper behavior (*śīlavipannaḥ ācaravipanna*), is surrounded by wives, sons, and daughters (*bhāryaputraduhitṛbhiḥ parivṛta*), has a robe covered in urine and excrement (*kāṣāyoccāraprasrāvaparipūrṇa*) and is not celibate (*asaṃvṛtteryāpatha*)."[14]

A passage such as this raises many questions and returns us to issues already raised in the introduction to the present work. There is no reason to assume that the practices of real-world preachers outside Buddhist sūtra texts correspond to the portraits of preachers found inside those texts. Yet even if we grant the notion that Buddhist sūtra texts are broadly normative in orientation, and that what actually happens need not correspond to what is held to be worth happening, we should not presume that the sūtras have nothing to teach us about history. To do so is to neglect the fact that normative texts can and do *affect* history, insofar as they delineate the terms in which people interpret and articulate their experiences. If models of preaching proffered *inside* Buddhist sūtra texts were propagated by successive generations of preachers *outside* those texts, then the accounts of preachers offered in texts surely had an impact on the ways in which preachers outside the texts conceptualized their own responsibilities, capacities, and activities. For this reason, passages from Buddhist sūtras that discuss dharma preachers are arguably of interest not only to students of Buddhist philosophy and rhetoric, but to historians of the tradition as well.

2. The Preacher "in Theory": Models of Teaching

In the final chapter of the extraordinary florilegium *Śikṣāsamuccaya*, the great eighth-century Buddhist author Śāntideva asks: "How should the gift of the dharma be given (*kathaṃ dharmadāno dātavyam*)?"[15] As a response to this question, he offers an excerpt from the thirteenth chapter of the *Saddharmapuṇḍarīkasūtra* that provides a vivid account of an idealized occasion of Buddhist instruction:

> A learned one, contemplating for a time, enters into his room;
> Having properly shut the door, having seen the dharma in an entirely correct way,
> Arising, with mind unafraid, he should expound the dharma.
> The learned one ever abides in happiness;
> Perfected in happiness, he also teaches the dharma, just as it is.
> Seated upon an elevated seat [that has been] well prepared [for him]
> In a place that is pure and pleasing,

He has donned a robe that is well dyed with a beautiful hue [and] clean,
A black dust cloak, properly prepared, and a long undergarment.
Having washed his feet well, he ascends and sits upon the dais,
Which is draped in various colored cloths and equipped with a footstool;
His face [is] radiant with oil.
Seated on that dharma seat, he teaches many discourses, various in kind
To the assembly of sentient beings who have grown attentive—
To the monks and nuns.[16]
Abandoning indolence, he should not think of quarreling;
Abandoning all displeasure, he should contemplate
The power of kindness in the assembly,
And he should speak [alt. cultivate] supreme teachings day and night.[17]
The learned one should thus satisfy and gladden the assemblies
With myriad diverse illustrations.
He should not wish for anything at all;
Accordingly, he should not worry over
That which is to be eaten and that which is to be enjoyed—food and drink,
Clothing, beds, robes, and medicines for the ill.
In the assembly, he should not want for anything.
On the contrary, the learned one continually should think:
"I myself and these sentient beings should attain awakening.
The dharma I teach, the basis for my own happiness—
I should let it be heard in the world for [the world's] benefit."[9]

In its original context of the *Saddharmapuṇḍarīkasūtra*, this passage purports to recount a moment in an ongoing dialogue between the Buddha and the bodhisattva Mañjuśrī. Such a dialogue format is quite typical of Mahāyāna sūtras (and, indeed, of Buddhist sūtra literature more generally). Typically, these texts begin by establishing a figure of authority—usually, though not always, a Buddha—as residing in a certain place, together with a retinue. An exchange is then recounted, in which one or more interlocutors—often members of the retinue—pose questions to the figure of authority, and the latter responds. The ensuing discourse may treat any number of topics; one topic that is sometimes broached is the matter of teaching and the shape it should take. When this occurs—as it does in the passage that Śāntideva quotes here—the resulting rhetorical situation is complex: the sūtra narrates a situation of teaching in which the subject of teaching is itself addressed. The speaker depicted *in* the passage here is plausibly read as a Buddhist preacher, while the speaker *of* the passage is Śākyamuni—and, notably, Śākyamuni describes a situation that is isomorphic with his own: both he, and the preacher he describes, are instructing others in Buddhist dharma. Śāntideva's citation of this text adds yet another layer of complexity, as he cites the passage as a response to a request for instruction as to how one ought to instruct others in the dharma ("How should the gift of the dharma be given?"). In the context of the *Śikṣāsamuccaya*, then, there are at least three distinct levels on which instruction is occurring or being modeled: Śāntideva is teaching *his* audience by appropriating a text purporting to recount the words of a Buddha teaching *his* audience about a Buddhist preacher teaching *his* audience the dharma. To the extent that Śāntideva's teaching is seen to correspond to the idealized situation that he (together with the *Saddharmapuṇḍarīkasūtra*) claims to have been described by the Buddha, Śāntideva's own utterance stands a good chance of being considered authoritative by his audience.

Although the passage does not employ a term that might reasonably be translated as "preacher," there can be little doubt that the situation it depicts is one of preaching; the learned figure at its heart corresponds well to the portrayal of preachers in texts such as the *Dharmasaṅgīti*, the *Daśabhūmika*, the *Suvarṇa(pra)bhāsottama*, the *Akṣayamatinirdeśa*, and the *Ratnamegha*. Each of these texts appears to have enjoyed considerable popularity among Indian authors working during the latter half of the first millennium, and each in its own way portrays the Buddhist preacher as a figure who actively *teaches*.[10] The preachers portrayed in these sūtras are not simply specialists in public recitation. They do not simply parrot texts that they have learned by heart, but they alternately analyze, paraphrase, summarize, elaborate, and tailor their teachings to suit the sensibilities and interests of particular audiences.

The qualities of the idealized dharma preacher (*chos smra ba po*) are extolled at length in the *Dharmasaṅgīti*, whose treatment of the figure comprises six parallel passages that extend over five folios in Tibetan translation.[11] Each of the first five of these passages adduces "ten undertakings in the way(s) of the dharma through which bodhisattvas achieve the mastery of the dharma preacher" (*byang chub sems dpas chos kyi tshul la 'jug pa bcus chos smra ba po khong du chud par bya*), while the sixth parallel passage adduces a set of ten things to which the dharma preacher may be compared: the earth, water, fire, wind, the sky, the moon, the sun, a solid boat, a bridge, and a lamp. According to the *Dharmasaṅgīti*, a dharma preacher is not simply a repository of faultless words (*sgra ngan pa med pa*), but also one whose utterances constitute explanations (or analyses: *rnam par 'byed pa*, Skt. **vibhaṅga*) of what is recondite (*gsang ba*, Skt. **guhya*).

The *Dharmasaṅgīti* also notes that the preacher is furnished with four discriminations (*pratisaṃvid*),[12] which together constitute what might today be termed a pedagogical skill set. The discriminations are widely discussed in Indian Buddhist literature. They appear in both Mahāyāna and non-Mahāyāna texts but are treated most extensively in certain sūtras associated with the Mahāyāna.[13] Close attention to the specifics of these treatments will afford us a more nuanced picture of pedagogical authority as normatively understood by Indian Buddhists.

2.1. Approaching the Four Discriminations

A useful place to begin is with the *Daśabhūmikasūtra*.[14] The *Daśabhūmikasūtra* charts the path to Buddhahood in terms of the ten gradational bodhisattva stages or levels—*bhūmis*—that its title references. On the way to becoming a Buddha, a bodhisattva passes through each of these levels in sequence, thus acquiring the particular characteristics associated with the level.[15] The levels are correlated with a traditional sequence of ten perfections (*pāramitā*), as in table 2.1.[16]

Among the perfections, the second—that of ethics or morality (*śīla*)—is typically associated with right speech: to speak rightly is to engage in moral action. It is thus no surprise to find that the qualities traditionally associated with right speech are initially broached in the *Daśabhūmikasūtra*'s treatment of the second bodhisattva level. These qualities are presented in the elaborate style that characterizes most of the sūtras of the *Avataṃsaka* corpus:

> [A second-level bodhisattva] abstains from speech that is wrong (*anṛta*); he is a speaker of what is true, correct, and appropriate. As he says, so he does. Even in a dream, when one's intention can wander [toward an inappropriate] view, receptivity, pleasure, wish, supposition, [or] reflection, he does not so much as utter an inappropriate word, much less speak deliberately [in such a way].[17]

TABLE 2.1 Perfections and Levels of the *Daśabhūmikasūtra*

Perfection (pāramitā)	*Level (bhūmi)*
1. Giving (*dānapāramitā*)	1. Joyful (*pramuditā*)
2. Ethics (*śīlapāramitā*)	2. Immaculate (*vimalā*)
3. Forbearance (*kṣāntipāramitā*)	3. Illuminating (*prabhākarī*)
4. Effort (*vīryapāramitā*)	4. Flaming (*arciṣmatī*)
5. Meditation (*dhyānapāramitā*)	5. Hard to Conquer (*sudurjayā*)
6. Insight (*prajñāpāramitā*)	6. Manifest (*abhimukhī*)
7. Skill in Means (*upāyakauśalyapāramitā*)	7. Far-Reaching (*dūraṅgamā*)
8. Vow (*praṇidhānapāramitā*)	8. Unmoving (*acalā*)
9. Power (*bālapāramitā*)	9. Excellent Intelligence (*sādhumatī*)
10. Knowledge (*jñānapāramitā*)	10. Cloud of Doctrine (*dharmameghā*)

Moreover, he abstains from speech that is malicious, practicing [speech that is] nondivisive and noninjurious among sentient beings. He does not repeat what he has heard here to the detriment of these, nor does he repeat what he has heard there to the detriment of those. He does not divide those who are in concord, nor does he encourage those who are divided. He takes no pleasure or delight in schism, nor does he utter speech—whether true or false—that prompts schism.

Moreover, he abstains from harsh speech—speech that is out of turn, cruel, rough toward others, offensive to others, faulty and inclined toward fault, vulgar, common, impure, not pleasing to the ear, uttered in anger and rage; [speech that] enflames the heart, sears the mind, is disagreeable, unwelcome, [and] not delightful, [and is] destructive to one's own mental continuum and the continua of others.

[Rather,] having abandoned such speech, [a second-level bodhisattva] utters speech that is gentle, soft, delightful, sweet, endearing, appealing, beneficial, pure, pleasing to the ear; [speech that] reaches the heart, is affectionate, urbane, articulate; [speech that] should be understood, heard, and relied upon; [speech that is] desired by multitudes, loved by multitudes, dear to multitudes, ingratiating, instructive, conducive to the benefit and happiness of all sentient beings, concentrated; [speech that] gladdens the mind, refreshes the mind, and engenders confidence in one's own mental continuum and in the mental continua of others.

Moreover, he abstains from idle chatter; his utterances are well-guarded, timely, [and] correct; he is a speaker of meaning (*arthavādī*), a speaker of the

> dharma (*dharmavādī*), a speaker of reason (*nyāyavādī*), [and] a speaker of discipline (*vinayavādī*). He utters speech possessed of a sound basis (*sanidānavatīvācaṃ bhāṣate*), [and he does so] at the right time and in an orderly sequence [of phrases].[18] He has also abandoned even the telling of legends from the past, to say nothing of confused speech.[19]

In this passage, stress is placed not so much on the activity of teaching as on the activity of speaking more generally. Although the speech of a second-level bodhisattva is said to be "instructive" (*vijñāpannā*), and although other qualities attributed to it clearly echo qualities attributed to the speech of Buddhas, the text largely refrains from presenting the idealized bodhisattva of the second level as an authoritative teacher, perhaps because he has not yet engaged in the practices that the tradition associates with learnedness. Such practices are specifically referenced in connection with the third bodhisattva level, termed "illuminating" (*prabhākarī*). On this level, the text tells us, a bodhisattva honors the Tathāgatas, arhats, and samyaksambuddhas, and listens to, grasps, and retains their teaching of the dharma.[20] Having abandoned all worldly interests, he "encounters no difficulties whatsoever, except those pertaining to the person of the dharma preacher (*dharmabhāṇakapudgala*) who teaches him even one word of the dharma."[21] Furthermore, the bodhisattva now also understands that the virtuous qualities of a Buddha are to be comprehended by practicing the dharma and those things that accord with it—and that practice of this kind should be understood to extend well beyond the cultivation of pure speech.

If the bodhisattva is assiduous in his efforts, he may eventually advance to the fifth level—"hard to conquer" (*sudurjayā*)—where he will acquire a wealth of qualities and skills that culminate in the inception of a new activity, that of propounding Buddhist dharma to others:

> [The fifth-level bodhisattva] is endowed with mindfulness, because he does not forget the dharma; and he is endowed with judgment, because his knowledge is well-ascertained; and he is endowed with comprehension, because he understands the meaning and the method of sūtras and utterances possessing a special intention (*saṃdhāyabhāṣita*); and he is endowed with modesty, because he protects himself and others; and he is endowed with constancy, because he does not abandon vows and cultivation; and he is endowed with intelligence, because

of [his] skill and excellent investigation of possibilities and impossibilities; and he has acquired knowledge, because he is not led by others; and he has acquired discriminative insight, because he is skilled in the terms that distinguish [what is] good from [what is] bad; and he has obtained realization of higher knowledge, because of his skill in the extensive realization of meditative cultivation; and he has obtained skill in means because he proceeds in accordance with the world. . . . He reveres the Tathāgatas, arhats, and samyaksambuddhas, and he respectfully [and] with great esteem listens to, grasps, and bears [in mind] their teaching of the dharma. Having heard [this teaching], he fulfills [it] insistently, with appropriate power [and] apportionment. And, to a great degree, he renounces [the world], according to instruction of the Tathāgatas. Following this renunciation, the one who bears in mind what he has heard becomes a dharma preacher (*dharmabhāṇaka*).[22]

The fifth-level bodhisattva thus begins to preach. However, he must continue through several additional bodhisattva levels before his preaching is perfected. It is only upon reaching the ninth—penultimate—level that a bodhisattva acquires the four discriminations: the discrimination of dharma (*dharmapratisaṃvid*), the discrimination of things (*arthapratisaṃvid*), the discrimination of expression (*niruktipratisaṃvid*), and the discrimination of eloquence (*pratibhānapratisaṃvid*).[23] Although each of the discriminations is discussed separately, all are said to be acquired simultaneously. Together, they provide a bodhisattva with the ability to proclaim and protect the treasury of Buddhist teaching.[24]

The tone in which the *Daśabhūmikasūtra* celebrates the bodhisattva's acquisition of the four discriminations is effusive, even by the standards of the *Avataṃsaka* corpus. Across ten ornate parallel passages, the *Daśabhūmikasūtra* proceeds to enumerate the numerous benefits that the discriminations grant to a bodhisattva who possesses them:

By the discrimination of dharma, [the ninth-level bodhisattva] knows the particular characteristics of dharmas;[25] by the discrimination of things, he knows the classification of dharmas; by the discrimination of expression, he knows the unmixed teaching of dharmas; by the discrimination of eloquence, he knows the uninterrupted continuity of dharmas.[26]

Moreover, by the discrimination of dharma, he knows dharmas to be bodiless;[27] by the discrimination of things, he knows dharmas to arise and pass away;

by the discrimination of expression, he teaches the dharma in which all dharmas are continually designated;[28] by the discrimination of eloquence, he teaches the dharma as being the limitless quiescence of such designation.[29]

Moreover, by the discrimination of dharma, he knows the present classification of dharmas; by the discrimination of things, he knows the past and future classification of dharmas; by the discrimination of expression, he teaches the dharma, not mixing past, present, and future; by the discrimination of eloquence, having begun at [any] particular time, he teaches the dharma via the limitless illumination of dharmas.[30]

Moreover, by the discrimination of dharma, he knows the analysis of dharmas; by the discrimination of things, he knows the analysis of things; by the discrimination of expression, he teaches the dharma with appropriate words; by the discrimination of eloquence, he teaches knowledge of appropriate intention.[31]

Moreover, by the discrimination of dharma, he knows skill in separating divisions in the knowledge of dharma; by the discrimination of things, he knows the correct differentiation of things, via knowledge of [their] connections; by the discrimination of expression, he explains [the dharma] in an unmixed way, considering conventional knowledge;[32] by the discrimination of eloquence, he teaches dharma with skill in the highest knowledge.[33]

Moreover, by the discrimination of dharma, he knows dharmas to be a single guide without discord; by the discrimination of things, he skillfully comprehends the true dependent arising of the aggregates, elements, and sense-fields; by the discrimination of expression, he explains, by means of sweet and venerable sounds and syllables, that which is comprehended by all people; by the discrimination of eloquence, he explains by way of the limitless, ever-increasing resplendence of dharma.[34]

Moreover, by the discrimination of dharma, he knows the multiplicity of attainments in the single vehicle; by the discrimination of things, he knows the variety of vehicles [as they are] divided; by the discrimination of expression, he explains all vehicles to be undivided; by the discrimination of eloquence, he teaches each individual vehicle as the limitless splendor of dharma.[35]

Moreover, by the discrimination of dharma, he is able to know the activity of any bodhisattva, awareness, or dharma; by the discrimination of things, he is able to differentiate and explain the ten levels; by the discrimination of expression, he explains in an unmixed way the appropriate provisions of the path with respect to the levels; by the discrimination of eloquence, he explains each individual level as limitless in aspects.[36]

> Moreover, by the discrimination of dharma, he awakens to the single characteristic of all Tathāgatas; by the discrimination of things, he comprehends various distinct times, substances, and characteristics; by the discrimination of expression, he explains awakening just as it is, via explanation and classification; by the discrimination of eloquence, he ceaselessly explains each individual word of the dharma for limitless eons.[37]
>
> Moreover, by the discrimination of dharma, he comprehends the speech of all Tathāgatas, together with [their ten] powers, [four] forms of fearlessness, [eighteen uncommon] Buddha characteristics, [their] great compassion, [their] use of the [four] discriminations, [their] turning of the wheel of dharma, and their omniscient awareness; by the discrimination of things, he knows the voice of the Tathāgata as it pertains to the diverse aims, faculties, and inclinations of sentient beings, who act in eighty-four thousand ways; by the discrimination of expression, he explains [the dharma] in the resounding voice of a Tathāgata, unmixed with the activities of all sentient beings; by the discrimination of eloquence, he teaches the dharma with zeal to the congregation by means of the radiant activity of a Tathāgata's awareness.[38]

The reader will undoubtedly have noted the rather forbidding style of these passages, a style that has been characterized by P. L. Vaidya as "abounding in sesquipedalian phraseology and gorgeous metaphor," and—less charitably—as "rather frightening."[39] Regardless of whether we find it appealing or appalling, however, the style here may be read as intimately connected to the claims that the text is making, as it arguably evinces several of the characteristics (e.g., the inexhaustibility and limitlessness of the teaching of dharma) that the sūtra holds the discriminations to facilitate. In describing a range of conditions—the discriminations—that authorize utterances and those who would make them, the sūtra at the same time underwrites its own authority by manifesting, in its rhetorical form, the very conditions it describes.

The *Daśabhūmikasūtra* account can be supplemented by other accounts drawn from several Indian Buddhist texts that appear to date from (very roughly) the middle centuries of the first millennium C.E. These texts allow us to sketch the discriminations in greater detail, but as we will see, they also introduce several thorny interpretive issues—issues that render suspect the notion that a uniform understanding of the discriminations was embraced across Buddhist scholastic communities during this time.

2.1.1. *DHARMAPRATISAṂVID* AND *ARTHAPRATISAṂVID*

As Har Dayal has pointed out, the traditional set of four discriminations appears to be an amalgam of two discrete sets of attributes that are sometimes listed separately in Buddhist sūtra literature.[40] The discrimination of dharma is elsewhere paired with the discrimination of things; the discrimination of expression, with the discrimination of eloquence.[41]

An exemplary treatment of the former pair is preserved in the eighth chapter of the *Saṃdhinirmocanasūtra*.[42] During an exchange between the Buddha and the bodhisattva Maitreya, the latter asks: "Blessed One, if a bodhisattva who has undertaken tranquility and insight [contemplation] possesses the discrimination of dharma . . . in what way does he do so?"[43] To this, the Buddha responds:

> Maitreya, the discrimination of dharma is of five kinds: name, phrase, syllable, [these taken] individually, and [these taken] together. What is a name? It is that which nominally designates the specific nature and characteristic of afflicted and purified dharmas. What is a phrase? It is that which is based upon a collection of those very names that are its basis and support, in order to speak conventionally of things that are afflicted and purified. What is a syllable? It is a phoneme: the basis for both [names and phrases]. What is the discrimination [that] takes them separately? [It is] discrimination by way of mental activity directed toward the unmixed. What is the discrimination [that] takes them together? [It is] discrimination by way of mental activity directed toward the mixed. All these together, as one, are called "the discrimination of dharma"; such is the discrimination of dharma.[44]

Maitreya asks also about the discrimination of things and is rewarded with a voluminous disquisition regarding the sorts of things on which this discrimination is understood to bear. Although the passage as a whole is too lengthy to be reproduced in its entirety here, a short excerpt will, I hope, suffice to give the flavor of the Buddha's response:

> Maitreya, a bodhisattva's discrimination of things is fivefold. What are the five kinds of things [upon which it bears]? [They are] a subject to be known, the thing to be known [about it], the knowledge itself, the attainment of the result of that knowledge, and the demonstration of that. Here, Maitreya, a subject that is to

> be known should be understood to be anything cognizable—for example, those things called "aggregates" or those things called "internal sense-fields" or those things called "external sense-fields," and so on. Here, Maitreya, the thing to be known is the way in which one knows that cognizable [subject] via some aspect. For example: the distinguishing characteristics of conventional and ultimate [truth], of fault and virtue, condition and time, birth, existence, and perishing, illness and so on, suffering, its arising, and so on, how things are and the true limit [of things], the realm of reality (*chos dbyings*, Skt. **dharmadhātu*), collections and divisions [of dharma], categorical responses to questions, analytical and questioning responses to questions, and the response of remaining silent [when questions are posed]; that which is secret and that which is widely proclaimed. One should understand these and similar things as things to be known. Here, Maitreya, knowledge is that which causes one to grasp both [of the previous two]; [i.e.,] the factors of awakening—e.g., the applications of mindfulness, the correct trainings, and so on. Here, Maitreya, the attainment of the result of knowledge is, e.g., the taming of greed, hatred, and delusion; the complete abandonment of greed, hatred, and delusion; the results of mendicancy and the virtues—mundane and supermundane, common and uncommon—of the disciples and the Tathāgatas that I have taught, having understood them directly. Here, Maitreya, the demonstration of that knowledge is the extensive and correct teaching to others of that liberating knowledge resulting from those very qualities that are realized. Maitreya, one may understand all things as included among these five things.[45]

These two passages help us to narrow what the Sanskrit terms *dharma* and *artha* should be understood to signal when used in connection with the discriminations. According to the *Saṃdhinirmocanasūtra*, when the term *dharma* occurs in the compound *dharmapratisaṃvid*, it should be understood to denote the linguistic components—names, phrases, and syllables—that constitute spoken or written Buddhist teaching. By contrast, the term *artha* in *arthapratisaṃvid* appears to denote things (whether meanings, objects, concepts, or aims) that names, phrases, and syllables are used to designate or characterize. Thus, the account given in the *Saṃdhinirmocanasūtra* presents the discrimination of dharma and the discrimination of things as forms of knowledge that bear upon distinct (if occasionally overlapping) objects. The first takes up the linguistic forms that make up instances of Buddhist teaching, while the second takes up what those forms are used to communicate.

This distinction closely tracks the distinction between knowledge of phrasing and knowledge of meaning explored in the previous chapter, and it is echoed in several roughly contemporaneous śāstric texts. Among them are the *Abhidharmasamuccaya*, attributed to Asaṅga; the *Mahāyānasūtrālaṃkārabhāṣya* and *Abhidharmakośabhāṣya*, both attributed to Vasubandhu; the *Mahāyānasaṃgrahopanibandhana*, attributed to Asvabhāva; and the *Abhidharmadīpavibhāṣāprabhāvṛtti*, of unknown authorship.[46] The uniformity of these accounts suggests that this way of understanding the discrimination of dharma and the discrimination of things was fairly common among Indian Buddhist intellectuals during the early centuries of the first millennium C.E. In what follows, I will refer to this view as the "Word and Object" view (with apologies to W. V. O. Quine). Although widespread, the Word and Object view had its rivals, as will soon become clear. Before discussing these rival views, however, we need to attend to the normative portrayal that the tradition offers regarding the second pair of discriminations: the discrimination of expression (*niruktipratisaṃvid*) and the discrimination of eloquence (*pratibhānapratisaṃvid*).

2.1.2. *NIRUKTIPRATISAṂVID* AND *PRATIBHĀNAPRATISAṂVID*

Like the two discriminations discussed previously, the discrimination of expression and the discrimination of eloquence are both presumed to facilitate the transmission of the dharma via language. If the discrimination of dharma and the discrimination of things pertain to *what* a dharma teacher comprehends regarding linguistic forms and the messages such forms should be used to convey, the discrimination of expression and the discrimination of eloquence pertain to *how* the teacher puts this knowledge to work in teaching. They provide him with the skills needed to express his knowledge in an effective and uninterrupted fashion.

The term *nirukti* is often used to index traditional etymological analysis—i.e., the practice of positing associations among Sanskrit terms (and, by extension, what those terms are employed to denote), based on perceived phonemic commonalities. Given this, one might presume that the compound *niruktipratisaṃvid* indexes the ability to engage in analysis of this kind. Some accounts of the discrimination do, in fact, interpret it along these lines. In the *Abhidharmasamuccayabhāṣya*'s explanation of *niruktipratisaṃvid*, for instance, two exemplary instances of *nirukti* are given:

the text informs us that the word *loka* ("world") should be understood to derive from the verbal root √*luj* ("break," "destroy"), while the term *rūpa* ("form") should be understood to derive from the verbal root √*rup* ("shatter").[47] Yet the text on which the author of the commentary is here commenting—the *Abhidharmasamuccaya*—appears to represent the compound *niruktipratisaṃvid* rather differently.[48] According to it, the discrimination involves the "correct attainment of being unimpeded with regard to the expression of the dharma in vernacular language" (*yul mi'i skad*, Skt. **janapadabhāṣā*).[49] The idealized dharma preacher is able to teach the dharma in multiple languages as occasion demands, and it is this skill that the discrimination is presumed to index or explain. The interpretive gloss offered in the *Abhidharmasamuccaya* is further corroborated by other Indian śāstric texts, among them the *Mahayānasūtrālaṃkārabhāṣya*, *Abhidharmakośabhāṣya*, and *Abhidharmadīpavibhāṣāprabhāvṛtti*; the *Bodhisattvabhūmi*, attributed to Asaṅga; and the somewhat later *Arthaviniścayasūtranibandhana*, attributed to Vīryaśrīdatta.[50] These texts are in agreement that *niruktipratisaṃvid* involves knowledge of forms of speech, and some supplement this description by explicitly referring to vernacular language. In consideration of these glosses, the translation "discrimination of expression" has been adopted here; though somewhat vague, it perhaps gains in accuracy what it loses in precision.

A relatively detailed account of the discrimination of expression, consistent with the accounts presented in the texts just noted, is preserved in the *Akṣayamatinirdeśa*.[51] The account reads:

> Here, what is the discrimination of expression? It is knowledge that understands the languages of all sentient beings, understanding the languages of gods, *nāgas*, *yakṣas*, *gandharvas*, *asuras*, *garuḍas*, *kiṃnāras*, *mahoragas*, humans, and nonhumans.[61] Having attained knowledge of the languages of all sentient beings born in the five realms—the thorough knowledge of their words, vowels, phrases, derivations, conventions, and the manner in which these are used—one proceeds to teach the dharma to particular beings in this or that language. And by means of such expressions, one teaches the dharma to these or those sentient beings, having perfectly understood their words. This is called "the discrimination of expression." . . .
>
> Thus, one knows the singular, dual, and plural [numbers], the masculine, feminine, and neuter [genders], the past, future, and present [tenses], [and] also knows [what is] superimposed onto a single letter, [what is superimposed] onto

> multiple letters, and [what] is without superimposition. This is called "the discrimination of expression."
>
> Moreover, [the discrimination of] expression is the knowledge of dharma via phrases that pertain to the cessation of all dharmas. This is called "the discrimination of expression."
>
> The expression of that [bodhisattva] is unhindered, nonerroneous, thoroughly presented, faultless, without severity, unconfused, exhaustive, clear; it is that which, accompanied by the meaning and the letter, satisfies the retinue in just the right way. It is of different kinds. Profound and appearing profound, it is adorned with the conventional and the ultimate. It is the realization of one's own mind, of knowledge and view; it is spoken by a Buddha [and] gladdens all sentient beings. This is called "the discrimination of expression."[62]

As described here, the discrimination of expression appears to parallel the discrimination of dharma when the latter is understood according to the Word and Object view. Both are presumed to bear on linguistic forms, as opposed to the content those forms are used to convey.

The final discrimination—the discrimination of eloquence (*pratibhāna-pratisaṃvid*, alt. *pratibhāṇapratisaṃvid*)—is defined in a number of different ways by Buddhist authors, and the accounts preserved in the sūtras are often far from clear.[63] Fortunately, previous work by Graeme MacQueen and Jens Braarvig has helped to illuminate aspects of Buddhist uses of the term *pratibhāna*.[64] MacQueen, in an influential two-part study of what he calls "inspired speech," has examined the use of the term *pratibhāna* in selected passages from the *Aṣṭasāhasrikāprajñāpāramitāsūtra*, concluding that the text—and Buddhist tradition more generally—preserves two distinct accounts of *pratibhāna*. One account holds it to be "a state of constant clarity attained through ascetical, moral, and meditational practice," while the other holds it to be "an occasional state of self-transcendence in which truth discloses itself and flows through one freely, finding immediate expression in language."[65] As MacQueen notes, Mahāyāna authors are rarely concerned to distinguish these two accounts; their interweaving may be glimpsed in the passage from the *Daśabhūmikasūtra* translated previously, in which the discrimination of eloquence is presented as a hard-won attainment that also facilitates the capacity to teach continually, unimpededly, and felicitously.[66]

In a separate study, Braarvig has drawn attention to the tradition's explicit linking of *pratibhāna* with the cultivation of concentration (*samādhi*) and mindfulness (*smṛti*).[67] These linkages are important, and they need to be explored further. The association of *pratibhāna* with *samādhi* tells us less than we might wish about the former term, given that the term *samādhi* is used by the tradition in so many different ways.[68] The same point holds for the connection that Braarvig finds between *pratibhāna* and *dhāraṇī*.[69] It is to be hoped that future scholarly work will help to clarify these connections and thereby advance our understanding of what Indian Buddhists presumed the term *pratibhāna* to index.

Perhaps the most extensive account of the discrimination of eloquence in the sūtra literature is presented in the *Akṣayamatinirdeśa*. This account is largely consonant with other Buddhist texts that discuss *pratibhānapratisaṃvid*, and it explicitly recapitulates many of the characteristics of "right speech" that we have already seen:

> Now, what is the discrimination of eloquence? It is, e.g., knowledge of [how to] teach a scriptural lesson without desire and [how to] teach a scriptural lesson continually and incontrovertibly. It is ready eloquence, eloquence that is swift and quick, eloquence that gets results, eloquence suitable to whatever question [may arise], eloquence that is undiverted and uncorrupted, eloquence that is coherent: the eloquence of realization. It is eloquence that delights in the dharma, eloquence that abides in the power of forbearance, eloquence regarding the profound. It is eloquence of various kinds; eloquence regarding the conventional and the ultimate; eloquence regarding giving, ethics, forbearance, effort, meditation, and discriminative insight; eloquence in teaching the divisions of phrases that pertain to all the dharmas of a Buddha; eloquence in the applications of mindfulness, in that which is abandoned, in the bases of magic, in the faculties, the limbs of awakening, and the profound path. It is eloquence regarding calm [meditation] and insight [meditation]. This is called "the discrimination of eloquence."
>
> It is eloquence regarding knowledge of the qualities of phrases—[a knowledge] that comes via thinking on expressions—and [eloquence] regarding the knowledge that understands absorption, liberation, concentration, equanimity, and truth. It is eloquence regarding all vehicles. It is eloquence that satisfies all sentient beings, by teaching [each] in the correct way—with phrases that are

> not inappropriate, stupid, or abusive; phrases that are reliable; phrases that are not harsh but instead are mild, pure, and thoroughly liberated, unobstructed, exhaustive, and warm. These phrases are neither inconstant nor agitated, but calm and virtuous. [They are] phrases that are relevant, phrases that apply [to circumstances], are not rigid, are very reasonable, and are not incomplete. [Such] phrases are renowned; they are gentle, and not phrases of reproach. They are phrases that are thoroughly collected, phrases that are spoken by all those who are noble, a reverberant sound enabling those in limitless [Buddha-]fields to comprehend [the teaching], a reverberant sound in the voice of Brahmā, enabling comprehension and understanding.
>
> One teaches with the eloquence of a Buddha's utterances, knowing some sentient beings to have faculties that are superior, and others to lack such faculties. A teacher of dharma acts toward these beings individually, ceasing their suffering and thereby liberating them. This is called "the discrimination of eloquence."[70]

Śāstric accounts of the discrimination of eloquence are more compressed, though they repeatedly stress the fluidity and cogency of speech that the discrimination is held to catalyze—or constitute—in the dharma preacher. In the words of the *Abhidharmakośabhāṣya*, the discrimination of eloquence allows a dharma preacher to manifest *yuktamuktābhilāpitā*: literally, the state of being one whose discourse is coherent and free.[71]

Having surveyed the discriminations individually, we are now in a position to summarize the main points raised in the accounts we have so far examined. The discriminations, according to these accounts, are paradigmatically associated with the preacher of Buddhist dharma. All index (or constitute) skills that are traditionally associated with effective instruction; the idealized preacher is also an idealized teacher. Moreover, all the discriminations are presumed to be simultaneously acquired on the cusp of Buddhahood, after extensive practice. According to the Word and Object view, the discrimination of dharma affords the idealized preacher the knowledge of Buddhist teachings, while the discrimination of things affords him knowledge of cognizable things. Both these forms of knowledge enable a dharma preacher to discern the requirements of (and possibilities for) a particular pedagogical situation and to tailor his preaching accordingly. Moreover, the discrimination of expression grants the preacher maximal linguistic flexibility, enabling him to preach among widely divergent groups of beings, in innumerable languages. Finally, the discrimination of eloquence grants the preacher the capacity to marshal the other discriminations and preach in a fluid and inexhaustible way, with discourse that is coherent and free.[72]

2.2. Perfect Preachers?

If real-world Indian Buddhist preachers held assumptions regarding dharma preachers that were informed by accounts such as these (as seems likely), then they may well have held the pedagogical discourse of a perfected preacher to be effectively indistinguishable from that of a Buddha. This claim is speculative, of course, but passages scattered throughout Mahāyāna sūtra literature lend support to the conflation of dharma preachers with Buddhas. As already noted, the *Dharmasaṅgīti* offers a set of ten similes for the dharma preacher; some of these similes bear a striking likeness to those offered elsewhere for Buddhas. Similarly, the *Akṣayamatinirdeśa* advises those who hear the teachings of dharma preachers to generate the idea that such preachers are (like) the teacher—that is, a Buddha.[73] The same sentiment is found at the conclusion of the *Ratnamegha*, where listeners are offered numerous protocols to observe in the presence of the preacher:

> You should generate the idea that the spot of earth on which the preacher (*chos smra ba*) abides is a place of veneration (*mchod rten*, Skt. *caitya*); you should generate the idea that the preacher is a superior; you should generate the idea that [the preacher] is a good friend; you should generate the idea that the preacher is the teacher of the path. Seeing the preacher, [you should] generate happiness, faith, and jubilation. You should commend the preacher, saying "Wonderful!" repeatedly.[74]

The *Suvarṇa(pra)bhāsottama* notes that the rhetorical power of the preacher can be so captivating that an audience who hears him elucidate the dharma may be unable to distinguish him from Samantabhadra, Maitreya, Mañjuśrī, or other embodiments of wisdom:

> One who hears this sūtra will know that an inconceivable mass of merit has been thus acquired by him . . . as soon as he has entered the monastery or cell, his ills depart from him, every evil dream and sign. . . . He should make there a seat resembling a lotus as the nāga kings revealed to him in his dream. And having sat

> on that seat, he should elucidate this sūtra. He should recite what is written and understand it just as it is. Getting down from the seat, he should go to another place. There, on that seat, miracles will be seen. And, at times the form of the dharma preacher will be seen there, at times the form of a Buddha, and at times a bodhisattva. Sometimes the forms of Samantabhadra or of Mañjuśrī, sometimes forms of Maitreya are seen on that seat. Sometimes merely a glow; sometimes the appearance of gods is glimpsed for a moment and then disappears.[75]

Along the same lines, the *Saddharmapuṇḍarīkasūtra* portrays the dharma preacher as endowed with "twelve hundred virtues of the tongue" (*jihvaguṇas*), associated also with Buddhas:

> The gentleman or lady who remembers, teaches, elucidates, copies out this dharma discourse shall be [endowed] with twelve hundred virtues of the tongue . . . and beings will be made joyful by the dharma he will utter in the midst of the assembly. They will be satisfied, utterly satisfied, exhilarated. A sweet, beautiful, delightful, deep voice will proceed from him, a tender voice that goes to the heart; beings will be satisfied and charmed by it. And after having heard his sweet voice, so beautiful and delightful, those among whom he teaches the dharma—even gods—will think [they should] approach [him] for [his] teaching, in order to venerate and adore him and hear the dharma. . . . So sweet will be the dharma delivered by that preacher, so truthful, just as it was spoken by the Tathāgata.[76]

The virtues mentioned here are counted among a larger class of virtues that the text respectively associates with the eye, ear, nose, body, and mind. Each is extensively discussed in the sūtra, and each is presented as an aim that aspiring bodhisattvas can, should, and (ideally) will achieve as a result of engaging in particular practices that the sūtra recommends. But the virtues of the tongue differ from the others in one respect: although the sūtra insists that each of the virtues it enumerates is achievable as a result of engagement with the text, only those of the tongue are held to be achieved in an unqualified manner. By contrast, the virtues of the eye that one achieves are explicitly stated to be those "of the corporeal eye, derived from one's mother and father" (*māṃsacakṣuṣā . . . mātāpitṛkasaṃbhunā*) and not those of the divine eye (*divyacakṣuḥ*) seen to be the exclusive possession of fully realized Buddhas. Similar qualifications are appended to the accounts the text offers of the virtues of the ear, nose, body, and mind—yet no such qualification is appended to the virtues of the tongue. The conclusion seems clear: the preacher portrayed in the sūtra is a being who delivers his discourses in a voice that has been utterly perfected in tone and rhetorical power, a voice indistinguishable from that of a Buddha.

None of this is particularly surprising. Given that these accounts of preachers were transmitted and interpreted via generations of actual preachers, it would be peculiar indeed if we were to find derogatory accounts of such figures. The accounts may strike us as a bit excessive, but they do appear to reflect (if somewhat hyperbolically) the institutional circumstances of Indian monasticism. As noted in the previous chapter, Xuanzang's testimony suggests that certain monks within large Indian monastic communities did indeed enjoy a level of prestige—and material reward—far greater than that granted to the majority of monks, and that this prestige was conferred on the basis of their skill in explaining the dharma.[77]

It is tempting to conclude, on the basis of accounts such as those so far surveyed, that historical Buddhist preachers either understood themselves to be Buddhas or did little to discourage such an understanding among those who came to hear them.[78] Yet not all sūtras present preachers in such a flattering light. Consider, for example, the following passage from the *Aṣṭasāhasrikāprajñāpāramitāsūtra*, cited by Śāntideva in the *Śikṣāsamuccaya*. The passage narrates a situation that some readers of this book are likely to find all too familiar:

> Furthermore, [students] will write and study with their minds on other things. Thinking, "We're getting no enjoyment out of this," they will rise from their seats and stride off. Thus, they will study—yawning and sneering. This is the work of Māra. . . . Furthermore, the dharma preacher will be eager to write and speak this profound Perfection of Wisdom—but the student of the dharma will be indolent. So, too, [may] the reverse [situation occur]. Or, suppose that the preacher will desire to go to another place, but the student of dharma will not; suppose that the preacher will be greatly willing, but the student less so. In brief, any unfavorable condition whatsoever between the preacher and the student of dharma is said to be the work of Māra.[79]

This passage provides a tempting opportunity for the application of what is sometimes called "the principle of embarrassment." The principle, as succinctly articulated by Jan Nattier, runs as follows: "When an author reveals, in the course of a discussion, something that is quite unflattering to the group or the position that he or she represents, there is a high degree of probability that the statement has a basis in fact."[80] Surely, this is so here: idealized preachers who are troubled by "works of Māra" (*mārakarman*) are, owing to that very fact, not Buddhas. Works of Māra do not trouble Buddhas; the attainment of Buddhahood is traditionally understood as the complete vanquishing of Māra.

3. The Preacher "in Practice": The Teaching of Models

If even idealized preachers were not presented as fully realized Buddhas, we can safely conclude that their real-world counterparts were sometimes less than perfect: prone at times to ambition, laziness, competitiveness, and other thoroughly human traits. Indeed, there is striking evidence to suggest that during the early centuries of the first millennium C.E. (and perhaps later), Buddhist preachers engaged in turf wars over regional discursive authority. A scenario of this sort is presented in the *Sarvadharmāpravṛttinirdeśa*, an extensive portion of which survives in Sanskrit as part of the Schøyen collection.[81] The sūtra recounts the story of a charismatic preacher named Viśuddhacāritra and his followers. The preacher, we are told, was "expert in knowing the excellent and weak abilities of living beings," while his followers, "as many as there were, all . . . excelled in their vows concerning the qualities of purification, and were experts in expedient means, having the tolerance of being without any preconceived views."[82] As the story opens, Viśuddhacāritra and his followers arrive at a monastery founded by a monk named Cāritramati. Cāritramati is portrayed as severe, judgmental, and virtuosic in his mastery of the vinaya; although he is an "expert in concentration" (*ting nge 'dzin la mkhas par gyur*), he is "not an expert on the behavior of a bodhisattva" (*byang chub sems dpa'i spyod pa la mkhas pa ma yin*). Cāritramati generously allows Viśuddhacāritra and his retinue to stay in his monastery, but a rivalry soon develops. The preacher and his retinue regularly leave the monastery to head into town, where they give teachings. As a result of this activity, "Viśuddhacāritra made many hundred thousand groups of beings believe, and his followers, as many as there were, became proficient in the art of religious leadership. Going to them they taught religion to the living beings, and they established many hundred thousands of living beings in the incomparable complete Awakening."[83] Cāritramati is displeased by these missionizing activities, and he chides the followers of Viśuddhacāritra for practicing without mindfulness and for talking too much. He tells them that they should abstain from going to town, reminding them that "the Lord has admonished us and praised us that we should live in seclusion."[84] But Viśuddhacāritra's disciples ignore Cāritramati and continue their objectionable behavior. The situation steadily grows worse. Finally, Cāritramati tells them that unless they stop going to town, they will no longer be welcome at his monastery. Viśuddhacāritra, apparently realizing the stakes, tells his followers to stop going to town, and they obey.

Cāritramati wins the battle, only to lose the war. A few months later, Viśuddhacāritra decides to leave the monastery with his followers and set up camp at another monastery close by. Again, the pattern of going to town resumes. Cāritramati spots this and again tries to cast aspersions on the activity of missionizing. But the eventual consequences reveal Cāritramati's actions to be wrongheaded: upon his death, he is plunged into the Avīci hell for billions of years. The text explains why:

> Those who do not wish to be connected with such hindrances of deeds should not have any hostility against any of the practices of another bodhisattva. They should rather have faith in all his undertakings. One should think thus: "I do not know the thoughts of others; the behavior of living beings is hard to understand." Considering the meaning of this, the Tathāgata taught the dharma thus: A person should not judge another. It is only for me, or someone like me, to judge another person. The one, son of good family, who wishes to protect himself should not question the practice of any other, nor should he criticize others, thinking: "This one is like this, this one like that." He should, rather, day and night, cultivate himself, intent on the religion of the Buddha, with a mind absorbed in religion.[85]

This passage is interesting both for what it says and for what it does not say. Cāritramati's fault is clearly not that he was an insufficiently aggressive proselytizer: the sūtra is not attempting to advocate a life devoted to preaching over a life devoted to meditation. On the contrary: the text appears to advocate a policy of abstaining from judgment (unless, of course, one happens to be a Buddha) as to which of these activities is properly preferable. Note, however, that this very move makes room for charismatic preaching of the sort in which Viśuddhacāritra engages. His conduct (*cāritra*) is indeed pure (*viśuddha*); a non-Buddha dismisses it only on pain of eons in Avīci.

Of course, it is difficult—perhaps impossible—to determine whether any part of the scenario sketched in the *Sarvadharmāpravṛttinirdeśa* accurately describes events that unfolded during the early centuries of the first millennium in India. But the principle of embarrassment suggests that its narrative may well recapitulate, however imperfectly, events on the ground. At least some Buddhist preachers—particularly those who engaged in widespread preaching to lay communities—may well have been, at times, viewed with suspicion by more conservative monastics and may have been censured for their activities. In describing Viśuddhacāritra as plagued by such censure, the *Sarvadharmāpravṛttinirdeśa* marks him as less than perfect. The path from renunciation to Buddhahood is a long one; the idealized preacher stands near, but not necessarily at, its end. The *Sarvadharmāpravṛttinirdeśa* will, however, go on to note that Viśuddhacāritra eventually does achieve Buddhahood: he is none other than the Buddha Akṣobhya.[86]

Indian Buddhists, in their struggles against works of Māra, routinely appealed to Buddhas and bodhisattvas for assistance. So, too, did preachers of the dharma. Gupta-period commentarial guides such as the *Vyākhyāyukti* and the **Vivaraṇasaṃgrahaṇī* emphasize that commentators should offer homage at the outset of teaching sessions, and a later text attributed to Atiśa (982–1054 C.E.), the **Adhyayanapustakapāṭhanapuraskriyāvidhi* (Preparatory ritual before recitation and reading), offers a revealing glimpse of a very human figure faced with the task of expounding Buddhist texts:

> Homage to all Buddhas and bodhisattvas.
>
> First, one who wishes to recite the dharma of the bodhisattvas and to read [it] from a book should supplicate [himself] before all the Buddhas and bodhisattvas of the ten directions. When the mind is completely focused, one should properly worship the bodhisattvas and great beings with the liturgy of the *Bhadracaripraṇidhāna*, in the manner of the seven-limbed prayer—prostration and so on. After that, resting the mind in goodwill toward all sentient beings, and with pure intent, one should repeat [the following] words attentively three times:

> "Whatever the meaning of a single phrase of the dharma spoken by the Blessed One may be—even if it pertains to all dharmas; even if, due to the shortcomings of my own acts, I am one of little insight and clinging mind; even if [my] memory is of such a kind, I will recite the pronouncements of the Blessed One that I have grasped. May a sentient being who hears the sound of the dharma gain the eloquence of a Tathāgata! Whatever the meaning of a single phrase of the dharma spoken by the Blessed One may be—even if [it pertains to] all dharmas; even if, due to the shortcomings of my own acts, I am one of little insight and clinging mind; even if [my] memory is of such a kind, I will read the dharma placed in [this] book. May a sentient being who hears the sound of the dharma gain the eloquence of a Tathāgata!"[87]

Atiśa exploits the polysemy of the term "dharma" here, using it to denote not only the words and phrases of Buddhist teaching, but also the content of that teaching. A bodhisattva may grasp the dharma in the first sense without grasping the dharma in the second sense; it is possible to know the proper phrasing of a teaching without understanding the content it conveys. In such cases, however, the benefits of recitation are not impeded. Even if a bodhisattva is unable to comprehend the meaning of what he recites, that recitation may still confer the benefit of eloquence (*spobs pa*, Skt. **pratibhāna*) among those fortunate enough to hear it.

The **Adhyayanapustakapāṭhanapuraskriyāvidhi* does not tell us much about the identity of the idealized reader it depicts: he (or she) may or may not be a dharma preacher. Nor does the text tell us much about the identity of the intended reader it targets: he (or she) may or may not be a monastic. The text clearly emphasizes the benefits to be incurred by rote recitation, but we should not be misled by this into thinking that the pursuit of a text's content or meaning is presumed to be unimportant. As Atiśa himself stresses elsewhere, grasping a teaching's lexical form is no substitute for striving to understand its meaning. Readers who do not know the meaning of the phrases they recite should not rest content with their lack of knowledge but should work toward grasping their meaning.

> Talking is delightful, but one should reflect on the meaning.
> The sugarcane husk has no essence whatsoever; the delightful taste is within.
> One who chews the husk cannot encounter the sweet taste of the sugar.
> Talking is like the husk, [but] thinking upon the meaning is like the taste.[88]

Like a sugarcane husk, the husk of talk is of uneven thickness; some texts offer more resistance than others. The idealized reader depicted in the **Adhyayanapustakapāṭhanapuraskriyāvidhi* appears particularly worried over his or her failure to comprehend teachings concerning all dharmas.[89] This phrase—"all dharmas" (*chos thams cad*, Skt. **sarvadharma*)—is regularly used in Buddhist sūtra literature, and it is also appropriated by commentators to serve various purposes, among them the explication of the discrimination of dharma (*dharmapratisaṃvid*). In the next section of this chapter, we will investigate commentarial attempts to come to grips with the meaning of the compound *dharmapratisaṃvid* and its relation to "all dharmas," in order to highlight the ways in which real-world Buddhist preaching in India reflected—and diverged from—its idealized counterpart.

3.1. Reading (with) the Discrimination of Dharma

Our focus in this section will be quite narrow: we will examine two additional accounts of the discrimination of dharma (*dharmapratisaṃvid*), together with their commentarial explications. One is drawn from the *Akṣayamatinirdeśa*; the other, from the *Arthaviniścayasūtra*. A strong case can be made that both these texts were in use in Indian Buddhist monastic complexes during the mid-to-late first millennium C.E. Their contents were known to at least some of the more learned monks at these sites: the *Akṣayamatinirdeśa* was often cited by such luminaries as Śāntideva (in his *Śikṣāsamuccaya*) and Kamalaśīla (in his *Bhāvanākramas*), whereas the *Arthaviniścayasūtra* appears to have been part of the pedagogical program in place at Nālandā during the late eighth century.[90]

As will become clear, the accounts of *dharmapratisaṃvid* offered in these texts do not agree with the Word and Object view—i.e., the view that the term *dharma* in *dharmapratisaṃvid* should be understood to index the *words and phrases* that make up a Buddhist teaching (versus the *things* indexed by *arthapratisaṃvid*). Given the enormous semantic flexibility of the Sanskrit *dharma*, the presence of divergent accounts is hardly surprising.[91] More surprising is what the texts' commentators make of this divergence: in both cases, they attempt to smooth over the implications of their root texts in favor of affirming the Word and Object view.

3.1.1. THE DISCRIMINATION OF DHARMA IN THE *AKṢAYAMATINIRDEŚA*(*ṬĪKĀ*)

In certain respects, the account of the discrimination of dharma given in the *Akṣayamatinirdeśa* squares with what we have already seen. Like the account offered in the *Saṃdhinirmocanasūtra* (and elsewhere), the *Akṣayamatinirdeśa*'s treatment of the discrimination of dharma links it to a bodhisattva's capacity for effective instruction. In other respects, however, the *Akṣayamatinirdeśa*'s presentation is very different. Formally, the text sequences the discriminations in a different order: the discrimination of dharma is discussed second, after the discrimination of things.[92] Moreover, close reading of the relevant section of the *Akṣayamatinirdeśa* reveals that the differences are not simply formal:

> Now, what is the discrimination of dharma? [It is] knowledge that penetrates into [i.e., understands] all dharmas: those that are virtuous and those that are not virtuous, those possessing evil and those lacking evil, those possessing corruption and those lacking corruption, those that are compounded and those that are uncompounded, those that are mundane and those that are supermundane, the beautiful and the vile, the afflicted and those that are auspiciously purified; it is the knowledge of the equanimity of the *dharmadhātu* regarding those who have passed into *saṃsāra* and *nirvāṇa*, the knowledge of the equanimity of awakening and the knowledge of the equanimity of the elements. This is the discrimination of dharma.[93]

In this account—placed in the mouth of the Buddha—no mention is made of "names, phrases, and syllables," nor is mention made of the "nominal designation" of particular qualities, as one finds in the *Saṃdhinirmocanasūtra* and in other texts that espouse the Word and Object view. Instead, the discrimination of dharma is held to afford a bodhisattva penetration into (i.e., understanding of) all dharmas (*chos thams cad la rjes su 'jug pa*, Skt. **sarvadharmānupraveśa*).

Although it is possible to interpret the phrase "all dharmas" in accordance with the Word and Object view—and thus to interpret it as indexing the entirety of Buddhist teaching—the way in which the sūtra goes on to unpack the phrase makes this reading highly implausible. It is doubtful (to say the least) that a Buddhist sūtra would proclaim the teaching of a Buddha to be, by turns, "virtuous" and "not virtuous," "possessing evil" and "lacking evil," "possessing corruption" and "lacking corruption," and so on. The view of the discrimination of dharma articulated in the *Akṣayamatinirdeśa* thus seems to differ dramatically from the Word and Object view; indeed, the two views look to be irreconcilable.

If the "dharma" in *dharmapratisaṃvid* does *not* here index the names, phrases, and syllables of Buddhist teaching, then how should it be understood? What is the discrimination of dharma, according to the *Akṣayamatinirdeśa*? One prima facie plausible reading is to see the term "dharma" as indexing various *qualities* that are possessed by various beings to whom (or perhaps about whom) a preacher might speak: their dispositions, modes of conduct, and so on. To read "dharma" in this way enables one to understand the relevant discrimination as conferring or constituting a preacher's ability to tailor his teachings to various listeners. On this reading, it is via the discrimination of dharma that a dharma preacher is made aware of the sensibilities of his audience.

This is not, however, the interpretive path that is taken by the author of the extant Sanskrit commentary on the text—the *Akṣayamatinirdeśaṭīkā*.[94] The commentary provides three different interpretations, each of which contrasts the discrimination of dharma with the discrimination of things.

> An *artha* (*don*) should be thought of as an object that is taught and comprehended. The dharma (*chos*) is that which teaches; think of it as what brings about comprehension.
>
> Alternatively, the dharma occurs in successive phrases, via terms such as "compounded and uncompounded"; an *artha* is the real object (*de nyid don*) that one investigates and analyses.
>
> Alternatively, the discrimination of things is the comprehension of the distinguishing characteristic(s) of all dharmas in a nonerroneous way; the discrimination of dharma is the knowledge of which terms are [correlated with] which dharmas.[95]

These interpretations make it clear that despite the discrepancies between the *Akṣayamatinirdeśa*'s account of the discrimination of dharma and the Word and Object view, the sūtra is being read as touting the latter. According to the first interpretation, the term "dharma" denotes the signifiers of

Buddhist teaching, as opposed to that which they signify. According to the second interpretation, the term denotes the phrasing of a teaching—e.g., terms such as "compounded and uncompounded." (Note the hermeneutic ingenuity here: in order to maintain that the discrimination of dharma bears on the linguistic components of Buddhist teaching, the commentator chooses to understand terms such as "unvirtuous," "evil," and so on not as descriptive adjectives characterizing the speech of Buddhas, but instead as terms that may be invoked by Buddhas to characterize phenomena.) Finally, according to the third interpretation, *dharmapratisaṃvid* consists in knowledge regarding the proper application of linguistic terms. In each case, the author of our commentary downplays certain implications of the passage on which he is commenting, in favor of articulating a view that our limited evidence suggests may have been more widely shared.

3.1.2. THE DISCRIMINATION OF DHARMA IN THE *ARTHAVINIŚCAYASŪTRA*(*NIBANDHANA*)

A rather different account of the discrimination of dharma is presented in the *Arthaviniścayasūtra*.[96] Extant in Sanskrit, this short text is divided into twenty-seven chapters, each of which is devoted to unpacking the constituent members of a particular Buddhist numbered list (e.g., the four noble truths, the five aggregates, the eighteen elements (*dhātu*) and so on). The section on the discriminations is extremely cursory and occurs near the end of the text, in its twenty-fourth chapter.[97] The speaker is again the Buddha: "What is the discrimination of dharma? [It is] incontrovertible knowledge regarding those dharmas that are uncontaminated."[98]

This account of the discrimination of dharma appears to diverge from both the Word and Object view and the view touted in the *Akṣayamatinirdeśa*. In contrast to the Word and Object view, linguistic forms are nowhere specifically mentioned. In contrast to the view expressed in the *Akṣayamatinirdeśa*, the discrimination no longer affords one understanding of all dharmas. Instead, the text unpacks the compound *dharmapratisaṃvid* by invoking a distinction routinely made in Buddhist abhidharma: a distinction between contaminated and uncontaminated dharmas (*sāsravānāsravā dharmāḥ*). According to the *Arthaviniścayasūtra*, the discrimination of dharma is a form of knowledge that bears exclusively upon uncontaminated dharmas—i.e., dharmas that are evaluated positively by the tradition.[99]

We now appear to have several distinct accounts of the discrimination of dharma in play. The first—touted in the *Saṃdhinirmocana*—is the Word and Object view. According to this view, the discrimination of dharma bears upon the names, phrases, and syllables of Buddhist teaching. The second—touted in the *Akṣayamatinirdeśa*—presents the discrimination of dharma as bearing upon all dharmas: those evaluated positively by the tradition and those evaluated negatively by the tradition. The third view—touted in the *Arthaviniścayasūtra*—occupies a kind of middle ground between the previous two, holding that the discrimination of dharma bears upon a specific range of dharmas: those identified positively by the tradition.[100]

Strikingly, however, the author of the *Arthaviniścayasūtranibandhana*—an otherwise unknown late-eighth- or early-ninth-century Nālandā monk named Vīryaśrīdatta—completely ignores this third view.[101] Instead, he chooses to begin his gloss of the discrimination of dharma with what looks like an egregious misrepresentation: "An elaboration [of the phrase] 'discrimination of dharma' is 'that which pertains to all dharmas.'"[102] Of course, this is not what the extant Sanskrit of the *Arthaviniścayasūtra* says; the text clearly restricts the discrimination's scope of operation to uncontaminated dharmas alone. But Vīryaśrīdatta has probably not made a mistake here. The gloss that he offers for the discrimination of dharma—"that which pertains to all dharmas" (*yatsarvadharmeṣu*)—is followed in his commentary by *iti*, a particle that is often used to mark direct quotation in Sanskrit.[103] This suggests that the elaboration may not be his own interpretive gloss on the original passage; it may instead be a gloss that he is quoting—one that was perhaps provided by the sūtra itself. In other words, we may be faced here with an instance of recensional variance: Vīryaśrīdatta's copy of the *Arthaviniścayasūtra* may have differed from our own. Whereas our text speaks of *uncontaminated* dharmas, Vīryaśrīdatta's text spoke of *all* dharmas. He continues:

> And here, by the word "dharma," one should understand "the dharma that is the teaching" (*deśanādharma*). The word "dharma" has many meanings. For example, "the dharma that is the teaching" [is that which is referenced in the statement]: "Monks! I will teach the components of dharma—good in the beginning, etc." [By contrast,] "the dharma that is activity" [is that which is referenced in the statement]: "What is dharma? [It is] the noble eightfold path." "The dharma that is the result [of the path, i.e.,] nirvāṇa" [is that which is referenced in the state-

> ment]: "In that way, I take refuge in the dharma." [Here, the discrimination of dharma should be understood as] "that which penetrates into [i.e., allows understanding of] all dharmas—those that are virtuous, those that are unvirtuous, and so on—by understanding those that are virtuous and so on just as they are."[104]

Vīryaśrīdatta notes the polysemy of the term "dharma," but he insists that in this case, the word is to be understood in the sense of *deśanā*: teaching. This fits uncomfortably (if it fits at all) with the implications of the passage that he is endeavoring to interpret. If Vīryaśrīdatta's version of the passage does in fact invoke "all dharmas" as the proper objects of the discrimination of dharma, and if we read the term "dharma" as he wishes us to read it here—i.e., as a term that denotes Buddhist teaching—then Vīryaśrīdatta effectively ends up advocating the position that Buddhist teaching is intermittently unvirtuous.[105]

Why would Vīryaśrīdatta choose to gloss this passage as he does? He may have simply erred here, but it is also possible to read his gloss as revealing the impact of commentarial tradition on those who would speak in and for that tradition. Those who hoped to be seen as traditional authorities have historically relied upon the testimony of those they presumed to be authoritative, and Vīryaśrīdatta is no exception. Indeed, his account is strikingly similar to the account of the discriminations given in Yaśomitra's subcommentary (*Sphuṭārthavyākhyā*) on Vasubandhu's *Abhidharmakośabhāṣya*:

> Here, the discrimination of dharma [refers to] the dharma that is the teaching. The word "dharma" has many meanings. For example: "Monks! I will teach the dharma—good in the beginning, good in the middle, and good in the end, with excellent meaning [and] excellent phrasing; I will reveal a holy life that is utterly perfect and pure." Here, "dharma" [is used in the sense of] "teaching." "What is dharma? [It is] the noble eightfold path." Here, "dharma" [is used in the sense of] "activity." "In that way, I take refuge in the dharma." Here, "dharma" [is used in the sense of] "the result [of the path, i.e.,] nirvāṇa."[106]

The similarity between Yaśomitra's text and Vīryaśrīdatta's text is unmistakable; it extends even to the particular examples adduced to illustrate the subordinate point that the term "dharma" is polysemic. But there is an important difference as well. Yaśomitra's root text here—the *Abhidharmakośabhāṣya*—interprets the discrimination of dharma according to the Word and Object view; Vīryaśrīdatta's root text does not.[107] Vīryaśrīdatta has imported Yaśomitra's gloss into a new commentarial context where it does not belong.[108] In so doing, he has disregarded the ways in which a shift in context can have an impact on meaning.[109]

We do not know—and will probably never know—what prompted Vīryaśrīdatta to adopt a "cut and paste" approach in this section of his commentary. The approach may, however, be read as suggesting a certain view of commentarial authority. Yaśomitra, the author of the *Sphuṭārthavyākhyā*, was a commentator whose works had already stood the test of time. He was a figure of authority within the community of monks at Nālandā, a commentator whose interpretations were sanctioned by wise monks. For this reason, Yaśomitra would likely have been held to be a trustworthy guide to the four discriminations; he, like a Buddha, might well have been understood to possess them.

4. Concluding Remarks

What we have so far seen suggests that Indian Buddhist tradition exerted a certain discursive pressure on those who endeavored to speak in its name. This pressure pointed in two directions at once. On the one hand, figures of pedagogical authority (preachers, teachers, and commentators) were presumed to bear responsibility for preserving the words of Buddhas; in the service of disseminating the teaching, these words were to be memorized and recited or transcribed accurately. On the other hand, these figures were presumed to bear responsibility for interpreting that which they had memorized. They did not simply recite the words of their predecessors, but also offered interpretations of those words to various audiences. To understand traditional Buddhist pedagogy requires that we keep these two responsibilities simultaneously in view. Indian Buddhist preachers and teachers of the dharma both were and were not the sources of the dharma they transmitted. What they said, in teaching, was inevitably an admixture of inheritance and originality—a fact that was not lost on Indian Buddhist audiences. This admixture was present not only in the commentarial literature, but also in the sūtra texts on which commentaries were composed.

Buddhist sūtra texts were (and are) transmitted from person to person; they offer—and present Buddhas as offering—divergent interpretations of

Buddhist teaching.[110] One such instance of divergence has been traced here, in the disparate—indeed, incompatible—accounts of the discrimination of dharma. Commentators faced with heterogeneity of this kind have traditionally dealt with it in different ways. A problematic teaching or interpretation might be denied authenticity; it might be classed as provisional (*neyārtha*), as opposed to definitive, or it might simply be left unacknowledged.[111] Each of these approaches allows a commentator to achieve a certain interpretive consonance, but it is consonance that comes at a cost: complexity is effaced. This effacement may or may not be seen as bearable; whether it is a necessary price to pay en route to savoring what Mātṛceṭa calls the "single taste" (*ekarasa*) of the dharma remains an open question.

What is unquestionable, however, is the fact that the paradigmatic form of the speech of a Buddha—the form in which statements taken to contain the utterances of Buddhas are traditionally couched—is that of reported speech. Buddhist sūtra texts traditionally commence with "Thus have I heard"—a rhetorical flourish signaling that what is to follow should be understood as the teaching of a Buddha. The "I" of "Thus have I heard" has traditionally been understood to point to the past; a preacher who utters the phrase thereby quotes a claim attributable to the compiler of the sūtra (often, though not always, presumed to be Ānanda).[112] Yet the "I" can also be understood to point to the present: to the figure of the dharma preacher, charged with transmitting a teaching to others. Read in this way, "Thus have I heard" is not simply a quotation; it is also an assertion. In uttering the phrase at the outset of a teaching, a dharma preacher facilitates the impression that the testimony of the sūtra compiler and the testimony of the dharma preacher are isomorphic. This isomorphism contributes to the authority of dharma preachers, but it also introduces the threat of instability. For as we have seen, dharma preachers may be afflicted by works of Māra. If the speech of a Buddha is no more than—and no less than—the testimony of dharma preachers, then this testimony, handed down through generations of preachers, might itself be seen as open to affliction by works of Māra.

The tradition is alive to this worry, or something like it; a note of skepticism regarding testimony is one that echoes through various Indian Buddhist texts. In the next chapter, we will explore its impact on issues of interpretation, as these issues are taken up and elaborated in Buddhist philosophical literature. Given that the idealized preacher is able to access not only what Buddhas say, but also what they mean or intend, and given that this access is routinely characterized in terms of knowledge (or unmistaken awareness: *jñāna*), one might reasonably wonder how a person is presumed to gain knowledge of a speaker's intentions. This is not simply an interpretive question; it is also an epistemological question, and it is to Buddhist epistemology that we now turn in search of an answer.

THREE

Models of Argument

Epistemology and Interpretation

IN A REMARKABLE passage that occurs late in the Mahāyāna *Mahāparinirvāṇasūtra*, Śākyamuni suddenly notices that his faithful and long-serving attendant Ānanda has gone missing:

> Then, the Blessed One, though knowing [the answer], said to Kauṇḍinya: "Where is Ānanda now?" Kauṇḍinya said: "O Blessed One, Ānanda is away from the *sal* forest, twelve *yojanas* from this assembly, and is surrounded by 64,000 billion Māras. All these Māras are transforming themselves into the Tathāgata. They say that everything is dependently arisen, or that everything is not dependently arisen; or that everything dependently arisen is eternal, or that everything dependently arisen is not eternal; or they say that the aggregates are real, or that they are illusory—and they elaborate on the sense-fields and the elements in the same way . . . they teach emptiness, the signless, the wishless. . . . Unable to rise up or to cry out, the monk Ānanda, caught in the noose of Māra, thinks: 'The utterances [spoken] by these Buddhas, these Blessed Ones, are in conflict. Which should I now take to heart?' O Blessed One, in this way the monk Ānanda is experiencing great suffering. Although he mentally attends to the Tathāgata, he can find no relief; due to this, he is not present among those assembled here."[1]

Kauṇḍinya's account vividly depicts a bewildered Ānanda, paralyzed by a barrage of apparently conflicting statements, each seemingly voiced by an awakened being. Ānanda has spent some twenty years in the company of Śākyamuni, yet Māra's illusions are so well crafted that even he can be fooled by them. Fortunately, his plight is swiftly resolved: the Buddha immediately dispatches Mañjuśrī to wrest Ānanda from Māra's clutches with the aid of a powerful *dhāraṇī*. This second spell breaks the first: Ānanda's speech-induced bewilderment is alleviated by another's speech, and he hastens to join the Buddha once again.

We do not know whether the target audience for the *Mahāparinirvāṇasūtra* found this resolution satisfying. There is, however, ample textual evidence to suggest that many Indian Buddhist thinkers were troubled by concerns similar to those that beset Ānanda here. A note of profound skepticism haunts the passage: if Māra is able to assume the form of a Tathāgata so effectively that even Ānanda is misled, what hope is there for others who encounter utterances purporting to issue from Buddhas—utterances such as those preserved in the *Mahāparinirvāṇasūtra* itself? How are they to determine which utterances, if any, to take to heart?

Indian Buddhist thinkers responded to concerns such as these not only by appealing to the power of *dhāraṇīs*, but also by elaborating and clarifying accounts of epistemic warrant and the means by which this warrant is properly conferred.[2] This chapter will explore the use made of such accounts by two influential Buddhist thinkers of the late eighth century C.E.: Śāntarakṣita and Kamalaśīla. Both of these thinkers appear to have thought that the conceptual tools supplied by Buddhist epistemological discourse can help us to answer interpretive questions: questions of what, and how, we can know from words. In this chapter, we will explore the aid they presumed these tools to provide. How do Śāntarakṣita and Kamalaśīla understand Buddhist epistemological theory to inform the work of textual interpretation? What account of the relation between epistemology and interpretive practice do they offer (or imply)? And what light, if any, does this account shed on the normative assumptions that historically shaped commentarial practice among Indian Buddhists?

To understand the position of Śāntarakṣita and Kamalaśīla on these matters will require familiarity with some of the basic concepts of Buddhist epistemology. For this reason, a brief introduction to the technical terms of the discourse is provided in section 1 of this chapter. Specialists may wish to skip ahead to section 2.

1. The *Pramāṇas*: A Brief Sketch

Most generally, the discipline of epistemology is concerned with knowledge: what it is and how we come to have it. In the Indian Buddhist epistemological tradition (as in Indian epistemological traditions more broadly), the question of how we come to have knowledge is answered by referencing what are termed the "means of correct cognition" (*pramāṇa*). Buddhist epistemologists ask not only how many means of correct cognition there are, but also how they work, with the answers to these questions shifting from author to author and from text to text. There are, however, certain features that Buddhist epistemologists typically associate with whatever they choose to identify as a *pramāṇa*. As means of correct cognition, *pramāṇas* are held to issue in unmistaken awareness (*avisaṃvādajñāna*).[3] Through their operation, doubt (*saṃśaya*) about an issue can be resolved, and one can properly speak of a view as "determined" (*adhyavasita*), "ascertained" (*niścita*), or "established" (*siddha*).

The means of correct cognition have their discursive home in traditions of intra- and intertraditional debates over doctrine, where they are routinely marshalled in the service of warranting claims to knowledge and justifying action founded on such claims.[4] Some accounts go further than this. At the outset of an early and seminal (albeit non-Buddhist) text for Indian *pramāṇa* thought, Vātsyāyana's commentary on the *Nyāyasūtras* of Akṣapāda Gautama, Vātsyāyana insists: "Without [the employment of] a means of correct cognition, there is no comprehension of an object. Without the comprehension of an object, there is no capacity to act. Having apprehended an object that a means of correct cognition causes one to know (*jñātārtham*), one desires to acquire or to avoid that [object]; the effort connected with the object that one desires to acquire or to discard is called 'activity' (*pravṛtti*)."[5] On Vātsyāyana's view, then, the means of correct cognition serve as indispensable conditions for our very capacity to act in the world.

This position is echoed in certain later Buddhist texts, where we find a similar insistence on the indispensable role that the means of correct cognition play in successful activity. So, for example, the opening lines of Dharmakīrti's *Nyāyabiṇḍu* read: "The attainment of every human aim is preceded by correct awareness (*samyagjñāna*); hence, this is discussed [here, in the *Nyāyabiṇḍu*]. Correct awareness is twofold: perception and inference."[6]

Here, Dharmakīrti emphasizes that correct awareness serves as a precondition for all successful human action, specifying that this awareness comprises two means of correct cognition: perception (*pratyakṣa*) and inference (*anumāna*). The difference between these means of correct cognition is presumed to track a difference in their respective objects: roughly speaking, perception is traditionally understood to bear on objects that are immediately present to our sense organs, while inference is understood to bear on things that are not immediately present to our sense organs.[7] Inference is further subdivided into inference for one's own purposes (*svārthānumāna*)—which need not involve explicitly articulated claims—and inference for another's purposes (*parārthānumāna*), in which the necessary components of an inference are presented, as claims, to another.[8]

When we infer, we move from immediately present evidence (*hetu*) to a conclusion (*sādhya*) to be established on the basis of that evidence. This move is rendered possible because a relation (*sambandha, pratibandha*) obtains between the evidence and what it allows us to conclude. In the wake of Dharmakīrti, this relation is usually presumed to take two forms: it can be either internal (*tādātmya*) or causal (*tadutpatti*).[9] These two forms are differentiated according to a difference in what is termed the "inferential locus" (*pakṣa, dharmin*). The locus of what one infers may be the same as, or different than, the locus of an instance of evidence. If the evidence and what one infers from it are brought into existence via precisely the same causal factors, then the two are said to share the same locus. If different causal factors are involved, then the two are said to occupy different loci.[10]

An internal relation is one in which the locus of evidence and the locus of what is to be inferred on the basis of that evidence are identical. The traditional example of such a relation is one that obtains between the property *being a śiṃśapā* (a kind of tree), and the property *being a tree*. If I observe something that possesses the former property, I have also observed something that possesses the latter (since, although there may be trees that are not *śiṃśapās*, there are no *śiṃśapās* that are not trees). Moreover, in order to explain the existence of a tree where that *śiṃśapā* stands, I do not need to seek additional causal factors over and above those that were involved in bringing that *śiṃśapā* into existence. Hence, the locus of the property to be inferred is identical to the locus of the property that supplies the basis for the inference. This internal relation secures the inference from "that is a *śiṃśapā*" (the evidence) to "that is a tree" (the conclusion).

A causal relation, on the other contrary, is one in which the locus of evidence and the locus of what is to be inferred from it are *not* identical. A stock example of this kind of inference is one in which, having observed the presence of smoke on a hill, I infer that fire is present there. The relation in this case is not internal, since fire and smoke do not share an identical locus; though they are both on the hill, they are not brought into existence via precisely the same causal factors. The presence of smoke requires fire as a causal condition, whereas the presence of fire requires that the causal conditions for fire (e.g., contact between lightning and dry grass) obtain.

Regardless of whether the evidence is internally or causally related to that which it allows us to infer, it must possess three features.[11] First, a particular instance of evidence must in fact exist in an inferential locus (in Sanskrit, this condition is traditionally termed *pakṣadharmatā*). In the standard example of seeing smoke on a hillside, the condition of *pakṣadharmatā* is satisfied if what is observed on the hillside is in fact smoke (and not, say, fog). The latter two features of inferential evidence are best understood as a pair; they are sometimes referred to as positive and negative concomitance (in Sanskrit, *anvayavyāpti* and *vyatirekavyāpti*, respectively). Positive concomitance requires the presence of that which is to be established on the basis of evidence in at least one "similar case" (*sapakṣa*)—that is, in at least one other case in which the evidence is likewise present. Negative concomitance requires that the evidence be absent when that which one seeks to infer on its basis is likewise absent.

These conditions become clearer when we consider them in light of the standard example. Seeing smoke on a hillside, we may infer the presence of fire there if fire has been present on other occasions when smoke has been present (where there is smoke, there is fire), and if smoke does not occur in the absence of fire (there is smoke *only* where there is fire—or, negatively, where there is no fire, there is no smoke). When these three features are present, an instance of evidence is said to be "triply qualified" (*trairūpya*). The three features are presumed to be jointly necessary for inference: an instance of evidence that is triply qualified may serve as the basis of a successful inference, but an instance of evidence that is not triply qualified cannot do so.[12]

2. The *Pramāṇas*: Means of Correct Interpretation?

The previous sketch, though admittedly very rough, provides us with the tools we need to take up questions regarding the role(s) assigned to the means of correct cognition in the work of interpretation. Did Buddhist epistemologists presume that we call upon the means of correct cognition when we listen to, understand, and act on the basis of texts? As we have seen, Dharmakīrti presents correct awareness as a precondition for successful goal-directed action and specifies that correct awareness is provided by (or is identical with) the means of correct cognition. Successful goal-directed actions can inarguably be undertaken on the basis of utterances: we can, for example, use a recipe to bake a cake or follow directions to reach a specified destination. In cases such as these, the means of correct cognition must somehow be involved. Perception is surely involved when we hear or read a text: we perceive sounds unfolding over time, marks laid out on a page, and so forth. When we hear or read a text, however, we also take the sounds or marks we perceive to be significant. Marks and noises may be perceived without comprehending their significance; as the tradition explicitly acknowledges, to have grasped a text's phrasing does not entail that one has grasped its meaning. This suggests that perception stops short of granting access to meaning.

In order to act successfully on the basis of utterances, we need more than correct awareness of marks and noises as they unfold—we also need access to what those marks and noises are being used to mean. Is this access secured inferentially? Recall that inference is presumed to require a relation between evidence and what we infer from it—a relation that is either internal or causal. The relation in this case is clearly not internal; the causal conditions that give rise to words are not generally the very same causal conditions that give rise to what those words may be used to mean. Perhaps, then, a causal relation obtains between words and what they may be used to mean. Were such a relation to be in place, it would entitle us to infer, on the basis of an utterance, the presence of a causal condition that is invariably concomitant with that utterance.

According to Śāntarakṣita and Kamalaśīla, there is such a causal condition: a speaker's *desire to speak* (*vivakṣā, vaktukāmatā*).[13] As Śāntarakṣita explains in the *Tattvasaṃgraha*:

Language does not cause one to know an external object in any way at all,
Since it is not the case that the word cannot occur otherwise.
Rather, it is an indicator (*gamaka*) of the desire to speak . . .
In the absence of the desire to speak, language is not used . . .

As has been stated, words do not cause one to understand directly (*sākṣāt*), since [they are] without relation to external objects.
Their presence indicates a desire to speak (*vivakṣā*).

On the basis of perception and nonapprehension, those [words] are ascertained as being effects of that [desire to speak].[14]
Therefore, it is clear that here [the relation] is one of cause and effect (*kāryakāraṇatā*).[15]

Śāntarakṣita here argues that acts of speaking are positively and negatively concomitant with desires to speak. When there is an utterance, its speaker possesses a desire to speak; when there is no desire to speak, an utterance will not occur. There is, however, no invariable concomitance between words and the objects to which those words refer. We can talk about objects not currently before us, objects that do not exist, and so on. For this reason, a distinction needs to be drawn between that to which words *refer* and that which we can *infer* from them. Words can refer to all sorts of things; what we can infer from words is, however, no more than—and no less than—that which is causally concomitant with them: a speaker's *vivakṣā*.

In translating the term *vivakṣā*, recent scholars have often used the term "intention."[16] This translation risks equating the term with another of considerable import to Buddhist hermeneutics: *abhiprāya* (a term that is almost always translated as "intention").[17] The latter term is routinely employed for interpretive purposes; commentators use it to present what a speaker means in speaking as he does. The relevant meaning need not be one we would identify as *obvious*; commentators also appeal to the notion of intention in order to explain or excuse particular utterances whose prima facie meaning is judged to be discordant and/or contradictory with what their speaker is judged to have intended—a meaning that may be significantly less obvious. Whether an *abhiprāya* is obvious or hidden, it appears to be loaded with—or identical to—a particular semantic content:

what is *intended* is what is *meant*.[18] No less an authority than Dharmakīrti appears to use the terms *vivakṣā* and *abhiprāya* interchangeably at times, and Śāntarakṣita's commentator Kamalaśīla also moves smoothly between them.[19]

If a desire to speak is understood to be equivalent to a meaningful intention (*abhiprāya*), then in affording access to the desire to speak, inference is granted an interpretive role: to infer a *vivakṣā* is to infer what a speaker means. What a speaker means may, of course, turn out to be false, but inference nevertheless supplies listeners with unmistaken awareness of that meaning.

What should we make, then, of those cases in which we err in construing what others mean? Did such cases trouble Śāntarakṣita and Kamalaśīla? Should they trouble us? Cases of this kind, which I will call rhetorical misfires, can for the purpose of analysis be grouped into two broad classes: *interpretive* and *performative*. Both types of misfire are acknowledged in Sanskrit literature. An interpretive misfire occurs when a speaker's utterance succeeds in conveying a meaning to an audience but nevertheless fails to convey what that speaker intends in speaking as he or she does. A charming instance of this sort of misfire enlivens the *Kathāsaritsāgara*'s story of the untutored king Sātavāhana. One warm spring day, Sātavāhana decides to splash his wives playfully with water:

> He sprinkled them with water from his cupped hands and they splashed back at him . . . [but] one of the queens, tired from the weight of her breasts, her body tender as a flower, wearied of the game. She could not bear to be splashed anymore and said to the king, "O king, don't splash me with water (*modakair deva paritāḍya mām*)!" The king immediately ordered some sweets (*modaka*) to be brought there, and the queen burst out laughing as she said, "What are we going to do with sweets in the lake? I told you not to splash me with water (*udakaiḥ siñca mā tvam mām*)! Don't you know how the words *mā* and *udaka* combine? How can you be so stupid as not to know this grammatical rule?" The king was deeply ashamed as his retinue burst into laughter when the queen, who was well versed in grammar, pointed out his mistake.[20]

Here, the queen's utterance of the Sanskrit sentence "modakair deva paritāḍya mām" can be interpreted either as "O king, pelt me with sweets!" or "O king, don't pelt me with water!" Although both are justifiable according to the sentence as it stands, only one was intended. The queen's words expressed what she intended to say, and the king did not fail to make *some* sense of them. Despite this, however, he did not grasp what she intended to say.

Sātavāhana's failure to understand his wife's intention may imply no more than what it was taken in the story to imply: that the king was a fool who lacked relevant background knowledge and inferential skill. The possibility of interpretive misfires need not count against the idea that desires to speak are loaded with intended content; nor need they count against the idea that when we come to know what someone has said, we do so inferentially.

There are, however, deeper problems on the horizon. These problems emerge when considering the second class of rhetorical misfire: the performative. Performative misfires occur when speakers fail to voice their intentions: when they fail to say what they intend to say.[21] In Indian literature, perhaps the best-known instance of performative misfire occurs following Tvaṣṭṛ's creation of Vṛtra.[22] As the story goes, the god Tvaṣṭṛ, angered by Indra's slaying of his son Triśiras, performs a sacrifice in order to create the terrible Vṛtra, foe of Indra. Tvaṣṭṛ addresses Vṛtra with the words "Indraśatrur varddhasva," intending by this to say "Grow, destroyer of Indra." But in speaking these words, he misplaces an accent, thereby shifting the compound from a *tatpuruṣa* to a *bahuvrīhi*. In giving voice to such a "faulty utterance" (*duṣṭaśabda*), he seals Vṛtra's fate: when the compound is read as *bahuvrīhi*, the meaning of the phrase becomes "Grow, [you] who have Indra as [your] destroyer."

The possibility of performative misfire challenges the notion that inference affords us access to what speakers mean in speaking as they do. For if performative misfire is possible, then *what I say* and *what I desire to say* become only fortuitously—not invariably—concomitant, and so we lose the invariable concomitance that the tradition presumes to be indispensable between inferential terms. A relation of invariable concomittance could be salvaged if we were to avoid assuming that when we infer the desire to speak from a particular utterance, we thereby also infer *what was said*. But when we pry the desire to speak apart from meaningful intention, we significantly limit what we are able to infer. On the basis of an utterance, we are now allowed to infer only *that a speaker desires to speak*. We cannot inferentially assign any content to this desire, unless we can be sure that the utterance in question perfectly expresses the speaker's intended meaning—i.e., that an instance of performative misfire has not taken place.[23]

We thus appear to be saddled with the following antinomy: on the one hand, if the desire to speak is equivalent to a speaker's intention, then what we say is invariably what we intend to say. Performative misfire is rendered impossible. Clearly, however, performative misfire *is* possible (it is, in fact, all too common). On the other hand, if the desire to speak is *not* equivalent to a speaker's intention, then we are allowed to infer desires, but at an impossibly high price: a desire that serves as the object of an inference must be stripped of determinate content and hence cannot conduce to—or justify—worldly action.

These worries may not apply to any and all inferences based upon utterances; perhaps perfectly realized Buddhas (unlike gods and humans) are not plagued by performative misfire.[24] For those of us who are not perfectly realized Buddhas, however, the gap between a text's phrasing and its meaning has widened into a chasm—and it is a chasm that inference cannot cross. We seem to be barred from using either of the admitted means of correct cognition to determine what a (nonawakened) speaker wishes to tell us.

Something like this worry appears to have been anticipated—and rejected—by Śāntarakṣita and Kamalaśīla. Śāntarakṣita, voicing the position of an objector, notes:

> [Someone may object:] An utterance of [someone who is] errant is seen to be one thing; that [speaker's] desire to speak, another.
>
> Therefore, that [utterance] in which there is a desire to speak in a certain way does not occur.[25]

Kamalaśīla elaborates:

> [On the view raised in this objection,] an utterance is unreliable even regarding a speaker's desire to speak, insofar as it [i.e., the utterance] does not reliably index a particular desire to speak (*vivakṣāviśeṣa*). [It is unreliable] because one can be led astray, since one sees someone who is confused saying one thing and desiring to say something else. As for a general desire to speak (*vivakṣāsāmānya*) [i.e., the general awareness that a speaker intends something], it is also unreliable, since it is without effect (*vaiphalyāt*). Indeed, the awareness merely that a speaker de-

> sires to say something does not allow for practical activity, since [one thereby obtains] no certainty about a particular state of affairs.[26]

In the first line of Śāntarakṣita's verse, an objector tries to break the relation of invariable concomitance that must characterize the terms of an inference. He does this by offering a hypothetical counterexample: a situation in which a particular utterance and a particular desire to speak fail to correlate. If we admit this possibility, we thereby also admit that we cannot be certain, on the basis of inference, what a speaker desires to say. We may, of course, infer *that* the speaker desires to speak—that is, that the speaker desires to say *something*. As the objector reminds us, however, this level of generality will not do for practical purposes. The general awareness that someone desires to say something is not determinate enough to allow us to act on the basis of an utterance, since we will not be certain just what—if anything—the speaker intends us to do.

On the objector's view, then, a speaker's desire to speak takes a particular form. This form may, from time to time, fail to reveal itself in the speaker's utterances. Instances of such failure pose a serious challenge to any attempt to understand interpretation in inferential terms. Unless the possibility of performative misfire can be decisively ruled out, inference cannot grant us access to the particular form taken by a given desire to speak. We would seem to need this access, however, if we are to engage in successful action on the basis of the utterance.

Śāntarakṣita responds to this objection by effectively brushing it aside:

> The difference between statements made by those who are errant (*bhrānta*) and those who are not is quite obvious (*parisphuṭa*). Clever people (*vidagdhāḥ*) are able to ascertain (*niścinvanti*) [this difference] from circumstance and so on (*prakṛtādibhyaḥ*).
>
> Those who do not understand the distinction among causes with respect to those [statements] are at fault. There is no fault, however, with the inferential sign.[27]

Śāntarakṣita here argues that clever people need not be worried over the issue the objector has raised, since this issue is not a live issue for them. They can distinguish the statements of those who are errant from the statements of those who are not. For Śāntarakṣita, the question of how clever persons are able to ascertain this distinction is not particularly pressing—the distinction is, after all, "quite obvious." Kamalaśīla elaborates:

> One has to accept that there is a difference between [statements] made by those who are errant and those who are not; otherwise, a difference in cause would not differentiate [them]. And skilled people (*kuśalāḥ puruśāḥ*) distinguish that difference from circumstance and so forth. "Circumstance" [means] context (*prakaraṇa*). From the words "and so on," one should understand such things as being nonagitated, having a peaceful facial expression, and so forth. How is there a difference between statements? . . . [Śāntarakṣita's response to this question] amounts to: due to difference in [their] causes. Thus, a properly individuated effect (*suvivecitaṃ kāryam*) does not deviate from a [particular] cause. Since this is definitely the case, [a statement] is authoritative (*prāmāṇyam*) with respect to a particular desire to speak.[28]

Kamalaśīla here emphasizes that, if there is no difference between the utterances of someone who errs and those of someone who does not, then our objector has nothing to which to object. Furthermore, if this distinction is collapsed, any cogency that the objection might possess is also vitiated: all speech acts become equally justified. All, therefore, become equally unjustifiable.

Kamalaśīla is arguably engaging in dialectical sleight of hand here. The objector has not denied that a meaningful distinction can be drawn between the utterances of those who are and are not errant. His point, rather, is simply that errant speech is possible—and that this possibility is sufficient to undermine the claim that we infer particular desires to speak on the basis of particular utterances. Śāntarakṣita and Kamalaśīla respond to this point by effectively stipulating that their account should properly be understood to apply only to the speech of a person who does not err (or, more precisely, is not currently erring). Duly qualified, their position now appears to be that we are able to infer particular desires to speak from particular utterances *in just those cases in which no performative misfire is ascertained to have occurred.*

Śāntarakṣita reassures us that clever persons will have no trouble figuring out which cases fit the bill; such persons need only attend to circumstance and so on (*prakṛtādi*). Kamalaśīla is more precise: speakers who do not err are nonagitated and bear peaceful facial expressions. It is not clear whether Kamalaśīla views these two characteristics as constituting inferential signs for a speaker's reliability. If he does, they are patently unconvincing; a non-agitated demeanor is hardly invariably concomitant with reliability. If he does not, one might reasonably wonder how a clever person might *ascertain* (as opposed to *surmise*) that an utterance does not involve performative misfire. Presumably, given the tight connection drawn between the means of correct cognition and ascertainment (*nis* + $\sqrt{}$*ci*), he or she would need to appeal to one or more of the means of correct cognition to rule out the possibility of error. It is not at all clear how this story would go.

Elsewhere in the *Tattvasaṃgraha*, Śāntarakṣita offers an account of the components of a speech-based inference:

> The presence of [the] three features [of an inference] is readily apparent (*vispaṣṭā*) regarding an intelligible desire to speak (*vivakṣāyām gamyāyām*):
>
> With respect to a [particular] person possessing the relevant property (*dharmin*), that [desire to speak] is what is to be established (*sādhyā*), via the utterance as effect.
>
> For example: That man is understood to possess the desire to speak of an object, a foot-drinker (*padapā*) [i.e., a tree],
>
> Because he has used the word "tree" (*vṛkṣa*), just as I [have] in prior situations.[29]

This brief passage makes several noteworthy points. First, speech-based inferences are not presumed to grant information about the world apart from the speaker; they merely allow us to attribute particular desires to speakers. Second, an inferred desire to speak may be expressed using phrasing that diverges from the phrasing of the utterance used as evidence for the inference. In the example here, a man is inferred to possess a desire to speak of a *padapā*; in his original utterance, the term used is *vṛkṣa*. We are, it seems, granted some interpretive latitude in assessing desires to speak and are not tied to rote repetition of the words and phrases originally used: that which is inferred can be paraphrased. (We will return to this point later.) Finally, Śāntarakṣita is also careful to note an exemplary instance (*dṛṣṭānta*)—i.e., a similar case (*sapakṣa*): he, too, has previously used the word that constitutes evidence for the desire he now seeks to infer.

Śāntarakṣita's exemplary instance renders explicit his familiarity with the linguistic conventions (*samaya*s, *saṃketa*s) that, on a traditional Buddhist view, govern our use of language and thereby render our desires communicable.[30] If a listener is unfamiliar with the conventions according to which a particular utterance is structured, he or she will be unable to infer a particular desire to speak, even if no performative misfire has taken place. An example will help to clarify this point. Presume that you are a skilled person, and that I do not appear to you to be errant—perhaps I am smiling and pacific. I now say to you, cryptically, "My grefla has tanquon sharboux." What can you gather from this? You may gather that I desire to say something about a grefla that I take to be in some sense mine: namely, that it—or he, or she—has tanquon sharboux. But this is not likely to be very helpful. Although my statement appears to be constructed according to rules of English syntax, and although it is peppered with English terms, I have told you very little about what a grefla might be (apart from it being the sort of thing that I can take myself to possess, and the sort of thing that I can take to have tanquon sharboux). Moreover, nothing in the form of the statement offers a means to distinguish a grefla that possesses the attributed feature(s) from a grefla that does not. Indeed, from this statement alone, you may be unable to tell whether *any* paraphrase of my words—or even the rote repetition of what I have said—correctly captures the form of my desire to speak. Without such an operable notion of correctness—of what it would be, under particular circumstances, to offer an adequate paraphrase of what I have said—I simply have not succeeded in saying anything. Such is the price of neglecting convention. Unless both a speaker and an interpreter are aware of (and observant of) relevant conventions, desires to speak cannot be paraphrased, and hence cannot be understood.[31]

In order to explain how determinate content is conferred upon our utterances, Śāntarakṣita and Kamalaśīla appeal to convention. Śāntarakṣita offers an account of how this process unfolds: "When there is awareness of diversity (*bhedajñāna*), a wish (*icchā*) [arises] with respect to the use/fashioning of a convention (*saṃketakaraṇe*). Then, its use/fashioning and the hearing of it [occur]; then, the experience (*ābhoga*) of it and the mental apprehension (*mati*) of it."[32] This passage admits of at least two divergent interpretations. On one reading (in which derivatives of √*kṛ* are translated as "use"), our conventions exist apart from and prior to our wishes and are invoked as circumstances demand. We thus employ conventions as we might employ pregiven tools, appropriating them in order to express what we desire to say. On another reading (in which derivatives of √*kṛ* are translated as "fashioning"), our conventions do not exist apart from and prior to our wish to invoke them. Rather, our wishes are constitutive conditions for, or aspects of, the very conventions that enable us to express what we desire to say.[33]

Kamalaśīla seems to waffle between these two interpretations. Elsewhere in his commentary on the *Tattvasaṃgraha*, he glosses the term "convention" as "existing just as (or by way of) one's own wishes," suggesting that his position on *saṃketa* is more closely captured by the second interpretation.[34] Yet in the same breath, he insists that convention serves to coordinate our wishes, thereby allowing communication to take place: "apart from convention, words [or sounds: *śabdānām*], by their nature, do not illuminate a meaning. If they did, then there would be the absurd consequence that even an uncultivated person [i.e., one who does not share the relevant convention(s)] would understand a meaning [from hearing a particular term used]."[35]

It is not clear that we need to choose between these two interpretations. Just as we fashion the tools that we employ, so each interpretation emphasizes an indispensable aspect of our linguistic practices. The former emphasizes their normativity: although present conventions could be otherwise, that fact does not make those conventions private, arbitrary, or capricious (we do, after all, succeed in communicating with one another).[36] The latter emphasizes their mutability: precisely because such practices and the conventions that allow for their intelligibility are not fixed, once and for all, they may, and do, *change*—new conventions may be created (and, importantly, may already be in existence among persons who do not share our own).

If we admit the point that shared conventions play an indispensable role in understanding, then an additional qualification needs to be added to Śāntarakṣita and Kamalaśīla's account of utterance-based inference. We may infer a particular desire to speak from a particular utterance if and only if (1) *the speaker is not currently erring* (this qualification targets performative misfire) and (2) *we are familiar with the linguistic conventions that structure the utterance* (this qualification targets interpretive misfire).

3. Concluding Remarks

Schematizing Śāntarakṣita and Kamalaśīla's account of utterance-based inference in this way enables us to read it as blending two distinct ideas. The first is the idea that the desire to speak constitutes an antecedent causal condition, accessible via inference, for any utterance whatsoever. The second is the idea that the desire to speak bears (or is) a particular semantic content fixed by convention; a particular desire to speak is individuated by this content. Slipping between these two ideas, Śāntarakṣita and Kamalaśīla argue that we—i.e., those of us who share linguistic conventions—are able to infer particular desires from particular utterances, at least so long as the possibility of errancy is ruled out. In doing so, we infer not *the general desire to speak*, but *a particular desire to speak*—and thereby infer what a speaker desires to say: a determinate, invariably concomittant, conventionally structured content.[37]

This, however, is a mistake. Even if it were possible to definitively rule out performative errancy for some subclass of cases, linguistic conventions (whether those of Sanskrit, English, or any other language) do not structure our utterances in a way that enables us to individuate *invariably concomitant* content, whether inferentially or by any other means. As Charles Travis has argued, this point holds not only for utterances that we are tempted to regard as ambiguous—e.g., "Mary had a little lamb"—but for most (perhaps all) natural language sentences.[38] Travis's point is perhaps best appreciated in light of a concrete example. Assume that you are told, "There is coffee all over the table." Assume, further, that the conditions for utterance-based inference have been satisfied: no performative misfire has occurred, and you are familiar with relevant linguistic conventions (you know what the term *coffee* can be used to refer to, understand how the word *table* is used, and so on). According to Śāntarakṣita and Kamalaśīla, you are now equipped to infer a content-bearing (i.e., paraphrasable) desire to speak: *what* the speaker, in producing this string of lexemes, desired to say. Yet a person who utters the sentence "There is coffee all over the table" might desire to say any of many different things. He might wish to tell you that a large assortment of bagged coffee beans is now present on the table; that a bag of coffee beans has ruptured, and that there are now loose beans spread across the table; that brewed coffee is splashed across the table's surface; that dozens of filled cups of brewed coffee are artfully arranged on the table; and so on. All these interpretations (and many others) are compatible with the utterance, even if only one such interpretation was intended by the speaker.

The point can be generalized. Shared knowledge of linguistic conventions does not enable us to fix one interpretation of a speaker's words as invariably concomitant with those words. To think otherwise is to misunderstand how linguistic conventions work. Just as the possibility of performative misfire ineluctably haunts our activity as speakers, the possibility of interpretive misfire haunts our activity as listeners or readers. One may feel forced to conclude from this that the gap between phrasing and meaning is therefore unbridgeable. But this conclusion is also a mistake, as is the assumption that makes it seem unavoidable: the assumption that interpretation is a matter of inference. As I hope to have made clear, that assumption is false.[39]

In saying this, I depart from the position advocated by Śāntarakṣita and Kamalaśīla, for whom interpretation is indeed a matter of inference. It is not clear how they would respond to the concerns I have raised in this chapter. Perhaps they would read them as implying that we cannot be certain of what other people intend on the basis of what they say—an implication that would be paralyzing only if they were to go on to insist that successful action in the world requires the kind of certainty afforded by the means of correct cognition. Interestingly, however, Kamalaśīla explicitly argues *against* this position in the opening pages of his commentary to the *Tattvasaṃgraha*, noting instead that we can and do act reasonably—even at times successfully—without such certainty.[40]

Although Kamalaśīla might have concerns over some of the issues raised in this chapter, I take it that he would not disagree with what I take to be the chapter's most crucial—and disarmingly simple—point. The capacity to understand another's words—like the capacity to understand another—is not simply a matter of perceptual or inferential acuity. It is informed by other resources: philosophical, practical, dialogical, meditative, and hermeneutic. This is not to claim that the means of correct cognition can play no role in the task of ascertaining meaning. The specifically *interpretive* role that the means of correct cognition are capable of playing, however, turns out to be minimal—despite what Buddhist epistemologists may once have desired to say. If we want a clearer picture of the resources from which traditional commentators drew in their attempts to interpret authoritative texts, we will need to look elsewhere. A useful place to start is with the extant corpus of Buddhist commentarial guides, which are explored in the next chapter.

FOUR

Models of Explication

Commentarial Guides

THE PREVIOUS CHAPTERS have surveyed numerous texts in which normative assumptions regarding the practices of commentary are stated and implied. These texts have ranged from devotional hymns to āgamic narratives; from vinaya literature to Mahāyāna sūtra texts; from abhidharmic treatises to scriptural commentaries. We have also examined Buddhist epistemological treatises in order to discover what they offer—and what resources they were presumed to offer—for answering interpretive questions. Taken together, these texts point toward a network of interconnected and shifting views regarding what it might mean to endeavor to speak for Buddhas. For all the richness of the texts we have explored so far, however, none has focused on formulating protocols for scriptural commentary per se. Indian Buddhist texts that do take up this task—a small, unjustly neglected corpus of commentarial guides—will be explored in the pages to follow.

A commentarial guide is a work (or section of a larger work) that is composed to provide an aspiring commentator with principles and procedures for elaborating on antecedent texts. Very few such guides survive today; of those that do, the best known are undoubtedly the Pali *Nettipakaraṇa* and *Peṭakopadesa*.[1] These two texts are not, however, the only extant texts of this kind, and in this chapter, we will look beyond them to investigate a set of commentarial guides attributed to Mahāyāna Buddhists.

Our main focus will be on an account of commentarial protocols preserved in Vasubandhu's fifth-century *Vyākhyāyukti*—a text whose title might be rendered as "The Logic of Explication."[2] Among subsequent Indian Buddhist authors, this account was very influential. Many of the great Indian Buddhist commentators of the post-Gupta and Pāla periods—among them Bhāviveka, Kamalaśīla, and Haribhadra—appear to have consulted the *Vyākhyāyukti*, using it to inform their views on the proper form, function, and content of scriptural commentary.[3] Sometimes, they cite passages from the *Vyākhyāyukti* directly; at other times, their indebtedness to the text is revealed in the formal structure of their commentaries and in the claims that they make about that structure. According to Jeffrey Schoening's pioneering survey of Indian Buddhist commentarial literature, no fewer than eleven of the sūtra commentaries preserved in the Tibetan *Bstan 'gyur* evince familiarity with the *Vyākhyāyukti* or with the account it presents.[4] To this number we may also add Vīryaśrīdatta's *Arthaviniścayasūtranibandhana*, preserved in Sanskrit, which quotes several unattributed verses that appear to have come from the *Vyākhyāyukti*.[5] This chapter attempts to facilitate further study of Vasubandhu's text, by providing a relatively detailed account of the contents and aims of the work.

Two other texts will figure heavily in the notes. The first is the *Abhidharmasamuccayabhāṣya*.[6] This work, whose authorship is uncertain, is an Indian commentary on the *Abhidharmasamuccaya*—a work that, as J. W. de Jong pointed out several decades ago, is "un des textes les plus importants de l'école Yogācāra."[7] The commentary is an indispensable aid to understanding the laconic root text on which it comments, and it appears historically to have been read in close conjunction with the root text.[8] One section of the commentary elaborates on the "ascertainment of explication" and thus provides an illuminating point of comparison to the project undertaken in the *Vyākhyāyukti*. So, too, does the **Vivaraṇasaṃgrahaṇī* (alt. **Vyākhyāsaṃgrahaṇī*)—a portion of the sprawling Yogācārabhūmi corpus, traditionally attributed to Asaṅga.[9]

Each of these three texts is of considerable interest to understanding Buddhist practices of exegesis; none, however, has yet received the attention it deserves. To encourage such attention, and to facilitate the work of comparing the three texts with one another, reference translations are provided in the appendixes herein. A more detailed comparative investigation of the similarities and divergences between these texts will have to wait until we have a fuller understanding of each on its own, but I hope here to provide materials that will aid scholars in further investigating these neglected—and, as yet, only partially understood—works.

1. On the *Vyākhyāyukti*

Vasubandhu's *Vyākhyāyukti* is a text whose importance to Buddhist tradition has recently begun to be appreciated, thanks in large part to the efforts of four scholars—José Cabezón, Jeffrey Schoening, Peter Skilling, and Peter Verhagen.[10] Each of these scholars has contributed mightily—and in different ways—to our understanding of the work. Cabezón has examined a section of the text in which Vasubandhu undertakes a spirited defense of the authenticity of the Mahāyāna sūtras; he has shown the ingenuity of Vasubandhu's argumentative moves and has highlighted the conceptual resources that they provide for thinking about questions of canon in Buddhist tradition. Schoening has offered a pioneering outline of the text's "five aspects" (*rnam pa lnga*, **pañcākāra*) and has charted the impact of the *Vyākhyāyukti* on several subsequent sūtra commentaries preserved in Tibetan translation, thereby enabling us to begin to appreciate the text's influence on later Indian Buddhist commentarial literature. Skilling has provided the first overview in a Western language of the contents of the text and has painstakingly traced many of the textual sources that it cites. Verhagen has likewise surveyed the text (in one of a series of valuable articles surveying works addressing what he terms "Indo-Tibetan Buddhist hermeneutics") and has speculated that the text may bear "some structural or historical relationship" to comparable Pali works such as the *Nettipakaraṇa* and *Peṭakopadesa*.[11]

Whether or not Verhagen's speculation as to the work's relationship(s) with the Pali guides turns out to be correct, the aims of the *Vyākhyāyukti* are surely comparable. Like the Pali commentarial guides, the *Vyākhyāyukti* is a text that aims to provide guidance for commentators. The need for such guidance was likely to have been one that was deeply felt by Vasubandhu, since he appears to have held a rather pessimistic view regarding his tradition's future. In the closing verses of the eighth chapter of the

Abhidharmakośa, he despairs over the unfortunate state of Buddhism and reminds his students to devote themselves tirelessly to practice:

> When the eye of the world, the teacher, is closed
> And the witness nearly gone,
> The teaching is thrown into confusion
> By persons who are unrestrained,
> Who have not seen the truth,
> And who argue poorly.
>
> When a self-realized one has departed to supreme peace,
> Together with those who bear the burden of his teaching,
> The world is leaderless.
> Here, today,
> The defilements, destroyers of multitudes,[12]
> Proceed uncontrolled and unchecked.
>
> Thus, having recognized that the teaching of the sage[13]
> Is in its last breath,
> And that the defilements are now gaining strength,
> Those who desire liberation should not be careless.[14]

These sentiments remain unchanged in the *Vyākhyāyukti*. Vasubandhu again closes his text by lamenting the general lassitude and incompetence that he finds among his fellow Buddhists and by repeatedly emphasizing the need to attend devotedly to Buddhist teaching.

> For the most part, those who hear turn away.
> For the most part, [they] fail to grasp the teaching thoroughly
> And, due to improper explications, are ruined.
> These days, good explication has come to an end . . .[15]
>
> These days, the speech of the sage is rarely spoken,
> One rarely distinguishes silver and gold;
> In that way, weak efforts are made
> Toward instruction and realization;
> The perfect, stainless sun of the Buddha is setting.

So, as long as it is not entirely gone,
One should work in discerning its meanings, just as they are.
When the sage's speech no longer appears,
Beings, utterly benighted, will be plunged into total darkness.[16]

If the ongoing transmission of a Buddha's speech is a lamp in the darkness, the *Vyākhyāyukti* is composed to fill it with oil. The work aims to provide, in Vasubandhu's own words, "brief instruction / to benefit those of lesser learning / who desire to expound the sūtras."[17] This instruction is both theoretical and practical: on the one hand, Vasubandhu stipulates formal characteristics that both commentators and the texts that they produce should properly possess; on the other hand, he adduces numerous examples of commentarial exegesis. The former approach provides the work with its topical structure, while the latter demonstrates the practical application of the elements of Vasubandhu's formal account to concrete instances of scriptural commentary.[18]

The *Vyākhyāyukti* is a difficult text. The Sanskrit original is no longer extant, and although it is sometimes possible to reconstruct the underlying Sanskrit from the Tibetan translation, the text bears all the trademarks of Vasubandhu's style: it is, as Skilling has noted, "confident and learned, replete with citations and allusions to canonical and other literature, and to the opinions of other teachers or schools."[19] The work is often as elusive as it is allusive, since Vasubandhu regularly cites texts in ways that impede our ability to identify both their source(s) and their content. Typically, he does not give the title of the text he is citing, and he almost never cites the whole of a passage. Fortunately, many—though by no means all—of the passages that Vasubandhu cites are anthologized in two indispensable supplementary texts: the *Vyākhyāyuktisūtrakhaṇḍaśata* and a lengthy commentary—the *Vyākhyāyuktiṭīkā*. The former text contains approximately one hundred short excerpts from Buddhist sūtra literature.[20] The latter text is the single extant commentary on the *Vyākhyāyukti*, attributed to Guṇamati.[21] By moving back and forth between the *Vyākhyāyukti* and these two supplementary texts, a reader can often gain a fuller understanding of the issues at stake in the passages that Vasubandhu chooses to cite. Without the assistance of the supplementary texts, the *Vyākhyāyukti* is often unintelligible—and even with their assistance, one sometimes feels set adrift on a textual sea without map or compass.

This is perhaps ironic, given that the text itself is intended to benefit would-be interpreters. It is not, however, surprising, since today's scholars, for the most part, fail to satisfy the prerequisites that the text demands of its audience. Despite his claim to target those of lesser learning, Vasubandhu is writing for Indian Buddhist monks; he presumes that his readers will possess a degree of highly specialized knowledge concerning both the source texts he cites and the scholastic categories he invokes. It is thus to be expected that a reader who approaches the text from a vantage point outside this community will feel somewhat disoriented, if not completely lost. Indeed, the personal cultivation provided by membership in such a community is one of the first topics Vasubandhu addresses in his text.

If authoritative commentaries are to be composed, authoritative commentators need to be trained in the craft of composing them. Vasubandhu suggests that the sensibilities and skills of a commentator should be developed and refined over the course of a prolonged period of apprenticeship: one learns how to speak for Buddhas in part by hearing others do so. In the opening pages of the *Vyākhyāyukti*, Vasubandhu stresses that a person who desires to expound the sūtras should possess three characteristics.[22] First, he should have "heard much"—i.e., he should have had extensive exposure to Buddhist teachings. Second, he should be "endowed with the basis of hearing"—i.e., he should be able to retain what he has heard.[23] Finally, he should endeavor to "accumulate what he has heard"—i.e., he should build up a storehouse of texts and teachings in his memory, to call upon as occasion demands. Vasubandhu discusses these three characteristics in a traditional—and traditionalist—fashion, working to ground his account in the sūtra literature itself: "How does one hear much, become endowed with the basis of hearing, and accumulate what has been heard? This is elaborated in a sūtra: 'the dharma—good at the beginning, in the middle, and at the end. . . .' "[24] The scriptural passage to which Vasubandhu here refers is similar to one that we have already encountered, in chapter 2; it is a stock passage that recurs throughout the āgamic literature. It is also the first passage to be included in the *Vyākhyāyuktisūtrakhaṇḍaśata*, where it is quoted in its entirety:

> One who, by means of verbal expressions, expresses the dharma—good at the beginning, in the middle, and at the end, [possessed of] excellent meaning and

> phrasing, unmixed, utterly complete, pure and refined, the pure practice—is one who has heard much, one who is endowed with the basis of hearing, and one who has accumulated what he has heard. Such a dharma as this is heard repeatedly, grasped, recited, comprehended by the mind, and thoroughly understood by personal observation.[25]

Vasubandhu immediately goes on to offer a commentary on this short scriptural passage. As he proceeds, he adduces additional scriptural passages to support his favored glosses of the terms of the root text on which he is commenting.

> In this [passage], "dharma" refers to the sūtras and so forth—i.e., [texts] that are correctly taught, whose meaning is grasped firmly and nonerroneously. "The pure practice" is the path to nirvāṇa. Nirvāṇa is "pure"—i.e., extraordinarily precious, since, as has been said, "one becomes pacified, cooled, and purified [upon attaining it]." "Pure practice" is that by which one is caused to practice, undertake, and obtain that, just as it is said that liquor causes intoxication.
>
> The "beginning, middle, and end" are, respectively, the first through the third of the components: ethics, contemplation, and discriminating insight. As it is stated extensively in a sūtra of the Kāśyapīyas:
>
> "Monks! I teach a dharma that is good at the beginning, good in the middle, good at the end! What is the beginning of pure practice? Spelled out more extensively, it is abiding ethically. What is the middle of pure practice? Stated more extensively, it is abiding in the separation from desire up to completion—the fourth absorption. What is the end of pure practice? It is the arising of liberation and the pristine cognition that comprehends liberation, having perfectly comprehended: 'This is the noble truth of suffering.' "
>
> [The teaching is] "good," since, being completely taintless, it is nonmistaken. [It manifests] "excellent meaning [and] excellent phrasing." Respectively, this is because of the excellence of [both] what is stated and the statements [themselves], since [the former] is nonerroneous and [the latter] cause one to understand. [The teaching is] "unmixed" and so forth respectively [as follows: it is "unmixed"] because it is not common. [It is "utterly complete"] because it is an antidote to all afflictions. [It is "pure"] because it is liberated [from defilement] via two forms of liberation: intrinsic [liberation] (*ngo bo nyid*) and [liberation of the] continuum (*rgyud*). Moreover, it is "good in the beginning, good in the mid-

dle, [and] good at the end," since it has excellent meaning, excellent phrasing, and is unmixed.[26]

In explaining a range of characteristics properly possessed by a person who desires to expound the sūtras, Vasubandhu adopts an approach that is paradigmatically commentarial. Lavishing attention on individual terms used in his root text, he works to interpret those terms via paraphrase, analogy, and explicit scriptural citation. In doing so, he shows that the three characteristics he discusses are anticipated in—and ratified by—the authoritative texts of Buddhist tradition. He also offers a paradigm case—the first of more than one hundred such cases scattered throughout the text—for what he takes the task of "expounding the sūtras" to demand. Moreover, he bolsters his own authority within the tradition by positioning himself as a figure possessing the very characteristics that his account identifies as normatively authoritative. In his extensive citation of scriptural sources, and in his application of those sources to interpretive occasions, Vasubandhu reveals himself to be one who has heard much, has retained what he has heard, and has accumulated a vast repository of Buddhist learning. The author of the *Vyākhyāyukti* thus portrays himself as an authoritative commentator and, as such, a reliable guide to commentarial practice.

2. The Five Aspects

After presenting an account of the traits possessed by an exemplary commentator, Vasubandhu turns to the topic of exemplary commentaries. These, he tells us, are characterized by five interrelated aspects.[27]

> How should one discuss the sūtras? [One should do so] via five aspects. One should state the purpose of the sūtra; the summary meaning; the meaning of the phrases; connections; and the two—objections and responses. . . . Why are these [five aspects] expressed? When one hears the greatness of the sūtra's meaning, one is spurred on to listen to and grasp [the text]; for this reason, the purpose is expressed. Moreover, the purpose may also be understood from the summary meaning of the sūtra, and the summary meaning from the meaning of

> the phrases. From the connections, [one may understand] that the meaning of the phrases is sequentially noncontradictory. From the objections and responses, [one may understand] that [the text] does not contradict reason and that there is no contradiction between those [texts] that are earlier [and] later. Thus, the summary meaning and so on should be stated.[28]

Vasubandhu presents an idealized scriptural commentary as a text that synthesizes the disparate details of the root text into one (or more) overarching topics and presents this "summary meaning" (*piṇḍārtha*) at its outset, thereby enabling an audience to understand the point of the sūtra with ease.[29] The summary meaning of a text is thus seen to be intimately connected with its purpose or point (*prayojana*): whereas the former briefly (and sometimes paraphrastically) recapitulates *what* a sūtra teaching says, the latter addresses *why* the teaching was originally—or is now again being—articulated. Additionally, the summary meaning is held to be intimately connected to the third aspect: the meaning of the phrases (*padārtha*). Just as one comes to understand the purpose of a teaching (its *prayojana*) when one understands, in broad outline, what is being taught—i.e., its *piṇḍārtha*—so, too, one understands the broad outlines of a teaching (its *piṇḍārtha*) by coming to understand the meaning of the individual phrases (*padārtha*) that the teaching contains.[30] These phrases reveal—and may be better understood by way of—connections (*anusaṃdhi*) to other passages and points of Buddhist doctrine. A commentary should trace and clarify these connections, thereby granting (or reminding a student of) the relevant background knowledge that is required to understand the root text. Finally, a commentary should entertain objections and respond to them (*codyaparihāra*), thereby acknowledging competing readings of the root text and arguing in support of favored views.

These five aspects collectively constitute a structural framework not only for commentary, but also for most of the *Vyākhyāyukti* itself. In large part, the work is devoted to analyzing the aspects, one by one, and showing how they apply to specific sūtra passages. In Book I, Vasubandhu treats the first two aspects—*prayojana* and *piṇḍārtha*—in their entirety, and he concludes the book with a preliminary treatment of the third aspect (*padārtha*). The whole of Book II is devoted to an extended treatment of *padārtha*. Drawing on the sūtra passages preserved in the *Vyākhyāyuktisūtrakhaṇḍaśata* as grist for his commentarial mill, Vasubandhu offers more than one hundred short exegeses that serve to demonstrate the manner in which the "meaning of phrases" is properly to be elucidated. In the first few folios of Book III, the fourth aspect (*anusaṃdhi*) is briefly discussed; the remainder of Book III and the whole of Book IV treat the fifth aspect (*codyaparihāra*). In Book V, having completed his discussion of the five aspects, Vasubandhu addresses the ways in which one can cultivate an attitude of devotion to (or respect for) a Buddha's teaching. He presents suggestions and techniques that a teacher can employ to convince his students that the activity of attending respectfully to the dharma is worthwhile, brings benefit, and should be pursued with concentrated effort. The work draws to a close with a brief appendix in which two additional verses that pertain to commentarial practice are cited and glossed.[31]

In the discussion to follow in this chapter, I have not attempted to discuss each book of the *Vyākhyāyukti* separately. Instead, I have organized the presentation along thematic lines: each of sections 2.1 though 2.5 discusses one of the five aspects; the conclusion (section 3) discusses, briefly, implications that may be drawn from Book V. Throughout, I have used the notes to reference parallel passages in the *Abhidharmasamuccaya* and **Vivaraṇasa ṃgrahaṇī*.

2.1. The Purpose

Vasubandhu's account of the purpose (*dgos pa*, **prayojana*) in the *Vyākhyāyukti* shares certain formal similarities with Kamalaśīla's later account of the same subject in his *Tattvasaṃgrahapañjikā*.[32] For both thinkers, the need to state the purpose of a text is intimately connected to the need to engage listeners and motivate them to act. "The purpose of a sūtra," Vasubandhu informs us, "should be understood under four aspects."[33] These aspects track particular audiences to which a teaching may be addressed; there are four kinds of audience, each of which may be further subdivided.[34] First are confused persons (*kun tu rmongs pa*, **saṃmoha*), for whom a sūtra provides correct instruction. Second are those who are careless (*bag med*, **pramāda*), for whom a sūtra provides guidelines for what is genuinely acceptable. Third are those who are dispirited (*zhum pa*, **līna*), for whom a sūtra provides genuine encouragement. Finally, there are those who are set out [on the path] (*yang dag par zhugs pa, *saṃprasthita*), for whom a sūtra provides genuine delight.

Having delineated these audiences, Vasubandhu turns to investigate the divergent ways in which they may come to understand the meaning of a sūtra text and teachings regarding it. Mulling over the distinction between phrasing (*tshig 'bru, *vyañjana*) and meaning (*don, *artha*), he raises a number of questions. Should one say that each phrase of the sūtra possesses only one meaning? Can a phrase have more than one meaning? What status should we grant to rhetorical strategies (*rnam grangs, *paryāya*)—i.e., variant terms and phrases that may be used to express the same meaning?[35] Further, why would the Buddha teach using such devices, instead of teaching in a single, definitive way?

Vasubandhu delays answering some of these questions until later in the text; at this point, he addresses himself to spelling out the pedagogical functions played by rhetorical strategies—a constitutive feature of the sūtra literature.[36] He enumerates "eight purposes for rhetorical strategies, owing to the variety among those who are trained."[37] Rhetorical strategies are pedagogical devices, used in order to facilitate the understanding of students (*slob ma rnams la go bar byed pas*) and in order to clear away hindrances to training (*'dul bar byed pa ni bgegs sel ba'i phyir*).[38] The particular purpose served by a rhetorical strategy will depend upon the nature of the audience to whom it has been—or is being—offered.

2.2. Summary Meaning

Vasubandhu has already noted that one may come to understand the purpose of a sūtra—i.e., the reason(s) for giving a particular teaching—by coming to understand the sūtra's summary meaning (**piṇḍārtha, bsdus pa'i don*)—i.e., the broad outlines of what it says.[39] Thus, in order to help his audience understand the purpose of a sūtra, a good commentator should render the sūtra's summary meaning explicit. Vasubandhu's treatment of the summary meaning is extremely cursory, taking up less than one folio side. He begins by noting that the summary meaning is "the corpus of the sūtra" (*mdo sde'i lus*), and he then proceeds to enumerate five subcategories: "Thus, in brief, a summary meaning is a teaching regarding some particular thing [and] how it is to be known, what such knowledge is, what the result of this knowledge is, and what is stated about that."[40] The account offered here is strikingly similar to one we have already encountered in chapter 2—namely, the *Saṃdhinirmocanasūtra*'s discussion of the bodhisattva's discrimination of things. There is no doubt that Vasubandhu was familiar with the *Saṃdhinirmocanasūtra* at the time he composed the *Vyākhyāyukti*: he cites passages from this sūtra more than once in his text.[41] If it is plausible to assume that Vasubandhu intended to invoke the *Saṃdhinirmocanasūtra* account here, then it is likely that he expected informed readers to draw a conclusion that he here leaves implicit: just as sūtra texts should be understood to evince a bodhisattva's discrimination of things, so, too, should the commentarial texts that elucidate them.

Vasubandhu expands on the five subcategories of summary meaning by appealing to an example. As his root text, he appropriates a passage from the *Saṃyuktāgama* that is reproduced in full in the *Vyākhyāyuktiṭīkā*:

> "Monks! Regarding the existence of matter/form (*gzugs*, **rūpa*), it is correctly viewed as impermanent; this is the arising of correct view regarding that. When one sees [this] correctly, desire is brought to an end, since [both] aversion and enjoyment are exhausted. Because [aversion], enjoyment, and desire are exhausted, the mind is totally liberated.
>
> "Monks! Regarding the existence of feeling, recognition, formation, and consciousness, [such existence] is correctly viewed as impermanent; this is the arising of correct view regarding that [existence]. When one sees [this] correctly, desire is brought to an end, since [both] aversion and enjoyment are exhausted. Because [aversion], enjoyment, and desire are exhausted, the mind is totally liberated. In this way, a monk, totally liberating his mind, can, if he wishes, exhaust his own [future] births."[42]

Vasubandhu comments:

> [In this passage,] what is to be known? That the noble truth of suffering includes form and so on. How [are form and so on] to be known? As being impermanent. What is this knowledge? Right view. What is the result of such knowledge? It is the complete liberation of the mind, in stages, from sorrow and so on. What is stated about this? "I have exhausted my own [future] births . . ." and so on.[43]

Vasubandhu's commentary on the *Saṃyuktāgama* passage suggests that in elucidating a summary meaning, a commentator may make use of both direct quotation and paraphrase to answer questions about what a particular sūtra says and implies. These answers should ideally be based on the commentator's thorough understanding of the meaning of the sūtra's constituent phrases—an understanding facilitated by commentarial activity.

2.3. The Meaning of Phrases

Vasubandhu begins this lengthy section—running to more than fifty folios—with a simple definition: "The meaning of phrases," he tells us, "is what should be said regarding what is said."[44] He then emphasizes two ways in which this meaning may be specified: via elaboration or condensation. As Vasubandhu puts it, "in some instances, a single [phrase] may possess multiple [meanings]; in some instances, multiple [phrases] may possess a single [meaning]."[45]

The treatment of the first theme—elaboration—is itself elaborated at considerable length. It is divided into two sections. The first is devoted to a discussion of three short scriptural passages regarding the nature of mind (or thought: *sems*, **citta*), whereas the second section comprises an investigation of thirteen specific Sanskrit terms and the various ways in which they can be interpreted.[46] Vasubandhu begins by elliptically citing a passage that he traces to the **Acandrikāputrasūtra* (*ma zla ba'i bu mo'i mdo las*). The passage is reproduced at greater length in the *Vyākhyāyuktiṭīkā*:

> [Śāriputra said:] "O son of *Acandrikā, Devadatta [taught the dharma] to the monks in this way: 'Venerable ones, the mind of a monk is thoroughly purified by means of the mind; a pure mind is free from desire, hatred, and delusion; it has the quality of lacking the subsidiary afflictions [associated with] desire, hatred, and delusion; it has the quality of not returning to the realm of desire, not returning to the realm of form, not returning to the realm of the formless.' "[47]

Vasubandhu immediately follows his citation with a commentary on its contents, adducing additional qualities that minds lacking desire, hatred, and delusion should be said to manifest: "In this case, one should understand that they are not characterized by those [afflictions]. On the basis of statements such as 'they are characterized by absence of yearning' and 'they do not turn back,' [one should understand them] as free from corruptions, and as not turning back, since they are free from the desires that beset outsiders and from qualities that do not accord [with the dharma]."[48]

Two additional sūtra passages are then cited and glossed. These also discuss characteristics properly associated with minds or thoughts that have been purified of afflictions. The first passage, from the **Pañcāṅgasthapatisūtra*, emphasizes that virtuous action is motivated by thoughts lacking desire, hatred, and delusion; thoughts that lack these qualities are endowed with certain others—e.g., detachment—and they conform to the *prātimokṣa* vows. The second passage, from the **Cetaḥparyāyābhijñānirdeśa*, emphasizes that a mind without desire is capable of knowing other minds just as they are. Again, the commentary gives the text in full:

> [Here, a monk] knows a mind that possesses desire just as it is: a mind possessing desire. He knows a mind that is separated from desire just as it is: a mind separated from desire. In the same way, he knows—just as they are—a mind possessing hatred and a mind separated from hated; a mind possessing delusion and a mind separated from delusion; a mind that is narrow and a mind that is broad; a mind that is timid and a mind that is lofty; a mind that is haughty and a mind that is not haughty; a mind that is not calmed and a mind that is calmed; a mind that is not concentrated and a mind that is concentrated; a noncontemplative mind and a contemplative mind; a mind that is not liberated and does not clearly apprehend liberation just as it is, and a mind that is liberated and correctly apprehends liberation just as it is.[49]

The ensuing discussion is formidably complex, involving an exchange of objections and rejoinders in which shifts in voice are not always explicitly signaled. The rhetoric of the passage makes it difficult at times to determine which of the views on offer represents Vasubandhu's considered position(s) on the issues at hand. Much additional work will be needed to determine which among the views propounded—and questions posed—should rightly be attributed to Vasubandhu himself.

The exchange focuses on two issues that are treated in a section of Vasubandhu's *Abhidharmakośabhāṣya* that is likewise characterized by a multiplicity of rhetorical voices.[50] The first has to do with what we might call relations of entailment between qualities: whether, for example, one is entitled to assume that a thought that is characterized by desire (*'dod chags dang ldan pa'i sems*, **sarāgacitta*) is ipso facto a thought or mind in which desire is presently occurring (*'dod chags dang mtshungs pa dang ldan pa'i sems*, **sarāgasaṃprayuktacitta*). The second issue stems from an apparent clash between two of the sūtra passages Vasubandhu has just cited. The excerpt from the **Acandrikāputrasūtra* characterizes a purified mind (*sems shin tu sbyangs pa*, **praśrabdhacitta*) as devoid of desire, hatred, and delusion. The excerpt from the **Cetaḥparyāyābhijñānirdeśa*, by contrast, notes that awakened beings—those whose minds are pure—possess the ability to know other minds, just as they are—*even if* those minds possess desire, hatred, and delusion. This raises a thorny question: How can the mind of a Buddha *know*—fully and accurately—that which the mind of a Buddha simultaneously (and definitionally) *lacks*? To answer this question fully would require investigating what is involved in the awareness of others' thoughts (*gzhan sems shes pa, paracittajñāna*), and exploring how the qualities possessed by a particular intentional object (*dmigs pa, ālambana*) might be known without these qualities being transferred to the awareness that knows them. In the *Vyākhyāyukti*, Vasubandhu resists being drawn into this discussion. His answer, in effect, is that we need not and should not worry too much about this issue, but should focus instead on liberation. The awareness of others' thoughts does not itself imply liberation and, in any case, is inconceivable, as the Blessed One himself has suggested.

Because Vasubandhu's discussion of these two issues is so detailed, it is easy to forget the point of their being raised at all. The discussion is, of course, polemical—it consists of a debate on the characteristics of the minds of awakened beings—but it is also (and just as importantly) exemplary. Vasubandhu is here aiming to provide aspiring commentators with a paradigm of exegetical elaboration to which they might appeal when they encounter a single phrase that possesses multiple meanings. He implies that one way to proceed is by distributing these multiple meanings across multiple rhetorical voices and placing those voices in dialogue with one another.

Before bringing his discussion of elaboration to a close, Vasubandhu devotes sustained attention to the polysemy of individual terms. Thirteen root terms are discussed. For each, Vasubandhu offers a brief mnemonic verse that specifies additional associated terms, followed by illustrative examples that show how these additional terms relate to the root term.[51] Most—though not all—of these additional terms can be used to express a meaning associated with the original term.

So, for example, the first of the thirteen terms discussed is **rūpa* (*gzugs*), for which Vasubandhu offers the following:

> The term **rūpa* (*gzugs*) pertains to the "aggregate of matter/form" (*gzugs phung*, **rūpaskandha*); "color" (*kha dog*, **varṇa*); "meditative states" (*bsam gtan*, **dhyāna*); and "aspect" (*rnam pa*, **ākāra*). [It pertains] to the "aggregate of matter/form" in phrases such as [the one that begins] "one searches for a self in matter (*gzugs*)" [and runs] to "[one searches for a self in] consciousness." [It pertains] to "color" in phrases such as "the eye sees colors (*gzugs rnams*)." [It pertains] to "meditative states" in phrases such as "desire for the form [realm] and desire for the formless [realm] (*gzugs kyi 'dod chags dang / gzugs med pa'i dod chags*)." [It pertains] to "aspect" in phrases such as "affliction in the [two] aspects of holding forms dear [and being averse to them] (*gzugs rnams kyi sdug pa'i gzugs dag la kun tu chags*)." [52]

Here, several exemplary phrases are given in which the term **rūpa* is employed in different ways, and the multiple meanings associated with **rūpa* are rendered explicit by additional terms: *varṇa*, *dhyāna*, and so on. This is Vasubandhu's standard procedure for the ensuing twelve terms. At times, however, the associations he draws are rather oblique. So, for example, in his treatment of the term "abandoning" (*spangs pa*, **prahāṇa*), he associates it with "negative predispositions" (*bag la nyal*, **anuśaya*) and goes on to note that it "pertains to correctly overcoming 'negative predispositions' in phrases such as 'due to abandoning three fetters, one is a stream-enterer.'"[53] Here, a loose conceptual connection between **prahāṇa* and **anuśaya*—well short of synonymy—is being noted: negative predispositions make up one class of things that Buddhists are enjoined to abandon.

Vasubandhu finishes this short subsection of the text by reminding us that all the phrases he has glossed "are no more than illustrative examples" (*dper brjod pa tsam du zad do*) of a more generalized phenomenon. This phenomenon places a considerable demand on the aspiring commentator. Because a single phrase can denote and connote different things depending on the way in which it is used, a commentator must be constantly attentive not only to the range of possible meanings that a term can bear (so as to select the particular *artha* that the term indexes in a particular context of use), but also to the conceptual connections that can be drawn between that *artha*—whatever it may be—and other meanings signaled by the phrases of Buddhist teaching.

Following this extensive treatment of elaboration, Vasubandhu turns to address the second theme: condensation. Here, rhetorical form again recapitulates content: the theme is granted only a single passing remark. Apropos of multiple phrases possessing a single meaning, Vasubandhu notes that synonymic terms provide examples of this.[54]

The *Vyākhyāyukti* then offers a second typology of meaning. It is threefold: the "meaning to be expounded regarding particulars" (*so so re re la brjod par bya ba'i don*), the "summary meaning" (*bsdus pa'i don*), and the "point" (*dgos pa'i don*). Vasubandhu's gloss of the first category closely parallels the gloss he has already given of the "meaning of phrases" (*tshig gi don*, **padārtha*): the meaning to be expounded regarding particulars is, he tells us, what should be said regarding what is said.[55] And indeed, this category appears to cover precisely the sort of exegetical elaboration that Vasubandhu has already treated in detail. Vasubandhu offers, as an example, the scriptural phrase "conditioned by ignorance, formations [arise]," noting that the meaning to be expounded regarding particulars should, in this case, be understood to include the responses given to particular questions—e.g., "what is ignorance?"

The second category of meaning shares its name with the second of the five aspects. Both the alternative typology's *piṇḍārtha* and the discussion of *piṇḍārtha* as the second aspect involve the appropriation of meanings culled from disparate phrases in a sūtra. In the alternative typology, the summary meaning is presented as "that meaning which is collected from phrases of diverse meaning"—an inversion of Vasubandhu's earlier observation that single phrases in scripture may flower into multiple phrases of exegetical elaboration.[56] Here, we see not elaboration, but synthesis: multiple phrases of scripture grouped under common headings. By way of example, Vasubandhu notes that phrases that teach the twelvefold chain of dependent arising may be understood as teaching three kinds of impurity.[57] This example (and there are others) demonstrates that discrete components of a teaching may be grouped together—organized under shared rubrics—and thereby serve pedagogical purposes above and beyond those they might serve when considered individually.

Vasubandhu's discussion of the third category—the point (*dgos pa'i don*, **prayojanārtha*)—is somewhat cryptic.[58] The treatment is, however, clear enough to indicate that Vasubandhu understands this category to involve making explicit the particular reason(s) a teaching has been given—the motives for, or consequences of, a Buddha's speech. As Vasubandhu puts it, "'Why is this teaching undertaken?' [In the event this question is posed,] the point must be stated."[59]

Each of the components of the alternative typology would seem, then, to parallel one of the five aspects. The alternative typology's "summary meaning" obviously parallels the second aspect, while the two remaining components of the alternative typology—"point" and "meaning to be expounded regarding particulars"—arguably parallel the first and third aspects, respectively. If we associate the three components of the alternative typology with the first three aspects in this way, the alternative typology looks to be little more than a reordering of old material. This reordering itself may, however, be significant. Whereas the order in which the aspects are treated conforms to the order in which they are presented in a well-ordered commentary, the order in which components of the alternative typology are treated conforms to the order in which they flower as the result of study. A student comes first to understand the meanings of individual phrases; doing so facilitates his subsequent synthesis of those meanings; and such synthesis in turn facilitates his understanding of the purpose of a sūtra. By placing the "meaning to be expounded regarding particulars" first in his alternative typology, Vasubandhu may be emphasizing that close attention to the meanings of particular phrases is a primary task for those who would be commentators.

Vasubandhu will soon turn to face this task directly, as he proceeds to comment on over one hundred different passages drawn from sūtra texts—all of which are anthologized in the *Vyākhyāyuktisūtrakhaṇḍaśata*. Before doing so, he concludes Book I by addressing the topic of enumerations (*grangs gsungs*)—i.e., teachings that treat topics by invoking numbered lists. Teachings of this sort are, of course, exceedingly common in Buddhist literature, and Vasubandhu discusses several examples, noting that enumerative statements "allow one a sure grasp of that which is enumerated."[60] With these examples, Book I comes to a close.

In Book II, the discussion of the "meaning of phrases" continues. Book II is entirely devoted to short commentaries on each of the

Vyākhyāyuktisūtrakhaṇḍaśata's passages; it thus provides the aspiring commentator with numerous exemplary instances of proper commentarial procedure. Vasubandhu does not, for the most part, explicitly discuss general procedural principles for commentarial interpretation. This point deserves emphasis. Skilling, in his study of the *Vyākhyāyukti*, has suggested that the text sets out "principles of exegesis or hermeneutics."[61] Although I do not wish to deny that the *Vyākhyāyukti* can be read as articulating such principles on occasion, most of the text amounts to a succession of examples, and general interpretive principles are not explicitly offered. Vasubandhu may have intended his audience to formulate such principles inductively—or he may have considered them of limited use (if he considered them at all). That is, he may have taken the task of interpreting the "meaning of phrases" to be one best learned by paying close attention to the shifting demands made by particular texts and audiences—not by internalizing a set of interpretive principles that could be applied across all texts and contexts.[62]

In the opening folios of Book III, Vasubandhu offers a few general reflections on how to discuss the meaning of phrases. He advocates the use of four tools: synonyms (*rnam grangs*, **paryāya*), distinguishing characteristics (*mtshan nyid*, **lakṣaṇa*), etymological explanations (*nges pa'i tshig*, **nirukti*), and analyses (*rab tu dbye ba*, **prabheda*).[63] Each of the first three tools is explicitly stated to involve names (*ming*, **nāman*): synonyms are said to consist in "other names" (*ming gzhan*, **paranāman*), and definitions offer "the name that pertains to an object" (*don gang la ming de yod pa*, **yadarthe tannāmabhāva*), whereas etymological explanation treats "the cause (sign) of names" (*ming gi rgyu mtshan*, **nāmanimitta*). The final component—analysis—is illustrated by means of representative examples. "One analyzes what is described into aspects: [something] possessing form, [something] that does not possess form, [something] demonstrable, [something] not demonstrable, and so on."[64]

Vasubandhu identifies a teaching in which these four tools are present as an "elucidation" (*yongs su bstan pa*, **paridīpanā*), and he notes that elucidations serve as grounds or contributing causes for the discriminations.[65] He finishes his discussion of the four components by offering a few short passages from scripture to illustrate the ways in which the Buddha taught by means of them. With this, Vasubandhu's treatment of the "meaning of phrases" concludes.

2.4. Connection

In contrast to the previous lengthy discussion, Vasubandhu's treatment of connection (*mtshams sbyar*, **anusaṃdhi*) is cursory, running to only two folios in its Tibetan translation.[66] Vasubandhu has previously noted that "connection" is that which allows readers to understand that the meaning of phrases is sequentially noncontradictory (*go rims mi 'gal ba*). Here, he notes two types of connection and offers a few examples of each. The first he terms "connection related to antecedent and subsequent meaning" (*don snga phyi 'brel ba'i mtshams sbyar*). In discussing this type of connection, Vasubandhu emphasizes the need for commentators to supply their audience with relevant background information. In the service of elucidating a textual connection (**anusaṃdhi*), a commentator proceeds by investigating (**anusaṃdhā*) the particular terms used in a passage, in order to clarify how these terms invoke or relate to points of Buddhist doctrine.[67]

The second type of connection that Vasubandhu identifies is "connection that pertains to the sequence of [what is] antecedent and subsequent" (*snga phyi nyid go rims kyi mtshams sbyar ba*, **pūrvottaratākramānusaṃdhi*). Once again, Vasubandhu emphasizes the need to furnish background information in order to aid comprehension. Here, however, the background information explicitly pertains to the order in which particular items are discussed in a scriptural text. As Vasubandhu explains,

> Connection [also] pertains to the sequence of [what is] antecedent and subsequent. For example, in the case of the noble truths, [one may ask] "why is the cause taught after the result?" . . . The connection pertaining to the four noble truths is in the way that they are realized. Having apprehended suffering as suffering, one determines its cause, [asking] "from what does this arise?" Then, [one determines] the ceasing of that, and then the way in which it is ceased. This is done in the way that one determines sickness, the basis of sickness, the absence of sickness, and the medicine [to be applied]. Since one discriminates each of these in sequence, the four noble truths are taught in the manner in which they are realized. This is the connection with that.[68]

Here, Vasubandhu notes that the order in which the four noble truths are presented may seem puzzling: the truths are not presented in an order that tracks the sequential unfolding of the phenomena they describe. A commentator can resolve this puzzlement by explaining that the truths are presented according to the order in which one comes to understand these phenomena. In the manner of a medical diagnosis, one proceeds backward: from an analysis of effects to an analysis of the conditions that give rise to those effects.

Thus, on Vasubandhu's account, "connection" marks two crucial commentarial techniques. First, a good commentator should show the ways in which particular passages of a root text relate to other Buddhist texts and doctrines, in order to enable his listeners or readers to understand each passage as one that informs and is informed by traditional concepts. Second, a good commentator should discuss not only what his text says, but also how the text is arranged and why passages in the text occur in the order that they do.

*2.5. Objections and Responses ('gal len, *codyaparihāra)*

Vasubandhu opens his discussion of objections and responses by distinguishing between two kinds of objection: objection to words (*sgra la brgal ba, *śabdacodya*) and objection to meaning (*don la brgal ba, *arthacodya*).[69] In discussing objection to words, Vasubandhu cites three short examples. These examples are somewhat obscure in translation but appear to illustrate objections pitched at the level of grammatical form. To object to words is to charge that a particular arrangement of words is a malapropism and therefore inappropriate to convey the real meaning of a teaching. So, for example, an objector versed in Buddhist metaphysical presuppositions could mount a protest to a statement such as "depending on the eye and forms, visual consciousness arises" (*mig dang gzugs la brten nas mig gi rnam par shes pa skye'o, *cakṣuḥ pratītya rūpāṇi cotpadyate cakṣurvijñānam*) on the grounds that it violates a rule of grammar. The relevant rule specifies that in a well-formed Sanskrit sentence, the agent who performs an action signaled by an absolutive form (*lyabanta*) must be the agent who performs the action signaled by a sentence's main verb.[70] Here, the objector's worry is perhaps generated by the characteristically Buddhist idea that phenomena are momentary: the consciousness that depends cannot be the consciousness that arises. In responding to objections of this kind, Vasubandhu appeals—and thereby suggests to prospective commentators that they appeal—to the force of counterexamples: statements to which the objector would presumably not object, despite the fact that they violate the grammatical strictures he proposes.

Vasubandhu then notes two forms of objection to meaning. He terms the first "objection as to contradiction between the antecedent and the subsequent" (*snga phyi 'gal bar brgal ba*). The objection purports to question the coherence of the Buddhist textual corpus—a corpus that is, as Vasubandhu acknowledges, heterogeneous. One aspect of a commentator's task is to show that although this corpus is heterogeneous, it is never incoherent; whereas textual passages may at times appear to contradict one another, they do not in fact do so. As an example of this first subtype of objection to meaning, Vasubandhu offers the following: "In some [sūtras, the Buddha] speaks of 'four noble truths'; in some, [he] speaks [of] 'the three truths of brahmans'; in some, he says 'truth [is] twofold: conventional and ultimate'; in some, he says 'truth [is] precisely one, without a second.'"[71] The Buddha is supposed to have spoken truly, but these accounts appear to contradict one another—and, as Vasubandhu himself will insist, "two mutually contradictory [accounts] cannot [both] be true."[72] How, then, is one to explain this apparent inconsistency? Vasubandhu's solution is to appeal to the intention (*dgongs pa*, **abhiprāya*) underlying the Buddha's utterances: the various accounts regarding truth found in the sūtra corpus do not contradict one another, since each such account is properly understood to be motivated by (and responsive to) particular audiences, aims, and interests; situational demands shape what a Buddha says.

The second form of "objection to meaning" is identified as "objection as to contradiction with reason." Vasubandhu glosses "reason" (*rigs*, **yukti*) in terms of three means of correct cognition: perception, inference, and authoritative speech (*yid ches pa'i gsung*, **āptavāda*). He informs us explicitly that "objections pertaining to contradiction with one or another of those [means of correct cognition] are objections pertaining to contradiction with reason."[73] He then offers a series of illustrative examples:

> "Monks! Past forms exist; future forms exist. That which [is] passed away, exhausted, destroyed, disappeared, transformed—it [nevertheless still] exists." This is in contradiction with perception, insofar as one perceives that past and future [forms] are nonexistent, like the hair of a tortoise, for example. . . .

> "The formless is liberated from form" is in contradiction with inference, since one sees feeling, etc., arise in dependence upon form. . . .
>
> "The Vaipulya group [of texts] is Mahāyāna" is a statement that is in contradiction with scripture (*lung*, **āgama*). Some say that books of sūtra containing lengthy expositions are Vaipulya, but not Mahāyāna. Why? [Because] that [class of texts] is not the speech of a Buddha. Why is it not the speech of a Buddha? Because of contradiction—[i.e.,] it contradicts what all groups acknowledge to be the speech of a Buddha.[74]

Vasubandhu answers each of these objections later. The first two are discussed in the latter part of Book III, whereas the third initiates a long discussion about the status of the Mahāyāna textual corpus—a discussion that has been analyzed in detail by Cabezón.[75] Cabezón's analysis is superb, and I will not attempt to recapitulate his discussion here. Instead, I want to call attention to a point that Cabezón, in focusing on the structure of Vasubandhu's arguments, does not stress—namely, the fact that the arguments offered in this section of the *Vyākhyāyukti* are not only polemical, but also *exemplary*. Vasubandhu is clearly concerned to challenge and defend particular claims about the canonicity of certain Buddhist sūtra texts, but he is also concerned to exemplify how the task of commentary is to be undertaken. On Vasubandhu's account, commentary properly involves a complex and agonistic interplay of voices; it is a forum in which competing claims to authority are to be acknowledged and engaged.

3. Concluding Remarks

The final book of the *Vyākhyāyukti* is rather different from what has gone before. Vasubandhu, having completed his discussion of the five aspects, now emphasizes the importance of listening devotedly to the dharma and encouraging others to do the same. Given that Book V follows immediately upon a lengthy discussion of objections and responses, the stress that it lays on listening devotedly (*gus par mnyan pa*) may come as something of a surprise, particularly if one assumes that an attitude of devotion toward a teaching implies the simple acceptance of what is taught. But Vasubandhu does not presume that devoted listening is incompatible with criticism: criticism characterizes explication, and by the act of explication, the knowledge acquired by devoted listening becomes pure (*yongs su byang bar 'gyur*).[76]

Transmission requires reception: students must be prepared to receive the dharma, and preachers and commentators must do what they can to prepare students toward this end. As Vasubandhu notes, "in the three worlds, though the dharma preacher may cause the rain of the dharma to fall, there may be no water of dharma. It may fall on deaf ears, due to distraction, stupidity, or sleep. Though falling, it may become polluted, since one may fail to attend to it in the right way. And [though it may fall and be pure], it may not remain, due to forgetfulness."[77] Throughout Book V, Vasubandhu offers prospective preachers a range of resources and suggestions for encouraging students to devote their full attention to the dharma. These resources include a range of picturesque similes for the Buddha and his teaching, mnemonic verses that describe the benefits of listening to the dharma (and the costs of failing to do so), and so on. To discuss these resources in the detail they deserve is a project for another time, but one aspect of Vasubandhu's treatment deserves our attention here, since it arguably has an impact on the way in which we read the *Vyākhyāyukti* as a whole.

Early in Book V, Vasubandhu offers a portrait of an awakened being in the act of teaching, listing five qualities that characterize "the voice of a Buddha, a Blessed One, when he is engaged in teaching dharma in an assembly" (*sangs rgyas bcom ldan 'das ni 'khor la chos ston par mdzad pa na dbyangs*). He then immediately juxtaposes this portrait with two scriptural citations. The first enumerates qualities possessed by an idealized dharma preacher, and its juxtaposition with the earlier passage suggests that Vasubandhu presumes a preacher's activity of preaching to resemble a Buddha's activity of teaching.[78] The second juxtaposed citation enumerates qualities possessed by idealized students. Its presence in a work explicitly aimed at "those who desire to expound the sūtras" suggests that Vasubandhu understands capable students, no less than capable teachers, to be integrally important to the event of textual transmission. To be an effective commentator is first to be an attentive student; to learn how to present the dharma to others requires that one first learn how to receive the dharma from others.

We have thus been brought full circle. Vasubandhu, having begun his text by focusing on those who would be commentators, has discussed the rhetoric of commentary at considerable length, only to return in Book V to the subject of the commentator—a person whose activity situates him as both student and teacher. The final pages of the *Vyākhyāyukti* emphasize this point, and in doing so they suggest that if the text's *abhidheya* is the rhetoric of commentary, its *prayojana* is, finally, the teaching of teachers. To those who would articulate—and be articulated by—the dharma, Vasubandhu offers paradigms for speaking authoritatively of authoritative speech: models of teaching for the teaching of models.

Conclusion

LIKE ANY READERS, Indian Buddhist commentators approached their texts already bearing interpretive presuppositions. These presuppositions served to guide their readings, influencing the questions they held to be worth asking, the answers they found acceptable, and their views regarding those to whom they might turn for guidance in these matters. In the previous chapters, I have sketched some of these presuppositions and their impacts on Indian Buddhist textual practice. I hope this material will help us to better understand not only Indian Buddhist scriptural commentaries, but also those who composed them—those who, for more than a millennium in India, disseminated the dharma by speaking for Buddhas.[1]

As we have seen—and as traditional and modern scholars are fond of emphasizing—Indian Buddhist tradition uses the term "dharma" in several different ways. Sometimes, the term is used to designate the specific words and phrases that constitute a teaching. At other times, it is used to designate the content of that teaching: that to which such words and phrases refer. The extension of the word "dharma" thus encompasses, and yet transcends, the linguistic forms in which the Buddhist teaching is encoded; the term ranges over what is responsive to, and what is dissociable from, the vicissitudes of circumstance. Buddhist authors routinely exploit this ambiguity, and they do not appear to have thought the two domains to be rigorously separable: on their view, the enduring teaching of the Buddha is encountered in and by way of evanescent teachings offered in particular idioms, languages, and dialects.

Regardless of how it is conveyed, the teaching will endure—so long as competent teachers are able to convey it. On the lips of incompetent teachers, however, the single taste of the dharma turns sour. Writing in the fourth or fifth century C.E., Vasubandhu chastises his contemporaries for failing to explicate Buddhist teaching effectively. In his view, a perfected message of supreme value has been—and may continue to be—abused by less-than-perfect messengers, as the dharma continues its decline and gradually disappears from the world. When it has disappeared completely, the possibility of liberation will vanish with it, and "beings, utterly benighted, will be plunged into total darkness."

In affirming the liberating power of Buddhist teaching, while simultaneously marking the fallibility of those who purport to preserve it, Vasubandhu voices an ambivalence that is both traditional and directed toward tradition. This ambivalence has intermittently surfaced in each chapter of the present work. In the story of Ariṭṭha discussed in chapter 1, we saw the tradition acknowledge that the teaching of the Buddha may be subject to misrepresentation in the mouths of wayward monks. But if the story of Ariṭṭha grants that monks can occasionally get things wrong, it also suggests that they can get things right. Those who correct Ariṭṭha are able to recognize his mistake as a mistake, and they work to disabuse him of his error: to teach him.

As we saw in chapter 2, one need not be a Buddha to teach as a Buddha does. This view, however, provides no guarantee that the dharma will remain uncorrupted as it is handed down over time. Even idealized teachers and preachers are understood to be vulnerable to works of Māra; they, like their real-world counterparts, are clearly not always (presumed to be) Buddhas. The tradition thus recognizes the fallibility of its own conditions of transmission, conditions in which the survival of a perfected message requires that it be taken up and taught over time by those who have yet to reach perfection. Viewed in this way, the very channels that allow for the historical transmission of tradition also serve to render the tradition suspect. Conditions of fidelity are conditions of fallibility; conditions of knowledge are conditions of uncertainty.[2]

Chapter 3 explored traditional responses to the worries generated by this picture—responses of avoidance and acknowledgment.[3] One can strive to avoid the specter of uncertainty by insisting that there are indeed methods for securing doubt-free awareness, or one can acknowledge uncertainty and downplay its impact. As Kamalaśīla himself notes, certain knowledge is not required for effective action. What *is* required is, we might say, ongoing exposure to and internalization of practices and attitudes that can be projected into new contexts: in a word, *training*. This training makes use of, and eventuates in, texts such as those explored in chapter 4. Commentarial guides are both products of and prompts to practices of self-cultivation that take on new urgency in light of the presumed decline of the dharma. Despite the tone of despair occasionally sounded in commentarial guides such as the *Vyākhyāyukti*, the existence of these texts can be understood to manifest guarded optimism. Although the light of the dharma is fading, the lamp can be rekindled—if students of the dharma are willing to redouble their efforts.

These different forms of ambivalence are recapitulated in the intentional ambiguity of the present work's title—a title that points both to concerns over how Buddhas speak and to concerns over how to speak in their stead. These concerns were shared by Indian Buddhist commentators, who struggled to characterize, interpret, and teach others to characterize and interpret the speech of a Buddha, while simultaneously demonstrating, by their example, the difficulty of speaking on a Buddha's behalf. Commentators negotiated the tensions generated by these dovetailing imperatives in different ways; the norms they named were sometimes present and sometimes absent in their performances of proxy.

The reader still may wonder, however, whether and to what extent these commentators saw themselves as represented in the texts they were charged with representing. In this brief concluding chapter, I want to take up this question and explore it in light of a short passage drawn from an eighth-century commentary attributed to Kamalaśīla on the *Śālistambasūtra*: the *Śālistambasūtraṭīkā*.[4] The root text for this commentary is a well-known Mahāyāna Buddhist scripture that purports to recount a teaching offered by the bodhisattva Maitreya to Śāriputra (a figure who is elsewhere represented as a teacher, but who here assumes the role of a student).[5] In the section of the commentary we will examine, Kamalaśīla is grappling with a passage in the introductory section of the sūtra. The passage recounts the first moments of an exchange between Śāriputra and Maitreya, and it sets up the context for the teaching that will unfold in the remainder of the text:

> At that time the venerable Śāriputra went to the bodhisattva-mahāsattva Maitreya's promenade. Upon his arrival, they exchanged many pleasantries; having done so, both sat down on a stone slab. Then, the venerable Śāriputra said this to the bodhisattva-mahāsattva Maitreya: "Maitreya, here today the Blessed One, after looking at a young rice plant, spoke this sūtra to the monks: 'Monks, he who sees dependent arising sees the dharma. He who sees the dharma sees the Buddha.' After that, the Blessed One said nothing more. Maitreya, what is the meaning of that sūtra spoken by the Blessed One?"[6]

The story that Śāriputra relates concludes with the silence of the Buddha. This silence makes room for commentary, and Kamalaśīla reads it as worthy of comment. Why, having issued such a cryptic pronouncement, would the Blessed One say nothing more?

For a commentator, this is a risky question to pose. Buddhas have their reasons, but the story of Ariṭṭha suggests that commentators need to tread very carefully in their attempts to delineate them. Within the unfolding narrative of the *Śālistambasūtra* itself, Maitreya allows the occasion to pass. He goes on to respond to Śāriputra's query by explicating the meaning of the Buddha's pronouncement, but he remains resolutely silent about the Buddha's silence. Kamalaśīla, by contrast, opts to forge ahead:

> It may be asked why the Blessed One did not speak [further]. Although one such as myself is not able to know the intentions of the Blessed One, nevertheless, having considered the matter, if I were to speak, [I would say that the Blessed One remained silent] in order to remove the pride of monks who are prideful—those who think, "I understand [what is said] with [only] a brief account." And [he remained silent] in order to express [the sūtra's] greatness (*che ba nyid*, **mahātmya*) to the bodhisattvas, by way of expounding an intention of exceedingly profound meaning. Thereby, the purpose [of the sūtra] stated [previously] is perfected.[7]

In this short but complex passage, Kamalaśīla begins by interpreting the Buddha's silence as motivated by two intentions. These intentions are aimed at benefiting two audiences that the sūtra has previously identified as members of the Buddha's retinue: monks and bodhisattvas.[8] The Buddha's silence benefits monks by removing the false pride of those who are overconfident in their own comprehension of dependent arising. On

Kamalaśīla's reading, the Buddha intends to throw these monks into a state of confusion—a state that stands to benefit them by revealing failures in their understanding that their pride might otherwise conceal. The Buddha's silence is also seen to benefit the bodhisattvas in his retinue, insofar as it serves to emphasize the greatness of the teaching that he has just offered. It is a teaching whose intention—which Kamalaśīla identifies as "of exceedingly profound meaning"—calls for their sustained reflection.

The passage concludes by associating the Buddha's silence with the perfection (*rdzogs pa, *saṃpanna*) of the sūtra's purpose. Previously in the *Śālistambasūtraṭīkā*, Kamalaśīla has identified the purpose of the *Śālistambasūtra* as twofold: it aims to remove obscurations and to facilitate activity on the path to nonabiding nirvāṇa.[9] When we compare Kamalaśīla's assessment of the dual purpose of the *Śālistambasūtra* with his provisional identification of the intentions underlying the Buddha's silence, a remarkable symmetry emerges. Just as the Buddha's silence aims for the removal of obscurations (in this case, pride), so, too, does the *Śālistambasūtra* itself. Just as the Buddha's silence provides an occasion for forms of reflection that facilitate advancement toward nonabiding nirvāṇa, so, too, does the *Śālistambasūtra*.

Kamalaśīla is thus suggesting that Maitreya's teaching and the silence of the Buddha share common aims. He invites us to understand Maitreya as a being who, though not yet a Buddha, possesses a Buddha's motivations. The motives that drive a Buddha to silence are the very motives that drive Maitreya to speech. If Maitreya's motives are those of a Buddha, what, then, of Kamalaśīla's motives? Notably, in composing a commentary on the *Śālistambasūtra*, Kamalaśīla is reiterating the very forms of speech that are represented in the text on which he is commenting. The *Śālistambasūtra* is *itself* a marriage of root text and commentary, in which a brief statement regarding dependent arising (i.e., a root text) is explicated at length by Maitreya. This leaves the way open for readers of Kamalaśīla's commentary to ascribe to him the motives he ascribes to Maitreya and the Buddha. Yet Kamalaśīla also explicitly acknowledges the limits of his own understanding: he is not able to know the intentions of the Blessed One.

In this acknowledgment, Kamalaśīla echoes a view of Buddhas voiced by the early authorities of Buddhist tradition. In the *Gopakamogallānasutta*, Ānanda is asked whether there exists "any single monk who possesses in each and every way all those qualities that were possessed by the Blessed One, accomplished and fully awakened."[10] He responds:

> There is no single monk, brahman, who possesses in each and every way all those qualities that were possessed by the Blessed One, accomplished and fully awakened. For the Blessed One was the arouser of the unarisen path, the producer of the unproduced path, the declarer of the undeclared path; he was the knower of the path, the finder of the path, the one skilled in the path. But his hearers (*sāvaka*) now abide following that path and become possessed of it afterward.[11]

Ānanda emphasizes the distinction between monks and Buddhas, but he also suggests that advancement on the path is possible. With such advancement, barriers to awakening are overcome, and a hearer's knowledge and skills grow. Advancement on the path is, as we have seen, normatively subject to the guidance of wise monks, and Kamalaśīla—the author of numerous commentaries on sūtras and śāstras as well as several guides to meditative cultivation—surely qualifies as such as monk. As we listen across the centuries to his attempt to speak for Buddhas, however, we may be struck by the way in which he articulates this wisdom: as an explicit acknowledgment that he still has much to learn. In this respect, Kamalaśīla is not unlike scholars of Buddhism today. Whether Buddhist or non-Buddhist, we would do well to heed the guidance he provides.

APPENDIX A

The *Vyākhyāyukti*, Book I

The following is a translation (from the Tibetan) of Book I of Vasubandhu's *Vyākhyāyukti*. The translation is based on the critical edition of the text prepared by Jong-Cheol Lee (2001). In view of the difficulty of obtaining this edition, pagination for the Derge edition (D) has been provided in square brackets. I have attempted to clarify the work's structure and facilitate cross-checking by using outline numbers; these are, however, absent in the original. Occasionally, the translation also notes variant readings from two other sources unavailable to Lee: the Golden Manuscript (G) and an incomplete xylograph edition held by the Institute of Mongolian, Buddhist, and Tibetan Studies of the Siberian Branch of the Russian Academy of Sciences (B).[1] Commentarial glosses and supplementary material have also been drawn from the first section of the *Vyākhyāyuktiṭīkā* (D, sems tsam *si*, 139b1–155a6), attributed to Guṇamati.

In the language of India, [this text is called] *Vyākhyāyukti*; in the language of Tibet, *rnam par bshad pa'i rigs pa.*

Homage to Mañjuśrī Kumārabhūta.

Dwelling in the assembly of those who are learned,
And having honored with my head the sage,
[Who is] awakened because [he has] eliminated confusion and torpor
And expanded [his] mind,
I offer here a brief instruction

To benefit those of lesser learning
Who desire to expound the sūtras.[2]

To begin with, one who wishes to expound the sūtras should have heard much, be endowed with the basis of hearing, and have accumulated what has been heard. How does one hear much, become endowed with the basis of hearing, and accumulate what has been heard? This is elaborated in a sūtra:

> One who, by means of verbal expressions, expresses the dharma—good at the beginning, in the middle, and at the end, [possessed of] excellent meaning and phrasing, unmixed, utterly complete, pure and refined, the pure practice—is one who has heard much, one who is endowed with the basis of hearing, and one who has accumulated what he has heard. Such a dharma as this is heard repeatedly, grasped, recited, comprehended by the mind, and thoroughly understood by personal observation.[3]

In this [passage], "dharma" refers to the sūtras and so forth—i.e., [texts] that are correctly taught, whose meaning is grasped firmly and nonerroneously. "The pure practice" is the path to nirvāṇa. Nirvāṇa is "pure"—i.e., extraordinarily precious, since, as has been said, "one becomes pacified, cooled, and purified [upon attaining it]." "Pure practice" is that by which one is caused to practice, undertake, and obtain that, just as it is said that liquor causes intoxication.

The "beginning, middle, and end" are, respectively, the first through the third of the components: ethics, contemplation, and discriminating insight. As it is stated extensively in a sūtra of the Kāśyapīyas (*'od srung ba'i sde pa dag gi mdo*):

> "Monks! I teach a dharma that is good at the beginning, good in the middle, good at the end! What is the beginning of pure practice? Spelled out more extensively, it is abiding ethically. What is the middle of pure practice? Stated more extensively, it is abiding in the separation from desire up to completion—the fourth absorption. What is the end of pure practice? It is the arising of liberation and the pristine cognition that comprehends liberation, having perfectly comprehended: 'This is the noble truth of suffering.'"

[The teaching is] "good," since, being completely taintless, it is nonmistaken. [It is possessed of] "excellent meaning [and] excellent phrasing." Respectively, this is because of the excellence of [both] what is stated and the statements [themselves], since [the former] is nonerroneous and [the latter] cause one to understand. [The teaching is] "unmixed" and so forth respectively [as follows: it is "unmixed"] because it is not common. [It is "utterly complete"] because it is an antidote to all afflictions. [It is "pure"] because it is liberated [from defilement] via two forms of liberation: intrinsic [liberation] (*ngo bo nyid*) and [liberation of the] continuum (*rgyud*). Moreover, it is "good in the beginning, good in the middle, [and] good at the end," since it has excellent meaning, excellent phasing, and is unmixed.

Furthermore, our own great teachings are stated to be antidotes to the teachings of outsiders. The teachings of outsiders do not instruct one in the beginning, middle, and end of pure practice, since [their] earlier and later [teachings] are contradictory. Moreover, those [teachings] are not good, since they are faulty in word and meaning. They are mixed, since they are common to others. They are not completely perfect, since they are trifling antidotes. They are impure, since they are sites for corrupt practices that occur at each stage [of training]. They are unrefined, since [at each stage] they are accompanied by latent tendencies for the afflictions that occur at other stages. Our teachings are the opposite of these.

Some recite, "accompanied by meaning, accompanied by phrasing" (*sārtham savyañjanaṃ*). [30a] Therefore, it is taught that it is good to recite "with meaning and with phrasing."

"By means of verbal expressions, expresses": [i.e.,] one demonstrates, one teaches the dharma that is expressed by those [verbal expressions]. Since the utterances that dispose one to practice are extraordinary (*rang bzhin ma yin pa*, **aprākṛta*), one is not able to understand the meaning by oneself. However, a lineage enables one to understand. Moreover, those [teachings] can be expressed by means of verbal expressions because they are of that nature. This is not to imply that they are expressed by means of verbal expressions [involving] a transformation of syllables; such a conclusion would be unwarranted.[4] Those things said to be expressed in verbal expressions are their meanings. Their meanings are the well-known meanings of terms [found] in one's own utterances. Yet this is not the case in expressions involving a transformation of syllables, as in this verse, spoken by Māra:

> Human life is long; a good person is not deceived.
> No death of the self is coming here; practice poorly and carelessly.[5]

It is said that one can expound this verse in another way, having transformed [its] syllables:

Human life is not long; good people are deceived;
One's own death will arrive here [soon]; one should not practice carelessly.[6]

Moreover, the pure practice is taught to be nothing other than what verbal expressions express.

[In the opening passage,] "heard [repeatedly]" up through "thoroughly understood by personal observation" [are phrases that] respectively refer to hearing, grasping, practicing, contemplating the meaning [of the dharma], and analyzing [it]. Regarding these, via the first two [terms, i.e., hearing and grasping], one [respectively] hears much and is endowed with the basis of hearing; via the remaining [terms], one accumulates what has been heard, in order to teach. As scripture (*lung*, *āgama*) states: "[One should understand the passage that runs] from "heard" up through "thoroughly understood by personal observation" [as referring to] grasping the teachings; reciting and reading them [aloud]; [30b] delighting [in them]; and analyzing them by apprehending them according to their class."[7] It is on the basis of exposition, accordingly, that one is [a person] who has heard much and so on. That [person] is suitable to be a teacher.

1. The Five Aspects

How should one discuss the sūtras? [One should do so] via five aspects. One should state the purpose of the sūtra; the summary meaning; the meaning of the phrases; connections; and the two: objections and responses. Regarding this, [the following] is said:

The purpose, together with the summary meaning, the meaning of phrases, connections, and objections and responses;
[These five aspects] should be stated by those who propound the meaning of sūtras.[8]

The two—objections and responses—are collapsed into one [aspect], since the responses offered pertain to the [particular] objections [raised].

Why are these [five aspects] expressed? When one hears the greatness of the sūtra's meaning, one is spurred on to listen to and grasp [the text]; for this reason, the purpose is expressed. Moreover, the purpose may also be understood from the summary meaning of the sūtra, and the summary meaning from the meaning of the phrases. From the connections, [one may understand] that the meaning of the phrases is sequentially noncontradictory. From the objections and responses, [one may understand] that [the text] does not contradict reason and that there is no contradiction between those [texts] that are earlier [and] later. Thus, the summary meaning and so on should be stated. Regarding this, it is said:

> Having heard the greatness of the meaning of the sūtras,
> A hearer should respectfully listen [to them] and grasp [them];
> So, at the outset, the purpose is stated.[9]
> One comprehends it from the summary meaning,
> And [one comprehends] the summary meaning from the meaning of the phrases,
> And [one comprehends] that the meaning of phrases is successively noncontradictory from the connections.
> From the objections and responses, [one comprehends] that there is no contradiction with reason, and no contradiction between earlier and later [teachings].

Moreover, from a statement of the purpose, one will know such things as the excellent results of the sūtra. From a statement of the summary meaning, [one will know] that which pertains to meaning. From a statement of the meaning of the phrases, [one will know] the summary meaning, dharma characteristics (*chos kyi mtshan nyid*), and intended characteristics (*dgongs pa'i mtshan nyid*). From a statement of the connections, [one will know] the sequential relation of the phrases [31a]. From a statement of the objections and responses, [one will know that the text] does not contradict reason or earlier and later [texts]. Regarding this, it is said:

> From the teaching of these five,
> One will know the excellent effect [and that which] pertains to [it], and
> Likewise [will know] the three: the summary meaning and so on.
> [One will know] relation and noncontradiction.

A dharma characteristic is, for example, "form is impermanent." By this phrase, a meaning is taught in terms of specific and general characteristics.[10] An intended characteristic is, e.g., "that which is impermanent is suffering."[11] The intention here pertains to that which possesses the afflictions and the suffering of conditioned states. In the same way, regarding the passage that runs "gain and renown is the skin" up to "the marrow," the intention is [to mark] the five faculties, since each of them—faith and so on—is correlated with skin and so on as one moves progressively inward, according to level of import (*gces rim*).[12] In a scripture, it is said: "By itself, faith is like skin, because it is delicate. Effort is like muscle, because it toils, continually undertaking [actions]. Mindfulness is like tendon, because it relates what is heard and an intended meaning. Concentration is like bone, because bad thoughts find it difficult to break. Wisdom is like marrow, because it abides in an equipoised mind."

1.1. The Purpose

Here, in brief, the purpose of a sūtra is to be understood under four aspects.

1. For those persons who are confused, a sūtra provides the genuine teaching.
2. For those who are careless, a sūtra provides guidelines for what is genuinely acceptable.
3. For those who are dispirited, a sūtra provides genuine encouragement.
4. For those who are set out [on the path], a sūtra provides genuine delight.

Just as each of these aspects is singular, so, too, can each be subdivided into four. Thus, genuine teaching, guidelines for what is genuinely acceptable, genuine encouragement, and genuine delight may apply to this or that [audience]. Each aspect references a specific [kind of] person and a certain form of ignorance with respect to a particular object.[13] [31b] Each "single" [kind of person] also encompasses four [kinds]: among those who are confused [should be counted also] ignorant ones, those who doubt, and those whose understanding is wrong. Among those who are careless [should be counted also] the indolent, those who lack earnestness, and those who calumniate. Among those who are dispirited [should be counted also] those who aim for what is trifling, those who are regretful of their own incapacities, and those who are fearful due to their many [negative] acts. And among those who are set out [should be counted also] those whose understanding is nonerroneous, those who possess equanimity, and those who are driven, lacking contentment.

The purpose turns one away from associating with the dark side (*nag po'i phyogs*, **kṛṣṇapakṣa*), or, alternatively, it leads to what is opposed [to it]—and so [to] what is genuinely acceptable.

[Q:] But how should these teachings and so on be understood? Do they pick out particular attributes? Or what is to be completely abandoned? Or what is to be relied on? Or what is distressing? Or what one has faith in? A sūtra says,"Two who lack faith rightly accept the excellence of faith; they are trained [in it], guided [to it], firmly placed [in it]."[14] Does each phrase [here] have a single meaning, or, alternatively, does each have various meanings?

[A:] What follows from this [line of questioning]?

[Q:] If each phrase has a single meaning, then there would be the fault of pleonasm; but if each phrase has various meanings, then the sūtra would have multiple purposes—viz., perfect teaching and so on.[15]

[A:] [These worries are unfounded.] Each [phrase] does indeed express a single meaning [i.e., its own]. Why would there be the fault of pleonasm pertaining to the meaning?[16]

[Q:] [What about the following objections?] That is meaningless (*don med pa*, **asadartha*).[17] If a term is used that has no meaning, why oppose it? Moreover, why would [a Buddha] teach using rhetorical strategies (*rnam grangs*, **paryāya*) but [not] teach in a definitive way?

[A:] If a single discourse spoken by the Buddhas were to be purposeless (*dgos pa med pa*, **niṣprayojana*), it would be a fault. Here, what is the purpose? There are said to be eight purposes for rhetorical strategies, owing to the variety among those who are trained.

[1.] In order to cause [a particular person] to grasp [the teaching] in this life or in a subsequent life. [32a]

[2.] In order to teach the meaning of that [teaching], via discursive strategies, to those who are distracted in this life—since others might disparage a statement as to what is in fact the case.

[3.] In order to characterize the meaning over and over again, so that inattentive persons will not forget it.

[4.] In order to eliminate ideas that bear on alternate meanings, in those cases in which a single phrase may possess multiple meanings.

[5.] In order to establish the meaning of that [teaching] via alternate phrasing, so as to use just the right words.

[6.] In order that dharma preachers (*chos sgrogs pa rnams*) will attain means and wisdom in expounding the meaning [of a teaching] and causing [its] comprehension.

[7.] In order to demonstrate that one possesses the discrimination of dharma (*chos so so yang dag par rig pa*, **dharmapratisaṃvid*).

[8.] In order to arouse the seeds of that [discrimination of dharma] in others.

The fault of pleonasm does not naturally apply, since all expositions using rhetorical strategies are [offered] in order to facilitate the understanding of students.

Alternatively, one could say that there are various meanings. "Do it in this way!" offers what one should "rightly accept"; one is "trained," since one attains a state of devotion; one is "guided," since one is established in practice; one is "firmly placed," since one does not waver, as one is not captivated [by distractions]. Moreover, rhetorical strategies are [used] in order to clear away hindrances to training.

[Q:] Does a sūtra not then have many purposes?

[A:] No, since it presents what is rightly to be accepted: the result of training and so on. So, by means of rhetorical strategies, [one may learn] the correct application of enticement (*nye bar 'dun bar 'byed pa*) and wrongful temptation (*'dun par zlog par byed pa*), [as one sees in the following statements]:

> "With respect to the teaching of the teacher, it is right that you should apply yourself; it is right that you should be vigilant; it is right that you should realize [this]."

> "Ānanda! Not good is the monk who savors distraction, who enjoys distraction, who strives for and abides in occasions for pleasure in distraction."

What is stated in such passages? [32b] With reference to those whose nature is to be careless (*bag med*), that which they should rightly accept [is stated]. With reference to those who are ignorant, that which is the "correct teaching" [is stated]—since they are correctly being taught what is right and wrong (*rigs pa dang ma rigs pa*, **yuktāyukta*).[18] Regarding this, the first sūtra fragment states that in which one is "trained"—[i.e.,] that upon which one relies for support, and that which one should do; the "enticement" is for these. On what does one rely? On the commencement of effort. What should one do? One should abandon things that do not conform [to the teaching] and rely upon those aspects that are allied [to it]. Moreover, the "enticement" should be understood as aimed at those who are dispirited in training, and at those who endeavor to obtain understanding so as to achieve wealth and renown, whether by merely listening [to the dharma], or merely exerting themselves in thinking [about it], or merely meditating [upon it]. Moreover, the "enticement" aims also at those who do not meditate, those who do not relish meditation, and those who do not know satisfaction by means of that alone.

From scripture: "Having respectively undertaken the three forms of training (*bslab pa gsum*). . . ."[19]

{The word *alam* can be seen as "ability" (*nus pa, *śakti*), [as in the following excerpt]: "one is unable to see or know this path." [20] [That is,] one cannot bear it; one has no capacity [for it]. It can also be seen as "opposition" (*bzlog pa, *vāraṇa*), as we find in the passage that runs from "O great king, each of my actions" [up to] "sufficient, because of delighting the mind"—i.e., all the formations are sufficient. It can also be seen as "ornament" (*rgyan, *bhūṣaṇa*), [as in the passage] "a rotting corpse adorned, like an eye freshly painted."[21] One also sees the meaning "fit" (*rigs pa, *paryāpti*), as in the passage: "*Senaka (dmag ldan pa) you are fit to be consumed by uncertainty and doubt"—i.e., doubt should consume you, doubt is born [in you]—"fit to grieve, fit to abandon the afflictions, fit to be completely liberated"—i.e., [it is] appropriate [that you experience these things].[22] One sees also the correct meaning of "application" in this.}

[33a1] From the second sūtra fragment [above, i.e., "Ānanda! Not good is the monk . . ."], one should understand the three phrases [as follows]: having commenced actions that are distracting as they arise in the present, in the past, and in the future, insofar as one savors, enjoys, and takes pleasure in them, one is said to enjoy their complete abandonment in the same way.[23]

1.2. The Summary Meaning

The summary meaning is the corpus of the sūtra (*mdo sde'i lus, *sūtrakāya, *sūtraśarīra*), as in sūtras such as [the following] from the *Saṃyuktāgama*: "Monks! Regarding that form which exists . . ."[24] Thus, in brief, a summary meaning is a teaching regarding some particular thing [and] how it is to be known, what such knowledge is, what the result of this knowledge is, and what is stated about that.

[With reference to the passage just cited,] what is to be known? That the noble truth of suffering comprises form and so on. How [are form and so on] to be known? As being impermanent. What is this knowledge? Right view. What is the result of such knowledge? It is the complete liberation of the mind, in stages, from sorrow and so on. What is stated about this? "I have exhausted my own [future] births . . ." and so on.

Furthermore, the summary meaning here is, in brief, seen to be the correct apprehension of things, just as they are; freedom from sorrow and desire; liberation, and the apprehension of liberating wisdom. The summary meaning of sūtras should be known as being of such a nature as this.

1.3. The Meaning of Phrases

The meaning of phrases is what should be said regarding what is said. In some instances, a single [phrase] may possess multiple [meanings]; in some instances, multiple [phrases] may possess a single [meaning].

1.3.1. A SINGLE PHRASE POSSESSING MULTIPLE MEANINGS

1.3.1.1. PART I

As an example of a single phrase that possesses multiple meanings, there is this passage from the **Acandrikāputrasūtra* (*ma zla ba'i bu mo'i mdo las*): "Their minds are free from desire, hatred, and delusion."[25] In this case, one should understand that they are not characterized by those [afflictions]. On the basis of statements such as "they are characterized by absence of yearning" and "they do not turn back," [one should understand them] as free from corruptions and as not turning back, since they are free from the desires that beset outsiders and from qualities that do not accord [with the dharma]. [33b]

From the **Pañcāṅgasthapatisūtra*: "These good, virtuous actions are motivated by thoughts. What are those thoughts? They are [thoughts] free from desire, free from hatred, free from delusion." One should understand [those thoughts] as characterized by presently occurring absence of attachment and so on.[25] They are not [thoughts] in which desire, etc., is absent [completely], and they are not [ethically] neutral, since they are subject to the *prātimokṣa* vows.

From the **Cetaḥparyāyābhijñānirdeśa*: "When a mind is free from desire, it correctly knows, just as it is, that mind is free from desire—and so, too, for freedom from hatred and delusion."[26] One should understand [the mind described here] as not being characterized by presently occurring desire and so on. [To say that it is] not characterized [is to say that such qualities] are absent [from it]. Yet [this mind] is not necessarily characterized by presently occurring nonattachment and so on.

[Q:] Why does not being characterized [amount to nothing more than the] absence [of presently occurring affliction]?

[A:] Because [otherwise] the fact that [one is] free from desire would imply that one is liberated.

[Q:] So?

[A:] This is not taught [even] among outsiders; [even] among [such] children, the higher forms of knowledge are not stated to be [completely] free from desire and so on, as liberation is.

If [the mind that is] free from desire and so on is not characterized by those [afflictions], then [the mind that] possesses desire is characterized by those [afflictions]. But this is not to imply that these [afflictions] are presently occurring [together].

[Q:] So?

[A:] [In the event that the afflictions never occurred separately,] they would not be spoken of as distinct; each [mind in which] one [occurred] would [then] possess [all] three. This [view] is not stated even among nonliberated outsiders.

If [the mind] is not characterized by freedom from desire, it is not right to say simply that it possesses—[i.e.,] is characterized by—desire; [34a] one should say that it is characterized by presently occurring desire.

[Q:] If [a mind] that accords with the dark side is characterized by presently occurring [afflictions], and [a mind] that accords with the white side lacks those [afflictions], what then?

[A:] Liberation is not said to be [that way] even among outsiders. It is not said to possess either the negative [quality] of being characterized by presently occurring desire, etc., or the positive [quality] of not being characterized [by them]. Nor is it said to be neutral.

[Q:] Now, how is the mind endowed with presently occurring afflictions and subsidiary afflictions spoken of? Do similar [considerations] apply?

[A:] Being subject to a mind that abides in the three kinds of feeling is due to [what should be] stated as the three roots of affliction.[27] One should speak of mind as precisely that in which these abide and as characterized by presently occurring afflictions and subsidiary afflictions, and other [qualities] that accord with subsidiary afflictions as well. One should not fail to speak of mind as characterized by presently occurring [afflictions].

[Q:] So, if [a mind] is not characterized by presently occurring desire, is it free from desire? If it is not characterized by presently occurring hatred, is it free from desire?

[A:] To grasp [the mind] in this way is to fail to understand. It is accordingly taught that one grasps [a mind] as possessing hatred precisely because one grasps that it is characterized by the presently occurring relevant [affliction].

[A mind that is] free from desire, etc., may be grasped differently: [it] can be free from that [desire] but characterized by presently occurring [affliction] of some kind. Yet other [afflictions need] not be presently occurring. [So, it] may be [grasped to be] not different, since it [need] not [be] characterized by any presently occurring [afflictions].

Some might argue as follows: if [a mind] is characterized by desire—i.e., if it possesses desire—it will wrongfully understand the minds of others. Why? Does that [mind] characterized by desire grasp the intentional object (*dmigs pa, *ālambana*) [of another's mind] or that [mind itself]? It does not grasp those two [together]. It cannot be the case that the awareness of another's mind bears on the intentional object of that [mind], when possession of that intentional object does not characterize [one's own] mind. [34b]

To such claims, one might respond by noting that the awareness of another's mind does not make one liberated. One should strive, accordingly, for that [i.e., for liberation]. How, then, should this [matter] be understood? [The answer is:] it is inconceivable. The Blessed One has said, "The object of a meditator's meditations is inconceivable." Even so, [a mind] possessing the latent impressions of desire and so on is grasped as specific.

1.3.1.2. PART II

Other examples [of single phrases possessing multiple meanings] include:

*1.3.1.2.1. *Rūpa*

The term **rūpa* (*gzugs*) pertains to the "aggregate of form" (*gzugs phung, *rūpaskandha*); "color" (*kha dog, *varṇa*); "meditative states" (*bsam gtan, *dhyāna*); and "aspect" (*rnam pa, *ākāra*). [It pertains] to the "aggregate of form" in phrases such as [the one that begins] "one searches for a self in form (*gzugs*)" [and runs] to "[one searches for a self in] consciousness." [It pertains] to "color" in phrases such as "the eye sees colors" (*gzugs rnams*). [It pertains] to "meditative states" in phrases such as "desire for the form [realm] and desire for the formless [realm] (*gzugs kyi 'dod chags dang / gzugs med pa'i dod chags*)." [It pertains] to "aspect" in phrases such as "affliction in the [two] aspects of holding forms dear [and being averse to them]" (*gzugs rnams kyi sdug pa'i gzugs dag la kun tu chags*).

*1.3.1.2.2. *Anta*

The term **anta* (*mtha*) [pertains] to "cessation" (*zad pa, *kṣaya*); "end" (*mjug, *avasāna*); "division" (*cha, *bhāga/*aṃśa*); "vicinity" (*nye ba, *sannikṛṣṭa*); "region" (*phyogs, *deśa*); [and that which is] "lowly" (*smad pa, *nindita*). The term *anta* [pertains] to "cessation" in phrases such as "bringing about the cessation of suffering." [It pertains] to [the] "end" [of something] in phrases such as "the end of subsistence is death" and "here, a living being [reaches] the end of the world." [It pertains] to "division" in phrases such as "the three divisions: the divisions of that which is perishable, the division of the origin of that which is perishable, the division of the destruction of that which is perishable." It pertains to "vicinity" in phrases such as "having arisen from the ground, he went to the water's edge."[28] It pertains to "region" in phrases such as: "to which region has [he] gone?" and "dwelling in one region." It pertains to [that which is] "lowly" in phrases such as "among livelihoods, begging is lowly"—i.e., "vile" (*tha chad*).[29]

*1.3.1.2.3. *Agra*

[35a] The term **agra* (*mchog*) pertains to the "supreme" (*gtso bo, *jyeṣṭha*); [that which is] "first" [i.e., foremost] (*dang po, *prathama*); "tip" (*rtse mo, *mūrdhāna*); "front" (*mdun kyi don, *purohita*); "phrase" (*tshig, *vacana*); "multitude" (*mang po, *bahu*); and "apprehension" (*dmigs, *upalambha*). It pertains to the "supreme" in phrases such as "Tathāgatas are said to be supreme among existing beings." It pertains to [what is] "foremost" in phrases such as "foremost seat" (*stan gyi thog ma*), "foremost water" (*chu gyi thog ma*), and "foremost alms" (*bsod snyoms kyi thog ma*). It pertains to "tip" in phrases such as "with the tip, or the best [portion], of the grass." It pertains to "front" in phrases such as "going in front." It pertains to "phrase" in phrases such as "seed phrase" (*tshig gi sa bon*). It pertains to "multitude" in phrases such as "[one for whom] there is a powerful multitude of warriors."[30] It pertains to "object" in phrases such as "the state of single-pointed mind and that which is not connected with mind" (*sems rtse gcig pa nyid dang sems mi 'brel ba zhes 'byung ba lta bu'o*). When affixed with a prefix, [the term *agra*] is seen to [pertain to other things, such as] "joy," as in phrases such as "one becomes glad (*mgo ba, *udāgra*), one becomes overjoyed"; "being single-minded," as in the phrase "look to those who concord with (*mthun pa, *samagra*) the monks who are hearers"; "common class," as in the phrase "the collection (*tshogs pa, *sāmagrī*) of conditions"; and "being youthful," as in the phrase "fresh (*lang tsho, *pratyagra*), endowed with youth."[31]

*1.3.1.2.4. *Loka*

The term **loka* (*'jig rten*) [pertains] to "sentient being" (*sems can, *sattva*); "receptacle" (*snod, *pātra*); "suffering" (*sdug bsngal, *duḥkha*); "living being" (*'gro ba, *gamana*); and "things desired" (*'dod pa rnams, *kāmāḥ*). It pertains to "sentient being" in phrases such as "for the world, these three qualities are not desired, not held dear, not excellent, displeasing to the mind." It pertains to "receptacle" in phrases such as "worlds as far as the world" (*'jig rten gyi bar gyi 'jig rten*). It pertains to "the truth of suffering" (*sdug bsngal gyi bden pa*) in phrases such as "What is the world? The five aggregates of appropriation." It pertains to "living being" in phrases such as "having come into this world once, [one] dispels suffering." It pertains to "things desired" in phrases such as "in the noble dharma [and] discipline, these five qualities of desire which are renounced are called 'the world.'"

*1.3.1.2.5. *Āmiṣa*

[35b] The term **āmiṣa* (*zang zing*) [pertains] to "worldly goods" (*rnyed pa, *lābha*); "desired qualities" (*'dod pa'i yon tan rnams, *kāmagunāḥ*); "form" (*gzugs, *rūpa*); [and] "food" (*zad/zas, *bhojana*). It pertains to "worldly goods" in phrases such as "Monks! I am [one who] practices and dwells according to a share in the dharma, but not [one who] practices according to a share in wealth (*zang zing*)." It pertains to "desired qualities" in phrases such as "the attachment of common people to worldly wealth (*'jig rten gyi zang zing*) is fierce." It pertains to "form" in phrases such as "What is the liberation possessing wealth (*zang zing*)? It is that which is endowed with form." It pertains to "food" in phrases such as "one should not grasp the water vessel with a hand polluted by food."[32] In the world, the word **āmiṣa* (*zang zing gi sgra*) also pertains to meat (*sha, *māṃsa*), as in the phrase "vegetarian food" (*sha med pa'i zas*).[33]

*1.3.1.2.6. *Bhūta*

The term **bhūta* (*'byung ba*) [pertains] to "beings" (*skyes pa, *jāta*); "truth" (*bden pa, *satya*); "such elements as earth" (*sa'i khams la sogs pa, *pṛthivīdhātvādi*); a "conditioned thing" (*'dus byas, *saṃskāra*); an "existent thing" (*yod pa, *sattā*); "sentient beings" (*sems can rnams, *sattvāḥ*); and "spirits" (*mi ma yin pa rnams, *amanuṣyāḥ*). In phrases such as "because four nutriments sustain those that have arisen," one should understand "beings" [to be designated]. It pertains to "truth" in phrases such as "furthermore, [an utterance that expresses things as they are (*yathābhūtavāda*)] is a timely utterance and a correct utterance." It pertains to "such elements as earth" in phrases such as "the four great elements" (*'byung ba chen po, *mahābhūta*). It pertains to "conditioned things" in phrases such as "a monk is one who has entered [the path] in order to consider that which has arisen (*byung ba, *bhūta*), so as to be free from afflictions and bring them to a halt." It pertains to an "existent thing" in phrases such as "as for the self, in what way is it properly said to be an existing thing?" It pertains to "sentient beings" in phrases such as "Regarding all sentient beings, one gives up the club [of punishment]." It pertains to "spirits" in phrases such as "those who have arisen (*'byung po gang dag*) remain here [upon] the earth or, if not, in the heavens"; "possessed by those who have arisen"; and "a benefit for those who have arisen" (*'byung pos zin pa dang 'byung po'i sman pa zhes 'byung ba lta bu'o*).

1.3.1.2.7. *PADA

The term *pada* (*pa da*) [pertains] to "nirvāṇa" (*mya ngan las 'das pa*); "foot" (*rkang pa*, *pāda*); "portion" (*cha*, *bhāga*); "moment" (*yud tsam*, *muhūrta*); "basis" (*gzhi*, *vastu*); "truths" (*bden pa rnams*, *satyāni*); "the region of the foot" (*rkang pa'i phyogs*, *pādadeśa*); "tracks" (*rjes*, *anu*); and "phrase." It pertains to "nirvāṇa" in phrases such as "the unsurpassable state of pacification" (*zhi ba go 'phang bla na med pa*, *anuttaraśāntipada*). It pertains to "foot" [36a] in phrases such as "sentient beings may lack feet, have two feet, or have [many] feet." It pertains to "portion" in phrases such as "the four classifications of dharma" (*chos kyi rnam grangs bzhi pa*, *caturdharmaparyāya [=caturdharmapada?]). It pertains to "moment" in phrases such as "moment to moment (*yud tsam yud tsam*, *muhūrtamuhūrtam*), the mind is overtaken by despair and conceptual constructions." It pertains to "basis" in phrases such as "one who is careful is one whose basis is not destroyed; one who is careless is one whose basis is destroyed." It pertains to "truths" in phrases such as "the bases of training (*slob pa'i gzhi*, *śikṣāpada*) are seen." It pertains to "the region of the foot" in phrases such as "Brahman, [you have] seen wheels at places where the feet of the one of the same lineage as Droṇodana, the Blessed One, have trod." It pertains to "tracks" in phrases such as "like the tracks of a bird in the sky, these are difficult to comprehend." It pertains to "phrase" in phrases such as "having understood the meaning of even a single phrase that is well-spoken. . . ."

1.3.1.2.8. *DHARMA

The term *dharma* (*chos*) [pertains] to "that which is knowable" (*shes bya*, *jñeya*); "path" (*lam*, *mārga*); "nirvāṇa"; "an object of the mind" (*yid kyi yul*, *manoviśaya*); "merit" (*bsod nams*, *puṇya*); "life" (*tshe*, *āyuṣ*); "scriptural text" (*gsung rab*, *pravacana*); [that which is] "occurring" (*'byung bar 'gyur*, *bhāvin*); "restraint" (*nges pa*, *niyama*); and "custom" (*chos lugs*, *nīti*). The word "dharma" pertains to "that which is knowable" in phrases such as "dharmas may be either conditioned or unconditioned; freedom from afflictions is said to be principal among them."[34] It pertains to "path" in phrases of explication such as "Monks! Wrong view is not the dharma; correct view is the dharma." It pertains to "nirvāṇa" in phrases such as "[I] take refuge in the dharma." It pertains to "an object of the mind" in phrases such as "the activity fields of dharma" (*chos kyi skye mched*, *dharmāyatana*)—those things that are, precisely, objects—and objects solely of mind—but are not supports. It pertains to "merit" in phrases of explication such as "practice the dharma when [you are] together with the queen's retinue and the young women (*gzhon nu ma rnams*)."[35] It pertains to "restraint" in phrases such as "the dharma is seen and experienced here; immature persons dearly grasp the dharma that is seen." It pertains to "instruction" in longer phrases such as "here, monks, the dharma is known in this way: the sūtra collection, the geya collection. . . ." [36b] It pertains to [that which is] "occurring" in phrases such as "conditioned substances: the dharma of those" and "accordingly, this body is [the site of] the dharma of old age." It pertains to the "holy life" in phrases such as "the four dharmas of a monk" and in longer phrases such as "in this way, monks, killing is not the dharma, and the abandonment of killing is dharma." It pertains to "custom" in phrases such as "the dharma of a place" (*yul chos*, **deśadharma*) and "the dharma of a clan" (*rigs chos*, **jātidharma*).

*1.3.1.2.9. *Prahāṇa*

The term **prahāṇa* (*spangs pa*) [pertains] to "relinquishing" (*gtang/btang ba*, **muci*); "freedom" (*bral ba*, **vipravāsa*); "subduing" (*gnon pa*, **ākramaṇa*); and "negative predispositions" (*bag la nyal*, **anuśaya*).[36] By **prahāṇa* one may intend both expulsion and such things as abandoning. The term **prahāṇa* pertains to "relinquishing" in phrases such as "having abandoned the heap of enjoyments, whether large or small." It pertains to "freedom" from a continuum (*rgyun dang bral ba*) in phrases such as "persons, having abandoned harmful, nonvirtuous qualities. . . ." It pertains to "subduing" via the worldly path in phrases such as "having abandoned longing for objects of desire, they therefore repeatedly abide and are born in the same class as [those who dwell in] the Brahmaloka." It pertains to correctly overcoming "negative predispositions" in phrases such as "due to abandoning three fetters, one is a stream-enterer." In this way, two aspects are distinguished [in phrases such as] "seen to be abandoned," "bereft of vows," "bereft of protection," [and] "bereft of concentration," [which are drawn] from two sūtras expounded to hearers.

*1.3.1.2.10. *Naya*[37]

The term **naya* (*tshul*) [pertains] to "truth"; "path"; "dependent arising" (*'brel 'byung*, **praītyasamutpāda*); "awarenesses" (*rig pa rnams*, **vidyāḥ*); "components that facilitate ascertainment" (*nges par 'byed pa'i cha*, **nirvedhabhaga*); "nirvāṇa"; "method" (*thabs*, **upāya*); and "correctness" (*rigs pa nyid*, **yuktitā*). One sees the term *tshul* to [mean] the truths, the path, and dependent arising in this [excerpt from a] summary verse: "Truth and the eight limbs and arising" (*bden dang yan lag brgyad dang* *'byung)*. It is seen also to pertain to "awarenesses" in phrases such as this: "Brahman, I have said that in this dharma and discipline of noble ones, you should understand the noble way (*'phags pa'i tshul*) as threefold." It is seen also to pertain to that which conforms to the "components that facilitate ascertainment" (*nges par 'byed pa'i cha dang mthun pa, *nirvedhabhāgīya*) [37a] in phrases such as "the four applications of mindfulness and that which does not accord [with them]: these, [respectively,] are proper to noble ones (*'phags pa'i tshul*) and those who do not accord with them." The word *tshul* is also seen to pertain to "nirvāṇa" in passages such as "one who is a householder, or a renunciate, or one who practices the correct technique (*yang dag sgrub byed*) [achieves] the unsurpassable dharma (*bla med tshul nyid kyi chos*), becoming completely liberated." It is seen also to pertain to "method" in phrases such as "when one undertakes effort in the way (*tshul gyi brtson 'grus*), no activity is difficult." It pertains to "correctness" in phrases such as "correct activity" (*tshul bzhin byed pa*).

*1.3.1.2.11. *Karmānta*

The term **karmānta* (*las kyi mtha'*) [pertains] to "wealth that is sought" (*nor tshol ba, *eṣaṇadhana*); "the threefold abandonment" (*gsum pa spangs pa*); and "the sevenfold abandonment" (*bdun spangs pa*). It pertains to "wealth that is sought" in phrases such as "whether in the fields or in the marketplace, that [person] enacts limits on action." It pertains to "the threefold abandonment" in the extensive passage that runs from "what are the correct limits on action in the world?" One abandons [those things enumerated in the passage] up to "killing"; [the latter] is wrong because it is the action of killing. Similarly, [we see the term to pertain to the abandoning of things enumerated] in passages such as the one that concludes ". . . sexual misconduct based on desire." The term pertains also to "the sevenfold abandonment" in passages such as "What is the perfection of limits on action? From "the abandonment of killing" up to "it is wrong because it is the action of killing." Similarly, [the term pertains to the abandoning of things enumerated] in passages such as that which concludes ". . . the action of speaking in phrases that are confused." The term **karmānta* also pertains to the [five] great offenses, since they are said to be limitlessly wrong actions (*log pa'i las kyi mtha' med pa nyid*), as has been extensively stated in a sūtra: "Based on this dharma [and] discipline, five persons are wrong and are those in whom evil is present; [they are] without merit and. . . ." The limits on action of those persons are wrong; the wrong limits on action are the five boundless offenses. In this case, the actions are limitlessly wrong: there are no limits on [how] wrong [they are]—the very substance of those [actions] is to lack such limits.

1.3.1.2.12. *Skandha

The term **skandha* (*phung po*) [37b] [pertains] to "heap" (*spungs pa*); "shoulders" (*phrag pa, *aṃsa*); "tree" (*sdong po, *druma*); and "component" (*cha, *bhāga*). The term **skandha* pertains to "heap" in phrases such as "collecting all these into one, one comes to reckon them as the 'aggregate of form.'" In the same way, [one finds the term used in this sense] in phrases such as "having attained a great heap of wealth, one dwells." It pertains to "shoulders" in phrases such as "the destroyer of men, having dismounted his horse [and] ascending from the ground to a lofty throne, rides upon the shoulders of an elephant."[38] It pertains to "tree" in phrases such as "the great trees—rooted and massive."[39] It pertains to "component" in phrases such as "one gives a gift in three components" (*sbyin par bya ba phung po gsum dag tu sbyin*).

1.3.1.2.13. *Saṃgraha

The term **saṃgraha* (*bsdu ba*) has six meanings: "essence" (*rang bzhin, *svabhāva*); "that which concords" (*rjes su mthun, *anuloma*); "delight" (*dga' ba, *tuṣṭa*); "that which is not lost" (*yongs su nyams pa med pa, *asampramuṣita*); "categorization" (*khongs su gtogs pa, *antarbhūta*); and "that which facilitates understanding" (*'dzin par byed pa, *grāhaka*). It pertains to "essence" in phrases such as "ten sense-fields are summarized (*bsdus*) under a single aspect: the aggregate of form." It pertains to "that which concords" with the essence [of a thing] (*rang bzhin dang rjes su mthun pa*) in phrases such as "the eightfold path of noble ones is summarized as three groups." It pertains to "delight" in phrases such as "those for whom there are four ways of gathering [adherents]" (*bsdu ba'i dngos po bzhi po dag*). It pertains to "that which is not lost" in phrases such as "this is a collection of those five faculties, i.e., the faculty of wisdom." It pertains to "categorization" in phrases such as "the mark of all those creatures fit to be born in the animal realm is [to be] assembled and gathered behind the elephant." It pertains to "that which facilitates understanding" in phrases such as "the general support is foremost among all the beams in a storied house, because it joins them."[40]

These are no more than illustrative examples.

1.3.2. MULTIPLE PHRASES POSSESSING A SINGLE MEANING

Multiple phrases can be associated with a single meaning. For example, synonymic terms may be used in this way.

1.3.3. MEANING: THREEFOLD TYPOLOGY

Moreover, meaning is of three kinds: the meaning to be stated regarding particulars; the summary meaning; and the point.

1.3.3.1. MEANING TO BE STATED REGARDING PARTICULARS

The meaning to be stated regarding particulars is what should be said regarding what is said. For example, [38a] [with reference to the phrase] "Conditioned by ignorance, formations [arise]," what is stated [includes responses to queries] such as "Regarding this, what is ignorance?"[41]

1.3.3.2. SUMMARY MEANING

The summary meaning is that meaning which is collected from phrases of diverse meaning. So, for example, by the phrases for the twelve branches of existence [i.e., the twelvefold account of dependent arising], three [kinds of] affliction—the afflictions of affliction, action and production/birth—are taught.[42] Similarly, by the phrases "those who lack faith, having accepted what is genuine with respect to perfect faith," up to "those who discriminate erroneously, [having accepted what is genuine] with respect to perfect discrimination," what is correct to accept may be taught in brief as the cause of exaltation and the ultimate good (*nges par legs pa*, **niḥśreyasa*), as passages such as the following state: "Having faith, one takes up ethics and so on.[43] Via ethics and forsaking [wrongful actions], one attains [a human] body and provisions; with these, one will obtain some degree of success. [But] by discriminating insight, one obtains the supreme excellence."

1.3.3.3. POINT

The point [encompasses synonyms, expoundings, and enumerations]:

1.3.3.3.1. Synonyms

The meaning to be stated regarding particulars and the summary meaning do not apply to these, since they are singular expressions, and since there is no difference in expressible meaning between phrases of teaching (*bstan pa'i tshig rnams*) and exposition (*bshad pa*) [in cases involving synonyms].

1.3.3.3.2. Expoundings

"Why is this teaching undertaken?" [In the event this question is posed,] the point must be expounded, just as in the **Bhikṣuṇīsūtra*: "Ānanda! Having directed the mind outwardly, one understands that his mind is directed outwardly, and one understands things just as they are, thinking 'my mind is released before and after, liberated.' "[44] This is a teaching; the remainder is exposition.

Likewise, "Monks! I ordained at a very young age" is a teaching.[45] [The ensuing phrases] "in the prime of youth" (*mchog tu gzhon nu*) and "quite young" (*rab tu gzhon nu*) are exposition, [offered] in order to completely expound youthfulness by the two particulars of nature and time. The remainder [38b]—the glorification of perfect happiness—is extensive exposition, [offered] in order to expound extensively those very [phrases]—"in the prime [of youth], very [young], quite [young]." In the same way, "What is dependent arising?" "Due to the existence of that, this arises; because that has been born, this is born." This is a teaching. "Conditioned by ignorance, formations [arise]. . . ." is extensive exposition.[46] Likewise, there is this teaching: "Venerable Ones! One who is born in favorable circumstances is equipped with twelve [aspects]."[48] Based on this, the so-called forms of excellence that pertain to oneself and to others are the teaching; the remainder is exposition. With the two—teaching and exposition—there are twelve.

In ways such as these, one must also expound the point regarding the phrases of the teaching.

1.3.3.3.3. Enumerations

[E.g.,] the five aggregates, the six internal sense-fields, and so on.

[Q:] Insofar as failure to understand a stated meaning does not occur, why should one state a point regarding enumerations in addition [to what has been said]?

[A:] [There is no need to do so.] The same holds for other phrases where the meaning to be stated is well known. One need only state the point of those [phrases] if [one's audience] is unable [to comprehend] that meaning [when it is not spelled out explicitly].

For example, take the meaning of the phrase "journeying in the vicinity of Śrāvastī." Here, the point to be explicated is well known in the world.

[Q.:] Why should one state the reasons that Buddha or hearers journeyed in the countryside and, similarly, why the Blessed One remained in [that place for] two and three fortnights [refusing to teach], why the venerable one Kauṇḍinya and the great venerable one Śāriputra went to that place, and so on?

[A.:] Regarding this, the point of the passages should be expounded over and above what has been previously stated. One is [thereby] caused to grasp the meaning connected with individual terms of teaching in the sūtra, since the meaning of the exposition is to be grasped as being just that of the teaching. [This is also done] in order that those monks who understand [the sūtra's meaning] at the very beginning might accept it afterward. In the case of others, [39a] [it is done] so that they will accumulate [the teaching] in an unmistaken way and easily understand [it]; so that the perfect teaching will possess the endowments that pertain to brief and extensive discussion; and so that that the seeds [of awakening] will be produced [in] others, due to contemplating such things.

[A passage] from scripture: "When a mere teaching [is given], the minds of yogis are directed to equanimity; hence, when the whole meaning is elaborated, direct [your mind] to equanimity!" It is toward this end that it is said, "one teaches by means of the two: teaching and exposition."

Enumerations allow one a sure grasp of that which is enumerated. For example, statements such as "[there are] five aggregates and six internal sense-fields" [are used] so that one will not forget [the teaching], [and] so that some persons will easily grasp [it].

For example: "A mind bearing upon certain objects is accompanied by twenty-one subsidiary afflictions; it is a mind possessing subsidiary afflictions." [An additional example is to be found in] the passage that begins "although actions arise in ten [ways], the dharma is singular; that which is essential is ornamented," and concludes "ten levels." Some [statements] must be expounded extensively so that those who are learned but do not cause [others] to listen and those who fear, owing to grasping, will undertake to listen.[49] For example, statements such as: "These are the three faculties: the female faculty, the male faculty, and the life force." Some [statements] are in order to bring joy to those who fear many things. For example, statements such as: "Monks! I proclaim that you must abandon one dharma in order for you to be a nonreturner. . . ."[50] Some [enumerations] are [offered] in order to teach that one thing implies another—for example, "When five become pure, three become pure; and when three become pure, five become pure." Some [enumerations] are [offered] in order to make known [the] extent [of something]—for example, the group of sixty excellent divisions. Some [enumerations] are [offered] in order to make known that one thing is another thing—for example, in order to [indicate that] "action bearing two qualities" and "sustaining and counteracting" are equivalent [phrases] in the context of the arising of the five obscurations.

Some [enumerations] are [offered] in order to correctly teach the meaning, just as the Blessed One himself had previously discriminated it.[51] [39b] Regardless of whether one correctly expounds in these ways or in others, such are the uses for enumerations.

Buddhas should be understood to journey for seven reasons:[52]

[1.] In order to train those who live in other locations.
[2.] Because those who live in those [lands] are afflicted by thirst.
[3.] So that hearers give up dwelling for an extended time in a single place.
[4.] In order to demonstrate nonattachment pertaining to just that.
[5.] In order to transform locations into shrines.
[6.] In order to generate merit [for] living creatures due to seeing and visiting [them] and so on.
[7.] In order to appease disasters such as epidemic disease, drought, and so on.

Summary verses:

Buddhas embark on journeys
In order to train [those in] other lands;
Because those who live there are subject to thirst;[53]
So that hearers will dwell [in] many [places];
In order to teach freedom from attachment,
To transform locations into shrines,
And for the merit of the embodied;
And in order to pacify epidemics and so on.[54]

Hearers should be understood as journeying for fifteen reasons, because the Blessed One taught five dangers [as follows]: "When one dwells for an extended time [in a single place], many are the tasks [there] and many the duties, many are the vessels and many the provisions, one yearns to remain there and settle down there; accordingly, one departs from that [place] possessing attachment [to it]."

In the same way, [hearers journey] because they lack robes and so on; because they suffer dissatisfaction; because they are tormented by illness; because they are tormented by afflictions; because they bring torment to the bodies and minds of others—whether human or nonhuman—due to their actions; because they crave gain and so on; out of fondness; in order to show sympathy for others and out of respect for the guru; in order to see wonders in [other] places and so on; in order to attain distinction in virtuous attributes; in order to confess failings; in order to esteem the three jewels; and in order to pay homage to shrines.

Summary verses:

Due to the five dangers, or because of lack,
Torment owing to discontent, illness, and passion,
Craving [for] gain and so on, [40a] fondness, sympathy,
Respect for the guru, [a distant] wonder, the pursuit of distinction, or because of transgression;
Due to esteem for the [three] jewels, and in order to pay homage to shrines—
[For these reasons,] monks undertake journeys.[55]

The Blessed One settled in [that place] for a fortnight and three [months] in order to make the hearers desire [the teaching]. Regarding this, [he said]:

"Presently, my compassion is not weak;
Moreover, I am not stingy with regard to dharma.
I have no [teacher's] fist, and no lack of ability;
I lack the essential characteristic of suffering,
My teaching is unobstructed.
I do not hope for anything from you;
But [you,] trainees, cannot understand me,
And, moreover, [you] lack devotion.
Therefore, I do not teach."
In order to make [them] understand and long for [the teaching],
The Blessed One rested therein
For a fortnight and three months.[56]

[As for why the venerable Kauṇḍinya and the great venerable one Śāriputra came to that place, it is said:]

Because of merit, wisdom, material offerings, refuge,
Delight, fault, investigation,
Knowledge, gratitude, and patronage.[57]
Because of compassion toward those and others,

Because of the two—horrors and wonders—and
In order that others follow.
For these fifteen reasons, they ardently desired to go [to that place];
That should be understood correctly.

[This concludes] the first book of the *Vyākhyāyukti*.

APPENDIX B

The *Abhidharmasamuccayabhāṣya* (Excerpt)

The following is a translation, from the Sanskrit, of the portion of the *Abhidharmasamuccayabhāṣya* that elaborates on the subject of the "ascertainment of explication" (*vyākhyāviniścaya*), discussed in the "Sāṃkathyaviniścaya" section of the *Abhidharmasamuccaya*. As in appendix A, outline numbers have been inserted; these are absent in the Sanskrit. The basis for the translation is the edition by Nathmal Tatia (1976:142–147). I have also made occasional use of the relevant portion of the Tibetan translation (by Jinamitra and Śīlendrabodhi; D 4053; sems tsam *li*, 105a6–110a3). The latter diverges considerably at times from the extant Sanskrit; I have not, however, noted all instances of such divergence here.

The ascertainment of explication is that by which one teaches the meaning of sūtras.

[1. Six Components]

That, moreover, is based on offering six components—the subject to be known and so on—as these are appropriate to a particular sūtra.[1] Regarding these, [the ascertainment of explication includes:]

1.1. The Subject To Be Known (parijñeyaṃ vastu)

[E.g.,] the aggregates and so on.

1.2. The Thing [or Meaning] To Be Known (parijñeyo 'rtha)

[E.g.,] impermanence and so on.

1.3. The Basis of Knowledge (parijñopaniṣad)

[E.g.,] ethics, the binding of the sense-doors and so on.

1.4. Knowledge (parijñā)

[E.g.,] the factors of awakening.

1.5. The Result of Knowledge (parijñāphala)

[E.g.,] liberation.

1.6. The Demonstration of That (tatpravedanā)

[E.g.,] the vision of liberating gnosis (*vimuktijñānadarśana*).

[2. Fourteen Approaches]

Moreover, there are fourteen approaches to explication.

2.1. Summary Explication (vyākhyāsaṃgrahamukha)

In which one delineates the purpose of the sūtra's delivery (*sūtrasyotpattiprayojana*), the meanings of its phrases (*padārtha*), the connection (*anusaṃdhi*), the intention (*abhiprāya*), and objections and responses (*codyaparihāra*).

2.2. Topical Summary (vastusaṃgrahamukha)

In which one propounds a sūtra regarding such topics as training and the noble truths.[2] For example, the way that the verse beginning "not practicing any evil" references the three trainings.[3]

2.3. Factors and Subsidiary Factors (aṅgopaṅgamukha)

In which a teaching by one phrase is explained by supplemental [phrases]. For example, in the *Dvādaśakṣaraṇasaṃnipātadeśanā*, two things—those [endowments] suited to oneself and those suited to another—are respectively taught, [each] by five terms.[4]

2.4. Successive Ordering (uttarottaranirhāramukha)

In which, due to being related in ordered succession, dharmas are taught accordingly. For example, the five faculties (*pañcendriya*). That is, faith having arisen, one undertakes perseverance; perseverance having been undertaken, mindfulness accrues; the mind is concentrated in that mindfulness which has accrued and, so concentrated, is discriminatively aware of things such as they are.

2.5. Rejection (pratikṣepamukha)

In which [one stresses that] having undertaken this, one rejects that. For example, in the *Vāsyaupamyasūtra*, [it is related that] having undertaken to destroy the afflictions, one rejects four [kinds of] person: (1) an outsider; (2) one satisfied with merely hearing and thinking over the dharma; (3) one weary of meditative cultivation; and (4) one whose provisions are incomplete.[5]

The first [such] person is rejected by means of a sūtra passage such as "for one who knows, for one who sees, I declare the destruction of the afflictions," and so on. The second [kind of person is rejected] by a passage such as "for one attentive to meditative cultivation . . ." and so on. The third [kind of person is rejected] by the axe simile; the fourth, by the simile of the boat.

2.6. The Transformation of Syllables (akṣarapariṇāmamukha)

In which syllables that are well known with respect to one meaning are transformed into another. An example is found in the verse that begins "one without faith and knowing the uncreated."[6]

2.7. [That Which Is] Eliminated and [That Which Is] Uneliminated (nāśānāśamukha)

This includes the eliminated; the uneliminated; the means for both; and the analysis of both.

2.7.1. AS EXEMPLIFIED IN THE *SUJĀTASŪTRA*

2.7.1.1. THE ELIMINATED

In the *Sujātasūtra*, the eliminated includes exterior and interior attachments, which are [both] brought to an end. Exterior [attachments] are such things as a house, wife, and so on; interior [attachments] are such things as the five aggregates of appropriation.

2.7.1.2. THE UNELIMINATED

This is the avoidance of clinging to either of these [types of attachment].

[2.7.1.3. THE MEANS FOR BOTH]

The means for the eliminated are nonrenunciation and, for one who has [already] renounced, negligence toward eliminating the afflictions. The means for the uneliminated should be obvious, since they are the opposite [of these].

[2.7.1.4. THE ANALYSIS OF BOTH]

The analysis of the eliminated is taught by the chanted verse:

> Excellent, indeed, is the tranquil monk without afflictions.

In this way, renunciation and the extinguishing of the afflictions are elucidated. Moreover, [there is this verse on] the extinguishing of afflictions:

> Without desire, unattached, without clinging, liberated,
> [He] bears [his] final body, having conquered the hosts of Māra.

That is, [he is without desire] because he lacks desire for the mundane path; [he is unattached] because he has abandoned attachment to lower elements via the supermundane path; [he is without clinging] because he has [also] abandoned attachment to higher elements; [and he is liberated] because he has abandoned internal attachments. Also, one should understand this teaching to reference the extinguishing of the cause and the result [of the afflictions]. The analysis of the uneliminated should be understood as being the opposite of this.

2.8. Classification of Persons (pudgalavyavasthānamukha)

This is stated insofar as persons are referenced. For example, in the *Audakopamasūtra*, persons are divided into two types, which are [further] differentiated into [groups of] three and four. It is said that there are worldly beings and those who see the truth. Worldly beings are of three sorts: those who lack merit, those who possess a small quantity of merit, and those who possess much merit. And those who see the truth are of four sorts: four who have set out [on the path]; four who possess the result; three who train; [and] one for whom there is no [more] training.[7]

2.9. Classification of Analytic Categories (prabhedavyavasthānamukha)

[These are cases] in which meaning is determined by inquiries that make use of such things as the four alternatives (*catuṣkoti*).

2.9.1. FOUR ALTERNATIVES: EXAMPLE 1

For example—in the *Anityasūtra*, [we read]:

> One who sees this correctly sees all form, or one who sees all form sees all [this] correctly.[8]

This has four alternatives:

2.9.1.1. The first alternative is one in which one apprehends what should be accepted and rejected [with respect to form, and] one does not impute the erroneous notions of permanence, purity, happiness, and a self onto the four [remaining] aggregates—feeling and so on.

2.9.1.2. The second alternative is one in which one apprehends what should not be accepted and rejected [with respect to form, and] one imputes the erroneous notions of permanence, purity, happiness, and a self onto [the aggregate of] form.

2.9.1.3. The third alternative is one in which one apprehends what should be accepted and rejected [with respect to form, and] one does not impute the erroneous notions of permanence, purity, happiness, and a self onto [the aggregate of] form.

2.9.1.4. The fourth alternative is one in which one apprehends what should not be accepted and rejected [with respect to form, and] one imputes the erroneous notions of permanence, purity, happiness, and a self onto the four [remaining] aggregates—feeling and so on.

Just as these four alternatives apply to form, so, too, should they be seen as applying to all [the remaining aggregates]: feeling and so forth.

2.9.2. FOUR ALTERNATIVES: EXAMPLE 2

> Anyone who has done what should be done does not know further existence.
> Anyone not knowing further existence has done what should be done.

There are four alternatives [here as well]:

2.9.2.1.The first alternative is for an individual who practices lifelong noble conduct.
2.9.2.2. The second is for those who have brought views and so on to an end.
2.9.2.3. The third is for one who needs no further training.
2.9.2.4. The fourth sets asides these aspects.

2.10. Methods (nayamukha)

In which the meaning [of a passage] is delineated by six methods: by the method regarding the real meaning (*tattvārthanaya*); by the method regarding obtaining (*prāptinaya*); by the method of teaching (*deśanānaya*); by the method of the exclusion of two extremes (*antadvayavivarjanānaya*); by the method regarding the inconceivable (*acintyanaya*); and by the method regarding intention (*abhiprāyanaya*).

Among these methods, the former three are to be understood by means of the latter three, in orderly sequence.

2.10.1 EXAMPLES, WITH REFERENCE TO THE *ĀSVĀDANASŪTRA*[9]

2.10.1.1 AND 2.10.1.4. REAL MEANING AND EXCLUSION OF EXTREMES

By passages such as "Monks, there is gratification with respect to form" and so on, the method regarding the real meaning is clarified, avoiding the extremes of denial (*apavādānta*) and superimposition (*samāropānta*). "There is gratification, misfortune, [and] escape"—by this [passage], the extreme of denial is avoided; ". . . in the case of form up through consciousness . . ."—[in this passage], the extreme of superimposition [is avoided]; ". . . there is affliction in the aggregates alone, and purification in the lack of a self."

2.10.1.2. AND 2.10.1.5. OBTAINING AND THE INCONCEIVABLE

By passages such as [the one that begins] "Monks! I am awakened [to] unsurpassable, perfect awakening" [and runs] up to "I inwardly knew," [the teaching] is elucidated by the method regarding obtaining and the method regarding the inconceivable, since [such passages] point to understanding that should be individually experienced.

2.10.1.3. AND 2.10.1.6. TEACHING AND INTENTION

The sūtra in its entirety is the method of teaching. That [method of teaching] is to be understood subsequently by [the method of] intention, encompassing the subject to be known, the thing to be known, knowledge, and the result of knowledge.[10] The sūtra is spoken with the intention to proclaim these.

In this case, the subject to be known has to do with form and so on; the thing to be known has to do with gratification and so on, since one knows form and so on as being that way. Knowledge is of the five aggregates of appropriation, comprehended accordingly just as they are: as transformed in three ways. By way of the result of knowledge, there is complete freedom from the afflictions: a liberation of insight [that occurs] from the world of gods down through the world of gods and men. This is announced [in the passage that begins] "I am awakened [to] unsurpassable, perfect awakening" [and continues] to "I inwardly knew."

2.11. Knowledge and So On (parijñādimukha)

[There are many components of this,] beginning with the mark of the real (*tattvalakṣaṇa*). One specifies the meaning [of the mark of the real] by means of the mark of knowledge (*parijñālakṣaṇa*); the mark of abandoning (*prahāṇalakṣaṇa*); the mark of direct action (*sākṣātkriyālakṣaṇa*); [the mark of meditative cultivation (**bhāvanālakṣaṇa*)];[11] the mark of sorting these—the mark of the real and so on—into kinds (*prakārabhedalakṣaṇa*); the mark of the connection between the basis and that which it supports (*āśrayāśritasaṃbandhalakṣaṇa*); the mark of dharmas that obstruct knowledge and so on (*parijñādīnām antarāyikadharmalakṣaṇa*); the mark of suitable dharmas (*ānulomikadharmalakṣaṇa*);[12] and the mark of the misfortunes that pertain to the lack of knowledge and the advantages [that pertain to knowledge] and so on.

2.11.1. EXAMPLES, WITH REFERENCE TO THE *ĀSVĀDANASŪTRA*

2.11.1.1. THE MARK OF THE REAL

The truth of suffering—the collected aggregates of appropriation.

2.11.1.2. THE MARK OF KNOWLEDGE

This is threefold: one knows, just as they are, gratification as gratification, and misfortune as misfortune, up through [knowing] escape as escape.

2.11.1.3–4. THE MARKS OF ABANDONING AND DIRECT ACTION

Liberation from all worlds. This occurs immediately upon the transformation of the basis, via the abandonment of obscurations.

2.11.1.5. THE MARK OF MEDITATIVE CULTIVATION

With a mind free from error, one repeatedly abides.

2.11.1.6. THE MARK OF SORTING INTO KINDS

2.11.1.6.1. [As It Pertains to the Mark of the Real]

The fivefold differentiation—from form through consciousness—of [the aggregates of appropriation that constitute] the mark of the real.

2.11.1.6.2. [As It Pertains to the Mark of Knowledge]

The threefold differentiation of the mark of knowledge. One has insight into things just as they are: one knows gratification as gratification [and misfortune as misfortune], up through [knowing] escape as escape.[13]

2.11.1.6.3–4. [As It Pertains to the Marks of Abandoning and Direct Action]

A twofold differentiation: liberation from the afflictions and liberation from suffering. Regarding this, liberation is no longer being born [into any world realm] from the world of gods down to the world of men, due to having been liberated from the afflictions; hence, in order to distinguish this, he said "escaped."

As it is said in another sūtra: "Liberation from what kinds [of afflictions]? The taming of desire by zeal, the abandoning of desire by zeal, the final transcending of desire by zeal." In this way, when one is separated from the afflictions and has ended future suffering, there is liberation from suffering. In order to specify this, he said "unattached, liberated."

2.11.1.6.5. [as it pertains to The Mark of Meditative Cultivation]

This is twofold: the path of insight (*darśanamārga*) and the path of cultivation (*bhāvanāmārga*). Regarding these, [the passage] "with a mind free from error" reveals the path of insight; [the passage] "one repeatedly dwells" reveals the path of cultivation.

2.11.1.7. THE MARK OF THE CONNECTION BETWEEN THE BASIS AND THAT WHICH IT SUPPORTS

One indicates that [those things] such as the mark of the real are, in each subsequent instance, the basis.

2.11.1.8. THE MARK OF THOSE THINGS THAT OBSTRUCT KNOWLEDGE AND SO ON

[It is owing to such obstructions that] one does not see things just as they are: as transformed in three ways.

2.11.1.9. THE MARK OF SUITABLE THINGS

Distinguishing, in appropriate circumstances, form and so on from gratification and so on.[14]

2.11.1.10. THE MARK OF THE MISFORTUNES THAT PERTAIN TO THE LACK OF KNOWLEDGE

Nonliberation, up to not being awakened to unsurpassable perfect awakening.

2.11.1.11. THE MARK OF THE ADVANTAGES [THAT PERTAIN TO KNOWLEDGE]

These should be known as the opposite [of the previous mark].

2.12. The Strong and the Weak (balābalamukha)

In a case in which [a hearer] would not comprehend a meaning from a single phrase being spoken, all of the individual phrases are explained in a suitable way. For example, in the *Pratītyotpādasūtra*: "when this exists, that exists; from the arising of that, this arises. Namely, conditioned by ignorance, formations arise" and so on. In the explanation of the characteristic [components] of dependent arising, each of the terms is to be understood just as in the previous [instance].

2.13. Abstraction (pratyāhāramukha)

In which, having grasped a single phrase of a sūtra, one teaches the meaning in an elaborated way. For example: "A monk equipped with six qualities may cause the snow-capped, wind-carved king of mountains to tremble—what to say of ignorance perfumed by karmic traces?"[15] With which six [qualities]? [1] Here, monks, a monk possesses skill in generating the mind [of abiding] (*cittasya utpādakuśala*). A monk dwells free from desires, having completed up to the fourth meditative state. In this way, a monk has skill in generating the mind [of abiding]. [2] And how does a monk possess skill in mental abiding (*cittasya sthitikuśala*)? Here, a monk, due to his devotion to service, performs a contemplation connected with hardship; that contemplation is connected to mental abiding. In this way, a monk possesses skill in mental abiding. [3] And how does a monk possess skill in arising (*vyutthānakuśala*)? Here, a monk, due to his devotion to service, performs the contemplation connected with mental abiding; that contemplation is connected to the particular [skill in arising]. In this way, a monk possesses skill in arising. [4] And how does a monk possess skill in increasing (*āyakuśala*)? Here, there are two correct abandonments; more fully, a monk [possesses skill in increasing those] skillful qualities that have not yet arisen. In this way, a monk possesses skill in increasing. [5] And how does a monk possess skill in decreasing (*apāyakuśala*)? Here [again], there are two correct abandonments; more fully, a monk [possesses skill in decreasing] evil, unskillful qualities that have arisen. In this way, a monk possesses skill in decreasing. [6] And how does a monk possess skill in means (*upāyakuśala*)? Here, a monk cultivates the four bases of supernatural power—more fully, the basis of supernatural power furnished with zealous concentration and the disposition toward abandoning.[16] In this way, a monk possesses skill in means.

2.14. Production (abhinirhāramukha)

In which each phrase is taught by means of such things as the fourfold group (*catuṣkādi*). Also, regarding the fourfold group and so on, each phrase should [in turn] be understood as producing another fourfold group and so on, endlessly. For example, in the *Buddhākṣepasūtra*, [we read]: "Bodhisattvas possess four qualities that thoroughly purify awakening: the meditative cultivation of emptiness, a mind that is unobstructed regarding all sentient beings, the constant ability to benefit bodhisattvas, and a mind, unconcerned with worldly pleasures, that elucidates the gift of the dharma." These four are acquired for their own benefit and for the benefit of others, so that awakening is thoroughly purified. They should be understood as antidotes to those things that oppose them. There are four such oppositions: gratification in concentration, enmity, conceit, and craving for gain and renown.

Alternatively, by the first quality, the antidote that is the abandonment of the afflictions [is taught]. By the remaining [three qualities], three reasons are elucidated as to why one should avoid the Hīnayāna: [1] because all beings are apprehended by the mind of awakening; [2] because one should develop those who have entered [upon the practice of the path]; [3] because one should cause those who have not entered to enter [upon such practice].

Alternatively, the provision of wisdom [is taught] by the first [quality, and] the provision of merit is elucidated by the [remaining] three, since one individually acquires merit in three particular [ways]—i.e., apprehension, development, and entry. Moreover, [one does so] for two reasons: due to intention and due to a benevolent mind. And practice is based on realization and the instruction of scripture (*āgama*).

Bodhisattvas who meditatively cultivate emptiness are equipped with four qualities: their unwavering minds are inwardly [turned], they generate the power of the discrimination of intention, they know all dharmas just as they are, and they are liberated from all obscurations. Here, the basis and the manner of meditative cultivation are elucidated [as follows]. What is the basis? [It is] the perfection of meditation (*dhyānapāramitā*). How do they cultivate [this]? They do so via the worldly path, [where] they generate the power of hearing and thinking on the dharma, and [also] by the path of trainees and the path of no more training.

Bodhisattvas whose minds are unobstructed regarding all sentient beings are equipped with four qualities: they cultivate benevolence, they are undisturbed in practice, they do not falsely imagine signs, [and] they endure distress. Here, the basis and the manner in which they possess unobstructed minds are eludicated [as follows]. What is the basis? [It is] the cultivation of benevolence in previous lives. How do they have unobstructed minds? Because, regarding those who abide in mistaken practices, [the bodhisattvas'] own minds are not disturbed; because, regarding things that are wrong, they do not falsely imagine the attribute "wrong"; and because they endure the great distress of effort in order to benefit others.

Bodhisattvas who have the constant ability to benefit bodhisattvas are equipped with four qualities: they consider the self, they set in motion the true teaching, they are perfumed by gentleness and happiness, and they provide offerings, goods, honor, and service. Here, the basis and the manner in which it provides are elucidated [as follows]. What is the basis? The destruction of their conceit. How does it provide? In three ways, as has been stated: for bodhisattvas who are lower [than themselves], those on a par [with themselves], and those who are elevated [above themselves], in that order.

Bodhisattvas who illuminate the gift of the dharma, [their] mind unconcerned with worldly pleasures, are equipped with four qualities: they felicitously know impediments; they are skilled in leading one out of stupidity and torpor; they provide joy to the mind,[17] and they delight in the dharma [they have] mastered. Here, the basis and the manner in which they illuminate are elucidated [as follows]. What is the basis? The knowledge that gain and renown are obstructions. How do they illuminate [the dharma]? Because, among those who are confused, they show what is right; among those who are indolent and fearful, they incite; among those who are dispirited, due to thinking of a self, [they offer] what is correct to assume; and for those who are perfected, they grant joy.[18] Quite naturally (*prakṛtyā eva*), they have joy in the dharma.

By analyzing the first phrase, another fourfold group [emerges]—[in this way,] one should understand [the method of] production.

APPENDIX C

The *Vivaraṇasaṃgrahaṇī

The following is a translation of the *Vivaraṇasaṃgrahaṇī* portion of the Yogācārabhūmi, attributed to Asaṅga. The translation is based largely on the Derge edition of the Tibetan translation (D, sems tsam *'i*, 48a1–68b5), with select variants from other editions noted. (The pagination of the Tibetan Buddhist Resource Center edition of G is unfortunately scrambled; readers wishing to make use of that edition are advised to consult table A.C.)

Balancing theoretical and practical concerns, the *Vivaraṇasaṃgrahaṇī* is constructed in two lengthy sections, each of which is further subdivided. The first (section A) treats all the topics listed in the opening programmatic verse (here translated as a list). The second (section B) offers an example of how these topics are to be applied in the course of commenting on the speech of a Buddha. As in appendix A, outline numbers have been inserted; these are absent in the Tibetan. Because the text is at times extremely laconic, certain passages have been paraphrased.

Homage to the three jewels.

What is the summary of explication? A general account [encompasses]:

1. The corpus (*lus*, **kāya*, **śarīra*, **āśraya*)
1.1. Phrasing (*tshig 'bru*, **vyañjana*)
1.2. Meaning (*don*, **artha*)
2. Explication (*rnam par bshad pa*, **vyākhyā*)
2.1. Teaching (*chos*, **dharma*)
2.2. Prompt (*kun nas slong ba*, **samutthāna*)

Table A.C Page Corrections for the Tibetan Buddhist Resource Center Scan of the Golden Edition of the **Vivaraṇasaṃgrahaṇī* (G sems tsam *yi* 70a–101b)

Page stamp number	*Tibetan folio number*	*Correct order*
139	70a	0 (title)
140	70b	1
141	71a	2
142	71b	3
143	72a	4
144	72b	5
145	73a	6
146	73b	7
147	74a	8
148	74b	9
149	75a	10
150	75b	11
151	76a	12
152	76b	13
153	77a	14
154	77b	15
155	78a	16
156	82a	24
157	79a	18
158	83a	26
159	80a	20
160	84a	28
161	81a	22
162	85a	30
163	78b	17
164	86a	32
165	79b	19
166	87a	34
167	80b	21
168	88a	36
169	81b	23
170	89a	38
171	82b	25
172	86b	33
173	83b	27
174	87b	35
175	84b	29
176	88b	37
177	85b	31
178, etc.	89b, etc.	39, etc.

2.3. Meaning (*don, *artha*)
2.4. Responding to objections (*rgol ba'i lan, *codyaparihāra*)
2.5. Connection (*mtshams sbyar ba, *anusaṃdhi*)
3. The dharma preacher ([*chos*] *smra ba*, *[*dharma*]*bhāṇaka*, *[*dharma*]*kathika*, *[*dharma*]*vādin*)
4. Exposition (*bshad, *deśanā*)
5. Assembly (*'khor, *gaṇa*)
6. Listening (*nyan pa, *śravaṇa*)
7. Brief and extensive praise of Buddhas (*sangs rgyas bsngags pa bsdus pa dang rgyas, *saṃkṣiptavistarabuddhapraśaṃsā*)
8. Rewards of training (*bslab pa'i phan yon, *śikṣānuśaṃsā*).[1]

[Section A]

The corpus has two aspects: phrasing and meaning. The phrasing is a basis and the meaning should be understood as based on it. Both of these should be known together. Explication has five aspects: the teaching; the prompt; meaning; responding to objections; and connection.

1. The Corpus

1.1. PHRASING

This has six aspects: the collections (*tshogs, *kāya,*sambhāra*) of names (*ming, *nāman*), phrases (*tshig, *pada*), and syllables (*yi ge, *akṣara*); speech (*ngag, *vāc*); aspect (*rnam pa, *ākāra*); and the teaching (*bstan pa, *deśanā, *śāsana*).

1.1.1. THE COLLECTION OF NAMES

These are verbal designations (*bla d(v)ags, *adhivacana*) that give rise to cognition. There are twelve subtypes:

1.1.1.1. Figurative Names[2]

Examples include terms used to designate phenomena that are internal, such as "sentient being" and "living being," and terms used to designate phenomena that are external, such as "pot" and "cloth."

1.1.1.2. Names for Things That Really Exist

Examples include sense faculties such as the eye, visible objects such as form, and so on.

1.1.1.3. Names Linked to Classes[3]

Examples include "sentient being," "form," "feeling," and "element."

1.1.1.4. Names Linked to Individuals[4]

Examples include "Buddhadatta," "Guṇamitra," "blue," and "yellow."

1.1.1.5. Secondary Forms

As in the case of "the figurative" (*gzugs su rung ba, *rūpaṇā*), [deriving from] "form" (*gzugs, *rūpa*); "the knowledgeable" (*tshor bar byed pa, *vedin*), [deriving from] "knowledge" (*tshor ba, vid*); "solar" (*nyin mor byed pa, *saurya*), [deriving from] the "sun" (*nyi ma, *sūrya*); and "inflamer" (*sreg par byed pa, *dāhaka*), [deriving from] "flame" (*me, *dahana*).

1.1.1.6. Idiomatic Expressions[5]

An example: calling a poor person wealthy.

1.1.1.7. Names That Are Well Known

These are terms that are well comprehended.

1.1.1.8. Names That Are Not Well Known

These are the opposite of the preceding category.

1.1.1.9. Names That Are Clear

These are terms whose meaning is understood.

1.1.1.10. Names That Are Not Clear

These are terms that are not understood. An example: terms used in Dravidian discourse (*'gro lding ba'i rigs sngags*).

1.1.1.11. Names That Are Short

These are terms of one syllable.

1.1.1.12. Names That Are Long
These are terms of many syllables.

1.1.2. THE COLLECTION OF PHRASES

[A phase] is that which perfects names and syllables. There are six kinds: incomplete phrases (*yongs su ma rdzogs pa'i tshig*); complete phrases (*yongs su rdzogs pa'i tshig*); phrases that establish (*bsgrub pa'i tshig*); phrases that are established (*sgrub pa'i tshig*); phrases of teaching (*bstan pa'i tshig*); phrases of exposition (*bshad pa'i tshig*).

1.1.2.1–1.1.2.2. Incomplete Phrases and Complete Phrases
Example: an incomplete phrase is "Any wrongdoing . . ." (*sdig pa thams cad, *sarvapāpa*). In order to complete the phrase, one should add "should not be done" (*mi bya, *akṛtya*).

1.1.2.3–1.1.2.4. Phrases That Establish and Phrases That Are Established[6]
Example: in the passage commencing "Alas! Compounded things are impermanent . . ." the phrase that establishes is "they have the quality of arising and perishing."

1.1.2.5. Phrases of Teaching
Example: "excellent ones."

1.1.2.6. Phrases of Exposition
Example [with reference to the example just given: "excellent ones" are] "those of correct conduct" [and] "noble persons."

> Phrases may be made up of names that are complete or incomplete.
> By means of these two, one attains the utmost (*mthar thug pa*).

1.1.3. THE COLLECTION OF SYLLABLES

There are forty-nine [syllables]. Names presuppose intent (*'dun pa, *chandas*); phrases presuppose names—and [both names and phrases presuppose] collections of syllables [49a]. Phrases involve both names and syllables. A single syllable is not a phrase. A syllable that does not itself constitute a short name is not, by itself, a name.

Why posit these designations [of collection of names, etc.]? [This is done] in order to cultivate the feelings that arise from contact with designations.[7] What is the meaning of the term "name"? "Name" is used since, in various ways, names cause proper understanding, and since they produce signs (*mtshan ma*, **nimitta*) [cognized] by the mind (*yid*, **manas*).[8] Moreover, they are "names" because they are stated together with phrases in order to indicate meanings that are [otherwise] hidden. Phrases [are stated] in order to designate boundaries by means of names.[9] The collection of syllables is for the clarification of names and phrases.

The Blessed One spoke extensively of "denominations (*tshig bla dags*, **adhivacana*) and the path of denominations." Denominations arise from divisional boundaries (*sde ba mtha' dag*); names are connected with class categories (*rigs pa*).[10] The path of denominations comprises these divisions, categories, and [also] intent, since the latter causes the arising [of denominations]. Linguistic expression/etymological analysis (*nges pa'i tshig*, **nirukti*) comprises that which establishes this or that teaching or explanation in specific cases; the path is the basis of this. Indication (*'dogs pa*, **prajñapti*) serves to indicate distinction based on particularity; the path is the basis of this. [An indication is] entrusted with intent that is inseparable [from it]. Phrases for those [intents]—producing indications—are the path. The basis of those—the collection of names and so on—should, in brief, be understood as sixfold: the dharma, the meaning, person, time, number, and occasion. These should be understood as taught in the *Śrutamayībhūmi*.[11]

1.1.4. SPEECH

In brief, one should understand speech [in two ways].

1.1.4.1. As Eightfold—Urbane, Beautiful, and So On[12]

[Speech is] "urbane" (*grong khyer ba*, **paurī*) insofar as it relates to the city of nirvāṇa. It is "beautiful" (*snyan cing 'jebs pa*, **valgu*) because it is sweet-sounding and lovely. It is "clear" (*rnam par gsal ba*, **vispaṣṭā*) [49b] because its phrases and syllables are well-connected. It is "worth listening to" (*mnyan par 'os pa*, *śrvaṇīyā*) because it is endowed with the dharma and the meaning. It is "independent" (*mi rten pa*, **aniśritā*) because it does not depend on acts of devotion. It is "nondiscordant" (*mi mthun pa med pa*, **apratikūlā*) because it is spoken in a measured way. It is "limitless" (*mi gtugs pa*, **aparyantā*) because it is extensive and learned.

In brief, one may understand these eight aspects of speech under three rubrics. The first aspect pertains to reference (*dbang du bya ba*, **vaśīkaraṇa*); the [next] two, to essence (*ngo bo nyid, *svabhāva[tā]*); those that remain, to application (*sbyor ba, *prayoga*).

1.1.4.2. As Qualities [of Speech] are Indicated via [a Familiar Passage] Beginning "Combination of Phrases and Syllables" and Running Through "a Collection of Components of Exertion"[13]

These are connected (*'byor ba, *yukta*) due to sequential application of the collections of names, phrases, and syllables. Moreover, they are connected insofar as they rely on the four modes of reasoning (*rigs pa, *yukti*). They are coherent (*'brel ba, *sahita*) because they cohere with reasons. They are concordant (*rjes su mthun pa, *ānulomika*) because they concord with what has been expounded. They are agreeable (*rjes su 'phrod pa, ānucchavika*) because they are clear and pure in their phrases and syllables. They are skillful (*thabs dang ldan pa, *aupayika*) because they penetrate to the heart; they are fitting (*'cham pa, *pradakṣiṇa*) because they fit the assembly; they are appropriate (*mthun pa, *pratirūpaka*) because of being endowed with the dharma and the meaning and being appropriate to [a particular] occasion. They are a collection of components of exertion (*'grus skyong gi yan lag gi tshogs, *nipakasyāṅgasambhāra*): "exertion" because of being done deliberately and continually, "components" due to comprising right view and so on.

1.1.5. ASPECT

[This comprises utterances that are] spoken by hearers, Tathāgatas, or bodhisattvas. They [i.e., the utterances] have to do with such things as the aggregates, elements, and sense-fields, dependent arising, correct and incorrect manners of abiding, and mindfulness and the foundations of mindfulness.

1.1.6. THE TEACHING

The teaching is that in dependence on which one expounds.

Moreover, one should understand persons as falling into twenty-seven categories; [these are determined] by analyzing their faculties and so on.[14] The analysis of "faculties" (*dbang po, *indriya*) divides persons into those possessing dull or keen faculties. The analysis of "conduct" (*spyad pa, *caryā*) is sevenfold—those whose actions [are impelled by] desire and so on; these are as taught in the *Śrāvakabhūmi*. [50a] Analysis by "position" (*phyogs*) [is twofold, and distinguishes between] householders and renunciates. Analysis by "resolve" (*smon lam, *pranidhāna*) [is threefold, and distinguishes between] hearers, solitary buddhas and bodhisattvas. Analysis by "those who are fit and unfit for attainment" [is twofold, and distinguishes between] those possessing the quality of final awakening and those who do not possess this quality. Analysis by "application" [is ninefold, and distinguishes between] those who those have not entered [the dharma] and those who have; [between] those who are confused and those who are not confused; [between] those who are not fully matured and those who are fully matured; [and between] those who are completely bound, those who are partially bound, and those without bondage. Analysis by "family" (*rigs, *kūla*) [is twofold, and distinguishes between] human and nonhuman beings.

All phrasing can be summarized under four rubrics. "Phrasing" [involves] what one teaches. [This is discussed previously] from "names and so on" up through the end of the section on aspect [i.e., in sections 1.1.1 through 1.1.5]. [It also involves those] to whom one teaches: in brief, one teaches to twenty-seven [types of] person [section 1.1.6]. [It also involves] that by which one teaches—i.e., via speech. [Finally, it involves those] who teach: Buddhas, hearers, and bodhisattvas. All of these things are indicated by means of the six aspects of phrasing [discussed previously]. If any one [of the aspects] is faulty, the meaning [of the teaching] will not be fully manifested. It is because meaning is fully illuminated by these that phrasing is called "that which illuminates."

1.2. MEANING

In brief, meaning should be viewed as having ten aspects: the meaning pertaining to levels (*sa'i don, *bhūmyartha*); the meaning pertaining to defining characteristics (*mtshan nyid kyi don, *lakṣaṇārtha*); the meaning pertaining to mental activity (*yid la byed pa'i don, *manasikārārtha*); referential meaning (*dbang du bya ba'i don, *vaśīkaraṇārtha*); the meaning pertaining to benefit (*phan yon gyi don, *anuśaṃsārtha*); the meaning pertaining to fault (*nyes dmigs kyi don, *adīnavārtha*); the meaning pertaining to harm (*mi mthun pa'i phyogs kyi don, *vipakṣārtha*); the meaning pertaining to antidote (*gnyen po'i don, *pratipakṣārtha*); summary meaning (*bsdus pa'i don, *piṇḍārtha*); and elaborated meaning (*rgyas pa'i don, *vistārārtha*).

1.2.1. THE MEANING PERTAINING TO LEVELS

This is fivefold, comprising levels of accumulation, of application, of seeing, of cultivation, and of completion. Analyzed more extensively, there are seventeen levels, from the level furnished with the collection of five forms of consciousness up through the level without attributes.

1.2.2. THE MEANING PERTAINING TO DEFINING CHARACTERISTICS

This is fivefold: the particular characteristic (*rang gi mtshan nyid, *svalakṣaṇa*); the general characteristic (*spyi'i mtshan nyid, *sāmānyalakṣaṇa*); the verbal characteristic (*brda'i mtshan nyid, *saṃketalakṣaṇa*); the characteristic pertaining to cause (*rgyu'i mtshan nyid, *hetulakṣaṇa*); the characteristic pertaining to effect (*'bras bu mtshan nyid, *phalalakṣaṇa*). The analysis of these is as taught in the *Cintāmayībhūmi.*[15] [50b] The absence of defining characteristics should also be understood [here] as it has been taught previously in the *Cintāmayībhūmi.*[16]

1.2.3. THE MEANING PERTAINING TO MENTAL ACTIVITY

As taught previously in the *Śrāvakabhūmi*, this is sevenfold: individuation of defining characteristics and so on.[17] There are ten [forms of] knowledge: knowledge of suffering, its origin, its cessation, and the path; knowledge of dharma; knowledge of subsequent realization; knowledge of the supreme; knowledge of the conventional; knowledge of exhaustion; and knowledge of nonproduction. The analysis of these is as taught in the *Śrāvakabhūmi.*[18] There are six categories of consciousness, from eye consciousness down through mental consciousness. These have been taught previously in the *Pañcavijñānakāyasamprayuktābhūmi* and the *Manobhūmi.*[19]

Perfected knowledge (*yongs su shes pa, *parijñāna*) is of nine types. The first is the perfected knowledge that abandons those things to be abandoned, having understood [forms of] suffering and its origin associated with the desire realm. The second is the perfected knowledge that abandons those things to be abandoned, having understood [forms of] suffering and its origin associated with the form and formless realms. The third is the perfected knowledge that abandons those things to be abandoned, having understood cessation in the desire realm. The fourth is the perfected knowledge that abandons those things to be abandoned, having understood cessation in the form and formless realms. The fifth is the perfected knowledge that abandons those things to be abandoned, having understood the path in the desire realm. The sixth is the perfected knowledge that abandons those things to be abandoned, having understood the path in the form and formless realms. The seventh is the perfected knowledge that abandons entanglements associated with the lower [realm]. The eighth is the perfected knowledge that extinguishes attachment to form, whereas the ninth is the perfected knowledge that extinguishes attachment to the formless. The analysis of these is as taught in the *Samāhitābhūmi.*[20] There are three gates of liberation: emptiness, wishlessness, and signlessness—and the analysis of these [51a] should also be known as taught in the *Samāhitābhūmi.*[21]

With respect to mental actions, one should engage in them purely; one should be aware of awareness as pure; one should discriminatively apprehend discriminative apprehension as pure; the doors of liberation should be liberated with purity. One should undertake to reflect on dharmas in this way.

1.2.4. REFERENTIAL MEANING[22]

In brief, this is threefold: reference to things, times, and persons.

1.2.4.1. Reference to Things

Reference to things is also threefold: the actual state (*dngos gzhi*, **maula*); the means for obtaining that; and compassion involving others.[23]

1.2.4.1.1. The Actual State

This is sixfold: good transmigrations (*bde 'gro*); bad transmigrations (*ngan 'gro*); decline (*nyams pa*); distinction (*khyad par*); saṃsāra (*'khor ba*); and nirvāṇa (*mya ngan las 'das pa*).

1.2.4.1.2. The Means for Obtaining That

This is twelvefold, insofar as there are twelve forms of conduct: conduct involving desire; conduct involving renunciation; virtuous conduct; nonvirtuous conduct; conduct that is arduous; conduct that is not arduous; conduct conducive to decline; conduct conducive to distinction; afflicted conduct; purified conduct; conduct for one's own benefit; and conduct for the benefit of others.

1.2.4.1.3. Compassion Involving Others

This is fivefold: turning away from desire [for harmful things]; instructing; inducing understanding; encouraging; and gladdening.

[Regarding 1.2.4.1.1:] "Good transmigrations" are human and divine transmigrations. "Bad transmigrations" are the miserable realms. "Decline" is of two kinds: that which depends and does not depend on others. As for these [two], the first should be understood to be the decline of one's own life—e.g., one's color, strength [51b], enjoyments, renown, happiness, confidence, and so on. The second comprises the decline of virtue; the decline of sovereignty of power; being well known as one of little consequence; lack of respect for one's speech; confusion of insight; the apprehension of lesser forms, sounds, scents, tastes, and tactile objects; and [a state in which] one's mind fails to encounter sublime enjoyments. Decline should be understood as associated with such things. The types of "distinction" should be understood as the opposite of these. "Saṃsāra" is the decline of good transmigration and these distinctions; "nirvāṇa"refers to the realm of nirvāṇa, with and without remainder.[24]

[Regarding 1.2.4.1.2:] "Conduct involving desire." This is desirous conduct that follows from being in the midst of ten forms of enjoyment. "Conduct involving renunciation": having understood that these forms of enjoyment are impermanent and so on, one renounces [them], undertakes ethics, and restrains one's senses. "Virtuous conduct" refers to the virtuous conduct—giving, ethics, cultivation, and so on—of one who possesses taints. "Nonvirtuous conduct" comprises the three kinds of negative conduct. "Conduct" that is arduous is [living] naked and uncovered and so on. "Conduct that is not arduous" [applies to cases in which] one abandons the extremes of devotion to sense-pleasures and asceticism, and relies [instead] on the middle path, taking up robes in accordance with the dharma, without abandoning the delight gained through the dharma. "Conduct conducive to decline" is conduct that impedes the forms of distinction in life and so on. "Conduct conducive to distinction" should be understood to be the opposite of that, as mentioned in the Parrot Sūtra (*ne tso'i mdo*). "Afflicted conduct," in brief, is itself threefold: affliction of action, affliction of affliction, and affliction of application [52a]. The basic roots of these should be understood as ninefold. Affliction of action comprises desire, hatred, and delusion. Affliction of affliction comprises the four errors. Affliction of application comprises ignorance and the craving for existence. Why? Because the affliction of action is produced in such a way by the three roots of nonvirtue, and the affliction of affliction is produced by the four errors. When these are produced, the affliction of application arises among renunciates on account of ignorance, and the affliction of application arises among householders on account of their thirst for existence. "Purified conduct," in brief, comprises the three trainings and the five levels—from the level of accumulation up to the level of completion—as [discussed] previously. The basic roots of this [purified conduct] should also be understood as ninefold. One is without desire, without hatred, and without delusion due to [training in] higher ethics and higher reflection. Four inerrancies occur on the levels of accumulation and application. Knowledge and liberation [are arrived at via] training in higher discriminating insight, and [on] the levels of seeing, cultivation, and completion. "Conduct for one's own benefit" is benefit that one attains for oneself, such as occurs among hearers and solitary buddhas; it is called "conduct for one's own benefit" because although one's activities may at times benefit others, one does not undertake them simply in order to benefit others. "Conduct for the benefit of others" is that which establishes benefit for others due to gladdening many sentient beings, such as occurs among bodhisattvas and Tathāgatas.

[Regarding 1.2.4.1.3:] "Turning away from desire" is that which condemns the six forms of dark activity and points out [their] faults. "Instructing" is pointing out four varieties of reasoning in order to induce understanding of forms of white activity [52b]. "Inducing understanding" pertains to establishing the basis of training for those who have been instructed and are resolved. Having done this, assuredly [such persons] will say "What should I now do? Please instruct me accordingly"—[and instructing] is what causes them to apply themselves correctly. "Encouraging" brings good fortune and power when one is discouraged with respect to understanding, attainments, or acquisitions, so that one's mind correctly grasps [the teaching]. "Gladdening" is praising one who has attained qualities that accord with the dharma.

[Moreover], "turning away from desire" can occur without "instructing" also occurring. Someone, by saying "Don't do this" or some other phrase, can cause turning away from desire. Or, one might threaten: "If you do this, then I will do this or that." Or, one might entreat: "Do this out of affection for me." Moreover, "instructing" can occur without "turning away from desire" occurring: one might instruct common people as to virtues and faults, though they may be unable to turn away from desires. [Finally], "turning away from desire" can occur together with "instructing," as in a case in which one instructs those who are living faultily and thereby induces them to turn away from desire. "Inducing understanding" and "encouraging" are employed so that who have not initially adopted the training will undertake it or so that those who are more advanced will further themselves. As for "gladdening," it brings five benefits. When one is gladdened, one becomes certain as to one's own realization; joy is produced in others with respect to virtues yet to be realized; those who bear animosity become faithful; common people who lack faith are brought to abide [on the Buddhist path]; and because of the faithful, [the teaching] spreads. Persons who are gladdened engage in actions that cause them to be reborn in the heavens of the beautiful gods. [53a] Wherever they may be born, they will experience beauty in that place and will not experience ugliness.

[Returning to 1.2.4.1.2:] "Conduct pertaining to desire" may either cause one to transmigrate to a fortunate realm, as when one engages in virtuous action out of attachment to future [virtuous results], or it may cause one to transmigrate to a lower realm, as when one is involved in desire [prompted] by evils. Via "nonvirtuous conduct," one transmigrates to lower realms. Via "arduous conduct" also, one transmigrates to lower realms, since one torments oneself because of relying on erroneous views. "Conduct that is not arduous" transforms into the assemblage [of prerequisites] for nirvāṇa. Via conduct "conducive to either decline or distinction," one goes to decline or distinction as appropriate. Saṃsāra occurs due to "afflicted conduct"; nirvāṇa, due to "purfied conduct." Via "conduct for one's own benefit," one proceeds to states of happiness, distinction, and nirvāṇa. Via "conduct for the benefit of others," one brings happiness, distinction, and nirvāṇa to both oneself and others.

Concluding Remarks on 1.2.4.1 and Its Subvarieities

[Again, the issues discussed previously] may classed under three rubrics: the "actual state", which encompasses six aspects, from good rebirth realms and so on up through final nirvāṇa; the "means for the attainment of that"—i.e., twelve [forms of] conduct; and "compassion for others," since when there is compassion for others, one engages in the twelve forms of conduct from the perspective of the actual state. As is appropriate, one practices "turning away from desire" through "gladdening." [53b]

1.2.4.2. Reference to Times

In brief, there are three categories of discourse (*gtam*): discourse concerning the past, discourse concerning the future, and discourse concerning the present—just as is stated in the sūtras.

1.2.4.3. Reference to Persons

This should be known as comprising the twenty-seven kinds of person—dull (*rtul po*) and so forth. In this way, discourses of Buddhas occur with reference to things, times, and persons—and so these are termed [forms of] reference.

1.2.5. THE MEANING PERTAINING TO BENEFIT

In brief, this is the extolling of praiseworthy qualities or persons.

1.2.6. THE MEANING PERTAINING TO FAULT

In brief, this is the condemnation of qualities and persons not worthy of praise.

1.2.7. THE MEANING PERTAINING TO HARM

In brief, this comprises all forms of afflicted conduct.

1.2.8. THE MEANING PERTAINING TO ANTIDOTE

In brief, this comprises all forms of purified conduct. [These are discussed in passages] such as: "lust is inimical and the antidote to it is repulsiveness. Hatred is inimical and the antidote to it is loving kindness."

1.2.9. SUMMARY MEANING

One teaches the dharma in connection with generalities.

1.2.10. ELABORATED MEANING

One teaches the dharma in connection with specifics. Moreover, one teaches the sūtras of provisional and definitive meaning.

Furthermore, summary meaning is twofold: summary phrasing and summary meaning—and elaborated meaning has a similar twofold division: elaborated phrasing and elaborated meaning. In a sūtra, the Blessed One says, "O Śāriputra, whether the dharma is taught summarily or in an elaborated fashion, those who understand it are very rare." In sūtras, the Blessed One teaches [by making use of] elaborated phrasing and summary meaning, whereas in verses (*tshig su bcad pa'i sde*, **gāthā*), he teaches using elaborated meaning and summary phrasing.

AN INTERIM VERSE:

> Levels; characteristics; mental activity;
> Reference; benefit; fault;
> Harm and [54a] the antidote;
> Summary and elaborated.

2. Explication

Having first investigated the corpus of *buddhavacana*, one should seek out all ten forms of meaning—or whichever is suitable—in the scriptural texts (*gsung rab*, **pravacana*). Having done so oneself, one should teach these to others. Accordingly, a dharma preacher should engage in the practice [of teaching] by explicating in five ways those sūtras that possess the corpus of phrasing and the corpus of meaning. First, he should expound the teachings. After that, he should expound the prompt. After that, he should expound the meaning. After that, he should expound responses to objections. After that, he should expound connections.

2.1. TEACHING

In brief, these are the twelve branches classified as scriptural texts—sūtras and so on.[25]

2.1.1. SŪTRAS (MDO)

These are explanations in prose by way of a stated meaning. For the most part, the intention (*dgongs pa*, **abhiprāya*) [in such texts] can be grasped.

*2.1.2. MELODIC VERSES (DBYANGS KYIS BSNYAD PA, *GEYA)*

[This category] is said to [apply to a text] that has verses sung at its conclusion and to a sūtra whose meaning is to be interpreted.[26]

*2.1.3. PROPHECIES (LUNG BSTAN PA, *VYĀKARAṆA)*

These are prophecies that elaborate on that which is taught in sūtras and prophecies as to the appearance of hearers of former times.

*2.1.4. VERSES (TSHIGS SU BCAD PA, *GĀTHĀ)*

These are expositions in verse; they may have anywhere from two to six metrical feet.

2.1.5. *INSPIRED UTTERANCES (CHED DU BRJOD PA, *UDĀNA)*

These are freestanding utterances that are stated in order to purify hearers, and as a means for establishing compassion in future beings—thus, they are called inspired utterances. As it has been said, "The Blessed One, with inspiration, uttered an inspired utterance."

2.1.6. *CIRCUMSTANTIAL NARRATIVES (GLENG BZHI, *NIDĀNA)*

These are stated in dependence [on particular circumstances]. [For example], it is said: "With reference to the black [deeds] of Mṛgāra, the Blessed One gave a dharma discourse to the monks," and "With reference to the *prātimokṣa* [vows], the Blessed One spoke a circumstantial narrative on this or that occasion pertaining to this or that brief point regarding training in the path of discipline." [54b]

2.1.7. *PARABLES (RTOGS PAR BRJOD PA, *AVADĀNA)*

These are sūtras that incorporate examples; by these, their meaning is purified (*des don de rnam par byang bar 'gyur ba'o*)

2.1.8. *ANCIENT NARRATIVES (DE LTA BU BYUNG BA, *ITIVṚTTAKA)*

These are [tales] of previous events, excluding accounts of former lives.

2.1.9. *ACCOUNTS OF FORMER LIVES (SKYES PA'I RABS, *JĀTAKA)*

These recount the conduct of bodhisattvas and the [Buddha's] own former births.

2.1.10. *EXTENSIVE SCRIPTURES (SHIN TU RGYAS PA, *VAIPULYA)*

These recount the bodhisattva path—the seven levels and the four activities of a bodhisattva, the qualities of a Buddha, the four purities in all their aspects, and the one hundred and forty unmixed qualities of a Buddha, up through perfected awareness [endowed] with all aspects. These are explicated [as] taught in the *Bodhisattvabhūmi*. They are called "extensive" because they are voluminous and expansive, and because they were accomplished over three immeasurable eons.

*2.1.11. FABULOUS ACCOUNTS (RMAD DU BYUNG BA, *ADBHUTADHARMA)*

These are texts that explicate marvels pertaining to Buddhas, hearers, and householders, such as those discussed in the *rmad du byung ba'i rgyu'i mdo.*[27]

*2.1.12. INSTRUCTIONS (GTAN LA PHAB PA, *UPADEŚA)*

These are matrices (*ma mo, *mātṛkā*) derived from the sūtras. All sūtras of definitive meaning are termed "matrices." [They are] those in which the Blessed One taught the characteristics of dharmas, and those in which hearers who have glimpsed the basis and dwell in realization teach the characteristics of dharma(s) without error. These are matrices; they are also the abhidharma. It should be understood that just as a syllabary (*yi ge phyi mo*) is primary in treatises on the arts and in speech more generally, so, too, should the characteristics of dharma(s) be expounded [as primary]. Just as syllables are unclear in the absence of a syllabary, so, too, are the twelve branches [of the teaching]—sūtras and so on—unclear when the characteristics of dharma(s) have not been presented. But they become clear when [such characteristics] are presented. [55a] Furthermore, the matrices are termed "abhidharma" because the characteristics are stated to be not different [from the dharma itself]. Other sūtras that should be explicated in dependence on these matrices are also termed "instructions."

2.2. PROMPT

The prompt is threefold. As appropriate to a given case, one should expound on things, times, and persons in order to cause this or that person with this or that conduct to turn away from desire; in order to instruct; and in order to gladden.

2.3. MEANING

Having expounded the prompt, one should expound the meaning. The meaning has two aspects: the summary meaning and the meaning of phrases.

2.3.1. SUMMARY MEANING

This has four aspects: summary presentations of sūtras of definitive meaning; teaching the limits of things; the practice; and the result. The practice also has two aspects: erroneous and correct. And the result likewise has two aspects: the result of correct practice and the result of incorrect practice.

2.3.2. THE MEANING OF PHRASES

This has four aspects: indicating synonyms; indicating the corpus via distinguishing characteristics; indicating etymological derivation; and analyzing into aspects.

2.3.2.1–2.3.2.2. Indicating Synonyms and Indicating the Corpus via Distinguishing characteristics

[Not discussed explicitly.]

2.3.2.3. Indicating Etymological Derivation

This has five aspects: sign; essential nature; action; quality; and cause and effect.

2.3.2.4. Analyzing Into aspects

There are five [kinds of analysis relevant here]: analysis of essential nature; analysis of realm; analysis of time; analysis of state (*gnas skabs, *avasthā*); and analysis of persons.

2.3.2.4.1. Analysis of Essential Nature

For example: form comprises the ten sense-fields possessing form; feeling is of three kinds; recognition is sixfold; formations are threefold; consciousness is sixfold. Analysis of essential nature should be understood to proceed along these lines.

2.3.2.4.2. Analysis of Realm

This comprises the realms of desire, form, and the formless.

2.3.2.4.3. [55b] Analysis of Time

This comprises the past, future, and present.

2.3.2.4.4. Analysis of State

This should be understood to have twenty-five aspects. States of being lesser, middling, and great; a state of happiness; a state of suffering; a state of neither happiness nor suffering; a state of virtue; a state of nonvirtue; a state of indeterminacy (with respect to virtue and nonvirtue); a state of listening; a state of reflecting; a state of meditatively cultivating; states of higher ethics, higher reflection, and higher discriminating insight; the state of being an insider [i.e., a Buddhist]; the state of being an outsider; the states of being grasped and of grasping; the state of the inimical and the state of the antidote; the state of being directly manifest;

the state of not being directly manifest; the state of the cause; and the state of the result.

2.3.2.4.5. Analysis of Persons

The analysis of persons should be understood as previously discussed—i.e., as involving the twenty-seven kinds of person.

2.4. RESPONDING TO OBJECTIONS

This involves responding to objections—whether the objections are expressed by oneself or by others.

2.4.1. OCCASIONS FOR OBJECTION

In brief, objections are of five kinds.

2.4.1.1. Not Understanding the Meaning

There is nonunderstanding of the meaning, where a person who has failed to understand inquires, "What is the meaning of this phrase?"

2.4.1.2. Verbal Contradiction

There is verbal contradiction, where [it is objected that] "what is said by the Blessed One here [contradicts] what he previously said on another occasion."

2.4.1.3. Contradiction with Reason

There is contradiction with reason, where a passage appears to contradict the four modes of reasoning.

2.4.1.4. Appearance [in] Multiple Parts

There is the appearance [of one meaning] across multiple parts [of a text or texts], as [when one hears], "The Blessed One taught this very meaning in this or that [place], with many synonyms."

2.4.1.5. Extremely Recondite Teachings

[Finally, one may encounter objections] due to an extremely recondite [teaching]—e.g., "What is the inner self? Does it exist, abiding as permanent, stable, eternal, and truly real?"

2.4.2. RESPONSES TO EACH

Responses to such objections/questions should also be understood as sequentially organized in terms of these five aspects.

2.4.2.1. Not Understanding the Meaning

In a case in which [the meaning] is not understood, [a person] should be brought to understand. [56a]

2.4.2.2. Verbal Contradiction

[Passages] should be made to concord via indicating the intention [underlying them]. One should proceed likewise in cases of appearance in multiple parts and extremely recondite teachings.

2.4.2.3. Contradiction with Reason

One should offer a response by indicating a *kālāpadeśa*, by indicating the four modes of reasoning, and by indicating the connection between the cause and the result, saying "This is the result of such-and-such a cause."[28]

2.4.2.4. Appearance [in] Multiple Parts

[See 2.4.2.2.]

2.4.2.5. Extremely Recondite Teachings

[See 2.4.2.2.]

A categorical response is [offered] in order to establish correctly the characteristics of dharmas for a questioner. An analytical response is [offered] so that those who inquire as to [what is] appropriate or inappropriate will come to understand the specific characteristics [of that which they desire to know]. A response that is itself a question is in order to prompt an assertion. Alternatively, one may respond by setting [the question] aside, for four reasons: "because [the answer] does not exist, because it is profound," etc.[29] As previously indicated in the *Cintāmayībhūmi*, responding to [questions such as] "Does the Tathāgata exist after death?" is inappropriate, whether [such responses are offered] in terms of either conventional or ultimate truth.[30] Therefore, it is said that this [sort of question] is "to be set aside." In this case, from the perspective of the ultimate, the Tathāgata does not exist essentially [before or after death], since [essences] do not exist. And from the perspective of the conventional, [questions] such as "Does the Tathāgata exist after death?" are unanswerable, both because they contradict [what is] appropriate, [what is] inappropriate, and the path, and because abandoning the result is not established [thereby].

2.5. CONNECTION

This is threefold: connection pertaining to completion, to explication, and to establishment. An example of connection according to these three aspects: the Blessed One said, "I ordained at a very young age, in the prime of youth, quite young."[31] Via this [statement], [the phrase] "very young" is completed. The passage "With my father Śuddhodana, [56b] I dwelled ensconced in a beautiful palace" is an explication of the reality of [his] youth. "Why did he renounce when very young?" "Because of apprehending qualities such as sickness and so on." This is connection pertaining to establishment. A summary presentation is indicated in a sūtra, in the statement "There are three feelings: joy, suffering, and neither joy nor suffering." It is precisely the connection pertaining to completion [that is evident] here: the utterance is brought to completion by means of the names that follow the term "feelings" itself. Just as in the case of feeling, the four noble truths and so on also should be understood as being sequentially explicated: subsequent phrases follow on, and concord with, an initial phrase. The connection pertaining to establishment is twofold: in some instances, later phrases may be established by earlier ones; in other instances, earlier phrases may be established by later ones. The connection pertaining to explication should also be viewed in the same way.

3. *The Dharma Preacher*

Regarding that, the preacher of dharma is endowed with ten qualities—complete in every aspect—and possesses both the dharma and the meaning. The dharma has six aspects; the meaning, ten.

3.1. TEN QUALITIES OF DHARMA PREACHERS[32]

Their utterances are expansive, because they have heard much, have grasped what they have heard, and have accumulated what they have heard. They are uncowed when in the midst of the assembly, not timid when teaching the dharma to royals/warriors (*rgyal rigs*, **kṣatriya*), and so on. For this reason, their voices do not tremble, nor do their armpits sweat; being attentive, they are unforgetful. They are repositories of virtuous names and actions, because, possessing names that manifest the eight features, they teach the dharma to the assembly by way of elaborations: names, syllables, connections, and so on. Names that manifest eight features are those that are urbane, soft, sweet, and so on. They [i.e., dharma preachers] are skilled in rhetoric (*gtam gyi sbyor ba*), because they make use of utterances with twenty aspects: timeliness, devotion, and so on.[33] They proceed with qualities that accord with the dharma, [57a] since they do not simply listen and pay lip service to the dharma, but act as they speak. Their behavior is perfected; when speaking, their hands and feet do not fidget, their brows are not creased, their heads, faces, and bodies remain steady. They are handsome in such things as coming and going. They strive to hear teachings that they have not yet heard, clarify teachings that they have heard, and ceaslessly practice yoga, mental application, and introspective calming meditation. They are indefatigable, since their minds do not become wearied by teaching the dharma to the four assemblies. They possess forbearance, since they do not become angry even [when confonted] by anger; they do not engage in fault finding even [when confronted] by fault finders; and they do not grow disturbed or commit an infraction even if insulted or belittled.

4. Exposition[34]

There are eight kinds of exposition: splendid (*brjid pa*); that which incorporates commentarial explanation (*rnam par 'grel dang ldan pa*); that which incorporates responses to objections (*rgol ba'i lan dang ldan pa*); that which incorporates analysis (*rab tu dbye ba dang ldan pa*); that which is associated with those (*de'i dang 'brel ba*); that which cites from [texts] other than those (*de las gzhan pa las drangs pa*); that which arises from inspiration (*spobs pa las 'byung ba*); and that which follows doctrinal tenets (*grub pa'i mtha' rjes su 'brang ba*).

4.1. SPLENDID DISCOURSE

Splendid discourse (*brjid pa'i gtam*) should be understood to have five aspects: it incorporates reasons and examples; its instrument is speech; it comprises various names and syllables; and it is readily intelligible.

4.2. DISCOURSE INCORPORATING COMMENTARIAL EXPLANATION

[This is offered] in order to clarify profundities, and in order to propound that what is clear also possesses profundity.

4.3. DISCOURSE INCORPORATING RESPONSES TO OBJECTIONS

In brief, this should be understood to dispel the five forms of objection [discussed previously].

4.4. DISCOURSE INCORPORATING ANALYSIS

[Here], one offers an analysis of individual dharmas into aspects, [as those aspects] proliferate from one to ten or more. [57b] [For example,] having undertaken [an analysis of] action as having three qualities, one details the four foundations of mindfulness by discussing [them] in this way.

4.5. DISCOURSE ASSOCIATED WITH THOSE

[Here], one is prompted to engage in explication based only on the corpora of sūtras, melodic verses, and so on, but not to draw summary conclusions from other [texts].

4.6. DISCOURSE THAT CITES FROM [TEXTS] OTHER THAN THOSE

This is an establishment [of claims] by means of sūtras other than those (*de las gzhan pa'i mdo sde*).

4.7. DISCOURSE ARISING FROM INSPIRATION

[In this form of discourse], one is equipped to expound on any meaning, as desired.

4.8. DISCOURSE FOLLOWING DOCTRINAL TENETS

[This form of discourse] is expounded relying on matrices or, alternatively, it is expounded relying on the the division of instructions (*gtan la bab par ston pa'i sde*) apart from those.

5. *Assembly*

There are five kinds of assembly: an assembly of householders, an assembly of renunciates; an assembly of the faithful; an assembly of those who are hostile; and an assembly of those [whose attitude is] in between [faith and hostility].

Before an assembly of householders, one should teach the dharma focusing on the condemnation of improper conduct and the praise of proper conduct, in order that they might turn away [from worldly existence] and enter [onto the path] based on this.[35] Before an assembly of renunciates, one should teach the dharma focusing on training, so that they might take up the three trainings of higher ethics and so in order as to attain [liberation] very swiftly. Before assemblies of the faithful and so on, one should engage in that discourse which possesses the greatness and power of the teaching, in order to further [their practice], encourage impartiality, and bolster their faith.

6. *Listening*

When a preacher teaches the dharma, others should apply [themselves] to listening devotedly. How is this done? By means of between one and ten factors.

First by means of one factor: because the teaching is that which conduces to reward and happiness. There are four possibilities here: [that which conduces to] reward but not with happiness [and so on]. This is as taught in the *Bodhisattvabhūmi*, in connection with the acceptance of the dharma.[36]

By means of two: so as to understand the supremacy of the holy dharma—a supremacy that should be understood, moreover, as [the dharma's] lack of faults and the greatness of its meaning. And also because the hardship of speaking and listening is connected to the result [of liberation]; were this not so, then one's own activity and [that of] others would be given up, since the hardships of speaking and listening [58a] would become pointless.

By three: because one might avoid bad transmigrations and secure good transmigrations, and because it is the cause by which one attains nirvāṇa. By listening devotedly, these three [ends] will be obtained.

By four: listening to the dharma devotedly, one comes to know the very qualities [discussed] in the sūtras and so on—for it is said [there] that one abandons nonvirtuous negative qualities in many ways and appropriates many virtuous qualities.[37] By listening to these [texts], one is caused to abandon [the former] and appropriate [the latter]. And due to having abandoned and appropriated [them], one is subesquently made to abandon the suffering that is caused by negative actions. And one obtains nirvāṇa, which is caused by abandoning those and appropriating virtues [in their stead].

By five: the Blessed One has said that the dharma "is associated with the basis, emancipation, teaching, the conversion of others, and the miraculous."[38] Extensive analysis of these phrases is as found in the *Paryāyasaṃgraha*.[39]

Again, by five: "what has not been heard should be listened to"; "what has been heard should be clarified"; "doubts should be dispelled"; "views should be straightened"; "one should understand the profound meanings and phrases [of the teaching] by means of discriminating insight." By means of these kinds [of phrase], the Blessed One taught the means for the purification of insight arising from hearing, reflection, and meditative cultivation. Via two [of the phrases just listed], he taught the method for purifying the discriminating insight arising from hearing; via two [more, he taught the method for purifying] the discriminating insight arising from reflection; via the last, he taught the method for purifying the discriminating insight arising from meditative cultivation.

By six: by that [listening devotedly], they repay and protect the teacher, thinking "great hardships were undertaken for the sake of the singular excellence of this dharma." And those who do not correctly see what is in their own interest think "those learned ones—who do see correctly, [58b] who are without illness and [teach] without ceasing, [who] are trustworthy, who present the meaning as they have seen it—they know this dharma of the Blessed One for themselves."

By seven: seven aspects of the dharma should be established by seven factors. Reflecting, one thinks "the dharma should be known," "the meaning should be known"—from this, up through thinking "persons who are supreme and not supreme should be known."[40]

By eight: the dharma is easily acquired, since it was explicated even to outcastes and so on. It is also easy [to practice]—whether one is walking, standing, sitting, or lying down—because it is approachable and meaningful; because its effects include fortunate rebirths and the supreme excellence; because it is virtuous in the beginning, middle, and end; and because it brings immediate joy and results in future joy.

By nine: with reference to liberation from the nine sources of harm, [the dharma] liberates one from the prison of saṃsāra, since it cuts the bonds of desire and so on. It reverses the lack of seven [kinds of] wealth, since it makes one a sovereign. It satisfies the hunger for acting virtuously and listening to the holy dharma, since it furnishes a fine harvest of holy dharma. It reverses the darkness of ignorance, since it generates the illumination of discriminating insight, and since one can traverse four rivers and proceed to the field of nirvāṇa [by means of it]. It cures one completely from the disease of the afflictions, because it liberates one from the enslavements of worldly existence and from the endless wilderness of saṃsāra. Moreover, among all these forms of bondage, the prison of saṃsāra is foremost. For this reason, it is noted first.

By ten: listening to the dharma devotedly enables them to attain the power of comprehension and thus to experience the benefits of this attainment. By means of the dharma, they obtain provisions [59a] and are not rash [in their actions]. In detail: when making use of provisions, they see faults [of saṃsāric existence] and [the rewards of] renunciation, [as one reads]: "they do not sorrow over their decline, they do not break down, they do not wail." In detail [again, one reads]: "they do not sorrow over the decline of their kinsmen, they do not break down, they do not wail." In detail [one reads]: "they do not sorrow over the decline of their health, youth, and life, they do not break down." Faithful persons, having seen these faults [of saṃsāric existence] and the rewards of renunciation, renounce [worldly existence], dwell in solitary places, [and perform other good acts] up to engaging in meditative practices. They listen to the dharma devotedly, and their realization accords with dependent arising, which is profound and appears profound. They attain a release that is difficult, supremely difficult, vast, and virtuous. The Blessed One said, "Hearken, O hearers, with single-pointed mind; listen to the dharma: you should perfect the abandonment of five qualities and the cultivation of seven qualities." Accordingly, they listen to the dharma devotedly. Having understood that all arisen dharmas cease, they generate the eye free from passion and devoid of defilement with respect to those dharmas, and they obtain provisions for achieving the [lesser] results [of practice], from stream-enterer up through the state of an arhat, or they obtain the provisions for the [greater] results of the state of the arhat or the self-arisen sage (*rang byung thub pa*), or they obtain the provisions of a bodhisattva, or they obtain the provisions of unsurpassed, supreme awakening, or they obtain worldly and transcendent meditative attainment, liberation, concentration, and equipoise.

7. *Brief and Extensive Praise of Buddhas*

[59b] At the very outset of preaching, one should first praise the Buddhas. This, moreover, may be done briefly or extensively.

7.1. BRIEF PRAISE

7.1.1. BRIEF PRAISE, ACCOUNT 1: FIVE ASPECTS

Brief praise should be understood to have five aspects [as it may pertain to] the beauty of [a Buddha's] physical form; [his] tranquility; [his] awareness; [his] attainment; and [his] power.

7.1.1.1. Beauty of Physical Form

This should be understood to comprise the thirty-two marks of the great man, as well as the eighty minor marks.

7.1.1.2. Tranquility

This includes such things as restraint of the senses and the complete victory over the afflictive emotions together with their latent propensities.

7.1.1.3. Awareness

This is based on unobstructed and unattached awareness of past, present, and future dharmas, as well as atemporal (*dus kyis ma bsdus pa*) dharmas.

7.1.1.4. Attainment

This should be understood as deriving from [his] perfected attainment of benefits for himself and others.

7.1.1.5. Power

This comprises the forms of higher knowledge of a Tathāgata.

7.1.2. BRIEF PRAISE, ACCOUNT 2: SIX ASPECTS

Alternatively, brief praise of a Blessed One can be understood as having six aspects, based on the totality of [his] virtues; [his] absence of faults, [his im]mutability, [his] peerlessness, [his] actions that benefit himself and sentient beings; and [his] capacity.[41]

7.2. EXTENSIVE PRAISE

As for the extensive praise of a Blessed One, it is limitless, since the virtues of a Blessed One are innumerable. He illuminates, since he brings about the light of knowledge; he disperses the darkness, since he overcomes the darkness of ignorance; he is endowed with vision, since he possesses three eyes; he perceives the ultimate, since he is aware of the incomparable noble truths; he is accomplished in conduct, because he is endowed with ethics and because his ethics are perfected. Supreme among those with two feet, he is utterly supreme among guides, a vibrant striver among strivers [60a], and a rare jewel in the world. Merciful and compassionate, he is one who wishes for the good, wishes for the beneficial, and acts in a compassionate way. He is conducive to wisdom, meaning, and the dharma; he teaches the clear meaning, and he relies on the meaning. He realizes the unrealized goal, because he initially realizes the eightfold path of noble ones, and because he does this himself [i.e., without the aid of a teacher]. He is a knower of the path, a teacher of the path, a speaker of the path, and a guide to the path, because he establishes the holy life that was not [previously] designated. He is a lion among men, because he is free from fear and that which has to do with fear. He is a bull among men, because he is a leader of the great assembly.[42] He is foremost among men, because he is the greatest in the assembly. He is a great elephant among men, because he lacks faults. He is a thoroughbred among men, because his heart is completely tamed. He is best among men, because he surpasses all persons in such things as family, lineage, and line (*rigs dang brgyud dang gdung la sogs pa*). He is highest among men, because he surpasses all men in such things as ethics, attainment, knowledge, and power. He is the white lotus among men, because he is unpolluted by worldly dharmas. He is peerless, because he is without equal. He is equal to the peerless, because he has no equal in the past or in the future. He is supreme, because he is supreme among all sentient beings. He is a great seer because of his ethics, because he has practiced noble conduct for a long time, and because he has comprehended the path as it was realized by the ancient great seers. He is victorious, because he has attained victory over all heretics and [over] the demons of the afflictions. He is a sage, because he is without thoughts of distraction, conceit, and so on, and because he is endowed with the three [qualities of] a sage. He is not led astray, because he is undiminished by any persons—false teachers and so on. He is cleansed, because he has been completely cleansed of all wrongdoing. [60b] He has arrived at the far shore, because he has passed beyond all worldly things. He is a Tathāgata, an arhat, completely awakened, learned and virtuous, well-gone, knower of worlds, an unsurpassed guide for persons to be tamed, teacher of gods and humans, awakened, blessed.[43] He has perfected the supreme dharma; he is omniscient, a master of all, one by whom the dharma is not forgotten, the heart of sentient beings, the finest, one whose mind is untouched by joys and sufferings. He is disciplined, because his sense-doors are guarded and because he is endowed with excellence. He is calm, because he has taken up ethics and because he is endowed with excellence. He is a comfort, because he has entered upon the definite stage (*nges pa'i sa, *niyata(ā)bhūmi*).[44] He has achieved complete nirvāṇa because he has attained awakening. He has removed the thorn, because he has removed the thorn of craving. He trains those who are untrained and calms [those who are restless], as previously discussed. He inspires those in need of inspiration, because he introduces ordinary persons to the results of the stream-enterer and the once-returner. He causes those who have not achieved complete nirvāṇa to do so, because he introduces the results of the nonreturner and the arhat to those who have achieved the first and second results. He has broken the locks; he has crossed the trench; he has traversed the pit; he has abandoned searching; he is noble; he has laid down the banner and dwells in greatness perpetually. So, too, is he an arhat: he has stopped the outflows; he has no afflictions; he has become powerful; his mind and insight are totally liberated. He is a thoroughbred; a great elephant; one who has done the deed; one who has done what is to be done. He has laid down the burden; he has attained his aim. His mind is liberated by correct insight; he has crossed to the far shore of the excellence of all mental faculties; he has completely exhausted entanglements with [saṃsāric] existence. [61a] So, too, has he "abandoned five aspects and acquired six aspects." [This claim is] more extensively [discussed in the passage that runs] "uncommon," down to "one who serves, the supreme person." So, too, [in the passage running] "knower of the dharma" down to "knower of the best among persons, and knower of those who are not the best."

Moreover, he is a renunciate; a brahman; stainless and free from stains; a doctor; a merchant captain; one who sees; the lord of the world; supreme among creatures. Regarding these [epithets]: he is stainless because he is purified of afflictive obstructions; he is free from stains because he has abandoned the obstructions to knowledge. Moreover, he is stainless because he has removed the bonds; he is free from stains because he has conquered the latent tendencies. He is one who sees, due to his overseeing of the world during the six phases of day and night.

So, too, do the characteristics of his body—beautified by the major and minor marks of a great man—manifest as completely pure in all aspects. He is powerful with the ten powers. He is unafraid, due to the four fearlessnesses. He possesses great compassion. His mindfulness is well established in the three foundations of mindfulness; he possesses the three forms of unguardedness; he is endowed with the quality of nonforgetfulness; he has completely conquered all afflicted latent tendencies; and he is a supreme knower of all aspects.[45] Regarding these [epithets], he possesses great compassion because of his attainment and mastery over a long period of three innumerable kalpas; and because he surveys all sentient beings, seeing all aspects of their suffering; and because, having met with all the aspects of the harm done by all sentient beings, he does not turn back [from helping them]; and because he treats all sentient beings as equal [in suffering].

Then, a dharma preacher should distinguish the characteristics of the dharma and briefly expound [them]. First, the phrasing and meaning should be investigated. As discussed previously, when teaching the dharma [61b], one should undertake to expound it to others according to five aspects. Furthermore, the dharma preacher himself should establish his endowment with the ten characteristics proper to teachers of the dharma—i.e., knowing the dharma, its meaning, and so on. Having established this for himself, discourse (*gtam*) and so on may occur among five kinds of audience as stated previously, and one should preach accordingly via eight aspects: in so-called "discourses" (*gtam de dag zer na*), one should employ [speech] that impresses the ear, and one should praise [the] teacher(s) at the outset. In this way, the dharma's possession of five aspects is taught. It is similar to music in bringing great delight to oneself and others, and it encourages practice so as to benefit oneself and others.

8. Rewards of Training

In the same way, one who becomes knowledgeable [in the dharma] obtains five rewards: one comprehends the meaning of a Buddha's teaching with little effort; one engages in discourses that are perfected in all aspects; one brings joy to the continua (*rgyud*) of oneself and others; one encourages many toward supreme joy, virtue, and renunciation; one's renown and fame as a virtuous renunciate spreads among gods and men, and one generates immeasurable merit.

[Section B: A Case Study]

[The case:]

> Monks! You should live with the training as the reward, [with discriminating insight as the highest, with liberation as the essence, and with mindfulness as the dominant principle].[46]

1. The Corpus

The corpus of this [passage] comprises the phrasing and the meaning.

1.1. PHRASING

Regarding that, "Monks! You should live with the training as the reward" comprises twelve syllables, four names, and one phrase. This is the collection of names, phrases, and syllables. The aspect is what is indicated: the basis of the training. The teaching is what is taught by the Tathāgata due to [questioning by] the monks. Speech is a saying spoken by the Tathāgata. These are the six aspects of phrasing. The phrases "discriminating insight as the highest" and so on [62a] should be viewed in the same way.

1.2. MEANING

1.2.1. THE MEANING PERTAINING TO LEVELS

The meaning is as taught in the *Śrāvakabhūmi*, [or one may think of it as encompassing] all five levels. "Training as the reward" references the level of accumulation; "discriminating insight as the highest," the level of application; "liberation as the essence," the levels of seeing, of cultivation, and of completion.

1.2.2. THE MEANING PERTAINING TO DEFINING CHARACTERISTICS

"Training as the reward" has the particular characteristic of ethics; "discriminating insight as the highest" has the particular characteristic of discriminating insight. The particular characteristic includes the corpus, together with its bases, accompaniments, and so on. The general characteristic is that which possesses the intentional object [of] discriminating insight. The particular characteristic of "liberation as the essence" comprises freedom from the afflictions and from the appropriation of bad abodes. The particular characteristic of "mindfulness as the dominant principle" is mindfulness. The meaning pertaining to defining characteristics is [elaborated] like this.

1.2.3. THE MEANING PERTAINING TO MENTAL ACTIVITY

Regarding this, [what is meant by] "training as the reward" is not some mental activity (*yid la byed ba, *manas(i)kāra*), but is elucidated as dependent on mental activity. "Discriminating insight as the highest" should be understood as mental activity comprising devotion and the discriminating awareness of characteristics. "Liberation as the essence" is elucidated as isolation, the collection of joy, the final practice, and the result of the final practice. "Mindfulness as the dominant principle" is the mental activity of analysis (*dpyad pa, *vicāra*). The meaning pertaining to mental activity is [elaborated] like that; one should apply this method also to awareness and so on.

1.2.4. REFERENTIAL MEANING

The reference [here] is to the pure practices that are, collectively, the basis of training with respect to nirvāṇa. Although practices such as appropriately applied encouragement toward correct apprehension—up through the generation of joy—are included here, the pure practices are the main thing. The reference to persons includes persons who are not householders. All persons—those who have weak faculties and so on—should be made joyful; those in the past and the present should be made joyful. At present, one teaches those who have properly taken up ethics. [62b] In the future, they should be encouraged and uplifted. The referential meaning is [elaborated] like that.

1.2.5. THE MEANING PERTAINING TO BENEFIT

Benefit is the cultivation perfected by means of the three trainings.

1.2.6. THE MEANING PERTAINING TO FAULT

When [the three trainings] are not properly undertaken, bad actions are not transformed and renunciation does not become valued.

1.2.7–1.2.8. THE MEANING PERTAINING TO HARM AND THE MEANING PERTAINING TO ANTIDOTE

Harm comprises faulty ethics, ignorance, forgetfulness, and the afflictions. The antidotes to these should be understood to be ethics and so on. Moreover, harm comprises all practices of [i.e., afflicted by] subsidiary affliction. The antidotes to those are the three trainings.

1.2.9–1.2.10 SUMMARY MEANING AND ELABORATED MEANING

That [passage]—"you should live with the training as the reward" up through "mindfulness as the dominant principle"—is a summary, since it is a brief teaching. An elaborated [teaching] should be understood as [a teaching] that unpacks that [summary teaching]. The summary and elaborated meanings [should be understood] along these lines; they are neither more nor less than these.

2. Explication

2.1. TEACHING

The dharma that is explicated in this [passage] is from the twelve-fold Buddhist scriptures. It should be viewed as included in the sūtra division and also the division of prophecies (*lung bstan, *vyākaraṇa*), since its meaning is definitive (*nges pa'i don, *nītārtha*).

2.2. PROMPT

The prompt should be expounded based on the basis. [In this case,] the sūtra was propounded because of the desire to teach the power of the path applicable to all beings. In addition, [it was propounded] so as to correctly teach abiding in training as the reward, as well as the benefits of the perfected three trainings for those whose effort is directed toward the pure practice of discipline, for those mixed up with material things, and for those devoted to those.[47]

Moreover, [it was propounded] so as to correctly teach four topics for monks. Regarding these, "training as the reward" [refers to] those who are monks [merely] in appearance and shape; it causes [them] to turn away from being hypocritical. "Discriminating insight as the highest" counters the aspiration to be a famous monk [who is the subject] of texts and encomia. Via "liberation as the essence" and "mindfulness as the dominant principle," [63a] one begins to grasp correctly what it really means to be a monk. In that way, [a monk] who desires fame and so on is caused to understand what he has heard via individual realization, in order to enable those whose discriminating insight is narrow and those who have not abandoned previous faults to practice correctly and so, in short, to enable them to correctly grasp liberation.

Moreover, [the sūtra is propounded] so that those who are satisfied with lesser [attainments] will undertake to achieve higher and higher [attainments]. "The training as the reward" is said for those who pursue mundane spells (*jig rten rgyang phan pa gsang tshig*) and those who are lazy. "Discriminating insight as the highest" is said for those who practice ethics but lack learning. "Liberation as the essence" is said for those content with mere hearing and reflection. "Mindfulness as the dominant principle" is said for those who become conceited regarding [their level of attainment in] ethics, wisdom, and liberation. The prompt should be expounded by way of such aspects, as appropriate.

2.3. MEANING

2.3.1. SUMMARY MEANING

Here, the summary meaning is taught to be the correct practice and the result [of such practice]. For example: the end of training comprises precisely those three—ethics and so on. Accordingly, by the statement "you should live," correct application as [applied to] four bonds (*rnal 'byor bzhi*, **caturyoga*) is briefly taught.[48] In this way, the phrase "the three trainings of those who live . . ." teaches the result of correct practice. Faith and zeal are the prerequisites for the correct adoption of ethics. At the time of grasping what has been heard, there is effort. Discriminating insight and so on are methods.

2.3.2A. THE MEANING OF PHRASES 1: "TRAINING"

2.3.2A.1. Indicating Synonyms

Here, the meaning of the phrases is [as follows]. Synonyms (*rnam grangs*, **paryāya*) for "training" include "practical application," "practicing as one is taught," "habituation," and "cultivation."

2.3.2A.2. Indicating the Corpus via Distinguishing Characteristics

Practice can be differentiated in terms of ethics—whose distinguishing characteristic is undertaking purity in body, speech, and livelihood—and in terms of forbearance (*bzod pa, kṣānti*). Thus, the term "training" [is used].

2.3.2A.3. Indicating Etymological Derivation

Moreover, it is "training" because one proceeds [in the practice] for the sake of calm. In this and in similar ways, [one should adduce] etymological derivations. [63b] Signs, nature, action, quality, cause, and effect are to be expounded as previously [stated].

2.3.2A.4. Analyzing Into Aspects

2.3.2a.4.1. Analysis of Essential Nature

To begin with, one analyzes essential nature (*ngo bo nyid, *svabhāva*): training as the reward is taught as the sevenfold ethics and the two hundred fifty grounds of training.

2.3.2a.4.2. Analysis of Realm

One analyzes the realms (*khams, *dhātu*): in the desire [realm], one practices the *prātimokṣa* vows; in the form and formless [realms, one practices] the vows pertaining to meditative states and the vow that is uncontaminated and disassociated.

2.3.2a.4.3. Analysis of Time

One analyzes the time (*dus,* kāla*): one should understand the training as the reward as being precisely this way in the past; precisely this way in the future; and precisely this way in the present.

2.3.2a.4.4. Analysis of State

One analyzes the state (*gnas skabs, *avasthā*): training as the reward [as it may concern] the state of the lesser—those persons have entered into training but who are not yet mature [in it]; the state of the middling—those who are maturing; and the state of the great—those who have reached maturity. Having individually investigated [these, one presents] training as the reward [as it may concern] the state of those who are suffering—[i.e.,] those who live according to the holy life yet are unhappy. [Or, one presents it as it may concern] the state of the joyous—those who are happy. [Or, one presents] training as the reward [as it may concern] the state of those who are neither suffering nor joyous—those who are not happy yet are not unhappy. All these [forms of] training as the reward pertain to the state of the virtuous but not to the nonvirtuous or to those whose state is indeterminate.

[One may speak of training as the reward as it pertains to] the state of hearing—[i.e.,] to those who grasp what is heard; and to the state of reflecting—to those who reflect; and to the state of cultivating—to those who practice meditative cultivation.[49] [One may speak of training as the reward as it pertains] solely [to] the state of [those who have obtained] higher ethics—i.e., those who have not obtained higher reflection and higher insight; or to the state of those who have obtained those [i.e, higher reflection and higher insight as well].

In this and similar ways, the analysis of state [is performed].

2.3.2a.4.5. Analysis of Persons

One also analyzes persons. [64a] Here, the intention pertains to the analysis of persons. On the one hand, there are those of dull faculties; on the other, there are those whose faculties are sharp. There are those whose conduct is desirous and so on, and there are those who enjoy equanimity. There are those with few afflictions. These are hearers but are not solitary buddhas or bodhisattvas, since solitary buddhas become awakened by themselves and since bodhisattvas are not taught to live in this [way, with] liberation as the essence. There are those who possess qualities of *parinirvāṇa* [but are not yet awakened]—namely, those who practice, who are undefiled, and who are subject to all or some bonds—they are not [yet] free from bonds. There are those born as humans, but not those born as gods. In this way, the analysis of persons [is conducted].

Summary Remarks on 2.3.2a.4

One should understand "discriminating insight as the highest, liberation as the essence, and mindfulness as the dominant principle" to be appropriately analyzable via these five aspects, in the same manner as "training as the reward."

2.3.2B. THE MEANING OF PHRASES 2: "REWARD"

2.3.2b.1. Indicating Synonyms

The terms "reward," "virtue," "the superior," and "excellence" are synonyms.

2.3.2b.2. Indicating the Corpus via Distinguishing Characteristics

"Having seen the ten rewards": this teaching references bodily benefits, and these are suitable to be praised.

2.3.2B.3. *Indicating Etymological Derivation*

Moreover, they are rewards because they are pursued by those for whom they properly arise, and they are rewards because they are connected with acts of praise.

2.3.2B.4. *Analyzing Into Aspects*

Analysis should be understood as tenfold [as referenced in the following phrases]: "in order to gather together the assembly, and in order that the assembly practice well" and so on.

2.3.2C. THE MEANING OF PHRASES 3: "MONKS"

2.3.2C.1. *Indicating Synonyms*

Regarding that, the terms "monks," "strivers," "renunciates," and "those who are not householders" are synonyms.

2.3.2C.2. *Indicating the Corpus via Distinguishing Characteristics*

[Not discussed explicitly.]

2.3.2C.3. *Indicating Etymological Derivation*

One is a "monk" in order to be separated from color and shape, in order to protect oneself from evil realms of rebirth, and in order to protect those who are nonaggressive.

2.3.2C.4. *Analyzing Into Aspects*

Regarding these, the analysis into aspects should be understood to pertain to the class of royals/warriors and so on, the classes of those who are exalted and those who are inferior, [64b] and the classes of those who are novices with respect to practice , those who are more experienced, and those who are elders.

2.3.2D. THE MEANING OF PHRASES 4: "YOU SHOULD LIVE"

2.3.2D.1. *Indicating Synonyms*

"You should live"—the synonyms here are "you should pass the time," "you should cultivate," and "you should repeatedly practice."

2.3.2D.2. Indicating the Corpus via Distinguishing Characteristics

The corpus of that is nothing other than the training, which has been well explained [previously].

2.3.2D.3. Indicating Etymological Derivation

The etymological derivation: you should live (*viharatha*) passing the time (*adhvagata*) in various (*citra/nānā*) paths of activity (*īryāpatha*).[50]

2.3.2D.4. Analyzing Into Aspects

The analysis should show distinctions between the paths, and the distinctions of abiding during the morning, at midday, in the evening, and at night.

2.3.2E. THE MEANING OF PHRASES 5: "DISCRIMINATING INSIGHT"

2.3.2E.1. Indicating Synonyms

Regarding this, discriminating insight (*shes rab, *prajñā*), gnosis (*ye shes, *jñāna*), seeing (*mthong ba, *darśana*), manifestation (*snang ba, avabhāsa*), and realization (*mngon par rtogs pa, adhigamana*) are synonyms.

2.3.2E.2. Indicating the Corpus via Distinguishing Characteristics

Moreover, they [refer to] a mental quality that analyzes distinguishing characteristics.

2.3.2E.3. Indicating Etymological Derivation

The etymological derivation: it is discriminating insight because it is essentially discriminating (*prabhedana*) and because it is the antidote (*pratipakṣa*) to ignorance (*ajña*). Moreover, it is discriminating insight insofar as it is awareness based on aspects, and it is discriminating insight because it definitively distinguishes the knowledge of those who are learned.

2.3.2E.4. Analyzing Into Aspects

Regarding this, analysis should be applied as stated previously, as appropriate.

2.3.2F. THE MEANING OF PHRASES 6: "LIBERATION"

2.3.2F.1. Indicating Synonyms

"Liberation," "abandonment," "dissociation," "purity," "cessation," "separation from desire," and so on are synonyms.

2.3.2F.2. Indicating the Corpus via Distinguishing Characteristics

The nature [of liberation] is the conquering of negative states and the abandonment of afflictions.

2.3.2F.3. Indicating Etymological Derivation

The etymological derivation: it is "liberation" because one is liberated from various kinds of bonds: desire and so forth. Moreover, it is "liberation" because it is stated by the Blessed One, since it is foundational for the two types of sage.

2.3.2F.4. Analyzing Into Aspects

The analysis: [there is] liberation pertaining to time and occasion, unshakeable [liberation], [liberation of] that which is to be abandoned via seeing, [liberation of] that which is to be abandoned via contemplation, and liberation from the afflictions pertaining to practice in the realms of desire, form, and the formless. In this way, the analysis should be understood in accordance with that which has been previously [stated].

2.3.2G. THE MEANING OF PHRASES 7: "MINDFULNESS"

2.3.2G.1. Indicating Synonyms

Regarding that, "mindfulness," "mental nonforgetfulness," and "discursivity" (*mngon par brjod pa, *abhi + √lap*) are synonyms.[51]

2.3.2G.2. Indicating the Corpus via Distinguishing Characteristics

The nature [of mindfulness] is that it is a quality arisen from the mind.

2.3.2G.3. Indicating Etymological Derivation

The etymological derivation: it is mindfulness (*dran pa, *smṛti*), because it possesses the dharma of recollection [or: because it is the recollection of dharma(s) (*chos rjes su dran pa, *dharmānusmaraṇa*)]. Moreover, [65a] it is mindfulness because, by way of mental practice which one makes habitual, discursivity is prompted.[52]

2.3.2G.4. Analyzing Into Aspects

Analysis of mindfulness: mindfulness should be understood to be sixfold: recollection of the Buddha, the dharma, the community, and so on. It should also be understood according to the divisions of the foundations of mindfulness. [Analysis] should be applied in a more extensive way as stated previously, as appropriate.

2.4. RESPONDING TO OBJECTIONS

If someone were to ask "What is the meaning of 'training as the reward'?," [one should respond:] this is a phrase that teaches seeing and abiding in the rewards of the training in higher ethics. If someone were to ask "What is the meaning of 'discriminating insight as the highest'?," [one should respond:] this is a phrase that teaches the supremacy of the faculty of discriminating insight over all other faculties. If someone were to ask "What is the meaning of 'liberation as the essence'?," [one should respond:] this is a phrase that teaches the abandonment of the afflictions that are to be abandoned via seeing and cultivation. If someone were to ask "What is the meaning of 'mindfulness as the dominant principle'?," [one should respond:] this is a phrase that teaches dissatisfaction with that which is merely lesser and inferior.

[Q:] When the Blessed One taught the three trainings in the proper order in other sūtras, why in this case does he not [here first] speak of the reward of the training in higher reflection and then teach the rewards of higher ethics and higher discriminating insight?

[The answer to this is as follows:] that very teaching, taught in a summary way as discriminating insight arising from hearing and so on, teaches progressive concentration—nonregret and so on—and so teaches the training of higher reflection. From among the five [faculties], the Blessed One also abridged—i.e., summarized—in this way: "[Regarding] the faculty of discriminating insight: a monk who possesses the faculty of discriminating insight should cultivate [the faculties] up through the faculty of concentration; in so doing, based on the faculty of discriminating insight, one becomes endowed [with the other faculties] up to the faculty of concentration." This is how it is stated. Therefore, [65b] in that sūtra, the Blessed One teaches the cause that guides concentration and the cause that guides the abandonment of afflictions. Higher reflection is taught together with the training of higher discriminative insight.

[Q:] When it is said that the cultivation of the three trainings becomes perfected, why is the cultivation of higher reflection not taught?

[A:] The way [this] should be viewed is precisely as stated previously.

[Q:] Why is it said that "you should live with training as the reward," but not said that "you should live with discriminating insight as the reward," or "you should live with liberation as the reward"?

[A:] "Reward" is stated for lesser [beings], in order to enable them also to begin to grasp the enjoyments of those who are subject to the discipline.[53] The ten communal rewards—"for the sake of assembling the community," "for the sake of the community's proper practice," and so on, are clearly taught so that [these beings] will train in pursuit of them.[54]

[Q:] Given that liberation is a quality unsurpassed by any [other], why is it said that "you should live with discriminating insight as the highest," but not said that "you should live with liberation as the highest"?[55]

[A:] "As the highest" is stated for lesser beings, to enable them also to begin to grasp the enjoyments of those who are subject to the discipline, and in order to instruct them in the distinctive uncommon liberation.

[Q:] What is distinctive here?

[A:] The essential point is that permanent liberation [is realized] by means of unsurpassed discriminating insight, which is impermanent.

[Q:] What is it to "live with training as the reward"?

[A:] Among those who possess the basis of training, to live with training as one's reward involves ten forms of reward; a state of ethics definitively and correctly seen; a state of ethics pertaining to teaching; a state of constant practice; and a state of constant application.[56]

[Q:] [Regarding the ten forms of reward:] what is the meaning of the phrases "so that the community assembles" and so on?

[A:] "So that the community assembles" is a phrase offering a teaching in brief. "So that the community practices correctly" [66a] is [a phrase spoken] so that those who desire merit will abandon the extreme of striving. "So that the community lives happily" is [spoken] so that [hearers] will abandon extremes of wearisome striving for their own [personal gains]. "So that the faithless gain faith" is [spoken] so that those who have not [yet] undertaken [practice] will do so. "So that the faithful gain [greater] faith" is [spoken] in order to ripen those who have already undertaken [practice]. "So that persons who injure and disrespect are subjugated" is [spoken] to prompt those whose ethics are faulty to observe [their commitments]. "So that those who feel shame will live happily" is [spoken] so that those who behave ethically will have no regrets. "So that miseries in this life may be controlled" is [spoken] so that [those who are] injured and entangled in the afflictions will be reconciled. "So that the miseries of future lives may be destroyed" is [spoken] in order to clarify abiding in the holy life that depends on vows, and in order that one accord oneself with abandoning negative tendencies. "My holy life brings extensive rewards to many living beings; it has been proclaimed correctly to gods and men, for the sake of establishing it for a long time" is [spoken] to secure the teaching's continuity.

Those ten rewards can be summarized in terms of three [rewards]; and the three can also [be discussed in terms of] the group of ten. [The three are:] states of abiding in which the community is not burdened by afflictions, is in contact with happiness, and undertakes [to practice] for an extended period.

Regarding these [three]: states of abiding in which the community is not burdened by afflictions and is in contact with happiness are indicated via the seven forms of guarding (*rjes su srung ba*, **anurakṣaṇā*): guarding against gain and renown; guarding against torment by fierce asceticism; guarding against the lack of necessities; guarding against mutual harm, guarding against thoughts of remorse; guarding against entanglement in the afflictions; [66b] and guarding against wrongful vows. The latter phrase(s) indicate(s) that the teaching should be undertaken for an extended period.

[Q:] How does one possess definitive ethics?

[A:] By not discarding the basis of training.

[Q:] How does one possess steadfast ethics?[57]

[A:] By not corrupting the basis of training.

[Q:] How does one engage in constant practice?

[A:] By not violating the basis of training.

[Q:] How does one engage in constant application?

[A:] By subsequently restoring [one's vows] in the event that one breaks them.

[Q:] How do those who have correctly taken up the basis of training train [themselves]?

[A:] By guarding the entirety of the training. Having heard the dharma, those endowed with definitive ethics and those endowed with steadfast ethics retire to a solitary place. Basing themselves on higher reflection and higher discriminative insight, they undertake [practice], reflect, consider, and investigate. In dependence on the discriminating insight arising from hearing, reflection, and meditative cultivation, they achieve contact with liberation. That liberation, moreover, is said to be the "essence" because its quality is incomparable and because it is the result of transcendent awareness.

Depending on the production of mindfulness, those yogis [recognize] whether or not they have perfected the component of ethics by the power of mindfulness, whether or not they have properly realized these dharmas by their own discriminating insight, and whether or not they have contacted their own liberation. It is they for whom the training becomes the reward, discriminating insight becomes the highest, and liberation becomes the essence. For this reason, mindfulness is

[also] the dominant principle [for them]. Moreover, mindfulness, in brief, should be viewed as of three kinds: that which depends on the teaching of the dharma, that which depends on personal counsel, and that which depends on one's individual realization regarding what should and should not be done.

[Q]: Given that the Blessed One has spoken of many kinds of ethics—the ethics of householders, the ethics of monks, the ethics of those following the one-day retreat, the ethics of meditation, the ethics of absorption, the ethics pleasing to noble ones and so on—[67a] which forms of ethics are those on the basis of which one is said to "live with training as the reward"?

[A:] Generally, on the basis of the ethics of monks.

[Q:] Given that the Blessed One has also said that discriminating insight is of various kinds—based on hearing, based on reflection, based on meditative cultivation, and so on—which forms of discriminating insight are those on the basis of which one is said to "live with discriminating insight as the highest"?

[A:] The three forms together.

[Q:] Given that the Blessed One has also said that liberation is of many forms—liberation pertaining to the worldly, the transcendent, [the paths of] learning and no more learning, the fluctuating and the nonfluctuating, and so on—which forms of liberation are those on the basis of which one is said to "live with liberation as the essence"?

[A:] The transcendent and the nonfluctuating.

[Q:] The Blessed One has also said that mindfulness is of many forms—one should establish mindfulness of the body, of states, of feelings, of mind, of dharmas, and, having done so, one should develop [it] for a long time. And based on what has been stated [previously], one should be mindful of one's development, just as one should [also] be mindful of teachings that are taught; and mindful of personal counsels; and mindful of what should and should not be done. And there is the mindfulness of a Buddha and so on as well. Given this, which forms of mindfulness are those on the basis of which "mindfulness as the dominant principle" is said?

[A:] In general, the individual realization of what should and should not be done.

2.5. CONNECTION

Here, the connection is as follows: in dependence on the ethics of a monk, one is caused to grasp what has been heard, and correct mental activity is generated. For one endowed with ethics, lack of regret occurs. Progressively, by way of this method—[involving] lack of regret and so on—discriminating insight is acquired, [and] concentration arises with respect to correct mental activity. These are, accordingly, the achievements of higher reflection. This is the connection pertaining to perfection, since one is perfected more and more [by way of it]. Training as the reward is for the purpose of discriminating insight as the highest, and [67b] discriminating insight as the highest is for the purpose of liberation as the essence.

How is there training as the reward [and so on] up through liberation as the essence? It has been said, "with mindfulness as the dominant principle"—that is the connection that is established. In the same way, "one who abides in the three trainings brings them to completion [via] cultivation"—that is the connection that is established.

3. The Dharma Preacher

[Not discussed explicitly.]

4. Exposition

[Not discussed explicitly.]

5. Assembly

[Not discussed explicitly.]

6. Listening

Among hearers, a teacher engages in teaching the establishment of what is to be done and what is not to be done. Moreover, he is a teacher because he engages in teaching in order to quell the suffering of many beings. Also, he is a teacher because of manifesting this [teaching] in order to revive those non-Buddhists (*mu stegs pa*, **tīrthika*) who are as good as dead. They are "hearers" because they listen and cause those other than themselves to propound.

[Q:] How do hearers in particular undertake practice?

[A:] Hearers are those who, becoming sons of the Blessed One, undertake practice as trainees. The dharma should be viewed to be "the collection of names, phrases, and syllables." The basis of training is taught to be the five root downfalls.

7. *Brief and Extensive Praise of Buddhas*

[A Buddha is said to be] merciful, because of living for a long time with measureless benevolence, etc., toward sentient beings. [He is] compassionate, because he dispels many qualities of suffering. He is one who aims at the goal, because he attains many felicitous qualities. He is one who aims at benefit, because he establishes many kinds of virtuous qualities. He is said to be one who brings about compassion, because he dispels many kinds of evil, nonvirtuous qualities. The holy life is said to benefit many beings, because [it benefits] lineages and groups such as royals/warriors and so on. It is "extensive" because these lineages of sentient beings undertake the practice, relying on those who have previously become proficient [in it]. "Gods down through men": this is because of the existence of power in these very [beings]; it is not that the compassion of the Blessed One is partial [to them]. "Instructs correctly"—[i.e., the instruction pertains to] things just as they are, and to the extent that they are. "A teacher of dharma"—[i.e., a teacher of] the whole of scripture in its twelve categories. [68a] Having memorized and studied it, he will bear it in mind. And the phrase "engage in advice" [refers to an action performed after] having gone to a solitary place. "To be realized definitively" [refers to] the dharma.

8. *Rewards of Training*

"For the sake of your reward" [refers to] that which concerns higher reflection. "For the sake of happiness" [refers to] those who experience sorrow and unhappiness through their own practices. "For the sake of reward and happiness" [refers to] practices of higher reflection and higher discriminating insight among those free from desire. It is a reward because it is virtuous; it is happiness because it brings benefit.

Moreover, "for the sake of [your] reward" is [a phrase] in which the Blessed One praises pure, virtuous qualities. "For the sake of happiness" references the granting of food endowed with excellent flavor [and] robes worth 100,000 *karṣapana* [coins]. "For the sake of reward and happiness" references the possession of the three forms of training.

"The Tathāgata has properly realized these dharmas by means of discriminating insight pertaining to this or that." [This refers to] those [dharmas] which are for the sake of reward and for the sake of happiness in the context of training for higher ethics, for higher reflection, and for higher discriminating insight.

Via these two causes, one is properly realized: via familiarization (*goms pa*, **abhyāsa*) over a long period and via unmistaken realization. "Liberated in this or that respect, one contacts the ultimate": this stems from higher reflection and higher discriminating insight. Regarding that, one contacts the ultimate via two causes: one is perfected (*mthar thug 'gro ba*, **niṣṭhāgata*), and one arrives at nonretrogression, due to the irreversibility [of one's attainment].

"[Their] own ethics unperfected": because their ethics is partial, or because they rely on ethics, but do not perfect the ethics associated with the level of equanimity. "Those dharmas that are not properly realized by oneself"—the specific characteristics [in this case should be understood] as being of two kinds, as stated previously. "They do not contact the ultimate": [again,] two kinds, [68b] as stated previously. "Accordingly, what I have said should be specifically expounded." [That is,] what is stated in the manner of a brief teaching should be understood as being a summary that [can be further] analyzed.

9. Appendix: An Alternative Account

Moreover, explication of the sūtras should proceed by way of these six aspects: knowledge of subjects (*dngos po yongs su shes pa*); abandoning faulty conduct, afflictions, and secondary afflictions; correctly adopting good conduct; the awareness [of suffering] according to aspects—sickness and so on; the realization of what has been learned; and the result of that together with the realization of that result by oneself and others.

In this way, via these aspects and in accordance with those previously established, explication of the sūtras should be undertaken.

Regarding this [alternative list]: "subjects" include the aggregates, the elements, the sense-fields, dependent arising, mindful abidings, complete abandonment, and so on. "The result of that" is the loss of faults and desire—[i.e.,] liberation, complete liberation. "The realization of the result of that by oneself and others" is the cessation of one's own birth. And so on.

That is the **Vivaraṇasaṃgrahaṇī*. The **Vivaraṇasaṃgrahaṇī* section of the *Yogācārabhūmi* is finished.

Notes

Introduction

1. Sharf 2002:16.

2. On cross-cultural application of the terms "scholastic" and "scholasticism," see Cabezón 1998.

3. *Dīgha Nikāya* (hereafter DN) 1, i.4–5; translation modified from Walshe 1995:68–69.

4. Cf. *Mānavadharmaśāstra* 12.6, and the six faults of brahmanical speech enumerated by Devala, cited in Aparārka's commentary to *Yājñavalkyasmṛti* 1.132 (Ganapati 1982:1.174): "harsh speech, abuse, rumor-mongering, falsehood, useless chatter, [and speech that is] cruel" (*parusavacanam apavādaḥ paiśunyam anṛtaṃ vṛthālāpo niṣṭhuram iti*). A word on the term "āgama" is perhaps in order. Throughout this study, I will use the terms āgama and āgamic to refer to the corpus of sūtra material held largely in common among four classes of texts (nikāya) of the Pali *Suttapiṭaka* (*Dīgha*, *Majjhima* (hereafter MN), *Saṃyutta* (hereafter SN), and *Aṅguttara* (hereafter AN) and their corresponding Sanskritic āgamas (*Dīrgha*, *Madhyama*, *Saṃyukta*, and *Ekottara*). As used here, the term "āgama" does not exhaust any single Buddhist's (or Buddhist school's) assessment of what should count as—and possess the authority of—the speech of a Buddha. Rather, it specifies a range of texts that monastic Buddhists would likely have agreed upon as constituting something like a common denominator, regardless of sectarian affiliation. For additional discussion of these points, see chapter 1.

5. The use of masculine pronouns to refer to Buddhas other than Gotama in this book is one of convenience and is intended to reflect the traditional idea that Buddhas are paradigmatically male. It should not be read as implying my assent to this idea.

6. DN 2, i.63–64. On the *Sāmaññaphalasutta*, see Bodhi 1989; Meisig 1987.

7. This emphasis is not, however, universal; some texts aver that awakened beings do not speak at all. In Buddhist sūtras and śāstras, we can discern two broad forms of the view that Buddhas do not speak. One form turns on a point about entities tout court. Consider, for example, verse 25.24 of Nāgārjuna's *Mūlamadhyamakakārikā*:

sarvopalambhopaśamaḥ prapañcopaśamaḥ śivaḥ /
na kvacid kasyacit kaścid dharmo buddhena deśitaḥ /
(de Jong 1977:40)

"Bliss [is] the quelling of all objectification, the quelling of vain thinking;
The Buddha never taught the dharma anywhere to anyone."

The latter half of this verse should be read in the context of Nāgārjuna's overarching argument in the *Mūlamadhyamakakārikā*. Here, as elsewhere in his text, Nāgārjuna wishes to deny a particular understanding of the Buddha's teaching and what it may be held to involve. His point is that such teaching may (wrongly) be seen to involve the representation, propagation, or both of substantially existent entities (views, words, sentences, and so on). We may be tempted, Nāgārjuna insists, to understand such entities as items radically distinct from the nexus of conditions that serve to bring them into being. But we should resist this temptation; the *Mūlamadhyamakakārikā* is dedicated to arguing that the notion of any such isolable, substantially existent entity is incoherent. Instead, we should understand all phenomena as dependent arising (*pratītyasamutpāda*). A properly contextualized reading of *Mūlamadhyamakakārikā* 25.24 thus tells us that if the Buddha's teaching is held to involve entities that are not dependently arisen, then the teaching did not occur (for, according to Nāgārjuna, it *cannot* have occurred). This position need not count against the claims made in the present work; my claims here do not require the existence of such hypostatized entities.

A second form of the objection turns on a point about Buddhas and the nature of their enlightened activity. In the *Laṅkāvatārasūtra*, for example, we read:

yāṃ ca rātriṃ tathāgato 'bhisaṃbuddho yāṃ ca rātriṃ parinirvāsyati, atrāntare ekam apy akṣaraṃ tathāgatena nodāhṛtam, na pravyāhariṣyati avacanaṃ buddhavacanam iti
(Vaidya 1963:58)

Between the night upon which the Tathāgata became supremely awakened and the night upon which he entered into *parinirvāṇa*, the Tathāgata uttered not even one syllable; nor will he discourse [in the future]. The speech of a Buddha (*buddhavacana*) is nonspeech (*avacana*).

This passage is a modification of a stock description found in āgamic texts concerning the truth of a Buddha's speech (on which, see chapter 1). The *Laṅkāvatārasūtra* immediately goes on to explain that the speech of a Buddha is properly characterized as nonspeech due to issuing from (or referring to) the nondiscursive realization that Buddhas achieve. Interestingly, however, the *Laṅkāvatārasūtra* attributes the passage to the Blessed One himself: the very being who informs us that Buddhas do not speak is himself a Buddha. Nowhere, then, does the text deny that a Tathāgata at least *appears* to speak. For further discussion of a Buddha's "nonspeech," see D'Amato 2009; Lugli 2010.

8. Bagchi 1967–1970:1.154: "sa ced aham āryayā vācā dharmaṃ deśayeyaṃ dvau cājñasyato dvau nājñāsyataḥ / sa ced dasyuvācā deśayeyam evam api dvau cājñasyato dvau nājñāsyataḥ / yat tv ahaṃ dvayor āryayā vācā dharmaṃ desayeyam / dvayor api dasyuvācā iti."

9. Cf. Vin ii.139, where Gotama permits monks each to "learn the speech of the Buddha by way of [his] own language" (*sakāya niruttiyā buddhavacanaṃ pariyāpunitun'ti*). For a summary discussion, see Brough 1980.

10. Cf. Caillat 1984; Heirman 2009.

11. Many of these commentaries are attributed to seminal figures in Indian Buddhism (e.g., Nāgārjuna, Asaṅga, Vasubandhu, Dignāga, Śāntideva, Haribhadra, Kamalaśīla, and Atiśa). Several of these attributions are probably spurious, but further study is required to determine precisely which are incorrect. For more extensive discussion, see Schoening 1995:15–47.

12. Dundas 1996:75. Recourse to the commentary as a favored mode of textual transmission and pedagogy is evinced in texts as early as the *Bṛhadāraṇyaka upaniṣad* (e.g., 1.3.28, 1.5.1–3, 2.2.3). See Pollock 1985, 1989a, and 1989b for discussion of śāstric textual protocols. On the rhetoric of commentary, see Bronkhorst 2006; Dreyfus 2003:183–186; Griffiths 1999:77–97; Preisendanz 2008. For remarks pertaining specifically to Indian Buddhist commentarial texts, see Eckel 1987a; Griffiths 1999:109–147; Schoening 1995:15–46, 1996.

13. This seems to have held true through at least the end of the eleventh century. The final Indian Buddhist sūtra commentaries preserved in the Tibetan Buddhist canon date from this period; one of the very last is the *Aṣṭasāh asrikāprajñāpāramitāvṛttimarmakaumudī* (Derge [hereafter D] 3805), attributed to Abhayākaragupta.

14. On this period of transmission, see Kapstein 2000 and sources cited therein. See also Kapstein and Dotson 2007; Walter 2009. The window granted by the extant imperial-period catalogues is partially obscured, insofar as they likely misrepresent the corpus of completed tantric translations. On this issue, see Herrmann-Pfandt 2002:143–144.

15. D 4364. The exhaustive study of Herrmann-Pfandt 2008 updates Lalou 1953. For more information on this text and the Tibetan historical accounts regarding it, see Herrmann-Pfandt 2002, 2008:11–83; Martin 1996:503; Schoening 1995:17–19; Tucci 1958:46–48 (n. 1); Vostrikov 1970:205–206. The other extant textual catalogue—the *Dkar chag 'phang thang (ka) ma*—has only recently come to light; an edition was published in 2003. Halkias 2004 provides a detailed survey of its contents. On its date, see Halkias 2004:51–54; Herrmann-Pfandt 2008:xxiv–xxvi.

16. Although the Derge and Peking (hereafter P) catalogues agree on the form *ldan dkar*, two alternate forms—*lhan dkar* and *lhan kar*—appear in the Dunhuang documents (Pelliot Tibetain 1085 and 1088, respectively). The text was probably composed shortly after the turn of the ninth century—perhaps in 800, 812, or 824 C.E. Cf. Herrmann-Pfandt 2008:xviii–xxii; Tucci 1958.

17. Herrmann-Pfandt 2008. Lalou 1953 largely follows the same structure.

18. Although it is obviously fallacious to presume that the total length of texts included under one of the categories enumerated in the *Catalogue* directly indexes the relative level of importance afforded to the textual category itself (or any text therein), there is little reason to doubt that learned Buddhists of this period held these three sorts of text in very high regard.

19. Such influences have long been acknowledged as occurring in Buddhist philosophical literature. On this point, see Dreyfus 1997a, 1997b; Dunne 2004:1–13; McCrea and Patil 2006.

20. In what follows, I will devote less attention to the specific lexical and syntactic features that characterize scholastic Sanskrit (on which, see Tubb and Boose 2007) than I will to a range of assumptions regarding exegetical practice and the ways that it should rightly be undertaken.

21. The paper, originally published in *History of Religions* 31, is reprinted in Schopen 1997a:1–22. The reprint will be cited in what follows.

22. Schopen 1997a:1.

23. Ibid.:13.

24. Mills 2003:xvi.

25. Ibid.

26. On this point, see Fussman 1980.

27. Bloch 1950:164–165; Sircar 1967:73.

28. Cf. in this regard Schopen's discussion of Buddhist presuppositions regarding the doctrine of karma and giving as attested in the inscriptions of Bhārhut and Sāñcī (Schopen 1997a:5–7). Schopen is right to note that "it has never been established that a strict doctrine of retribution of acts was ever actually recognized outside of texts." However, the textual story may be somewhat more complex than this comment suggests, since ideas that run counter to a strict doctrine of retribution of acts are occasionally manifested in texts as well (cf. verses 7–8 of the *Tirokuḍḍasutta* in the Pali *Khuddakapāṭha*).

29. Schopen 1997a:14.

30. This point is further discussed in chapter 1.

31. See Sastri 1929–1930. Cf. also the inscriptional evidence pertaining to preachers at Bhārhut and Sāñcī, discussed in chapter 2.

32. This is not to gainsay the valuable discussion of so-called Protestant Buddhism in Gombrich and Obeyesekere 1988; in this work, the phrase is used to describe a rather different phenomenon.

1. Models of Speaking

1. There are two translations of this work into English: Li 2000 and Takakusu 1966. Cf. also Chavannes 1894; Fujishima 1888. Yijing's commentary is one of a pair of extant seventh-century travelogues composed by Chinese pilgrims; the other is that of Xuanzang (Li 1996; Beal 1969; see also Li 1995). These records afford us invaluable, although undoubtedly limited, accounts of Indian Buddhist institutions in the seventh century.

2. Both texts are known to the tradition under multiple titles, and their authorship has also been the subject of debate. The transliterated title *Śatapañcāśatka* is preserved in the Tibetan translation, although Sāṃkṛtyāyana relates that the colophon of the Nepalese manuscript reads *Adhyarddhaśataka*. D. R. S. Bailey has argued for the alternative titles *Prasādapratibhā* or *Prasādapratibhodbhāva*. The Tibetan translation of the *Śatapañcāśatka* attributes it to Aśvaghoṣa, whereas the colophon of the extant Sanskrit manuscript attributes the work to Mātṛceṭa (as does Yijing). The *Catuḥśataka* is also known under the title *Varṇārhavarṇastotra* (Hymn in praise of the praiseworthy). On this work, see Bailey 1950, 1951a; Hartmann 1987.

The portion of the *Śatapañcāśatka* discussed in this chapter has been preserved in manuscript fragments found in Eastern Turkestan, on which see Hoernle 1916:58–70; La Vallée Poussin 1911. For the translation here, I have used the romanized Sanskrit edited by Bailey (1951b). The edition is printed alongside Tibetan and Chinese translations of the text, and it incorporates a commentary attributed to Dga' byed snyan pa (*Nandipriya/*Rāmapriya/*Nandapriya). The Tibetan canon also preserves an elaboration on the text of the *Śatapañcāśatka*, attributed to Dignāga, which interweaves new verses with Mātṛceṭa's own. Titled *Miśrakastotra*, it has received scant scholarly attention; the Tibetan of the text is included as an appendix to Bailey 1951b.

3. Translation slightly modified from Li 2000:140–142; cf. Takakusu 1966:156–158. On Mātṛceṭa, see Bailey 1951b:1–27; Chattopadhyaya 1980:130–136; Hartmann 1987:12–22; Obermiller 1932:136; Warder 1974:235–243.

4. On these points, see Dreyfus 2003:93–97.

5. Aspects discussed in the *Śatapañcāśatka* include a Buddha's attainment of six perfections, his uniqueness, his deeds, his form, his compassion, his speech, his teaching, his vow, the adaptability of his path, his hardships, his skill, and his discharge of debt to living creatures. Aspects discussed in the *Catuḥśataka* include the impossibility of doing justice to all that a Buddha represents; a Buddha's consecration of fools; his omniscience, powers, and forms of fearlessness; his purity of speech, absence of disputation, accord with brahmanical norms, beneficence, and boundless generosity; the perfection of his physical attributes, his large tongue, and his ability to awaken distress toward saṃsāric existence.

6. The compound *arthasiddhyā* fails to specify the identity of the being whose aims are accomplished; the passage may be taken to refer to the Buddha, to his utterances, to his audience, or to sentient beings more broadly. In opting to treat the term *artha* as plural, I have followed the commentary, which specifies that two aims are referenced here: (rebirth in) a higher realm (*mtho ris*, **svarga*) and liberation (*thar pa*, **mokṣa*).

7. "When pondered" follows the Tibetan *rnam brtags na* (pointing to an underlying Sanskrit **vimarśe*). The extant Sanskrit reads *vimarde* ("when crushed"). Bailey opines that the latter is "apparently a metaphor borrowed from the compounding of medicines" (1951b:165); his translation ("when pounded down [in the mind]") attempts to bridge the senses of the Sanskrit and Tibetan.

8. Bailey 1951b:84–95: supadāni mahārthāni tathyāni madhurāṇi ca / gūḍottānobhayārthāni samāsavyāsavanti ca / kasya na syād upaśrutya vākyāny evaṃvidhāni te / tvayi pratihatasyāpi sarvajña iti niścayaḥ / prāyeṇa madhuraṃ

sarvam agatyā kiṃcid anyathā / vākyaṃ tavārthasiddhyā tu sarvam eva subhāṣitaṃ / yac chlakṣṇaṃ yac ca paruṣaṃ yad vā tadubhayānvitaṃ / sarvam evaikarasatāṃ vimarde yāti te vacaḥ / aho supariśuddhānāṃ karmaṇāṃ naipuṇaṃ param / yair idaṃ vākyaratnānāṃ īdṛśaṃ bhājanaṃ kṛtaṃ / asmād dhi netrasubhagād idaṃ śrutimanoharaṃ / mukhāt kṣarati te vākyaṃ candrād dravam ivāmṛtaṃ / rāgareṇuṃ praśamayad vākyaṃ te jaladāyate / vainateyāyate dveṣabhujaṅgoddharaṇaṃ prati / divākarāyate bhūyo 'py ajñānatimiraṃ nudat / śakrāyudhāyate mānagirīn abhividārayat / dṛṣṭārthatvād avitatham niṣkleśatvād anākulam / gamakaṃ suprayuktatvāt trikalyāṇaṃ hi te vacaḥ / manāṃsi tāvac chrotṝṇāṃ haranty ādau vacāṃsi te / tato vimṛśyamāṇāni rajāṃsi ca tamāṃsi ca / āśvāsanaṃ vyasaninām trāsanaṃ ca pramādinām / saṃvejanaṃ ca sukhināṃ yogavāhi vacas tava / viduṣāṃ prītijananaṃ madhyānāṃ buddhivardhanaṃ / timiraghnaṃ ca mandānāṃ sārvajanyam idam vacaḥ / apakarṣati dṛṣṭibhyo nirvāṇam upakarṣati / doṣān niṣkarṣati guṇān vākyaṃ te 'bhipravarṣati / sarvat rāvyāhatā buddhiḥ sarvatropasthitā smṛtiḥ / avandhyaṃ tena sarvatra sarvam vyākaraṇaṃ tava / yan nādeśe na cākāle naivāpātre pravartase / vīryaṃ samyag ivārabdhaṃ tenāmoghaṃ vacas tava.

9. The Sanskrit of this portion of the *Catuḥśataka*, where it is extant, is fragmentary. I have relied chiefly on the Tibetan translation (available in Hartmann 1987), checking it against the Sanskrit of Hartmann's edition where possible.

10. This follows the commentary's gloss of *ro gcig pa nyid* as *thar pa gcig gi mtha'*. The attributes that Mātṛceṭa enumerates are representative but do not by any means exhaust the qualities that the authors of Buddhist śāstras have characterized as the speech of a Buddha. Cf. the sixty-fold list enumerated by Asaṅga (*Mahāyānasūtrālaṃkāra* 12.9 [Lévi 1907:79–80]) and Vasubandhu (*Vyākhyāyukti*, folios 118b3–119a2). Although each of these authors references his source text for the list somewhat differently (Asaṅga citing the *Guhyakādhipatinirdeśa*, Vasubandhu the *Tathāgataguhya*), both citations seem to refer to the same text: the *Tathāgatācintyaguhyanirdeśa* (D 47). However, the list offered in the extant editions of the *Tathāgatācintyaguhyanirdeśa* (at D, dkon brtsegs *ka*, 133a6–b6) diverges slightly from the list cited by Asaṅga and Vasubandhu. Cf. also *Mahāvyutpatti* 444–504.

11. Classical sources discussing the "single taste" of the Buddhist dharma—or the liberation to which it leads—are numerous. Perhaps the best-known is found in *Cullavagga* 9.1.4 (a passage repeated in the *Aṅguttaranikāya*, and one that echoes a metaphor deployed also in non-Buddhist contexts [e.g., *Chāndogya upaniṣad* 6.13]).

12. On the use of simile and imagery in Buddhist texts, see Collins 1982:165–176, 1998:213–233; Rhys-Davids 1907–1908. On simile as discussed in Sanskrit literary criticism, see Gerow 1977.

13. See Enomoto, Hartmann, and Matsumura 1989 and sources cited therein; Lamotte 1988a:152–164.

14. As Lamotte notes, "The number of pericopes is not the same: some are added, others deleted, and yet others re-located" (1988a:156). For a detailed comparison of the contents of selected Pali suttas (sūtras) with āgamic material, see Akanuma 1958; Anālayo 2006, 2008; Anesaki 1908; Bingenheimer 2008, 2009; Chou 1991.

15. Lamotte 1988a:156.

16. Unless otherwise noted, all passages cited herein are paralleled by Chinese āgamic texts, as reported by www.suttacentral.net.

17. Cf. Schopen 1989a. These texts were sometimes labeled *vaipulya*; on this category, see Skilling 1997a:31–42.

18. This is, of course, a very slippery slope—but the advantages of attempting to stand on it seem to me to outweigh the advantages of playing it safe.

19. On this distinction, see the contributions of Houben and Bronkhorst to Auroux et al. 2000–2001.

20. "So dhammaṃ deseti ādikalyāṇaṃ majjhekalyāṇaṃ pariyosānakalyāṇaṃ sātthaṃ sabyañjanaṃ kevalaparipuṇṇaṃ parisuddhaṃ brahmacariyaṃ pakāseti." The corresponding Sanskrit is preserved in a number of Mahāyāna sūtras, among them the *Samādhirājasūtra* (Vaidya 1961a), *Lalitavistara* (Vaidya 1958), and *Rāṣṭrapāla paripṛccha* (Finot 1901:2). A recitational divergence in this passage is noted by Vasubandhu in the opening pages of the *Vyākhyāyukti* (see appendix A).

21. On this sense of *vyañjana*, see Edgerton 1953:2.514.

22. Cf. MN 22, i.133–134, 70, i.479–480.

23. Translation modified from Walshe 1995:432ff. DN 29, iii.128.

24. On Buddhist accounts of the decline of the dharma, see Nattier 1991.

25. DN 29, iii.122–126. Deference to the learned is a theme that arises also in Mahāyāna texts; a representative passage from the *Pratyutpannabuddhasaṃmukhāv asthitasamādhisūtra* tells us that bodhisattvas "should be respectful and reverent . . . enthusiastic about doing honor to teachers and preceptors" (translation Harrison 1990:81).

26. Trans. Li 1996:57–58. Cf. Beal 1969:1.80–81.

27. Trans. Li 1996:58. Cf. Beal 1969:1.81.

28. This point also applies to uses of Xuanzang's text, though I am presuming that it applies to a lesser degree.

29. Cf. Edgerton 1953:1.1–2. On the views of the Sanskrit grammarians, see Auroux et al. 2000–2001 (the contributions of Cardona, Houben, and Bronkhorst); Cardona 1990; Coward and Raja 1990; Staal 1972.

30. The esteem accorded knowledge of Sanskrit appears to have been accorded at times to knowledge of Magadhī. On this point, see Granoff 1991.

31. Li 2000:145–155. Cf. Takakusu 1966:169–180. Takakusu's translation of this section has been reprinted, with helpful annotations, in Staal 1972:11–17. That a screening process for applicants was in place at Nālandā is clear from Xuanzang's account of the site. See Li 1996:283; Beal 1969:2.170–171.

32. It is possible that the monks of Nālandā did not need to venture outside the monastic gates to encounter the representatives of brahmanical tradition against whom they debated. Iconographic and inscriptional evidence from the site suggests that such people may well have been residents at the monastery: in addition to the numerous stone reliefs of non-Buddhist deities found at the site, the Shahpur stone inscription of Ādityasena refers to Nālandā not as a *mahavihara*, but as a *mahāgrahāra*—a term traditionally used to denote a land grant to brahmans. On this point, see Sastri 1986:83.

33. Trans. Li 2000:149. Cf. Takakusu 1966:177.

34. Trans. Li 2000:150. Cf. Takakusu 1966:178.

35. The promotion of scholars trained at prestigious monastic complexes such as Nālandā likely continued well beyond the seventh century. For a summary account of Pāla-era patronage at Nālandā, see Huntington 1984:108–109. See also the inscriptional material collected in Sastri 1986.

36. Lamotte 1976a:12 charts the occurrence of this passage and its Mahāyāna variants through the sūtra literature. The citation here is taken from the *Pāsādikasutta* (translation Walshe 1995:436). DN 29, iii.135.

37. Trans. Ñāṇamoli and Bodhi 1995:635. MN 77, ii.9.

38. Cf. MN 114, iii.47–49.

39. For further discussion of this point, see Nance (forthcoming).

40. AN 4.4.4.3; translation modified from Woodward 2006:179–180.

41. Jha 1999:1.378: "satyam brūyāt priyaṃ brūyān na brūyāt satyam apriyam / priyaṃ ca nānṛtaṃ brūyād eṣa dharma sanātana." Cf. Nāgārjuna, *Suhṛllekha*, verse 18: "The victor declared that the words of people who speak in three ways—pleasingly, truthfully, and wrongly—are [respectively] like honey, flowers, and excrement. The last should be abandoned." D, spring yig *nge*, 41b2–3: "rgyal bas snying la 'bab dang bden pa dang / log par smra ldan skyes bu rnams kyi [Golden (hereafter G) and Narthang (hereafter N) here read *kyis*] ni / sbrang rtsi me tog mi gtsang lta bu'i tshig / rnam gsum bka' stsal de las tha ma spang [G, N *spangs*]."

42. The ninth/tenth-century commentator Medhātithi, commenting on this passage in his *Manubhāṣya*, offers amusing examples of agreeable and disagreeable utterances (Jha 1999:1.378). An utterance that is agreeable is, e.g., "Brahman, a son is born to you!" (*brāhmaṇa putras te jāta*). A disagreeable utterance—one that should not be spoken even if true—is, e.g., "Brahman, your maiden daughter is pregnant!" (*brāhmaṇa kanyā te garbhiṇī*).

43. Cf. the discussion of truth (*bhūta/taccha*) and benefit (*atthasaṃhita*) pertaining to covert speech (*rahovāda*) at MN 139, iii.234.

44. Translation modified from Ñāṇamoli and Bodhi 1995:499–500. MN 58, i.394–395. Cf. the comparable passage in the Mahāyāna *Mahāparinirvāṇasūtra* (D, mdo sde *nya*, 257b1–4).

45. In this regard, the passage parallels the account of proper brahmanical speech given in the *Yājñavalkyasmṛti* (Ganapati 1982:106), in which we are told that what is wrong (*anṛtam*), disagreeable (*apriyam*), and unbeneficial (*ahitam*) should not be uttered. Such parallels between the *Yājñavalkyasmṛti* and Buddhist literature are suggestive but have yet to be extensively explored by modern scholarship. For a pioneering contribution, see Schopen 1994.

46. Here, the āgamic account differs markedly from the view—attributed to Asaṅga/Maitreya (c. fourth century)—according to which speech may be untrue and yet benefit its hearers, if it is spoken by a bodhisattva with proper intent (cf. Dutt 1966:114–115; Tatz 1986). A similar position is advocated in a passage from the *Tathāgataguhyakośasūtra* cited by Bhāviveka in the fourth chapter of the *Tarkajvāla* (see Eckel 2008:144, 332–333). For further discussion of these points, see Nance (forthcoming).

47. Davidson 1990:294. This idea—which is found in Pali texts as well (cf. SN 5.12.4.1)—is exploited in arguments mounted in the fourth chapter of Bhāviveka's *Tarkajvāla* (Eckel 2008:148ff.) and in Vasubandhu's *Vyākhyāyukti* in support of the

claim that Mahāyāna teachings contain the speech of a Buddha. On the latter, see Cabezón 1992.

48. Cf. DN 3, i.105–106ff., 4, i.114ff., 5, i.132, 14, ii.16ff., 30, iii.143; MN 91, ii.136–137, 95, ii.167. Several Mahāyāna sūtras also mention the thirty-two marks, although not all enumerate the list in its entirety. Among them we may count the *Lalitavistara*, *Vajracchedikā*, *Vimalakīrtinirdeśa*, *Saṃdhinirmocana*, and *Saddharmapuṇḍarīka*. For additional sources and discussion, see Burnouf 1925:2.553–583; Griffiths 1994:97–101; Kawara 1972:18–19, 53–55; Lamotte 1981a:271–281; Lopez 2005:13–36; Powers 2009:12–19, 235–237.

49. Cf. *Bodhisattvabhūmi* (Dutt 1966:259–260, cited in Griffiths 1994:215).

50. Translation modified from Walshe 1995:206. DN 14, ii.20. See also DN 30, iii.174.

51. Translation modified from Walshe 1995:108. The response here is a stock one, found in various texts—e.g., DN 2, i.85.

52. We know little about this figure, apart from the fact that he lived during the late first millennium C.E. and was well read in the *jātaka* and *avadāna* literature, from which he quotes liberally. See Bailey 1951b:23–25; Chattopadhyaya 1980:148. For the relevant section of *Nandipriya's commentary, see Bailey 1951b:85.

53. DN 15, ii.55. Translation modified from Walshe 1995:223. Cf. SN 2.1.6.10.

54. DN 34, iii.285. Translation modified from Walshe 1995:517. Cf. MN 33, i.223.

55. See, for example, AN 2.1.2.4 and 3.1.4.3.

56. See MN 135, iii.203, 18, i.110, 133, iii.193–194, 138, iii.223.

57. Cf. AN 1.14.1.10. Mahākaccāna is credited by the Theravādin tradition with the authorship of the *Nettipakaraṇa*, on which, see Bond 1980, 1988; Ñāṇamoli 1962:7–64.

58. Translation slightly modified from Ñāṇamoli and Bodhi 1995:1078–1079. MN 138, iii. 229.

59. See SN 2.1.3.4, 2.1.4.1, 2.1.4.2, 4.1.4.4.6, 4.3.2.5, 4.2.3.8, 4.8.10. The implications of this will be explored more fully in the next chapter.

60. Recent scholarship on the Mūlasarvāstivāda *Vinayavastu* has been dominated by the numerous and pioneering studies of Gregory Schopen (see, for example, 1994, 1996, 1997a, 1997b, 1998, 2004, 2005, 2008). See also the contributions of Chung, Hüsken, Matsuda, and Vogel to Kieffer-Pülz and Hartmann 1997; Panglung 1981; Silk 2008; Clarke 2009a, 2009b.

61. On this text, see Prebish 1975. The Sanskrit text of the Mūlasarvāstivāda *Prātimokṣasūtra* is extant but incomplete; it was found among the Gilgit manuscripts recovered in 1931 (cf. Chandra 1960). An edited edition has been published by Bannerjee (1977); the edition restores the lacunae of the Gilgit manuscript by making use of the Tibetan translation.

62. Because the commentators with which I am concerned in this book were male, I will here address only vows applicable to monks. For comparative discussion, see Lamotte 1988a:165–179; Pachow 2000.

63. See Clarke 2009a, 2009b.

64. I have omitted reference to the third and fourth sections here, since they do not present rules bearing on speech.

65. The precise number of speech offenses is a matter of debate, since some of the fifty-nine offenses that I enumerate here could be characterized somewhat

more broadly as offenses of personal comportment that are only incidentally concerned with speech. So, for example, it would be wrong to read the prohibition against admonishing nuns in the evening (V.22) as a rule that endorses the mixing of monks and nuns in the evening, so long as no admonishment occurs. If the list errs, it errs on the side of inclusiveness. For a comparable list surveying speech-related vows of the *Dharmaguptakavinaya*, see Heirman 2009.

66. Letter codes following each entry will be explained later.

67. See Nance (forthcoming).

68. One vow (VII.53) is a simple directive not to speak with one's mouth full; it can, I think, be safely ignored.

69. The Gilgit manuscript has several lacunae here, and Bannerjee's reconstruction of these portions is sometimes less than faithful to the Tibetan translation. In what follows, I have interposed the relevant sections of the Tibetan translation in brackets. The crucial portion reads:

> yaḥ punar [corrected from Bannerjee 1977, which reads punanar] bhikṣur evaṃ vadet tathāhaṃ bhagavato dharmaṃ deśitam ājānāmi yathā ye antarāyikā dharmā uktā bhagavatā te pratisevyamānā nālam antarāyāyeti / [dge slong de la dge slong rnams kyis] idam syād vacanīyo mā tvam āyuṣman evam vocas tathāhaṃ bhagavato dharmaṃ desitam ājānāmi yathā ye antarāyikā dharmā uktā bhagavatā te pratisevyamānā [bar du gcod par mi 'gyur te] / mā bhagavantam abhyācakṣu na sādhu bhavati bhagavato abhyākhyānam na ca punar bhagavān evam [corrected from Bannerjee 1977, which reads bhagavānnevam] āha.

70. This relation between vows and explanatory stories need not be presumed to work in only one direction; in some cases, stories may also have been elaborated as ex post facto rationalizations for antecedently existent vows.

71. MN 22, i.130.

72. Translation slightly modified from Ñāṇamoli and Bodhi 1995:224ff. The language here is highly repetitive; certain passages have been elided. Cf. the elaboration of the protocols for Ariṣṭa's censure found in the *Pāṇḍulohitakavastu* (Dutt 1984:vol. 3, part 3, pp. 30–32; Bagchi 1967–1970:14–15). Versions of this story are also appropriated in several Indian commentaries on the *Prātimokṣasūtra* extant in the Tibetan canon. See *Prātimokṣasūtrapaddhati* (D, 'dul ba *du*, 185b3–187a2); *Prātimokṣasūtraṭīkāvinayasamuccaya* (D, 'dul ba *phu*, 210b3–217a1); *Prātimokṣasūtravṛtti* (D, 'dul ba *bu*, 201a3–b6). See also Ganeri 2007:40–43.

2. Models of Instruction

1. This is, however, beginning to change. Several studies that take up Buddhist preaching practices—largely focused outside India—have recently been published (Blackburn 2001; Deegalle 2006; Hubbard 1999; Kaminishi 2004; Mair 1988; McDaniel 2008; Teiser 2006; Veidlinger 2006). These provide rich resources for further comparative reflection. See also Adikaram 1946; Collins 1992; Cousins 1983, 1992; David-

son 2005:249–257; Deegalle 1997, 1998, 2006; Drewes 2009; Gummer 2000; MacQueen 1981, 1982; Mori 1990; Nance 2008; Norman 1983; Strong 1992.

2. Scholars have not been able to arrive at a consensus on the way(s) in which this transmission was effected. See Allon 1997; Cousins 1983; Skilling 2009; Wynne 2004.

3. These terms are found in inscriptions preserved in Sri Lanka, as well as in paracanonical and commentarial Pali texts.

4. Cf. Collins 1992; Mori 1990; Norman 1983. The phrase "*bhāṇaka* system" is drawn from Norman 1983.

5. Cf. Takakusu and Nagai 1934:789.

6. Collins 1992:125. The distinction that Collins is attempting to draw here is worth pondering; it is not clear why public recitation should be understood as falling outside the domain of textual transmission.

7. This is not to downplay the considerable importance that Indian Buddhist tradition continued to place on memorization more generally (see Griffiths 1999:chaps. 2, 3, 5).

8. Norman 1983:111.

9. See Paranavitana 1970, inscriptions 330, 407, 666, 708, 852; Paranavitana and Dias 2001, inscription 171A.

10. See Lüders et al. 1963, inscriptions A39, A59, A61, A62, A63, A54, A54a; Bühler 1894a, inscription 36. Occasionally, additional epithets (e.g., *navakammika*, *bhicchuna*) are added, making it clear that the preachers referenced in these inscriptions were formal members of the monastic community. On the *navakammika*, see Silk 2008:75–99.

11. Specializations may have been recognized among the Buddhists in south India as late as the third century C.E.: a pillar inscription at Nāgārjunikoṇḍa references "masters . . . who are preachers and preceptors of the *Dīgha*, the *Majjhima*, and the five *mātukas*" (Vogel 1929:17: *dīgha-majhima-pa[ṃ]ca-mātuka-osaka* (read *desaka)-vācakānaṃ ācariyānaṃ*). We also find reference made to a *samyuktabhānaka* (Dutt 1931:640).

12. Theravāda tradition may have recognized a division of labor between the *dhammabhāṇaka* (whose principal role, it appears, was to recite memorized texts) and another figure—the *dhammakathika*—whose principal role it was to explicate the texts so recited (Deegalle 2006:39, 46–47). If these terms mark a division of labor, this division does not seem to have been widely observed across Buddhist traditions during the first millennium C.E.

13. The term *chos smra ba* appears to have been used to render *dharmavādin* in translating the opening of the sixtieth chapter of the Gilgit *Aṣṭadaśasāhasrikāprajñāpāramitā* (Conze 1962:69): "atha śakro devānām indro bhagavantam etad avocat: kaścid ahaṃ bhagavann evaṃ bhāṣamāṇa evaṃ upadiśann uktavādī ca bhagavato *dharmavādī* ca dharmasya cānudharmatāṃ samyak vyākurvaṃ vyākaromi." This is rendered into Tibetan (by an unknown translator) as follows (D, sher phyin khri brgyad *kha*, 264a5–6): "de nas bcom ldan 'das la lha'i dbang po brgya byin gyis 'di skad ces gsol to / bcom ldan 'das bdag gis de skad smras shing / de skad bstan pa bcom ldan 'das kyis gsungs pa'i rjes su smra zhing *chos smra ba* dang / chos kyi rjes su 'thun pa'i chos yang dag par brjod pa lags sam." For the use of the term *chos sgrogs pa* to render

dharmabhāṇaka, see the Tibetan translation of Kuladatta's *Kriyāsaṃgraha*, where the phrase *dharmabhāṇakaṃ pūjāpratyekaṃ* (Rani 1977:199) is rendered as *chos sgrogs pa rnams la so so'i mchod pa* (D, rgyud *ku*, 225b6). For the use of both terms to render a single underlying Sanskrit term (the identity of which is unclear), see the Tibetan translation (attributed to Viśuddhasiṃha, Sarvajñadeva, and Devendrarakṣita) of a passage from the *Vyākhyāyuktisūtrakhaṇḍaśata* (D, sems tsam *shi*, 23a3–4): "tshe dang ldan pa dag dge slong *chos smra ba pos* chos kyi gtam byed pa na rnam pa nyi shu po 'di dag dang ldan pas gtam bya ste." The same passage is quoted in Guṇamati's *Vyākhyāyuktiṭīkā*, where it is translated (by Viśuddhasiṃha, Śākyasiṃha, and Devendrarakṣita) as follows (D, sems tsam *si*, 207a3): "tshe dang ldan pa dag dge slong *chos sgrogs pas* chos kyi gtam byed pa na rnam pa nyi shu po 'di dag dang ldan pas gtam bya ste."

14. Vaidya 1961c:298, paraphrased in Studholme 2002:145–146.

15. The *Śikṣāsamuccaya* is extant in Sanskrit, and it is available in two editions: the superior Bendall 1902, and Vaidya 1961b. In categorizing the text as a florilegium, I am following Griffiths 1999, though this categorization should perhaps be qualified: the textual genre of the *Śikṣāsamuccaya* is not yet fully understood (cf. Harrison 2007).

16. Here, the Tibetan translation reinserts verse 13.30, absent from the Sanskrit text.

17. The Tibetan here (*sgom*) reads a derivative of *bhū* for *bhāṣet*. Bendall notes two manuscript readings that are closer to the Tibetan: *bhāveya* and *bhāve ca*; Vaidya reproduces Bendall's reading without noting variants.

18. Although the excerpt may appear to be seamless, it is in fact a selection of verses, in three discontinuous sections: Śāntideva has omitted 13.25 and 13.30–13.31. Bendall 1902:352–354: "kālena co cintayamānu paṇḍitaḥ praviśya layanaṃ tatha ghaṭṭayitvā / vipaśya dharmaṃ imi sarvayoniśo utthāya deśeta alīnacitaḥ / sukhasthito bhoti sadā vicakṣaṇo sukhaṃ niṣaṇṇas tatha dharma bhāṣate / udāraprajñapta karitva āsanaṃ caukṣe manojñe pṛthivīpradeśe / caukṣaṃ ca so cīvara prāvaritvā suraktaraṅgaṃ ca prasannaraṅgaiḥ / āsevakaṃ kṛṣṇa tathā daditvā mahāpramāṇaṃ ca nivāsayitvā / sapādapīṭhasmi niṣadya āsane vicitradūṣyehi susaṃstṛtasmin / sudhautapādaś ca upāruhitvā snigdhena śīrṣeṇa mukhena cāpi / dharmāsane tatra niṣīdiyānaḥ ekāgra satveṣu samaṃ vipaśyan / upasaṃharec citrakathā bahūś ca bhikṣūn atho bhikṣunikās tathaiva / kilāsitāṃś cāpi vivarjayīta na cāpi utpādayi khedasamjñāṃ / aratiṃ ca sarvāṃ vijahīta paṇḍito maitrībalaṃ parṣadi bhāvayec ca / bhāṣec ca rātriṃ divaṃ agradharmān dṛṣṭāntakoṭiniyutaiḥ sa paṇḍitaḥ / saṃharṣayet tāṃ ca tathaiva toṣayet na cāpi kiñcit tatra jātu prārthayet / khādyaṃ ca bhojyaṃ ca tathā 'nnapānaṃ vastrāṇi śayyāsanacīvarāṇi / gilānabhaiṣajya na cintayet saḥ na vijñapet parṣadi kiñcid anyat / anyatra cinteya sadā vicakṣaṇaḥ bhaveya buddho 'ham ime ca sattvāḥ / etac ca me sarvasukhopadhānaṃ yaṃ dharma śrāvemi hitāya loke."

19. Evidence for the popularity of these texts is not difficult to find. As noted later, each appears in the *Catalogue* (discussed in the introduction herein). Śāntideva repeatedly cites them in his *Śikṣāsamuccaya*; Kamalaśīla cites the *Dharmasaṅgīti*, *Ratnamegha*, and *Akṣayamatinirdeśa* numerous times in the *Bhāvanākramas* and in the *Madhyamakāloka* (where he also cites the *Daśabhūmikasūtra*); and Prajñākaramati

cites the *Dharmasaṅgīti*, the *Akṣayamatinirdeśa*, and the *Ratnamegha* in his commentary to Śāntideva's *Bodhicaryāvatāra*.

20. D 238; the work is number 94 in the *Catalogue* (Herrmann-Pfandt 2008:54; Lalou 1953:321). The extant Tibetan translation is attributed to Mañjuśrīgarbha, Vijayaśīla, Śīlendrabodhi, and Ye shes sde (ninth century). The passage noted here occurs at D, mdo sde *zha*, 16b5–20a3.

21. On the discriminations, see Dayal 1970:263ff.; MacQueen 1982; cf. also Braarvig 1985, Harrison 2003. The term *pratisaṃvid* itself presents serious translation difficulties, not least among which is scholarly uncertainty regarding the root from which it derives. The Sanskrit term obviously derives from √*vid* ("know," "understand"), and this sense is preserved in various attested Tibetan translations—e.g., *so so yang dag par rig pa* and *tha dad pa yang dag par shes pa*. The Pali *paṭisaṃbhidā* appears to derive from *bhid* ("divide," "split"). It is difficult to tell which term was original (see Childers 1976:366–367; Dayal 1970:259–267; Edgerton 1953:2.370), and there has been little consensus on the translation of the Sanskrit.

22. On the discriminations as discussed in Pali canonical and extracanonical sources, see the appendix to Aung and Rhys-Davids 1960:377–381, and Buddhaghosa's discussion in *Visuddhimagga* XIV.21–31 (trans. Ñāṇamoli 1999:439–442).

23. A useful introduction to the *Daśabhūmikasūtra* is Yuyama 1996. In what follows, translations from the text are made principally on the basis of the Vaidya edition (1967), which reproduces the editions of Rahder (1926) and Rahder and Susa (1931–1932). I have also consulted the edition prepared by R. Kondō (1936) and have noted textual divergences where they occur. For a complete translation from the Sanskrit, see Honda 1968.

24. For further discussion of the ten levels, see Dayal 1932:270–291; Hirakawa 1990:307–308; Kawara 1972:49; Lamotte 1980:2373–2445; Lopez 1988b.

25. This list of ten perfections contains a shorter traditional list of six, to which a list of four additional perfections (levels 7–10) has been added. For additional material on the perfections, see the sources cited in Edgerton 1953:341–342; cf. also Dayal 1932:165–265; Hirakawa 1990:299–300; Huntington 1989:69–104; Kawara 1972:38–39; Lamotte 1981b.

26. The translation here is conjectural; the Sanskrit of this portion of the text, although uniform across the published editions, is rather convoluted: "so 'ntaśaḥ svapnāntaragato 'pi vinidhāya dṛṣṭiṃ kṣāntiṃ ruciṃ matiṃ prekṣāṃ visaṃvādanābhiprāyo nānṛtāṃ vācan niścārayati kaḥ punar vādaḥ samanvāhṛtya." The Tibetan translation of the passage (at D, phal chen *kha*, 188a5) omits the offending portion entirely.

27. The word *nidāna*, here translated as "sound basis," is used in several different ways in Buddhist texts. Sometimes, it indexes the occasion—place, time, retinue, and so on—at/for which is teaching is offered. At other times, it indexes the reason(s) for offering the teaching. Finally, it may be used to index the section of a sūtra in which such specifics are delineated, preparing the way for the teaching to follow. Thus, the term *nidāna* may be used to index where, when, why, and/or how a teaching is transmitted. All of these senses of *nidāna* may be in play here.

28. Vaidya 1967:15–16 (cf. Kondō 1936:38–39): "anṛtavacanāt prativirataḥ khalu punar bhavati satyavādī bhūtavādī kālavādī yathāvādī tathākārī / so

'ntaśaḥ svapnāntaragato 'pi vinidhāya dṛṣṭiṃ kṣāntiṃ ruciṃ matiṃ prekṣāṃ visaṃvādanābhiprāyo nānṛtāṃ vācaṃ niścārayati kaḥ punar vādaḥ samanvāhṛtya / piśunavacanāt prativirataḥ khalu punar bhavati abhedāviheṭhāpratipannaḥ sattvānām / sa netaḥ śrutvā amutrākhyātā bhavaty amīṣāṃ bhedāya / na amutaḥ śrutvā ihākhyātā bhavaty eṣāṃ bhedāya / na saṃhitān [Kondō: saṃhitāṃ] bhinatti na bhinnānām anupradānaṃ karoti / na vyagrārāmo bhavati na vyagrarato na vyagrakaraṇīṃ vācaṃ bhāṣate sadbhūtām asadbhūtāṃ vā / paruṣavacanāt prativirataḥ khalu punar bhavati / sa yeyam vāg adeśā karkaśā [Kondō inserts paruṣā] parakaṭukā parābhisaṃjananī anvakṣānvakṣaprāgbhārā [Kondō: anakṣā anakṣaprāgbhārā] grāmyā pārthagjanakī [Kondō: pārthagjanikī] anelā akarṇasukhā krodharoṣaniścāritā hṛdayaparidahanī [Kondō inserts manyujananī] manaḥsaṃtāpakarī apriyā amanāpā amanojñā / svasaṃtānaparasa ṃtānvināśinī / tathārūpāṃ vācaṃ prahāya yeyam vāg snigdhā mṛdī [Kondō: mṛdvī] manojñā madhurā priyakaraṇī manāpakaraṇī hitakaraṇī nelā karnasukhā hṛdayaṃgamā premaṇīyā paurī varṇavispaṣṭa (paurīvarṇavispaṣṭa) vijñeyā [Kondō: vijñāyā] śravaṇīyā niśritā [Kondō: amiśritā] bahujaneṣṭā bahujanakāntā bahujanapriyā bahujanamanāpā vijñāpannā sarvasattvahitasukhāvahā samāhitā mana-utplāvanakarī [Kondō: manautplāvanakarī] manaḥprahlādanakarī [Kondō omits manaḥprahlādanakarī] svasaṃtānaparasaṃtānaprasādanakarī tathārūpāṃ vācaṃ niścārayati / saṃbhinnapralāpāt prativirataḥ khalu punar bhavati suparihāryavacanaḥ kālavādī bhūtavādī arthavādī dharmavādī nyāyavādī vinayavādī sa nidānavatīṃ vācaṃ [Kondō: sanidānavatīvācaṃ] bhāṣate kālena sāvadānām / sa cāntaśa itihāsapūrvakam api vacanam parihāryam pariharati kaḥ punarvādo vāgvikṣepeṇa."

29. Cf. Vaidya 1967:22: "tāṃś ca tathāgatān arhataḥ samyaksaṃbuddhān paryupāste / teṣāṃ ca dharmadeśanāṃ satkṛtya śṛnoti udgṛhṇāti dhārayati." Following *dhārayati*, Kondō here inserts *vācayati*. There is no evidence to support this addition in the Tibetan translation (folio 201a2: *chos nyan to / len to 'dzin do*). The relevant line is unintelligible in Matsuda 1996, Manuscript A, but there is also no trace of the addition in Manuscript B (cf. Matsuda 1996:66, folio 20a, line 6).

30. Vaidya 1967:20: "na ca tasmād duṣkarasaṃjñī bhavati anyatra tasminn eva dharmabhāṇakapudgale duṣkarasaṃjñī bhavati yo 'syaikadharmapadam api deśayati."

31. Ibid.:28–29: "smṛtimāṃś ca bhavati asaṃpramoṣadharmatayā matimāṃś ca bhavati suviniścitajñānatayā gatimāṃś ca bhavati sūtrārthagatisaṃdhāyab hāṣitāvabodhatayā hrīmāṃś ca bhavati ātmaparānurakṣaṇatayā dhṛtimāṃś ca bhavati saṃvaracāritrānutsargatayā buddhimāṃś ca bhavati sthānāsthānakauś alyasuvicāritatayā jñānānugataś ca bhavati aparapraṇeyatayā prajñānugataś ca bhavati arthānarthasaṃbhedapadakuśalatayā abhijñānirhāraprāptaś ca bhavati bhāvanābhinirhārakuśalatayā upāyakuśalaś ca bhavati lokānuvartanatayā . . . tāṃś ca tathāgatān arhataḥ samyaksaṃbuddhān paryupāsate teṣām ca sakāśād gauravacitrīkāreṇa satkṛtya dharmadeśanāṃ śṛṇoti udgṛhṇāti dhārayati / śrutvā ca yathābalaṃ yathābhajamānaṃ pratipatyā saṃpādayati / bhūyastvena ca teṣāṃ tathāgatānāṃ śāsane pravrajati / pravrajitaś ca śrutadhārī dharmabhāṇako bhavati."

32. Later, my translation choices for these four terms will be discussed in more detail. For the sake of readability, I have opted to translate each of the compounds

dharmapratisaṃvid, arthapratisaṃvid, niruktipratisaṃvid, and *pratibhānapratisaṃvid* into English as though the relation between their constituent terms were *ṣaṣṭhī tatpuruṣa*. These compounds are, however, repeatedly glossed in the commentarial literature as *saptamī tatpuruṣa*; hence they might be more literally translated as "discrimination regarding [i.e., that bears upon] dharma," and so on.

33. Cf. Vaidya 1967:51.

34. Here and in the ensuing pages, I have refrained from translating the term "dharma" in order to preserve its polysemy.

35. Vaidya 1967:51: "sa dharmapratisaṃvidā svalakṣaṇaṃ dharmāṇāṃ prajānāti / arthapratisaṃvidā vibhaktiṃ dharmāṇāṃ prajānāti /niruktipratisaṃvidā asaṃbhedadeśanāṃ dharmāṇāṃ prajānāti /pratibhānapratisaṃvidānuprabandhān upacchedatāṃ dharmāṇāṃ prajānāti."

36. Cf. the Tibetan (D, phal chen *kha*, 254b4): "chos rnams kyi rang bzhin myed pa rab tu shes so (*dharmāṇāṃ abhāvasvabhāvaṃ prajānāti)": "he knows dharmas to lack essences."

37. Alternatively, "he teaches the doctrine that continually designates all dharmas."

38. Vaidya 1967:51: "punar aparaṃ dharmapratisaṃvidā abhāvaśarīraṃ dharmāṇāṃ prajānāti / arthapratisaṃvidā udayāstagamanaṃ [Kondō: udayāstaṃgamanam] dharmāṇāṃ prajānāti /niruktipratisaṃvidā sarvadharmaprajñaptyavacc hedanadharmaṃ [Kondō: sarvadharmaprajñaptyavacchedena dharmaṃ] deśayati / pratibhānapratisaṃvidā yathāprajñaptyavikopanatāparyantatayā [Kondō: yathāprajñaptyavikopanatāyā aparyantatayā dharmaṃ] deśayati."

39. Ibid.:51: "punar aparaṃ dharmapratisaṃvidā pratyutpannavibhaktiṃ dharmāṇāṃ prajānāti / arthapratisaṃvidātītānāgatavibhaktiṃ dharmāṇāṃ prajānāti / niruktipratisaṃvidātītānāgatapratyutpannāsaṃbhedato dharmaṃ deśayat i / pratibhānapratisaṃvidā ekaikam adhvānam ārabhyāparyantadharmālokatayā dharmaṃ deśayati."

40. Ibid.: "punar aparaṃ dharmapratisaṃvidā dharmaprabhedaṃ prajānāti / arth apratisaṃvidārthaprabhedaṃ prajānāti / niruktipratisaṃvidā yathārutadeśanatayā dharmaṃ deśayati / pratibhānapratisaṃvidā yathānuśayajñānaṃ deśayati [reading pratibhānapratisaṃvidā yathāśayajñānaṃ deśayati, following Kondō 1936:161 and the reading of all Chinese editions of the text (cf. Honda 1968:246)]." The Tibetan (D, phal chen *kha*, 255a2) diverges slightly, reading "ji bzhin du shes pas chos ston to (*yathājñānena dharmaṃ deśayati)": "he teaches the dharma via correct knowledge."

41. The Sanskrit compound translated here is *saṃvṛtijñānasaṃdarśanāsaṃbhed atayā*. A diametrically opposed translation of this compound is also possible: "as being unmixed with considerations pertaining to conventional knowledge." The Tibetan (D, phal chen *kha*, 255a3) rules out the latter but also diverges from the Sanskrit editions: "kun rdzob kyi rgyus yang dag par bstan pas chos ston to." Cf. Honda 1968:246: "he explains with un-disorderedness, though he shows conditioned knowledge."

42. Vaidya 1967:51: "punar aparaṃ dharmapratisaṃvidā dharmajñānavibhakty asaṃbhedakauśalyaṃ [Kondō: dharmajñānavibhaktyasaṃbhedakauśalaṃ] prajānāti / arthapratisaṃvidā anvayajñānatathātvavyavasthānaṃ prajānāti / niruktipra-

tisaṃvidā saṃvṛtijñānasaṃdarśanāsaṃbhedatayā nirdiśati / pratibhānapratisaṃvi dā paramārthajñānakauśalyena dharmaṃ deśayati."

43. Ibid.: "punar aparaṃ dharmapratisaṃvidā ekanayāvikopaṃ dharmāṇāṃ prajānāti /arthapratisaṃvidā skandhadhātvāyatanasatyapratītyasamutpādakauśalyānugamam avatarati / niruktipratisaṃvidā sarvajagadabhigamanīyasumadhuragirinirghoṣākṣarair nirdiśati / pratibhānapratisaṃvidā bhūyo bhūyo 'paryantadharmāvabhāsatayā nirdiśati."

44. Ibid.: "punar aparaṃ dharmapratisaṃvidā ekayānasamavasaraṇanānātvaṃ prajānāti / arthapratisaṃvidā pravibhaktayānavimātratāṃ prajānāti / niruktipratisaṃvidā sarvayānāny abhedena [Kondō: asaṃbhedena] nirdiśati / pratibhānapratis aṃvidā ekaikaṃ yānam aparyantadharmāvabhāsena deśayati."

45. Vaidya 1967:52: "punar aparaṃ dharmapratisaṃvidā sarvabodhisattvacarijñānacaridharmacarijñānānugamam avatarati / arthapratisaṃvidā daśabhūmivyavasthān anirdeśapravibhaktim avatarati / niruktipratisaṃvidā yathābhūmimārgopasaṃhāra saṃbhedena nirdiśati / pratibhānapratisaṃvidā ekaikāṃ bhūmim 'paryantākāreṇa nirdiśati."

46. Ibid.: "punar aparaṃ dharmapratisaṃvidā sarvatathāgataikalakṣaṇānubodham (Kondō: sarvatathāgataikakṣaṇānubodham) avatarati / arthapratisaṃvidā nānākālav astulakṣaṇavibhaṅgānugamaṃ prajānāti /niruktipratisaṃvidā yathābhisaṃbodhiṃ [Kondō: yathābhisaṃbodhaṃ] vibhaktinirdeśena nirdiśati / pratibhānapratisaṃvi dā ekaikaṃ dharmapadam aparyantakalpāvacchedena nirdiśati."

47. Ibid.: "punar aparaṃ dharmapratisaṃvidā sarvatathāgatavāgbalavaiśāradyabuddhadharma-mahākaruṇāpratisaṃvitprayogadharmacakrānupravartamān asarvajñajñānānugamaṃ prajānāti / arthapratisaṃvidā caturaśītasattvacaritasahasrāṇāṃ yathāśayaṃ yathendriyaṃ yathādhimuktivibhaktitas tathāgataghoṣaṃ prajānāti / niruktipratisaṃvidā sarvasattvacaryāsaṃbhedatas tathāgataghoṣānuraveṇa nirdiśati / pratibhānapratisaṃvidā tathāgatajñānaprabhācaryāmaṇḍa lādhimuktyā [Kondō: tathāgatajñānaprabhāsacaryāmaṇḍalādhimuktyā] dharmaṃ deśayati. My translation of the final clause is conjectural. The Sanskrit here diverges considerably from the Tibetan translation (at D, phal chen *kha*, 256a1–2): "spobs pa tha dad pa yang dag par shes pas / de bzhin gshegs pa'i ye shes 'od gsal ba dang / spyod pa'i dkyil 'khor la mos pas chos ston to."

48. The former quotation is from Vaidya 1967:1; the latter, from Vaidya 1960d:vii.

49. Dayal 1970:263.

50. As will be discussed later, the order in which these attributes are listed is not constant among texts.

51. On the *Saṃdhinirmocanasūtra*, see Lamotte 1935:1–29; Powers 1992, 1993. The Sanskrit is lost; translations herein have been based on the Tibetan edition provided in Lamotte 1935. The work is number 117 in the *Catalogue* (Herrmann-Pfandt 2008:66; Lalou 1953:322). The sūtra has been translated in its entirety into French (Lamotte 1935) and English (Powers 1995; Keenan 2000). Portions have also been translated into German (Frauwallner 1956:284–296). See also Tillemans 1997.

52. Lamotte 1935:98: "bcom ldan 'das byang chub sems dpa' zhi gnas dang lhag mthong bsgom pa / chos so sor yang dag par rig pa . . . lags na / ji ltar chos so sor yang dag par rig pa lags."

53. Ibid.: "byams pa rnam pa lngas [chos] so sor yang dag par rig pa yin te / ming dang tshig dang yi ge dang so so ba dang bsdus pas so / ming gang zhe na / kun nas

nyon mongs pa dang / rnam par byang ba'i chos rnams la ngo bo nyid dang / bye brag gi ming du bya bar btags pa gang yin pa'o / tshig gang zhe na / kun nas nyon mongs pa dang / rnam par byang ba'i don rjes su tha snyad gdags pa'i phyir gnas dang rten ming de dag nyid kyi tshogs la brtan pa gang yin pa'o / yi ge gang zhe na / de gnyis ka'i gnas kyi yig 'bru gang yin pa'o / de dag so so las so so yang dag par rig pa gang zhe na / ma 'dres pa la dmigs pa'i yid la byed pas so so yang dag par rig pa gang yin pa'o / bsdus pa las so so yang dag par rig pa gang zhe na / 'dres pa la dmigs pa'i yid la byed pas so so yang dag par rig pa gang yin pa'o / de dag thams cad gcig tu bsdu na chos so so yang dag par rig pa zhes bya ste / de ltar na chos so so yang dag par rig pa yin no."

54. Ibid.: "byams pa yang byang chub sems dpa' rnam pa lngas don so so yang dag par rig pa yin te / don rnam pa lnga gang zhe na / yongs su shes par bya ba'i dngos po dang / yongs su shes par bya ba'i don dang / yongs su shes pa dang / yongs su shes pa'i 'bras bu thob pa dang / de rab tu rig par byed pa'o / byams pa de la yong su shes par bya ba'i dngos po ni shes bya thams cad yin par blta bar bya ste / 'di lta ste / phung po rnams zhes bya ba 'am / nang gi skye mched rnams zhes bya ba 'am / phyi rol gyi skye mched rnams zhes bya ba 'am / de lta bu la sogs pa dag go / byams pa de la yongs su shes par bya ba'i don ni rnam pa ji snyed kyis shes bya de ji lta ba bzhin shes par bya ba ste / 'di lta ste / kun rdzob dang / don dam pa dang / skyon dang yon tan dang / rkyen dang / dus dang / skye ba dang / gnas pa dang / 'jig pa'i mtshan nyid dang / nad la sogs pa dang / sdug bsngal dang / kun 'byung ba la sogs pa dang / de bzhin nyid dang / yang dag pa'i mtha' dang / chos kyi dbyings dang / bsdu pa dang / dbye ba dang / mgo gcig tu lan gdab pa dang / rnam par dbye ba dang / dris te lan gdab pa dang / gzhag pa dang / gsang ba dang / bsgrags pa dang / de lta bu dang 'thun pa ni yongs su shes par bya ba'i don yin par rig par bya'o / byams pa de la yongs su shes pa ni de gnyis ka 'dzin par byed pa / byang chub kyi phyogs dang 'thun pa'i chos gang yin pa dag ste / 'di lta ste / dran pa nye bar bzhag pa rnams dang / yang dag par spong ba rnams dang / de la sogs pa'o / byams pa de la yongs su shes pa'i 'bras bu 'thob pa ni 'di lta ste / 'dod chags dang / zhe sdang dang / gti mug 'dul ba dang / 'dod chags dang / zhe sdang dang / gti mug ma lus par spong pa dang / dge sbyong nyid kyi 'bras bu rnams dang / ngas nyan thos dang / de bzhin gshegs pa'i yon tan 'jig rten pa dang / 'jig rten pa las 'das pa thun mong dang thun mong ma yin pa gang dag bstan pa de dag mngon du bya ba gang yin pa'o / byams pa de la rab tu rig par byed pa ni mngon sum du byas pa'i chos de dag nyid las rnam par 'grol bar shes pa dang / gzhan dag la 'ang rgya cher ston pa dang / yang dag par ston pa gang yin pa ste / byams pa don lnga po de dag gis kyang don thams cad bsdus par rig par bya'o."

55. For a translation and edition of the relevant passages of the *Abhidharmasamuccaya* and *Mahāyānasūtrālaṃkārabhāṣya*, see Griffiths et al. 1989:141–142, 313–315. The relevant material in the *Abhidharmakośabhāṣya* is presented in Shastri 1998:860. For the account preserved in the *Abhidharmadīpavibhāṣāprabhāvṛtti*, and useful (if brief) comments on the geneaology of the discriminations, see Jaini 1977:62–65, 393.

56. Cf. Tatia 1976:128.

57. On the authorship of the *Abhidharmasamuccayabhāṣya*, see chapter 4, note 7.

58. Griffiths et al. 1989:313: "yul mi'i skad dang chos kyi nges pa'i tshig la thogs pa med pa yang dag par 'byor pa." On *janapada*, see Inden 1990:218–220ff.

59. Cf. *Mahāyānasūtrālaṃkārabhāṣya* 18.34 (Lévi 1907:138–139, cf. also 185); *Abhidharmakośabhāṣya* on *Abhidharmakośa* 7.38 (Shastri 1998:860); *Abhidharmadīpavibhāṣāprabhāvṛtti* (Jaini 1977:393); *Bodhisattvabhūmi* 17 (Dutt 1966:176); *Arthaviniścayasūtranibandhana* 24 (Samtani 1971:275–278).

60. D, mdo sde *ma*, 79a1–174b7. The work appears in the *Catalogue* as number 93 (Herrmann-Pfandt 2008:52–53; Lalou 1953:321). The *Akṣayamatinirdeśa* is no longer extant in Sanskrit; all translations here are based on the critical edition of the Tibetan text (a translation attributed to Dharmatāśīla) edited by J. Braarvig (1993a; for a translation and study, see 1993b). Much of the *Akṣayamatinirdeśa* closely parallels the *Bodhisattvapiṭaka*; the relation between the two texts is discussed in Pagel 1994. Cf. also Pagel 1995.

61. For further discussion of the categories of beings listed here, see DeCaroli 2004.

62. For the Tibetan, see Braarvig 1993a:112–113.

63. The term is obviously related to another important term with an extraordinarily rich history in Indian religious, grammatical, and literary thought: *pratibhā*. See Gonda 1963.

64. Braarvig 1985; MacQueen 1981, 1982. See also Harrison 2003.

65. MacQueen 1982:60.

66. Thus, the discrimination of eloquence is often linked to the quality of discursive fearlessness—a gloss reflected in the Tibetan translation of *pratibhāna: spobs pa* ("courage," "daring").

67. On the use of the term *smṛti* in Buddhist discourse, see the essays collected in Gyatso 1992. See also Harrison 2003.

68. Some early Mahāyāna texts associate the term with a host of disparate characteristics and skills, typically presenting these in long lists. So, for example, the *Samādhirājasūtra* lists approximately 330 discrete aspects of its favored *samādhi*, while the second chapter of the *Pratyutpannabuddhasaṃmukhāvasthitasamādhisūtra* enumerates a list of over 150 aspects of the *samādhi* that graces its title (Harrison 1990:26–30). Later tantric materials complicate the issue still further. Consider, for example, the *Vajrapañjara*'s remarkable assessment, quoted in Davidson 2003:193 (trans. Davidson): "The Blessed One replied . . . 'Samādhi is known as disputing with Tīrthikas, rooting out those who dispute with you, and firmly announcing the texts of one's own school.'" ("Bcom ldan 'das kyis bka' stsal pa / ... / mu stegs can sun dbyung ba dang / rgol ba rnams tshar gcod pa dang / rang gi sde'i gzhung brjod pa zhes bya ba'i ting nge 'dzin.")

69. These observations are not intended to impugn the quality of Braarvig's scholarship, which is uniformly excellent. On *dhāraṇī*, see Braarvig 1985; Davidson 2009; Gyatso 1992:172–213; Hirakawa 1990:300–302; Inagaki 1999; Lamotte 1976b:1854–1864.

70. For the Tibetan, see Braarvig 1993a:113–114.

71. The full gloss given in the *Abhidharmakośabhāṣya* is: "The discrimination regarding eloquence is the clear exposition of one who possesses the power of concentration, when [his] discourse is coherent and free, and the incontrovertible knowledge regarding that [clear exposition]" (Shastri 1998: 860: "yuktamuktābhilāpitāyāṃ samādhivaśisamprakhyānam tatra ca avivartyaṃ jñānaṃ pratibhānapratisaṃvit").

Cf. also the similar gloss in the *Abhidharmadīpavibhāṣāprabhāvṛtti* (Jaini 1977:393). The compound *yuktamuktapratibhāṇaḥ* is found also in the Mūlasarvāstivāda *Vinayavastu* (Bagchi 1967–1970:2.86, 101), and in the twenty-third chapter of the *Divyāvadāna* (Cowell and Neil 1886:329). In both places, it is associated with the figure of the *dharmakathika.*

72. Cf. appendix C, section 3.1.

73. D, mdo sde *ma*, 172b5: "bcom ldan 'das chos smra ba de dag la bdag cag gis ston par 'du shes bskyed par bgyi." Braarvig translates this passage as "Lord, we will produce the concept that these preachers of religion are like the Teacher." The term "like" is not, however, explicitly signaled in the Tibetan.

74. This text is number 89 in the *Catalogue* (Herrmann-Pfandt 2008:51; Lalou 1953:321). D 231 is a translation attributed to Rin chen 'tsho and Chos nyid tshul khrims (Dharmatāśīla). The passage translated here is D, mdo sde *wa*, 112a3–4: "sa phyogs gang na chos smra ba de gnas pa de la yang mchod rten du 'du shes bskyed par bya ste / chos smra ba de la yang bla mar 'du shes bskyed par bya'o / dge ba'i bshes gnyen du 'du shes bskyed par bya'o / lam ston par 'du shes bskyed par bya'o / chos smra ba de mthong na dga' ba dang / dad pa dang / rangs pa bskyed par bya'o." On the influence of the *Ratnamegha*, see Pagel 2008. Cf. Schopen 1975:158ff., where a short passage from the *Kāśyapaparivarta* that mentions "doing homage to the preacher of the Tathāgata's dharma" (*de bzhin gshegs pa'i chos smra ba la bkur sti byed pa*) is translated and discussed briefly.

75. Translation slightly modified from Emmerick 1970:66. Cf. *Suvarṇa(pra)bhāsottamasūtra*, "Yakṣāśrayarakṣāparivarta," verses 9, 11, 13–17. The Sanskrit (Nobel 1937: 157; cf. Bagchi 1967: 84 [hereafter B.]) is as follows: "tadā [B. yadā] sa eva jānīyād yas taṃ [B. yat tatra] sūtraṃ śruṇīyate [B. śrūyate] evam acintiyaṃ mahyam puṇyaskandhaṃ samārjitam // . . . samantarapraviṣṭasya vihāraṃ layanaṃ eva ca [B. layanaṃ tathā] / apagacchanti [B. apagacchati] pāpāni sarvaduḥsvapnalakṣaṇam [B. sarvaduḥsvapnalakṣanā] // . . . tādṛśaṃ āsanaṃ tatra kurvīta padmasaṃnibham / yādṛśaṃ nāgarājebhi [B. nāgarājaiśca] darśitaṃ supināntare / tatrāsanopaviṣṭaś ca [B. tatrāsanopaviṣṭasya] idaṃ sūtraṃ prakāśayet / likhitaṃ vācayec caiva tathaiva paryavāpnuyāt / avatīryāsanād eva anyadeśe gato bhavet / dṛśyante prātihāryāṇi tatrāsanagatāni ca / dharmabhāṇakarūpaṃ ca kadācit tatra dṛśyate / kadācid buddharūpaṃ [B. buddha rūpaṃ] ca bodhisattva [B. bodhisattvaṃ] kadācana / samantabhadrarūpāṇi kvacin mañjuśriyas tathā / kvacin maitreyarūpāṇi dṛśyante tatra āsane / kvacit kevalam ābhāsaḥ [B. ābhāsaṃ] kvacid devatadarśanam [B. devopadarśanam] / muhūrtenāb hidṛśyante punaś cāntarahāyiṣu." On the *Suvarṇa(pra)bhāsottamasūtra*, see Gummer 2000. See also the introductions to Emmerick 1970, Nobel 1937, and Bagchi 1967.

76. Vaidya 1960a:218: "sa kulaputro vā kuladuhitā vā imaṃ dharmaparyāyaṃ dhārayamāṇo deśayamānaḥ prakāśayamāno likhamānas tair dvādaśabhir jihvāguṇaśataiḥ . . . yaṃ ca dharmaṃ vyāhariṣyati parṣanmadhyagataḥ tena tasya te sattvāḥ priṇitendriyā bhaviṣyanti tuṣṭāḥ paramatuṣṭāḥ prāmodyajātāḥ / madhuraś cāsya valgumanojñasvaro gambhīro niścariṣyati hṛdayaṃgamaḥ premaṇīyaḥ / tenāsya te sattvās tuṣṭā udagracittā bhaviṣyanti / yeṣāṃ ca dharmaṃ deśayiṣyati te cāsya madhuranirghoṣaṃ śrutvā valgumanojñaṃ devāpy upasamkramitavyaṃ maṃsyante darśanāya vandanāya paryupāsanāya dharmaśravaṇāya ca . . . tāvan

madhuraṃ sa dharmabhāṇako dharmaṃ bhāṣiṣyate yathābhūtaṃ yathoktam tathāgatena."

77. Li 1996:57–58; cf. Beal 1969:1.80–81.

78. If such preachers were monks who took the Vinaya seriously (and this is not to say that all Buddhist monks did), then they would need to be careful to avoid incurring the *pārājika* offense of "intentionally and falsely representing oneself as one who has seen or known things which are seeable and knowable only by persons of consummate attainment (*uttaramanuśya*)." But such a charge, were it ever to be brought, might easily be avoided: a dharma preacher could protest that the laudatory accounts of preachers presented inside sūtra texts ought not be understood as representing his own view of himself.

79. Bendall 1902:49: "punar aparam anyavijñānasaṃjñino likhiṣyanti yāvat paryavāpsyanti / na vayam atrāsvādaṃ labhāmahe ity utthāyāsanāt prakramiṣyanti / evaṃ vijṛmbhamāṇā uccagghanto yāvat paryavāpsyantīti mārakarma // . . . punar aparaṃ dharmabhāṇakaś chandiko bhaviṣyati imāṃ gambhīrāṃ prajñāpāramitāṃ lekhayituṃ yāvad vācayituṃ dharmaśravanikaś ca kilāsī bhaviṣyati / evaṃ viparyayāt / dharmabhāṇakaś ca deśāntaraṃ gantukāmo bhaviṣyati dhārmaśravaṇikāś ca neti neyam / evaṃ dharmabhāṇako maheccho bhaviṣyati dhārmaśravaṇiko 'lpeccha iti neyam / saṃkṣepād dharmabhāṇakadhārmaśravaṇikayor yā kācid vidhuratā sarvaṃ tanmārakarmety uktaṃ." This passage does not precisely match the corresponding section of Vaidya's published edition of the *Aṣṭasāhasrikāprajñāpāramitā* (cf. 1960c: 120–121). Cf. Sparham 2006–2009:3.32–33; 161–164.

80. Nattier 2003:65. For a contrasting view, see Silk 2008:7.

81. Much of the *Sarvadharmāpravṛttinirdeśa* has been translated and discussed by Braarvig (2000:81–166), who characterizes it as belonging to "the middle period of Mahāyāna sūtra literature—after the Prajñāpāramitā literature." It is quoted in Śāntideva's *Śikṣāsamuccaya* and Atiśa's *Mahāsūtrasamuccaya* (cf. Mochizuki 1995).

82. Trans. Braarvig 2000:130.

83. Trans. Braarvig 2000:130–131.

84. Trans. Braarvig 2000:131.

85. Trans. slightly modified from Braarvig 2000:133. Cf. Braarvig 2000:132: "ye kulaputraivaṃrūpeṇa karmāvaraṇenānarthikāḥ / tair na dvitīyasya bodhisatvasya sarvvacaryāsu vipratipattavyam / sarvvāḥ kriyās tasyādhimoktavyāḥ/ evañ cittam utpādayitavyaṃ na ahaṃ paracittaṃ jāne durvijjñeyā satvacaryā / idañ ca khalu kulaputrārthavaśaṃ saṃpaśyaṃs tathāgata evandharman deśayati na pudgalena pudgalaḥ pramātavyaḥ / ahaṃ vā pudgalaṃ praminuyāṃ yo vā syān mādṛśaḥ / yaḥ kulaputrātmānaṃ rakṣitukāmas tena na kasyacic caryā vivecayitavyā / na pareṣāṃ vikuṭṭanā karttavyā / ayaṃ īdṛśo 'yam īdṛśa iti / buddhadharmābhiyuktena bhavitavyaṃ rātrindivaṃ dharmapaliguddhamānaseneti."

86. Braarvig 2000:131.

87. D, dbu ma *gi*, 255b3–256a2: "sangs rgyas dang byang chub sems dpa' thams cad la phyag 'tshal lo / dang po re zhig byang chub sems dpa' chos kha ton du bya bar 'dod pa dang glegs bam du bya ba [G: byas pa] klog par 'dod pas phyogs bcu'i 'jig rten gyi khams kyi sangs rgyas dang byang chub sems dpa' thams cad la gsol ba btab ste / yid kyis kun du dmigs la/ byang chub sems dpa' sems dpa' chen po kun

du bzang po'i spyod pa'i smon lam gyi cho gas / phyag 'tshal ba la sogs pa yan lag bdun gyi tshul du mchod pa rnams kyi yang dag par mchod do / de'i rjes la sems can thams cad la byams pa'i sems nye bar gzhag ste / yang dag pa'i lhag pa'i bsam pas de ltar bsams pa'i rjes la / tshig lan gsum brjod par bya ba ni / bcom ldan 'das kyis gsungs pa'i chos kyi tshig gcig gi don gang yin pa de ni chos thams cad kyi yang yin na / 'on kyang bdag ni rang gi las kyi nyes pas shes rab chung zhing blo zhen [G: zhan] te / de lta [G here inserts "na"] yin du zin kyang / gang bcom ldan 'das kyi [G: kyis] gsung rab bzung nas des bdag gi kha ton byas te / chos kyi sgra de sems can gang gi rna lam du grag pa de / de bzhin gshegs pa'i spobs pa thob par gyur cig / bcom ldan 'das kyis gsungs pa'i chos tshig gcig gi don gang yin pa de ni / chos thams cad yang yin na / 'on kyang bdag ni rang gi las kyi nyes pas shes rab chung zhing blo zhen [G: zhan] te / de ltar [G: lta] yin du zin kyang / gang bdag gis glegs bam du byas pa'i chos klag [G: bklags] par bya ste / chos kyi sgra de sems can gang rnams kyi rna lam du grag pa de dag / de bzhin gshegs pa'i spobs pa thob par gyur cig ces lan gsum du brjod par bya."

88. Atiśa, **Mahāyānapathasādhanavarṇasaṃgraha* (D, dbu ma *khi*, 299a5–302b6). The Tibetan, from Sherburne 2000:454: "smra la dga' yang don bsam bya / bu ram shing shun snying po ci yang med / dga' bar bya ba'i ro ni nang na 'dug / shun pa zos pas mis ni bu ram ro / zhim po rnyed par nus pa ma yin no / shun pa de bzhin 'di la smra ba ste / ro lta bu ni 'di la don sems yin." This verse is very similar to one from the *Adhyāśayasañcodanasūtra* that Atiśa cites with approval in the fifth chapter of his *Bodhimārgapradīpapañjikā* (cf. Sherburne 2000:196).

89. The Tibetan here is compressed, and other readings are possible. Cf. Sherburne 2000:527.

90. Based on the colophon of the *Arthaviniścayasūtranibandhana*, on which see note 101 of this chapter.

91. Note that the flexibility of the term "dharma" is apparent even in the passage from the *Saṃdhinirmocanasūtra* that articulates the Word and Object view. The passage specifies that the discrimination of dharma is of five kinds, among which are names, phrases, and syllables, yet it immediately goes on to use the term "dharma" to denote the various qualities that may be designated by those names, phrases, and syllables.

92. This order (i.e., *arthapratisaṃvid* followed by *dharmapratisaṃvid*) is also found in Pali texts. Dayal (1970:264) argues that the difference here signals a chronological shift (from *artha*, dharma to dharma, *artha*) and speculates that the shift may reflect an evolution in Buddhist doctrine. Both orders are, however, attested in texts that Buddhist tradition and modern scholarship agree may be attributed to a single author: Candrakīrti varies the order in which he discusses the discriminations in his *Madhyamakāvatārabhāṣya* and *Yuktiśāstikāvṛtti*.

93. The account is quite lengthy; only its opening section is cited here. For the Tibetan, see Braarvig 1993a:111.

94. D 3994. See Braarvig 1993a:v, xiii–xiv, 1993b:cxvii–cxxx; Schoening 1995:1.31, 34, 43. Little is known about the provenance of this commentary, although we know from its presence in the *Catalogue* (Herrmann-Pfandt 2008:305; Lalou 1953:332 [number #536]) that it was among the first works to be translated into Tibetan during the early propagation of Buddhism in Tibet. It is one of a large number of works

attributed by later Tibetan tradition to Vasubandhu, though the attribution may be spurious (Braarvig 1993b:cxxvii–cxxx).

95. *Akṣayamatinirdeśasūtraṭīkā* (D, mdo 'grel *ci*, 209a5–6): "don ni bstan cing rtogs pa'i yul lta bur rig par bya'o / chos ni ston cing rtog par byed pa lta bur rig par bya'o / yang na chos ni 'dus byas dang 'dus ma byas la sogs pa'i ming gis 'og nas smos pa rnams la bya'o / don ni de nyid don yongs su dpyod cing bye brag tu dbye ba la bya'o / yang na chos thams cad kyi mtshan nyid phyin ci ma log par rtogs pa ni don so so yang dag par rig pa'o / chos de dang de dag gi ming gang dang gang yin pa shes pa ni chos so so yang dag par rig pa'o."

96. All translations of the *Arthaviniścayasūtra* and the *Arthaviniścayasūtranibandhana* are based on Samtani 1971. For more information on these works, see Samtani's helpful introduction to that edition. For a translation, see Samtani 2002.

97. As in the *Akṣayamatinirdeśa*, the first two discriminations are presented in the order *artha*, dharma.

98. Samtani 1971:51–52 (here, I have translated the Sanskrit of Samtani's edition, though he is careful to note the wide divergences among the extant manuscripts at this point in the text—a point to which we will return later): "dharmapratisaṃvit katamā / anāsraveṣu dharmeṣu yad avaivartyajñānam." The Sanskrit diverges here from the Tibetan translation of the *Arthaviniścayasūtra* (D 317), which simply lists the four discriminations without offering any explanatory gloss (at D, mdo sde *sa*, 184b7–185b1).

99. Although the uncontaminated dharmas are not discussed at length in the *Arthaviniścayasūtra* itself, a succinct account is presented in the *Abhidharmakośa* (1.4–1.6) and discussed in the *bhāṣya* thereon (Shastri 1998:13–20). After first dividing all dharmas into two groups—those that are contaminated (*sāsrava*) and those that are uncontaminated (*anāsrava*), Vasubandhu enumerates four uncontaminated dharmas: the truth of path (*mārgasatya*), space (*ākāśa*), cessation through realization (*pratisaṃkhyānirodha*), and cessation through nonrealization (*apratisaṃkhyānirodha*).

100. Unlike the view touted in the *Akṣayamatinirdeśasūtra*, the latter account is not irreconcilable with the Word and Object view: the names, phrases, and syllables of Buddhist teaching could be counted among the uncontaminated dharmas.

101. The *Arthaviniścayasūtranibandhana* is one of very few Buddhist sūtra commentaries that survive in Sanskrit; its remarkable colophon allows us to situate the text with a degree of geographical and temporal precision that is extraordinary for a medieval Indian treatise. The relevant portion of the colophon reads: "There once reigned a most powerful Buddhist king, lord of his people, famed as Dharmapāla. In the kingdom of this great one, in the noble monastery of Nālandā, there was a monk, conqueror of sense-faculties, named Vīryaśrīdatta, who compiled this commentary." (Cf. Samtani 1971:312: "āsīt sa saugato nāthaḥ prajāyāḥ pṛthuvikramaḥ / dharmapāla iti khyāto rājye tasya mahodaye / śrīnālandāvihāre 'smin bhūto bhikṣur jitendriyaḥ / vīryaśrīdattanāmnedaṃ kṛtaṃ tena nibandhanam.") Scholars disagree about the precise dates of Dharmapāla's reign; however, most who discuss the issue hold his rule to have commenced sometime in the late eighth century (c. 780–790) and to have ended in the early ninth century (probably between 810 and 820). Cf. Basham 1963:71; Davidson 2003:52–53; Kulke and Rothermund 1998:111; Samtani 1971:133–134; Sinha 1954:337–367. This text should not be

confused with the unattributed commentary on the *Arthaviniścayasūtra* preserved in the Tibetan canon (D 4365; sna tshogs *nyo*, 1b1–192a7); the two texts are not the same.

102. Samtani 1971:276: "dharmapratisaṃvid iti yatsarvadharmeṣv iti vistaraḥ."

103. On the ways in which this particle may be employed in commentaries, see Tubb and Boose 2007:215–223.

104. Ibid.:276–277: "dharmaśabdena cātra deśanādharmaḥ pratigṛhyate / anekārtho hi dharmaśabdaḥ / tadyathā dharmaskandho bhikṣavo deśayiṣyāmy ādau kalyāṇam iti deśanādharmaḥ / tathā dharmaḥ katamaḥ āryāṣṭāṅgo mārga iti pratipattidharmaḥ / tathā dharmaṃ śaraṇaṃ gacchāmīti / phaladharmo nirvāṇam / yat sarvadharmeṣu kuśalākuśalādiṣu anupraveśaḥ kuśalādyavagamena tattatheti."

105. Note the parallelism with the opening phrase of the *Akṣayamatinirdeśasūtra*'s description of *dharmapratisaṃvid*, discussed previously. Cf. also the gloss found in the *Arthaviniścayasūtraṭīkā* (D, sna tshogs *nyo*, 187a7–b2). The latter does not mention dharma in the sense of teaching, but again interprets the discrimination of dharma in terms that are remarkably similar to those of the *Akṣayamatinirdeśasūtra*.

106. Shastri 1998:860: "dharmapratisaṃvid iti / iha deśanādharmaḥ / anekārtho hi dharmaśabdaḥ / tadyathā dharmaṃ vā bhikṣavo deśayiṣyāmi ādau kalyāṇaṃ madhye kalyāṇaṃ paryavāsane kalyāṇam svarthaṃ suvyañjanaṃ kevalaṃ paripūrṇaṃ pariśuddhaṃ brahmacaryaṃ saṃprakāśayiṣyāmi ity atra deśanādharmaḥ / dharmaḥ katamaḥ / āryāṣṭāṅgamārgaḥ ity atra pratipattidharmaḥ / tathā dharmaṃ śaraṇam gacchāmi ity atra phaladharmo nirvāṇam ity ādi."

107. See *Abhidharmakośabhāṣya* on *Abhidharmakośa* 7.37–7.38 (Shastri 1998: 860): "nāmapadavyañjanakāyeṣv arthavācitā avivartyajñānam dharmārthaniruktipratisaṃvido yathākramam." The extant Sanskrit may be corrupted here; the Tibetan translation by Jinamitra and Dpal brtsegs rakṣita (D, mngon pa *khu*, 59b3) reads: "chos dang don dang nges pa'i tshig so so yang dag par rig pa rnams ni go rims bzhin du ming dang tshig dang yi ge'i tshogs rnams dang / don dang ngag la thogs pa med par shes pa yin no."

108. See Gombrich 1987 for a parallel case.

109. Ironically, the very passage from Yaśomitra that Vīryaśrīdatta has chosen to graft is one that emphasizes the polysemy of the term "dharma" and highlights the fact that a single term can admit of multiple readings.

110. It is tempting to presume the point regarding interpersonal transmission to be closely related to the point regarding interpretive divergence, but it is perhaps worth noting that neither of these points entails the other.

111. On these strategies—sometimes grouped together under the general rubric of "Buddhist hermeneutics"—see the essays collected in Lopez 1988a.

112. Cf. Lamotte 1981a:84ff.; Schoening 1995:1.201–202.

3. Models of Argument

1. The translation here has been condensed from a longer passage that runs from D, mdo sde *ta*, 299a6–300b1: "de'i tshe bcom ldan 'das mkhyen bzhin du tshe dang

ldan pa kau ṇḍi nya la dge slong dga' bo da ltar gang na 'dug ces bka' stsal to / tshe dang ldan pa kau ṇḍi nyas gsol pa / bcom ldan 'das dge slong dga' bo ni da ltar shing sā la'i tshal 'di nas dpag tshad bcu gnyis kyi pha rol na bdud drug khri bzhi stong snyed kyis yongs su gtse zhing mchis so / bdud de rnams de bzhin gshegs pa'i gzugs su sprul nas / la la ni chos thams cad rten cing 'brel te 'byung ba yin no zhes smra / la la ni chos thams cad rten cing 'brel te 'byung ba ma yin no zhes smra / la la ni rten cing 'brel te 'byung ba'i chos thams cad rtag pa yin no zhes smra / la la ni rten cing 'brel te 'byung ba'i chos thams cad mi rtag pa yin no zhes smra / la la ni phung po lnga bden pa yin no zhes smra / la la ni sgyu ma yin no zhes smra / de bzhin du skye mched dang / khams dang / rgyas par ro / la la ni rten cing 'brel te 'byung ba yod / la la ni rkyen bzhi 'ba' zhig yod do zhes smra / la la ni chos thams cad sgyu ma lta bu dang / sprul pa lta bu dang / smig rgyu lta bu'o zhes smra / la la ni thos pa'i rgyu las chos thob bo zhes smra / la la ni bsams pa'i rgyu las chos thob bo zhes smra / la la ni bsgoms pa'i rgyu las chos thob bo zhes smra / . . . / la la stong pa nyid dang / mtshan ma med pa dang / smon pa med pa smra / 'dus byas song [sic] pa nyid dang / 'dus ma byas stong pa nyid dang / . . . rang gi mtshan nyid dang / byang chub stong pa dang / lam stong pa dang / mya ngan las 'das pa stong pa dang / stong pa nyid stong pa nyid dang . . . kyang ston to / . . . / langs sam smra 'am ci bgyi ba'i gtol ma mchis so / dge slong dga' bo ni bdud kyi zhags pas zin pa yang 'di snyam du sangs rgyas bcom ldan 'das rnams kyis gsungs pa ni so sor mi 'thun na / bdag gis da gang gzungs snyam sems so / bcom ldan 'das dge slong dga' bo ni de ltar sdug bsngal zhen po myong ste / de bzhin gshegs pa yid la dran yang dpung gnyen 'gyur ba ma mchis pas / 'khor gyi dkyil 'khor 'dir ma mchis pa lags so."

2. For evidence of the breadth and depth of current scholarship in this area, see the numerous papers collected in Balcerowicz 2003; Katsura 1999; and Steinkellner 1991. See also the lengthy bibliographies provided in Dreyfus 1997a; Dunne 2004; Patil 2009; and Steinkellner and Much 1995.

3. Cf. *Tattvasaṃgrahapañjikā* on *Tattvasaṃgraha* verse 1487 (Shastri 1997:370); *Pramāṇavārttika* II.3, III.1.

4. On this point, see McClintock 2010:56–57.

5. *Nyāyasūtrabhāṣya*, opening section: "pramāṇam antareṇa nārthapratipatt iḥ / nārthapratipattim antareṇa pravṛttisāmarthyam / pramāṇena khalv ayaṃ jñātārtham upalabhya tam īpsati vā jihāsati vā / tasyepsājihāsāprayuktasya samīhā pravrttir ity ucyate."

6. *Nyāyabiṇḍu*, 1.1–1.3: "samyagjñānapūrvikā sarvapuruṣārthasiddhir iti tadvyutpādyate / dvividham samyagjñānam / pratyakṣam anumānaṃ ca." The first verse is quoted in part by Kamalaśīla in the *Tattvasaṃgrahapañjikā* (Shastri 1997:9).

7. The qualifier "roughly speaking" is important in both cases. The scope of *pratyakṣa* is somewhat broader than the English "perception" suggests. Though *pratyakṣa* encompasses the deliverances of the five sense organs, it extends also to the deliverances of the mind (since the mind is traditionally counted as a sixth sense organ by Buddhist thinkers). Moreover, the description of the objects of *anumāna* offered here sidesteps the question of whether fully fledged inferences can afford access to so-called *atyantaparokṣa* (radically inaccessible) objects. On these issues, see Dunne 2004:23–25; Tillemans 1999:37–51.

8. For a concise overview of the structure of inference as understood by Buddhist thinkers, see Dunne 2004:26–35; Patil 2009 offers a more detailed account.

9. See Dunne 2004:chap. 3.

10. See Hayes 1987.

11. Cf. *Pramāṇasamuccaya* II.1; *Pramāṇavārttika* I.1; *Nyāyabindu* II.5; *Tattvasaṃgrahapañjikā* on *Tattvasaṃgraha* 1361–1362. The scope of *anumāna* is narrower than the connotations of the English "inference" suggest. We speak of sound and unsound inferences, but it would make little sense to speak of an unsound *anumāna*; an *anumāna* is, by definition, a means of correct cognition. "Unsound *anumāna*" is thus an oxymoron: if what we claim to know is, in fact, false, then our claim is not—cannot be—warranted by a means of correct cognition.

12. To say that the three features are necessary is not to imply that they are sufficient. See Patil 2010:177–183.

13. For Dharmakīrti's elaboration of this point, see Gillon and Hayes 2008. The term *vivakṣā* is borrowed from the Sanskrit grammatical tradition; on the grammarians' deployment of the term, see Radicchi 2002; Scharf 1995, 2002; van Nooten 1983. For an early Buddhist discussion of some of the issues raised here (a discussion that does not deploy technical terms of Buddhist epistemology), see *Kathāvatthu* IX.10 (Taylor 1979:416–417; trans. Aung and Rhys-Davids 1960:240–241).

14. I have followed Kamalaśīla in interpreting *pratyakṣānupalambhataḥ* as a *dvandva* compound. Compare, however, *Nyāyasūtrabhāṣya* on *Nyāyasūtra* 2.1.49, which sets forth a Buddhist *pūrvapakṣa*: "Testimony is inference; it is not a separate means of correct cognition. Why? Because the meaning of a word is to be inferred [on its basis]. For what reason [do we say that the meaning is] to be inferred? Since [it] is not perceptively apprehended (śabdo anumānaṃ na pramāṇāntaram kasmāc chabdārthasyānumeyatvāt / katham anumeyatvaṃ pratyakṣato 'nupalabdheḥ)."

15. This quotation juxtaposes *Tattvasaṃgraha* 1408–1409 and 2618–2619: "śabdas tu jñāpayaty arthaṃ naiva bāhyaṃ kathañcana / anyathāsambhāvābhāvād vivakṣāgamakas tv asau / ... vivakṣāsammukhībhāve na hi śabdaḥ prayujyate . . . sākṣāc chabdā na bahyārthapratibandhavivekataḥ / gamayantīti ca proktaṃ vivakṣāsūcakāstvamī / tasyāḥ kāryatayā te hi pratyakṣānupalambhataḥ / niścitā iti tenātra kāryakāraṇatā sphuṭā." On the *Tattvasaṃgraha(pañjikā)*, see Funayama 1992, 1995; Kapstein 2001; Kellner 1997; McClintock 2000, 2003, 2010; Steinkellner 2004. Passages from the *Tattvasaṃgraha* are here indexed by verse number; passages from the *Tattvasaṃgrahapañjikā* are referenced according to the pagination of the Shastri edition (1997). I have followed D. Shastri's numbering of the verses, which differs slightly from the Gaekwad edition (Krishnamacarya 1926): for verses above 525, the reader should add one to the verse number(s) given here to determine referenced verse(s) in the Gaekwad text. (The latter edition was used as the basis for Jha's English translation (1937–1939)—so, if referencing that translation, adjustments should be made accordingly.)

16. McClintock 2010; Seyfort Ruegg 1989; Taber 1996; Tillemans 1999, 2000.

17. On Buddhist uses of *abhiprāya*, see especially Broido 1984, 1988; Collier 1998; Seyfort Ruegg 1989:26–35.

18. This is not to say that the terms *abhiprāya* and *artha* are simply interchangeable, any more than it is to say the same of the English terms "intention" and "meaning." On this point, see Cavell 1985:524.

19. Cf. *Pramāṇavārttikasvopajñavṛtti* on *Pramāṇavārttika* I.213. The verse reads: "nāntarāyakatā 'bhavāc chabdānāṃ vastubhiḥ saha / nārthasiddhis tatas te hi vaktrābhiprāyasūcakāḥ." Dharmakīrti's gloss of *vaktrābhiprāyasūcakāḥ* reads "vaktur abhiprāyasya vivakṣāyās te śabdāḥ sūcakāḥ." Cf. also Manorathanandin's commentary on *Pramāṇavārttika* II.3cd (Shastri 1994:5), and Kamalaśīla's *Tattvasaṃgrahapañjikā* 4: "[An objector might protest:] those who desire to speak in one way (*ye yathā vivakṣanti*) [sometimes] do not act, when the time comes, in just that way. Thus, one whose intention is misleading (*visaṃvādanābhiprāyasya*) might compose a treatise that does not accord with [his own] position (*pratijñā*)." ("Na hi ye yathā vivakṣanti te tathaiva anuṣṭhānakāle kurvanti visaṃvādanābhiprāyasya anyathā pratijñāyā 'py anyathā śāstraracanāsambhavāt.") The source of the objection raised here may have been Arcaṭa, to whom Kamalaśīla's discussion appears indebted (see Funayama 1995). On issues raised by the opening section of the *Tattvasaṃgrahapañjikā*, see Eltschinger 2007; McClintock 2010: 47–111. Cf. also Wezler 1998.

20. Translation (slightly modified in parts) from Sattar 1994. The Sanskrit story from which this excerpt is taken is well known from Lanman's *Sanskrit Reader* (1967:49–53).

21. Cf. the discussion of *Fehlleistung*, or parapraxis, in Freud 1914.

22. See, among other places, the ninth verse of the fifth book of the *Mahābhārata*. The story is very old; it is recounted more than once in Vedic texts: Mādhyandina *Śatapathabrāhmaṇa* 1.6.3.1–1.6.3.10; Kāṇvīya *Śatapathabrāhmaṇa* 2.6.1.1–2.6.1.10; *Taittirīyasaṃhitā* 2.4.12.1. On "Indraśatrur varddhasva" as faulty utterance, see the *paspaśāhnika* of Patañjali's *Mahābhāṣya* and commentaries thereon; *Vākyapadīya* 3.10.5.

23. Cf. *Pramāṇavārttika* IV.28ff. (Tillemans 1999:47–54), where Dharmakīrti, commenting on (and reinterpreting) a remark made by Dignāga at *Pramāṇasamuccaya* III.2, explicitly unpacks the inferential thesis (*sādhya*) as something that is "accepted" (*iṣṭa*). See also Iwata 2007.

24. Cf. *Tattvasaṃgraha* 3593–3595. See, however, an intriguing passage from the *Aṅgulimālasutta* (MN 86, ii.103), where the Buddha appears to be portrayed as misspeaking.

25. *Tattvasaṃgraha* 1515: "bhrāntasyānyavivakṣāyāṃ vākyaṃ ced anyad īkṣyate / yathāvivakṣam apy etat tasmān naiva pravartate." Cf. Krishnamacarya's version of *padas* c and d: "tathā vivakṣāsāmanye tasmān naiva pravartate."

26. Shastri 1997:376–377: "nanu ca vivakṣāyām api śabdasya naiva prāmāṇyaṃ yuktam / tathā hi na tāvad vivakṣāviśeṣe prāmāṇyam vyabhicārāt / bhrāntasy ānyavivakṣāyām anyavākyadarśanāt / nāpi vivakṣāsāmānye vaiphalyāt / na hi vivakṣāmātravijñānaṃ kvacid vyavahārāṅgatāṃ pratipadyate tato 'rthaviśeṣāniścayāt."

27. *Tattvasaṃgraha* 1516–1517: "bhrāntābhrāntaprayuktānāṃ vailakṣaṇyam parisphuṭam /vidagdhāḥ prakṛtādibhyo niścinvanti girām alam / vailakṣaṇyena hetūnāṃ viśeṣaṃ tāsu ye na tu / avagacchanti dośo 'yam teṣāṃ liṅgasya nāsti tu."

28. Shastri 1997:377: "avaśyam hi bhrāntābhrantaprayuktānāṃ vailakṣaṇyam aṅgīkartavyam anyathā na kāraṇabhedo bhedakaḥ syāt / tac ca vailakṣaṇyaṃ kuśalāḥ puruṣā niścinvanty eva prakṛtādibhyaḥ / prakṛtam prakaraṇam / ādiśabd enāvyākulatā mukhaprasannatādi gṛhyate / vailakṣaṇyam eva girāṃ katham / . . . kāraṇabhedād iti yāvat / tasmāt suvivecitaṃ kāryaṃ na kāraṇaṃ vyabhicaratīti bhavaty eva vivakṣāviśeṣe prāmāṇyam."

29. *Tattvasaṃgraha* 1520–1521: "vivakṣāyāñ ca gamyāyāṃ vispaṣṭaiva trirūpatā / puṃsi dharmiṇi sā sādhyā kāryeṇa vacasā yataḥ / pādapārthavivakṣāvān puruṣo 'yaṃ pratīyate / vṛkṣaśabdaprayoktṛtvāt pūrvāvasthāsv ahaṃ yathā."

30. On *saṃketa*, see Arnold 2006. The idea of language as governed by convention is an old one in the Buddhist tradition, as is the idea that conventions are multiple, and that to be a Buddha is to have obtained perfect mastery over them. (See, for example, the tale of four kings from the Mūlasarvāstivāda *Vinayavastu*, cited in the introduction herein.) A passage in the *Tathāgatācintyaguhyanirdeśa* (D, dkon brtsegs *ka*, 141b4–142a4) notes that "although linguistic conventions are diverse, the Tathāgata, speaking the appropriate language, articulates truths via various terms (brda yang tha dad pa der yang de bzhin gshegs pas skad kyi 'jug pa ji lta ba bzhin du ming tha dad pa rnams kyis bden pa dag rnam par bkod de)." The passage goes on to identify forty-seven varieties of the Tathāgata's speech. Some are identified by referencing particular locations across South, Southeast, East, and Central Asia (e.g., *yul ka sha, kam bo dza, ya ba na, tho gar yul, yul mthas gtugs pa, rgya yul, glo bkra*). Others are identified by referencing particular groups (*bram ze, rgyal rigs, rje'u rigs, dmangs rigs*). This intermingling of geography and social class implies something noteworthy about the concept of *saṃketa* as formulated in the *Tathāgatācintyaguhyanirdeśa*: discrete linguistic conventions are held to structure not only languages and dialects, but also what we might term "sociolects."

31. See Shastri 1997:597 (commenting on *Tattvasaṃgraha* 2618), where Kamalaśīla acknowledges this point by noting that although particular utterances are invariably *effects of* particular desires to speak, they do not *express* those desires: "[Utterances] do not propound the desire to speak as [what is] to be expressed [by them]. What, then [do they do]? They index [the desire to speak] by being inferential signs [for it] (vivakṣām api na vācyatayā pratipādayanti kim tarhi liṅgatayā sūcayanti)." Cf. Kamalaśīla's similar contrast between *śabda* as *gamaka* and *śabda* as *vācaka* (Shastri 1997:354, commenting on *Tattvasaṃgraha* 1408ab).

32. *Tattvasaṃgraha* 772: "bhedajñāne satīcchā hi saṃketakaraṇe tataḥ / tatkṛtis tacchrutiś cāsyābhogas tanmatis tataḥ."

33. Jha's translation of the passage (1937–1939:1.438) renders the derivatives of √kṛ as "set up," thereby privileging the second interpretation and resolving (i.e., obscuring) the ambiguity in the Sanskrit.

34. Shastri 1997:82, commenting on *Tattvasaṃgraha* 206: "svatantrecchāmātrabhāvī hi saṃketaḥ."

35. Ibid.: "na hi saṃketam antareṇa śabdānām prakṛtyā 'rthaprakāśanam asti / avyutpannasyāpi tato 'rthapratītiprasaṅgāt."

36. Cf. *Pramāṇavārttika* IV.109.

37. For a telling example of such slippage, see *Tattvasaṃgraha* 1478–1480 and Kamalaśīla's commentary thereon.

38. See Travis 1989, 1996, 1997, 2000. The ensuing example is used also in Putnam 1999:87–88.

39. This is not a strike against so-called "semantic inferentialist" accounts (e.g., Brandom 2000), since the model of inference presumed in such accounts is considerably more flexible than the model of inference discussed here.

40. Shastri 1997:5–7. For additional discussion, see Eltschinger 2007. As Dunne has noted (2004:375), this point is anticipated in Śākyabuddhi's *Pramāṇavārttikaṭīkā*.

4. Models of Explication

1. These two texts are translated and discussed in Ñāṇamoli 1962, 1964. They have received a measure of scholarly attention—chiefly through the pioneering studies of George Bond (1980, 1982, 1988)—though their structural complexity and forbidding metalanguage have served to discourage many from close investigation of their contents.

2. D 4061 (sems tsam *shi*, 29a2–134b2). The text is number 649 in the *Catalogue* (Herrmann-Pfandt 2008:361–362). A critical edition of the *Vyākhyāyukti* was published in Japan in 2001 by Lee. The Tibetan reproduced in the notes has been drawn from this edition; however, in consideration of the difficulty of obtaining it, I have opted to supplement page references to it with page references to D. Discrepancies between the critical edition and D will be noted when they occur.

3. On the influence of the *Vyākhyāyukti* upon subsequent commentarial literature, see Schoening 1995:138–43; Skilling 2000:330–334.

4. Schoening 1995:1.39.

5. See appendix A herein; Skilling 2000:330–33; Samtani 1971, 2002.

6. Tatia 1976. The root text and commentary are both attested in the *Catalogue*. See Herrmann-Pfandt 2008:385–386.

7. "One of the most important texts of the Yogācāra school" (de Jong 1973:339). Modern scholars have often attributed the *Abhidharmasamuccayabhāṣya* to Sthiramati, following an attribution that is found in some Chinese sources. In support of this attribution, Pradhan has noted that several passages in the text of the *Abhidharmasamuccayabhāṣya* very closely replicate passages from the *Triṃśikāvijñaptibhāṣya*—also attributed to Sthiramati—and, on this basis, has unequivocally stated that "it is Sthiramati who has written the *Bhāṣyas* on both the *Triṃśikā* and the *Abhidharmasamuccaya*" (1950:19). Pradhan's confidence may, however, be misplaced. The presence of parallel passages in two texts is not evidence that those texts were authored by the same individual; at best, such parallelism signals only that one author was familiar with the work of another—hence, Pradhan's attribution of authorship on the basis of such "evidence" is conjectural. The tenability of this conjecture is eroded by two further considerations. First, the attribution to Sthiramati is not shared by all traditional sources: the Tibetan translation of the text attributes it to Jinaputra (rgyal ba'i sras), and N. Tatia and M. Shinoda have called attention to a competing Chinese attribution according to which the text was authored

by neither Sthiramati nor Jinaputra, but by a figure named Buddhasiṃha (cf. de Jong 1973:340–341). Second, the author of the *Abhidharmasamuccayabhāṣya* at times appears unfamiliar with Vasubandhu's interpretations of certain technical terms. (For an example of one such divergence, compare the treatments of the "transformation of syllables" (*akṣarapariṇāma*) offered in appendix A and appendix B.) We would not expect such ignorance from Sthiramati, who is generally presumed to have known Vasubandhu's work quite well. Of course, neither of these considerations offers anything like conclusive proof that the author of the *Triṃśikāvijñaptibhāṣya* was not the author of the *Abhidharmasamuccayabhāṣya*, but they weigh against uncritically accepting the attribution in the absence of further supporting evidence.

8. Also extant (though unattested in the *Catalogue*) is a text bearing the title *Abhidharmasamuccayavyākhyā*, which for the most part interweaves the root text of the *Abhidharmasamuccaya* with the text of the *bhāṣya*. Kritzer (2005) has stressed certain points of divergence between the *vyākhyā* and the *bhāṣya*, and his points are well taken. However, the passages from the *bhāṣya* examined here correspond very closely to those of the *vyākhyā*. I wish to thank Alberto Todeschini for alerting me to Kritzer's study.

9. D 4042 (sems tsam 'i, 48a1–68b7). The **Vivaraṇasaṃgrahaṇī* may be the text attested as number 619 in the *Catalogue* (Herrmann-Pfandt 2008:348). On the Yogācārabhūmi, see Kritzer 2005:xii–xvii; Silk 2001. I wish to thank Stephen Hodge for kindly providing me with his preliminary translation of the **Vivaraṇasaṃgraha ṇī* (still unpublished, to my knowledge). The translation in appendix C is my own.

10. See Cabezón 1992; Schoening 1995, 1996; Skilling 2000; Verhagen 2005. Nearly a decade before Cabezón's study appeared, L. W. J. van der Kuijp drew attention to the need to study the *Vyākhyāyukti* and *Abhidharmasamuccaya* with a view toward determining their impact on Buddhist hermeneutics (1983:258, n. 10).

11. Verhagen 2005:568.

12. Here, the Tibetan and Chinese translations read *guṇa* ("virtuous qualities") for *gaṇa* ("multitudes").

13. Although the Sanskrit "of the sage" (*muneḥ*) is singular, the Tibetan translation explicitly marks it as plural (*thub pa dag gi*).

14. *Abhidharmakośa* 8.41–8.43: "nimīlite śāstari lokacakṣuṣi kṣayaṃ gate sākṣijane ca bhūyasā /adṛṣṭatattvair niravagrahaiḥ kṛtaṃ kutārkikaiḥ śāsanam etad ākulam / gate hi śāntiṃ paramāṃ svayambhuvi svayambhuvaḥ śāsanadhūrdhareṣu ca / jagaty anāthe gaṇaghātibhir malaiḥ niraṅkuśaṃ svairam ihādya caryate / evaṃ kaṇṭhagataprāṇaṃ viditvā śāsanaṃ muneḥ / balakālaṃ malānāṃ ca na pramādyaṃ mumukṣubhiḥ."

15. Vasubandhu himself comments on this verse in the *Vyākhyāyukti* as follows: "In brief, corruption is of two kinds. There is corruption of scripture (*lung yongs su nyams pa*, **āgamaparihāṇi*)—[its] phrasing and meaning—and there is corruption of realization (*rtogs pa yongs su nyams pa*, **adhigamaparihāṇi*). Moreover, hearing is corrupted, since most who hear [the teaching] turn away [from it] and most fail to grasp the teaching thoroughly. Correct understanding is corrupted, since [the teaching] is explained improperly. Correct contemplation is corrupted, since one is ruined. [The phrase] 'These days, good explication has come to an end . . .' refers to the disappearance [of the teaching]. Accordingly, having understood that the teach-

ing of the Buddha is corrupted and will not remain for long, those who have faith in listening, grasping, and attaining the consistent meaning [of the dharma] should exert themselves for this short time [that they possess] a [human] body." Cf. Lee 2001:282–283 (D, sems tsam *shi*, 124b5–125a1).

16. Lee 2001:282 (D, sems tsam *shi*, 124b1–125a2): "nyan pa'i skye bo dag ni phal cher phyir phyogs dang / yongs su 'dzin par byed pa phal cher 'das pa dang / nyes par rnam par bshad pa dag gis mthu bcom pas / deng sang legs par bshad pa mthar gyur to / . . . / deng sang thub pa'i gsung ni smra bar byed pa'ang nyung / dngul dang gser du 'byed par 'gyur ba'ang nyung bar gyur / de ltar lung dang rtogs pa dag la 'bad zhan pas / sangs rgyas nyi ma mthar phyin dri ma med 'di nub / de lta bas na ji srid thams cad ma nub pa / de srid ji bzhin don rnams dbye la 'bad par gyis / thub pa'i gsung gi snang ba nub par gyur na ni / 'gro ba kun du mun pa gcig pu'i thibs por 'gyur."

17. Ibid.:1 (D, sems tsam *shi*, 29a3): "blo chung ba / mdo rnams 'chad 'dod de dag la / de la phan par bya ba'i phyir man ngag cung zad bstan par bya."

18. A similar twofold approach can be seen even more clearly in the structure of the **Vivaraṇasaṃgrahaṇī* (translated in appendix C). A distinction between "theory" and "practice" is not, however, explicitly thematized in these texts.

19. Skilling 2000:298.

20. D 4060, sems tsam *shi*, 17b1–29a2. Unattested in the *Catalogue*.

21. D 4069, sems tsam *si*, 139b1–301a7. The text is number 650 in the *Catalogue* (Herrmann-Pfandt 2008:362). In D, the sections of the commentary that correlate with the five books of the original text are as follows: Book I: 139b1–155a6; Book II: 155a6–248a1; Book III: 248a1–265a3; Book IV: 265a3–278a7; Book V: 278a7–301a7. Guṇamati—who, according to Xuanzang, hailed from south India (Li 1996:236)—is held by Tāranātha to have been a student of Guṇaprabha (himself reportedly a student of Vasubandhu) and to have had as students both Vasumitra and Sthiramati. Nakamura (1999:280) hypothesizes Guṇamati's dates as c. 420–500 C.E.; Frauwallner (1961:858–859) places him somewhat later, although he does not specify precise dates. Cf. Mejor 1991:49–51; Skilling 2000:313–314; Verhagen 2005:564–565.

22. Cf. the **Vivaraṇasaṃgrahaṇī*'s extensive description of the idealized dharma preacher (appendix C, section 3).

23. The **Vivaraṇasaṃgrahaṇī* presents a comparable list of qualities, substituting *thos pa 'dzin pa* for Vasubandhu's *thos pa'i gzhi can*. See appendix C, section 3.1. Cf. the *Vyākhyāyuktiṭīkā*, which stresses that one becomes endowed with the basis of hearing due to grasping what one has heard (D, sems tsam *si*, 141b4).

24. Lee 2001:2 (D, sems tsam *shi*, 29a3–5): "ji ltar na thos pa mang ba dang / thos pa gzhi can dang / thos pa bsags pa yin zhe na / chos gang dag thog mar dge ba zhes bya ba mdo las rgya cher ji skad bstan pa lta bu'o."

25. Ibid. (D, sems tsam *shi*, 17b1–3): "chos gang dag thog mar dge ba / bar du dge ba / tha mar dge ba / don bzang po / tshig 'bru bzang po / ma 'dres [D: 'bres] pa / yongs su rdzogs pa / yongs su dag pa / yongs su byang pa / tshang [G: tshangs] par spyod pa / mngon par brjod pas mngon par rjod par byed pa ni mang du thos pa dang / thos pa'i gzhi can dang / thos pa bsags pa yin te/ de chos de lta bu mang bo thos pa dang / bzung [D: gzung] ba dang / kha ton [Peking (hereafter P): don] byed pa dang / yid kyis brtags pa dang / mthong bas shin tu rtogs pa yin no zhes bya ba."

26. Ibid. (D, sems tsam *shi*, 29a5–b6): "de la chos ni mdo la sogs pa ste / rigs pa ston pa'i don dang / don phyin ci ma log par nges par 'dzin pa'i don gyis so / tshangs par spyod pa ni mya ngan las 'das pa'i lam yin no / mya ngan las 'das pa ni mchog tu gtso bo yin pa'i don gyis tshangs pa yin te / zhi ba dang bsil bar gyur pa dang tshangs par gyur pa zhes gsungs pa'i phyir ro / der gang gis spyod par byed pa dang / 'gro bar byed pa dang / thob par byed pa de ni tshangs par spyod pa yin te / 'dis myos par 'gyur bas chang zhes bya ba bzhin no / de'i thog ma dang bar dang tha ma dag ni tshul khrims dang / ting nge 'dzin dang / shes rab kyi phung po dag yin te / 'di ltar 'od srung ba'i sde pa dag gi mdo las / dge slong dag khyed la ngas chos thog mar dge ba / bar du dge ba / tha mar dge ba dag bstan pa yin te tshangs par spyod pa'i thog ma gang zhe na / tshul khrims dang ldan par gnas pa dang zhes rgya cher 'byung ba dang / tshangs par spyod pa'i bar gang zhe na / 'dod pa dag las dben pa zhes bya ba nas rgyas par bsam gtan bzhi pa'i bar tu rdzogs par byas te gnas pa yin no zhes 'byung ba dang / tshangs par spyod pa'i tha ma gang zhe na / 'di ni sdug bsngal 'phags pa'i bden pa yin no zhes yang dag pa ji lta ba bzhin du rab tu shes pa nas / rnam par grol ba la rnam par grol lo snyam tu ye shes mthong ba 'byung ba yin no zhes bya ba'i bar du rgya cher 'byung ba yin no / dge ba yang yongs su nyams pa med pas mi slu ba'i phyir ro / don bzang po tshig 'bru bzang po ni / go rims bzhin tu phyin ci ma log pa dang go bar byed pa gnyis kyis brjod par bya ba dang / rjod pa phun sum tshogs pa'i phyir ro / ma 'dres pa la sogs pa ni thun mong pa ma yin pa'i phyir dang / nyon mongs pa thams cad kyi gnyen po'i phyir dang / ngo bo nyid dang rgyud rnam par 'grol ba gnyis kyis rnam par grol ba'i phyir te / go rims gzhin no / gzhan yang thog ma dang bar dang / tha mar dge ba ni don bzang po dang tshig 'bru bzang po dang / ma 'dres pa la sogs pa yin pa'i phyir ro."

27. See ibid.:6–249; D 30b2–114a6. Cf. the *Abhidharmasamuccayabhāṣya*'s discussion of summary explication (*vyākhyāsaṃgraha*), in appendix B, section 2.1, and the **Vivaraṇasaṃgrahaṇī*'s discussion of the fivefold protocol that a dharma preacher should follow in presenting the dharma to others, in appendix C, section 2. Schoening 1996 notes that Vasubandhu's list may be indebted to a fourfold list—the *anubandhacatuṣṭaya*—that is often found at the opening of non-Buddhist Sanskrit śāstras and may have influenced aspects of the notion of *dgos 'brel* (on which, see Broido 1983; Schoening 1995:33–34). Although more research in this area is needed, the fivefold list of aspects may also inform another list of textual features that later non-Buddhist commentators will emphasize: the components of a structurally sound śāstric section (*adhikaraṇa*), typically held also to be five in number. On the rhetoric of the śāstric preamble, see the papers collected in Slaje 2008.

28. Ibid.:6 (D, sems tsam *shi*, 30b2–3, 30b4–6): "ji ltar mdo sde rnam par bshad par bya zhe na / rnam pa lnga dag gis te / mdo sde'i dgos pa dang / bsdus pa'i don dang / tshig gi don dang / mtshams dbyar ba dang / brgal ba dang / lan gnyis brjod par bya'o // . . . ci'i phyir 'di dag brjod par bya zhe na / mdo sde'i don gyi che ba nyid thos na nyan pa dang 'dzin pa la 'bad par byed pas dgos pa brjod par bya'o / dgos pa de'ang mdo sde'i bsdus pa'i don las rtogs par 'gyur ro / bsdus pa'i don yang tshig gi don las so / tshig gi don gyi go rims mi 'gal ba ni mtshams sbyar ba las so / rigs pa dang mi 'gal pa dang / snga phyi mi 'gal ba ni brgal ba dang lan las yin pas na bsdus pa'i don la sogs pa yang brjod par bya'o."

29. Cf. the discussion of the outline (*uddeśa*) at the opening of Vīryaśrīdatta's *Arthaviniścayasūtranibandhana*: "The outline is presented for the student's ease of comprehension. Indeed, a person who has understood the overall meaning [of a text] can easily learn the meaning of each part, just as a horse fearlessly traverses ground that it has already seen" (Samtani 1971:73: "uddeśaḥ punaḥ śiṣyasukhāvabodhārthaṃ kriyate / avabuddhasamudāyārtho hy avayavārthaṃ sukhena pratipadyate / dṛṣṭab hūminiḥsaṃgāśvaprasarpaṇavad iti").

30. Commentators may sometimes locate these aspects of the commentarial act in the sūtra text upon which they are commenting, and thus the formal features of commentary may be understood to recapitulate the formal features of sūtra texts. Such recapitulation is explicitly acknowledged in Vīryaśrīdatta's discussion (in the *Arthaviniścayasūtranibandhana*) of the ways in which the *Arthaviniścayasūtra* itself manifests aspects that functionally parallel those identified in the *Vyākhyāyukti*: "Moreover, [in the *Arthaviniścayasūtra*] the explanation (*nirdeśa* [cf. *padārtha*]) is offered [by the Buddha] in order to analyze what has been briefly outlined, since they are commentary and aphorism, as it were. That is, the explication is, as it were, a commentary; the outline (*uddeśa* [cf. *piṇḍārtha*]), an aphorism. The summary meaning of the outline—the sūtra—is easily understood when analyzed via the explication—the commentary" (Samtani 1971:73: "nirdeśo 'pi saṃkṣiptenoddiṣṭavibhajanārthaṃ kriyate vṛttisūtr abhūtatvāt / vṛttibhūto hi nirdeśaḥ / sūtrabhūta uddeśaḥ / sūtrabhūtasyoddeśasya piṇḍībhūto 'rtho vṛttibhūtena nirdeśena vibhajyamānaḥ sukhaṃ gamyate"). Cf. also the distinction drawn often in the *Vyākhyāyukti* between passages that constitute "teachings" and passages that constitute "expositions" (an instance of this can be seen in appendix A, section 1.3.3.3.2).

31. The first of these is explicitly stated to occur in the (*Mahāyāna*)*sūtrālaṃkāra*, though I have not been able to locate a corresponding verse in that text. The **Vivaraṇasaṃgrahaṇī* likewise ends with a brief appendix specifying an alternative approach to explication (see appendix C, section 9).

32. See Lee 2001:8–12 and D 30b4–33a2 for Vasubandhu's treatment of the purpose. For discussion of Kamalaśīla's treatment of *prayojana*, see Eltschinger 2007; McClintock 2010:105–111.

33. Lee 2001:8 (D, sems tsam *shi*, 31a5): "mdo sde'i dgos pa ni bsdu na rnam pa bzhir rig par bya ste."

34. Cf. the *Abhidharmasamuccayabhāṣya*'s "classification of persons" (appendix B, section 2.8), and the **Vivaraṇasaṃgrahaṇī*'s mention of twenty-seven [kinds of] persons (appendix C, conclusion of section 1.1 and section 5).

35. A term with a wide semantic range, the Sanskrit *paryāya* may be used in the sense of "arrangement," "discourse," or "figurative expression," among other things. Often rendered into English as "synonym," it marks not the relation of synonymy as conceptualized in modern semantics, but close conceptual affiliation between two terms (as is often the case for ordinary, nontechnical uses of the English term "synonym" as well). Edgerton (1953:2.335) has called attention to the fact that the term is often employed in Buddhist literature to mean something very close to *upāya*, or "(skill in) means." Such seems to be the case in this particular context; I have therefore opted to translate the term *paryāya* in this case as "rhetorical strategy." For additional pertinent remarks, see Davidson 2009; Hallisey 1994:131–133; Sasaki 1962.

36. That this feature is constitutive does not imply that it is also distinctive. The term *paryāya* also features in the title of one of the earliest foundational treatises of Sarvāstivādin Abhidharma—the *Saṅgītiparyāya*, attributed to Mahākauṣṭhila. On this text, see Frauwallner 1995:13–15.

37. Lee 2001:10 (D, sems tsam *shi*, 31b7): "dgos pa dag ni brgyad de rnam grangs gsungs pa ni 'dul ba tha dad pa'i phyir te."

38. Ibid.; D, sems tsam *shi*, 32a3–4.

39. See ibid.:13 (D, sems tsam *shi*, 33a2–6) for Vasubandhu's treatment of the summary meaning.

40. Ibid. (D, sems tsam *shi*, 33a2–3): "de las ni bsdu na gang zhig ji ltar yongs su shes par bya ba dang yongs su shes pa gang yin pa dang / yongs su shes pa'i 'bras bu gang yin pa dang / de rjod par byed pa gang yin pa ni bsdus pa'i don to." The sevenfold presentation of the summary meaning in Kamalaśīla's *Śālistambasūtraṭīkā* (see Schoening 1995:194–198) appears heavily indebted to the account offered here. Cf. also the *Abhidharmasamuccayabhāṣya*'s discussion of "six components" (appendix B, section 1) and the alternative account preserved in the **Vivaraṇasaṃgrahaṇī* (appendix C, section 9).

41. Ibid.:225, 239 (D, sems tsam *shi*, 105b6, 106a1, 111a1).

42. D, sems tsam *si*, 146a1–4: "dge slong dag gzugs yod pa 'di la mi rtag par yang dag par rjes su lta ba de la ni yang dag pa'i lta ba de 'byung ste / yang dag par mthong na skyo zhing dga' ba zad pa'i phyir 'dod chags zad par 'gyur la / dga' ba dang 'dod chags zad pa las sems shin tu rnam par grol ba yin no zhes smra'o / dge slong dag dge slong tshor dang / 'du shes dang / 'du byed rnams dang / rnam par shes pa yod pa 'di la mi rtag par yang dag par rjes su lta ba de la ni yang dag pa'i lta ba de 'byung ste / yang dag pa mthong na skyo shing dga' ba zad pa'i phyir 'dod chags zad par 'gyur la / dga' ba dang 'dod chags zad pa las sems rab tu rnam par grol ba yin no zhes smra'o / de ltar dge slong sems yang dag par shin tu rnam par grol na / gal te 'dod na bdag nyid kyis bdag nyid la bdag gi skye ba zad do."

43. Lee 2001:13 (D, sems tsam *shi*, 33a3–6): "ci zhig yongs su shes par bya zhe na / gzugs la sogs pa sdug bsngal gyi bden pas bsdus pa'o / ji ltar yongs su shes par bya zhe na / mi rtag par ro / yongs su shes pa gang shes na / yang dag pa'i lta ba'o / yongs su shes pa'i bras bu gang zhe na / skyo ba la sogs pa'i rim gyis sems shin tu rnam par grol ba nyid do / de rjod par byed pa gang yin zhe na / bdag gi skye ba zad do zhes bya ba de lta bu la sogs pa'o."

44. Ibid.:13 (D, sems tsam *shi*, 33a6): "tshig gi don ni rjod pa gang gi brjod par bya ba gang yin pa." See Lee 2001:13–163 (D, sems tsam *shi*, 33a6–84a5) for Vasubandhu's treatment of the meaning of phrases.

45. Ibid.: "de yang kha cig ni gcig la du ma 'byung ba dang / kha cig ni du ma la gcig 'byung ba."

46. Vasubandhu may have intended to discuss fourteen terms. See appendix A.

47. D, sems tsam *si*, 147a5: "ma zla ba'i bu mo'i bu lhas byin dge slong rnams la 'di ltar tshe dang ldan pa dag dge slong sems kyis sems shin tu sbyangs pa de'i sems de ni 'dod chags dang bral ba dang / zhe sdang dang bral ba dang / gti mug dang bral ba yin te / kun du chags pa ma yin pa'i chos can / kun du zhe sdang ba ma yin pa'i chos can / kun du gti mug pa ma yin pa'i chos can / 'dod pa'i srid pa dang / gzugs kyi srid pa dang / gzugs med pa'i srid par mi ldog pa'i chos can yin no." Cf. AN 9.1.3.6.

48. Lee 2001:14 (D, sems tsam *shi*, 33a7–b1): "de dag dang mi ldan par shes par bya ste / kun tu chags pa ma yin pa'i chos can zhes bya ba la sogs pa gsungs pa'i phyir / phyir mi ldog pa'i chos can zhes gsungs pa'i phyir te / yongs su nyams pa med pa dang / phyir ldog pa med pas phyi rol pa'i 'dod chags dang bral ba dang chos mi mthun pa'i phyir ro."

49. D, sems tsam *si*, 146b6–147a3. As Skilling (2000:341) has pointed out, this passage closely parallels one from the *Saṃghabhedavastu* (cf. Gnoli 1978:248). Cf. also SN 2.5.9. A similar passage is also cited in Yaśomitra's *Sphuṭārthavyākhyā* (Shastri 1998:1107): "sarāgaṃ cittam sarāgaṃ cittam iti yathābhūtaṃ prajānāti / vigatarāgaṃ cittaṃ vigatarāgaṃ cittam iti yathābhūtaṃ prajānāti / sadveṣaṃ vigatadveṣaṃ samohaṃ vigatamohaṃ saṃkṣiptaṃ vikṣiptaṃ līnam pragṛhītam uddhatam anuddhatam avyupaśāntaṃ vyupaśāntaṃ samāhitam asamāhitam abhāvitaṃ subhāvitam avimuktam vā cittam avimuktaṃ cittam iti yathābhūtaṃ prajānāti."

50. Cf. *Abhidharmakośabhāṣya* on *Abhidharmakośa* 7.11 (Shastri 1998:818–825).

51. Typically, all of these associated terms are included in the initial brief mnemonic verse; occasionally, however, the terms found in the verse are supplemented by others (interpolations?) in the ensuing discussion.

52. Lee 2001:17 (D, sems tsam *shi*, 34b3).

53. Ibid.:22 (D, sems tsam *shi*, 36b4): "bag la nyal yang dag par bcom pa la ni kun tu sbyor ba gsum spangs pa las / rgyun tu zhugs pa yin no zhes 'byung ba lta bu'o." Cf. MN 118, iii.81.

54. Ibid.:25 (D, sems tsam *shi*, 37b6): "tshig du ma la don gcig pa ni dper na rnam grangs kyi tshig lta bu'o."

55. Ibid.:26 (D, sems tsam *shi*, 37b7): "de la so so re re la brjod par bya ba'i don ni rjod pa gang gi brjod par bya ba yang yin te [D: no]."

56. Ibid.:26 (D, sems tsam *shi*, 38a1): "bsdus pa'i don ni don tha dad pa'i tshig rnams kyi don bsdus pa gang yin pa ste."

57. Cf. the threefold typology of *pratītyasamutpāda* that Vasubandhu offers at *Abhidharmakośa* 3.26 (Shastri 1998:349).

58. Regrettably, Guṇamati opts to pass over the difficulties raised by this section of the text.

59. Lee 2001:26 (D, sems tsam *shi*, 38a1): "ci phyir bstan pa byas zhes dgos pa'i don brjod dgos te."

60. Ibid.:29 (D, sems tsam *shi*, 39a2–3): "grangs gsungs pa ni kha cig ni bgrang bar bya ba nges par gzung ba'i phyir."

61. Skilling 2000:336.

62. Of course, this may itself be understood as an exegetical principle, albeit a rather formal one. A detailed investigation of the contents of Book II and the assumptions that undergird its construction is a desideratum, but it is outside the scope of the present work. (A full, annotated translation of the whole of the *Vyākhyāyukti* is, however, currently in preparation [Nance in preparation b].)

63. Cf. appendix C, section 2.3.2. I have previously used the phrase "rhetorical strategies" to render *rnam grangs* (**paryāya*). Vasubandhu clearly wants to use the term in various ways, and I have tried to capture these variant uses with shifts in English terminology. Here, *paryāya* is being used in a sense roughly comparable to that of the English "synonym," as is clarified by Vasubandhu's ensuing gloss and

example—cited in Lee 2001:162; D, sems tsam *shi*, 83b7–84a1: "de dang de la yang dag pa ji lta ba bzhin du mi shes pa dang / mi mthong ba dang / mngon par ma rtogs pa dang / mun khung dang / kun tu rmongs pa dang / ma rig pa dang / mun pa gang yin pa di ni ma rig pa zhes bya'o zhes 'byung ba lta bu'o."

64. Lee 2001:162 (D, sems tsam *shi*, 83b6): "rab tu dbye ba ni brjod par bya ba de gzugs can dang / gzugs can ma yin pa dang / bstan du yod pa dang / bstan du med pa la sogs pa'i rnam par rab tu dbye bas so."

65. Ibid.: "so so yang dag par rig pa'i rgyu yang byas pa." Editions of the Tibetan text vary here. C, D read *sa* (**bhūmi*), whereas Lee (with G, P, and Guṇamati across editions) reads *rgyu* (**hetu*). At D, sems tsam *si*, 248a3–4, Guṇamati associates each of the four components with one of the four discriminations: synonyms serve as a contributing cause (*nye rgyu*, **upakaraṇa*) for the discrimination of dharma, definitions for the discrimination of things, etymological explanation for the discrimination of expression, and analysis for the discrimination of eloquence.

66 . See ibid.:163–167 (D, sems tsam *shi*, 84a5–85b4) for Vasubandhu's treatment of connection.

67. The *Abhidharmasamuccayabhāṣya* also mentions connection (*anusaṃdhi*), but the text does not go on to discuss the topic explicitly. However, its treatment of "successive ordering" (appendix B, section 2.4) appears to share certain commonalities with Vasubandhu's account of connection. The **Vivaraṇasaṃgrahaṇī* briefly discusses connection as well (appendix C, section 2.5).

68. Lee 2001:164 (D, sems tsam *shi*, 84b1): "snga phyi nyid kyis [D: phyi kyi] go rims kyi mtshams sbyar ba ni dper na 'phags pa'i bden pa rnams las ci'i phyir 'bras bu'i 'og tu rgyu bstan . . . 'phags pa'i bden pa rnams kyi bshad pa'i mtshams sbyar ba ni ji ltar mngon par rtogs pa bzhin du yin te / sdug bsngal la sdug bsngal nyid du mthong [D: mthongs] nas 'di ga las byung zhes rgyu tshol bar byed do / de nas de 'gog pa la'o / de nas 'gog pa'i thabs la ste / de ltar na nad dang de'i gzhi dang / nad med pa nyid dang / sman tshol ba'i tshul gyis snga ma snga ma la rnam par dpyod pa'i phyir 'phags pa'i bden pa rnams ji ltar mngon par rtogs pa de ltar bshad pa yin te / 'di ni de'i mtshams sbyar ba yin no."

69. See ibid.:167–249 (D, sems tsam *shi*, 85b4–114a6) for Vasubandhu's treatment of objections and responses. Cf. **Vivaraṇasaṃgrahaṇī*, appendix C, section 2.4.

70. Cf. *Aṣṭādhyāyī* 3.4.21: *samānakartṛkayoḥ pūrvakāle*. For further discussion of the implications of this grammatical rule for Buddhist philosophical analysis, see Salvini 2011. The concerns raised here appear to be similar to those discussed in the portion of the *Abhidharmakośabhāṣya* dealing with the first two *pada*s of *Abhidharmakośa* 3.28—a section that Yaśomitra elaborates in a manner closely paralleling the discussion in the *Vyākhyāyukti* (Shastri 1998:360–361). Cf. also *Vyākhyāyuktiṭīkā* 258a1ff.

71. Lee 2001:170 (D, sems tsam *shi*, 86b1–3): "kha cig las 'phags pa'i bden pa bzhi dag ces gsungs pa dang / kha cig las bram ze'i bden pa gsum dag ces gsungs pa dang / kha cig las bden pa ni gnyis te kun rdzob kyi bden pa dang don dam pa'i bden pa'o zhes gsungs pa dang / kha cig las bden pa ni gcig kho na ste gnyis pa med do zhes gzungs pa."

72. Ibid.:192 (D, sems tsam *shi*, 94a5–6): "gnyis phan tshun 'gal ba dag ni bden par bya bar mi nus so."

73. Ibid.:173 (D, sems tsam *shi*, 87b4): "de dag las gang yang rung ba zhig dang 'gal bar brgal ba yang rig pa dang 'gal bar brgal ba yin par bya'o." Vasubandhu's account here intersects with—but is less broad than—that of the **Vivaraṇasaṃgrahaṇī* (see appendix C, sections 2.4.1.3 and 2.4.2.3), which presents reason in terms of the four modes of reasoning (on which see Kapstein 1988; Nance 2007).

74. Ibid.:173–176 (D, sems tsam *shi*, 87b3–5, 87b7, 88a5–7): "dper na dge slong dag gzugs 'das pa yod do / gzugs ma 'ongs pa yod do / 'das pa dang / zad pa dang / 'gags pa dang / bral ba dang / yongs su gyur pa gang yin pa de yod do zhes bya ba ni mngon sum dang 'gal ba yin no / 'di ltar 'das pa dang ma 'ongs pa ni med pa nyid yin par mngon sum yin te / dper na rus [D: ru] sbal gyi spu bzhin no / . . . gzugs rnams kyi nges par 'byung ba ni gzugs med pa'o zhes bya ba ni rjes su dpag pa dang 'gal ba yin te / tshor ba la sogs pa rnams ni gzugs la rag las te skye bar mthong ba'i phyir ro / . . . kha cig na re mdo sde'i le'u grangs rgyas pa rnams ni shin tu rgyas pa'i sde yin gyi theg pa chen po ni ma yin no zhes zer [D: no zer] te / ci'i phyir zhe na / de ni sangs rgyas kyi gsung ma yin no / ji ltar sangs rgyas kyi gsung ma yin zhe na / 'gal ba'i phyir te / de ni sde pa thams cad la grags pa'i sangs rgyas kyi gsung dang 'gal ba yin no."

75. Cabezón 1992. Cf. Verhagen 2005:587–593; *Abhidharmakośabhāṣya* 8 (Shastri 1998: 934).

76. Cf. Lee 2001:258 (D, sems tsam *shi*, 117a2–3).

77. The translation here is rather free. Lee 2001:255 (D, sems tsam *shi*, 116a4): "snod gsum dag tu chos smra bas chos kyi char phab kyang / chos kyi chu'i bya ba mi byed de / rnam par g.yeng [D: g.yengs] ba dang / rmugs pa dang / gnyid dag gis mi nyan pa'i phyir / gang du mi 'bab pa dang / tshul bzhin yid la mi byed pa'i phyir / gang du bab kyang skyon can du 'gyur ba dang / dran pa brjed ngas pa'i phyir gang du mi gnas pa'o."

78. For a translation, see appendix C, note 33.

Conclusion

1. The degree to which the findings here may be generalized is not yet clear. They may—or may not—shed light on the exegesis of tantric texts (a subject not addressed here). On interpretive practices applied to (and in) tantric discourse, see Arènes 1998, 2002; Broido 1988; Davidson 2003:236–292; Hodge 2003; Steinkellner 1978; Thurman 1988.

2. This point is explored more extensively in Nance (in preparation a).

3. The language used here is indebted to Cavell 1979.

4. Schoening 1995. As Schoening has noted (1995:38–39), the structure of Kamalaśīla's commentary appears indebted to the commentarial protocols articulated in the *Vyākhyāyukti*.

5. On the *Śālistambasūtra*, see Reat 1993:1–23; Schoening 1995:1–13. The text of the *Śālistambasūtra* is extant in its entirety in Tibetan; some has also been preserved, via citation, in Sanskrit. La Vallée Poussin 1913 offers an edition of the Tibetan text together with an attempted Sanskrit reconstruction; Vaidya 1961c:101–106 provides another reconstruction, and Reat 1993 yet another. Although the work was

composed in Sanskrit, Jeffrey Schoening's painstaking diplomatic edition of the Tibetan (based on manuscripts recovered from Dunhuang) seems to me at least as reliable a guide to the Sanskrit as any modern reconstruction. I have therefore based the translation here on the Tibetan edition of the sūtra offered in Schoening 1995:vol. 2.

6. Schoening 1995:391: "de'i tshe na tshe dang ldan ba sha ri'i bu / byang chub sems dpa' sems dpa' chen po byams pa'i bgrod par bya ba'i sa ga la ba der song ste / phyin nas / phan tshun yang dag par dga' bar bya ba'i gtam rnam pa mang po byas nas / 'dus te gnyis ka rdo leb la 'khod do / de nas tshe dang ldan ba sha ri'i bus / byang chub sems dpa sems dpa chen po byams pa la 'di skad ces smras so / byams pa deng 'dir bcom ldan 'das gyis sa lu ljang pa la gzigs nas / dge slong rnams la mdo 'di gsungs so / dge slong dag sus rten cing 'breld par 'byung ba mthong ba des chos mthong ngo / sus chos mthong ba des / sangs rgyas mthong ngo / zhes de skad bka stsald nas / bcom ldan 'das cang myi gsung bar gyurd na / byams pa bde bar gshegs pas bka' stsald pa'i mdo de'i don ji." Much of this passage is also extant in Sanskrit, preserved in Yaśomitra's *Sphuṭārthavyākhyā* (cited in Schoening 1995:701): "āyuṣmān śāriputro maitreyaṃ bodhisattvam etad avocat / śālistambam avalokya bhikṣubhyaḥ sūtram idam uktam yo bhikṣavaḥ pratītyasamutpādaṃ paśyati sa dharmaṃ paśyati yo dharmaṃ paśyati sa buddhaṃ paśyatīti uktvā bhagavāṃs tūṣnīm babhūva / tad asya bhagavatā bhāṣitasya sūtrasya ko 'rthaḥ."

7. Ibid.:461: "ji'i phyir bcom ldan 'das cang myi gsung bar gyur / ce na / bdag lta bus bcom ldan 'das kyi dgongs pa shes par myi nus mod kyi / 'on kyang brtags sthe brjod na / dge slong gang dag nged ni mgo smos pas go ba'o snyam du nga rgyal byed pa de dag gi nga rgyal spang ba dang / byang cub sems dpa' rnams shin du zab mo'i don gyi dgongs pa yang 'chad pas che ba nyid brjod pa dang / de tsam kyis bshad pa'i dgos pa' yongs su rdzogs pa'i phyir ro."

8. Ibid.:200–201, 390. The sūtra does not suggest that these two audiences are mutually exclusive.

9. Ibid.:198.

10. Translation slightly modified from Ñāṇamoli and Bodhi 1995:880–881. MN 108, iii.8.

11. Ibid.

Appendix A

1. On B, see Bazarov 2008:2.

2. Translation tentative; the grammar of the opening verses is underdetermined in the Tibetan translation.

3. This passage is quoted elliptically in the *Vyākhyāyukti*, but it is cited in full in the *Vyākhyāyuktisūtrakhaṇḍaśata* and *Vyākhyāyuktiṭīkā*.

4. Cf. appendix B, section 2.6 herein; Tatia 1976:143, 155–156.

5. The translation of this final line is tentative; the Tibetan reads " 'phyar ba dang ni bag med spyod" across editions. The *Mahāvyutpatti* lists the term *'phyar ba* as a translation for the rare Sanskrit term *vyāseka*. I have assumed *vyāseka* to be an antonym of the Pali *avyāseka*. This reading does not, however, correspond well to the

semantic range of the Tibetan *'phyar ba* ("to hold aloft, raise, lift up"). Cf. Edgerton 1953:2.518–519.

6. Cf. SN 1.4: "dīghamāyu manussānaṃ na naṃ hīḷe suporiso / careyya khīramattova natthi maccussa āgamori / appamāyu manussānaṃ hīḷeyya naṃ suporiso / careyyādittasīsova natthi maccussa nāgamoti."

7. Cf. *Kīṭāgirisutta* (MN 70, i.479–480, trans. Ñāṇamoli and Bodhi 1995:582–583).

8. Cf. Vaidya 1960c:277: "prayojanaṃ sapiṇḍārthaṃ padārthaḥ sānusaṃdhikaḥ / sacodyaparihāraś ca vācyaḥ sūtrārthavādibhiḥ iti / pañcabhir ākāraiḥ sūtraṃ vyākhyātavyam iti vyākhyāyuktau nirṇītam."

9. Cf. Samtani 1971:72: "śrutvā sūtrasya māhātmyaṃ śrotur ādarakāritā / śravaṇodgrahaṇaṃ syād ity ādau vācāṃ prayojanam."

10. The *Vyākhyāyuktiṭīkā* (D, sems tsam *si*, 142b1) clarifies: "In this teaching, the specific characteristic (*rang gi mtshan nyid*, **svalakṣaṇa*) is 'form'—that which is suitable to be a form; the general characteristic (*spyi'i mtshan nyid*, **sāmānyalakṣaṇa*) is 'impermanent,' and so on."

11. The translation's "intended characteristic" reads with G and the critical edition: *dgongs pa'i mtshan nyid* against B, C, D: *dgos pa'i mtshan nyid*.

12. On the five faculties, see *Abhidharmakośabhāṣya* on *Abhidharmakośa* 2.3 (Shastri 1998:111); *Mahāvyutpatti* 977–981. Cf. appendix B, section 2.4.

13. Translation tentative: "gang zag kha cig gcig bu yin yang don kha cig la kun tu rmongs pa."

14. Cf. *Vinayavibhaṅga* (D, 'dul ba *ca*, 76b2, 130a5).

15. Editions of the commentary here substitute "intention" (*dgongs pa*) for "purpose" (*dgos pa*).

16. The objector's worry appears to presume a strained interpretation of the phrase "each statement has a single meaning"—viz., that each statement has the same meaning as every other statement. Interpreted in this way, the objection is thus that the extensive corpus of Buddhist sūtra literature—containing multiple statements—consists of nothing more than the Buddha repeating himself, thereby incurring the fault of pleonasm (*zlos pa nyid kyi skyon*).

17. The pronominal reference is unclear here.

18. The translation's "with reference to those who are ignorant" reads with B, G, and the critical edition: "kun tu rmongs pa'i dbang tu mdzad nas" against D: "kun tu rmongs pa'i dbang tu mjad nas."

19. On the three forms of training, see *Abhidharmakośabhāṣya* on *Abhidharmakośa* 6.45 (Shastri 1998:762); *Mahāvyutpatti* 929–932.

20. The whole of this bracketed section makes little sense in this context and is ignored by Guṇamati. It appears to be either an interpolation or a scribal confusion, albeit one found across all extant editions of the text. The passage may belong in the section of the text devoted to the discussion of polysemic terms (see later). Cf. *Amarakośa*, "Nānārthavarga" 252ab (Dādhimatha 1997:442): "alaṃ bhūṣaṇaparyāpti śaktivāraṇavācakam."

21. Cf. *Udānavarga* 27:25 (Bernhard 1965:345).

22. I have assumed the critical edition's "dmag ltan pa" to be a typographical error; all editions concur in reading "dmag ldan pa."

23. This rather compressed account is expanded by Guṇamati in the commentary, at 145b1–6. He interprets Vasubandhu to be respectively correlating the three

superior trainings to the three times (present, past, and future) and to the three forms of enjoyment taken in distraction that are mentioned in the sūtra passage referenced earlier.

24. The passage that Vasubandhu cites in passing is quoted more fully by Guṇamati at D, sems tsam *si*, 146a1–4.

25. Cf. D, sems tsam *si*, 147a5–7.

26. The phrase "presently occurring X" is used to translate *X dang mtshungs par ldan pa* (**X-saṃprayukta*). On this usage, see *Abhidharmakośabhāṣya* on *Abhidharmakośa* 7.11 (Shastri 1998:818–825).

27. The passage referenced here is reproduced in the *Vyākhyāyuktiṭīkā* (D, sems tsam *si*, 116b6–117a3). For the relevant Sanskrit, see chapter 1, note 19.

28. On the three kinds of feeling, see *Abhidharmakośabhāṣya* on *Abhidharmakośa* 1.14 (Shastri 1998:39).

29. Translation conjectural: "sa slangs [according to G, P, and the critical edition; cf. B, C, D: blangs] nas chu'i mthar 'gro'o zhes byung ba lta bu'o."

30. The *Mahāvyutpatti* offers the Sanskrit *pratikṛṣṭa* as the underlying term for the Tibetan *tha chad*; the term reappears in the *Vyākhyāyuktiṭīkā* (D, sems tsam *si*, 150a6), though no gloss is provided.

31. The Tibetan here is *khrom gyi ru*—a phrase that appears in the *Mahāvyutpatti* under the section titled "mi'i rim pa'i ming" (a section devoted, for the most part, to listing titles of those in government service). The Csoma de Körös edition of the *Mahāvyutpatti* offers *ghatavolagra* as a translation equivalent for *khrom gyi ru*; Minayev's reading of *bhatavolāgra* is little improved. I have assumed the underlying Sanskrit to be **bhaṭabalāgra* and have translated accordingly.

32. The translation's "overjoyed" reads with G and the critical edition: *yid rangs pa nyid*, against B, C, D: *yi rangs pa nyid*.

33. The term *zang zing* does not appear in this exemplary phrase.

34. The association of *āmiṣa* with *māṃsa* may be an interpolation. It is not anticipated in the initial verse that summarizes the section on *āmiṣa*, and it is ignored in the *Vyākhyāyuktiṭīkā*.

35. The translation's "that which is knowable" reads with B and the critical edition: *shes bya ba*, against C, D, P, and G: *zhes bya ba*.

36. G here has a blank space where one would expect to find the feminizing *ma*, reading instead: *gzhon nu rnams*.

37. The translation's "subduing" reads with P and the critical edition: *gnon pa*, against B, C, D, and G, which all read *gnod pa* in the verse and *gnon pa* in the gloss.

38. Skilling (2000:338) identifies the Sanskrit term translated here as **nyāya*. *Nyāya* is one—but not the only—Sanskrit term for which Tibetan translators have appropriated the term *tshul*; the latter is used also to translate the Sanskrit *naya*. Complicating matters still further, one of the exemplary sentences used to illustrate the varying uses of the term *tshul* cites the phrase *tshul bzhin*—a term routinely used to translate the Sanskrit *yoniśas*.

39. The translation's "ascending" reads with G: *'dzegs nas* against B, C, D and the critical edition: *'jog nas* and P: *'jegs nas*.

40. The term *phung po* does not appear in this passage.

41. Translation conjectural: "khang pa brtsegs pa'i phyam dgu bo dang dag yin pa de dag gi mchog."

42. G adds "What are formations?" (*'du byed rnams gang zhe na*).

43. Cf. *Abhidharmakośa* 3.26 and the commentary thereon (Shastri 1998:349–350).

44. G and P omit "and so on."

45. Cf. SN 5.3.1.10 (v. 154–158).

46. Cf. **Vivaraṇasaṃgrahaṇī* (D, sems tsam 'i, 56a7, and appendix C herein), where the same passage is adduced to illustrate "connection" (*mtshams sbyar*).

47. Cf. appendix B, section 2.12.

48. See the sources cited in appendix B, note 4.

49. The Tibetan here is elliptical: "kha cig ni gang dag rgyas par bshad par dgos pas nyan par mi byed pa mang du mnyan pa dang / gzung pas 'jigs pa nyan du gzhugs pa'i phyir te."

50. The commentary identifies the dharma referenced here to be attachment (*chags*).

51. The translation is tentative and augments what is explicit in the Tibetan with material from the commentary: "kha cig ni [bcom ldan 'das] nyid la snga nas so so yang dag par rig par gyur pa'i don gsung ba nyid du yang dag par bstan pa'i phyir." For *snga nas*, G and D read *lda nas*.

52. This concluding section of the text has been edited, translated, and studied in Prapod and Skilling 1999. I wish to thank Peter Skilling for kindly providing me with a copy of this paper.

53. Reading with G and the critical edition: *de na 'khod pa skom bya'i phyir*, against B, C, D: *de na 'khod pa bsgom bya'i phyir*. The critical edition does not note this variant.

54. On summary verses (*saṃgrahaśloka*), see Mimaki 1980. As pointed out in Prapod and Skilling 1999, a slightly different version of this verse is quoted by Haribhadra in his *Abhisamayālaṃkārāloka*: (Vaidya 1960c:271). The Sanskrit reads: "deśāntaravijñeyārthaṃ tatsthānaṃ tarpaṇāya ca / śrāvakānekavāsārtham anāsaktiṃ ca darśayan / deśānāṃ caityabhāvārthaṃ puṇyārthaṃ caiva dehiṇāṃ / ītyādiśamanārthaṃ ca buddhaś carati cārikām."

55. Cf. Haribhadra's *Abhisamayālaṃkārāloka* (Vaidya 1960c:274): "pañcādīnavav aikalyāratirāgādighaṭṭitaḥ / lābhāditṛṣṇāpriyatā 'nukampāgurugauravaiḥ / kautū halād viśeṣārtham āpattyā ratnakāraṇāt / caityādivandanārthaṃ ca bhikṣuś carati cārikāṃ." See also Sparham 2006–2009:1.181.

56. Cf. Haribhadra's *Abhisamayālaṃkārāloka* (Vaidya 1960c:554): "na kṛpāmandatedānīṃ na ca me dharmamatsaraḥ / nācāryamuṣṭir nāśaktiṛ na ca me duḥkhaśīlatā / na ca me niṣṭhitaṃ śāstraṃ tarkayāmi tavāntikāt / ājñātuṃ na ca me śaktā vineyā na ca sādharāḥ / na deśayāmi yeneti jñāpayan paritarṣayan / dvau māsau [*sic*; Prapod and Skilling (1999) suggest reading 'trimāsān'] pratisaṃlīno bhagavān ardham eva ca."

57. The translation's "fault" reads with B, G and the critical edition: *klan ka*, against C, D: *slan ka*. The translation's "knowledge" reads with B, C, D: *shes*, against P and the critical edition: *bshes* (cf. G: *bshos*).

Appendix B

1. Cf. the treatment of *arthapratisaṃvid* in the *Saṃdhinirmocanasūtra* discussed previously (in chapter 2).

2. Where I have written "sūtra," the Sanskrit reads *sūtramukhaṃ*. The Tibetan translation ignores the latter term of the compound entirely: *mdo sde*.

3. The Tibetan translation here cites the whole verse: "Not practicing any evil, attaining what is virtuous, controlling one's own mind—this is the teaching of the awakened ones" (*sdig pa thams cad mi bya ste//dge ba phun sum tshogs par bya//rang gi sems ni yongs su 'dul//'di ni sangs rgyas bstan pa'o*). Cf. Bannerjee 1977:55: "sarvapāpasyākaraṇaṃ kuśalasyopasaṃpadā/svacittaparidamanam etad buddhānuśāsanam."

4. The Sanskrit text does not elaborate further; the Tibetan translation explicitly lists both groups, which are discussed at greater length in the *Śrāvakabhūmi* (Shukla 1973:5–8) and in Guṇamati's *Vyākhyāyuktiṭīkā* (D, sems tsam si, 153a7–b4).

5. Cf. SN 3.1.5.9 and Bodhi 2000:959–961.

6. Cf. the opening portion of appendix A herein. The passage referenced here appears to be *Dhammapada*, v. 97 (*assadho akataññū ca sandhicchedo ca yo naro/hatāvakāso vantāso sa ve uttamaporiso*). The author discusses the passage more extensively at a later point (Tatia 1976:155–156); Hara 1992 examines this discussion in detail. Cf. also Norman 1979.

7. Cf. *Mahāvyutpatti* 5131–5138.

8. Translation tentative. Tatia 1976:143: "yaḥ sadidam samanupaśyati sarvo 'sau rūpaṃ samanupaśyati yo vā rūpaṃ samanupaśyati sarvaḥ sa sadidam samanupaśyati iti." The Tibetan translation here reads "gang gis 'di legs par mthong ba des gzugs thams cad mthong ngam/gang gis gzugs thams cad mthong ba des thams cad legs par mthong ngam." Cf. the final verses of *Udānavarga* 27 (Bernhard 1965:1.350–352). On gender correlation in Buddhist Sanskrit, see Edgerton 1953:40.

9. Cf. MN 13 (*Mahādukkhakkhandasutta*); MN 109 (*Mahāpuṇṇamasutta*).

10. Prior to "intention," the Sanskrit of Tatia's edition omits "method" (*sa ca abhiprāyeṇa anugantavyaḥ*). The corresponding Tibetan does not: "de yang dgongs pa'i tshul gyis khong du chud par bya ste."

11. Although present in the Tibetan translation, the mark of meditative cultivation is not listed in Tatia's Sanskrit text. I have reinserted it, translating from the Tibetan: "sgom pa'i mtshan nyid."

12. Corrected from Tatia's *āmulomikadharmalakṣaṇa* on the basis of the Tibetan: "rjes su mthun pa'i chos kyi mtshan nyid."

13. The Tibetan inserts "and misfortune as misfortune" (*nyes dmigs la nyes dmigs dang, *ādīnavañ ca ādīnavataḥ*); the phrase is missing in the Sanskrit.

14. The Tibetan here diverges, reading **ādīnavādi* (*nyes dmigs la sogs pa*) for *āsvādādi*.

15. The translation here is tentative and free. Tatia's Sanskrit reads: "tadyathā ṣaḍbhir dharmair samavāgato bhikṣur himavantam api parvatarājaṃ mukhavāyunā cālayet kaḥ punar vādaḥ savāsanāyā avidyā[yāḥ]." The Tibetan translation reads: "dper na chos drug dang ldan pa'i dge slong ni kha'i dbugs kyis ri'i rgyal po gangs ri yang 'thor na ro lta bu'i (*śavopamāyā) ma rigs pa lta smos kyang ci dgos." Cf. AN 6.1.3.4.

16. Tatia's edition reads *pradhāna*; the translation amends this to *prahāna*, following the Tibetan and the standard formulation of the four bases (cf. *Mahāvyutpatti* 967–975). For more on the *ṛddhipādāḥ*, including an extensive list of textual citations, see Lamotte 1970:1124–1125.

17. Or, "they are provided with mental joy." This passage is missing from the Sanskrit; the Tibetan reads "yid bde ba nye bar sgrub pa."

18. Cf. appendix A, section 1.1. The Sanskrit of Tatia's edition is a bit jumbled here: "saṃdarśanato mūḍhānāṃ samādāpanataḥ samuttejanataś ca pramādasaṅgānātmaparibhavena [*sic*; read pramādasaṅgānāṃ ātmaparibhavena] vā līnāṃ saṃpraharṣaṇataḥ samyakpratipannānām." The translation here follows the formal order of presentation found in the Tibetan (D, sems tsam *li*, 110a1), pairing *samādāpanataḥ* with *līnāṃ*—though the Tibetan here diverges from the published Sanskrit edition in other ways as well.

Appendix C

1. I have shifted the order in which these topics are listed in the opening verse to track the order in which they are treated in detail in the ensuing text.

2. This subtype appears to comprise internal and external phenomena (of whatever sort) that do not ultimately exist according to classical Buddhist abhidharma.

3. This subtype apparently comprises any and all terms that may be used as collective designations for a multiplicity of underlying phenomena. Whereas subtypes 1.1.1.1 and 1.1.1.2 are complementary, subtype 1.1.1.3 overlaps with both: "form" is a class term used to refer to things that really exist; "sentient being" is a class term that is figurative.

4. This subtype appears to incorporate proper names and primitive color terms. On the contrast between primitive and derivative colors, see *Abhidharmakośabhāṣya* on *Abhidharmakośa* 1.10 (Shastri 1998:26). Subtype 1.1.1.4 again overlaps with subtypes 1.1.1.1 and 1.1.1.2: proper names fall into the former category (since the selves that they putatively denote do not ultimately exist), whereas primitive color terms fall into the latter.

5. The Tibetan here is *tha snyad*, which likely signals an underlying Sanskrit **vyavahāra*, a term meaning "custom" or "convention." The ensuing explanation of this category reveals, however, that the author of the *Vivaraṇasaṃgrahaṇī* may have in mind instances in which customary expectations are violated.

6. A "phrase that establishes" would appear to be a phrase that is adduced as a reason supporting a claim; the claim itself is the phrase that is established.

7. Contact (*sparśa*) is commonly stipulated as the condition for feeling (*vedanā*) in the well-known twelvefold formulation of dependent arising (*pratītyasamutpāda*).

8. The author is here offering a *nirukti*, analyzing a term by referring to other Sanskrit terms that echo its phonemes. I have not attempted to replicate this in translation.

9. The translation's "in order to designate boundaries by means of names" reads with C, D: *ming gis mtha' blangs pa'i phyir* against G: *ming gi mtha' blangs pa'i phyir*.

10. Translation tentative. The term *sde ba* may point to an underlying **nikāya*, whereas the term *rigs pa* here likely renders **kula* or **jāti*. All of these Sanskrit terms can be rendered in a variety of ways—e.g., *nikāya* can mean, among other things, "division," "class," "set," "sect"; "community"; *jāti* can mean "universal," "lineage," "rank," "caste," "tribe"; *kula* likewise has a wide range of meanings.

11. See D, sems tsam *tshi*, 161a2–200b5.

12. Comparable lists are presented (in slightly altered form) in two successive sūtra fragments preserved in the *Vyākhyāyuktisūtrakhaṇḍaśata* (D, sems tsam *shi*, 23b2–5). These fragments both substitute "luminous" (*gsal ba*, **prabhāsavara*) for "urbane" (though, interestingly, the *Vyākhyāyukti* cites the fragments as though they read "urbane"). The fragments also both add a virtue curiously omitted here: that of being "instructive" (*rnam par shes par bya ba*, **vijñāpanīya*).

13. The passage referenced here may be drawn from the *Bodhisattvabhūmi*: "A bodhisattva . . . teaches the dharma with phrases and syllables that are reasoned, coherent, concordant, agreeable, skillful, exemplary, fitting, appropriate, a collection of components of exertion." Dutt 1966:101: "bodhisattvaḥ . . . dharmaṃ deśayati yuktaiḥ padavyañjanaiḥ sahitair ānulomikair ānucchavikair aupayikaiḥ pratirūpaiḥ pradakṣiṇaiḥ nipakasyāṅgasaṃbhāraiḥ."

14. Cf. sections 1.2.4.3 and 2.3.2.4.5 herein. The following three paragraphs are not explicitly anticipated in the text's opening programmatic verse.

15. For the relevant Sanskrit, see the Yogācārabhūmi Database, available at http://ybh.chibs.edu.tw/ui.html. The Tibetan is at D, sems tsam *tshi*, 201a3–204b4.

16. See D, sems tsam *tshi*, 204b4–5.

17. See Shukla 1973:279.

18. Ibid.:195.

19. See D, sems tsam *tshi*, 2a3–5, 106a1–3.

20. Ibid.:120b2–159a6.

21. Ibid.:142a6–143a3.

22. In this section, the author begins by offering a brief (though complex) account of subcategories before moving on to consider each category in greater detail. We are thus faced with a nested scholastic enumeration ("the first has three subcategories, of which the first subcategory has three subdivisions; the second, twelve; and the third, five"). Once the author reaches the end of the categories so enumerated, he returns to the first in order to offer a more elaborated account, and then proceeds back through the list in order.

23. The translation of the final phrase has purposefully been left vague. Whereas the Tibetan is fairly clear (reading *gzhan gyis rjes su snying brtse ba*), the underlying Sanskrit is probably the compound form **parānukampā*, which can be read in various ways.

24. The translation's "nirvāṇa" reads with G: *mya ngan las 'das pa ni*, against C, D: *mya ngan las 'das pa nas*.

25. Cf. the treatment of the twelve branches in the *Śrāvakabhūṃi* (Shukla 1973:136–139).

26. Translation tentative: "de la dbyangs kyis bsnyed pa'i sde ni tha mar tshigs su bcad pa'i dbyangs kyi bsnyad pa gang yin pa dang / mdor bstan par gzhag pa nges pa'i don ma yin pa gang yin pa'o." Cf. Shukla 1973:137: "geyaṃ katamat | yasyānte paryavasāne gāthā abhigītā, yacca sūtraṃ neyārthamidamucyate."

27. The identity of this text is uncertain; it may be D 319.

28. On uses of the term *kālapadeśa* (usually offered together with the term *mahāpadeśa*), see La Vallée Poussin 1938:159–160.

29. On the four responses, cf. DN 33 (*Saṅgītisutta*), iii.229; AN 4.1.5.2.

30. Cf. D, sems tsam *tshi*, 204b2–3; for the Sanskrit, see the relevant section of the Yogācārabhūmi Database (http://ybh.chibs.edu.tw/ui.html).

31. Cf. the *Vyākhyāyukti*'s discussion of this passage, translated in appendix A.

32. Several comparable tenfold lists are provided in the *Dharmasaṃgītisūtra* (cf. D, mdo sde *sha*, 16b5–20a3). None is identical with the list given here.

33. Cf. *Vyākhyāyuktisūtrakhaṇḍaśata* (D, sems tsam *shi*, 23a3–6) : "Venerable Ones, monks who are preachers of the dharma should be spoken of as endowed with twenty aspects in [their] speaking of the dharma: it should be said that (1) [they know what is] timely; (2) [they possess] devotion; (3) [they teach in the proper] sequence; (4) [their teachings are] relevant, (5) concordant, (6) pleasing, (7) desirable, (8) delightful, (9) productive of joy, (10) nondisparaging, (11) reasoned, (12) coherent, (13) uncorrupted, (14) endowed with dharma, and (15) suited to [their] audience; (16) [their] thoughts are benevolent, (17) [turned toward] benefit, and (18) compassionate; (19) they do not rely on [or are not supported by: *mi rten pa*] wealth, honor, and verses [of accolade]; and (20) when expounding statements, they do not praise themselves and do not denigrate others." ("tshe dang ldan pa dag dge slong chos smra ba pos chos kyi gtam byed pa na rnam pa nyi shu po 'di dag dang ldan pas gtam bya ste / dus su dang / gus pa dang / go rims dang / 'tshams sbyar ba dang / rjes su mthun pa dang / dga' bar bya ba dang / 'dod par bya ba dang / mgu bar bya ba dang / spro ba skyed pa dang / mi smad pa dang / rigs pa dang / 'brel pa dang / ma 'dres pa dang / chos dang ldan pa dang / 'khor ji lta ba bzhin dang / byams pa'i sems dang / phan pa sems dang / snying brtse ba'i sems dang / rnyed pa dang / bkur sti dang tshigs su bcad pa la mi rten pa dang / gtam de dag brjod pa na bdag la bstod par mi bya zhing gzhan la smad par mi bya la gtam yang bya ba ste / rnam pa nyi shu po 'di dag dang ldan pas gtam bya'o zhes bya ba dang.") For Vasubandhu's gloss of this sūtra fragment, see D, sems tsam *shi*, 63a5–64a6; cf. also 115a4.

34. The author briefly treats the topics of exposition and assembly together before tacking back to treat each in greater detail. In the translation, the detailed treatment of each has been moved to follow the corresponding brief account.

35. The translation's "praise of proper conduct" renders G: *legs par spyad pa bstod pa*, against C, D: *legs par spyad pa stong pa*.

36. Cf. Dutt 1966:15; *Mahāvyutpatti* 1560–1564.

37. The translation's "comes to know" renders G: *rnam par shes par 'gyur ba*, against C, D: *rnam par 'gyur ba*.

38. The translation's "conversion of others" reads with C, D: *pha rol gnon pa dang bcas pa*, against G: *pha rol gnod pa dang bcas pa*.

39. See D, sems tsam *'i*, 22b1–47b7.

40. Cf. AN 7.2.2.4: "dhammaññū ca hoti atthaññū ca attaññū ca mattaññū ca kālaññū ca parisaññū ca puggalaparovaraññū ca."

41. Regarding "[his im]mutability": all editions agree here in reading *g.yo ba'i phyir*, though one would expect *g.yo ba med pa'i phyir* (or *mi g.yo ba'i phyir*).

42. On uses of the epithet "bull among men," see Powers 2009.

43. On this list of epithets ("a Tathāgata, an arhat..."), see Griffiths 1994:60–65.

44. Cf. *Mahāvyutpatti* 2331; Dutt 1966:195.

45. The items in this list are standard; many are discussed extensively in the tenth chapter of Asaṅga's *Mahāyānasaṃgraha* and its commentaries (see Griffiths et al. 1989:128ff.).

46. Cf. *Itivuttaka* 2.2.9 (*Sikkhānisaṃsasutta*): "sikkhānisaṃsā, bhikkhave, viharatha paññuttarā vimuttisārā satādhipateyyā."

47. The pronominal reference is unclear here.

48. The specific components of the set referenced here are not clear. I suspect that the reference is not to any of the variant lists of four yogas found in later tantric literature, but rather to a standard list (found at AN ii.10, DN iii.230, and in the *Abhidharmasamuccaya*) that reads the four yogas in negative terms, construing them as coextensive with four outflows (Pali *ogha*, Skt. *āsava*).

49. D: *bsbroms pa* [*sic*]; the translation follows G and C.

50. The *nirukti* is unclear; the translation equivalents noted here are those attested in the *Mahāvyutpatti*. The Tibetan reads "spyod lam sna tshogs kyi dus yol bar gnas so."

51. Cf. G: *mngon par brjed pa*.

52. Translation tentative: "yang ji ltar 'dris pa'i dngos po yid la byed pa 'dis mngon par rjod par byed pa'i phyir."

53. The translation's "for lesser beings" reads with C, G: *dman pa la*, against D: *de man pa la*.

54. The relevant Sanskrit is available in the *Mahāvyutpatti* (8346–8356). The *Vinayasaṃgraha* section of the Yogācārabhūmi (D, sems tsam 'i, 4b7–5b2) discusses these ten more extensively, as does the *Prātimokṣasūtrapaddhati* (D, 'dul ba *du*, 39a3–40a5). A portion of this section of the text is also preserved in Tibetan among the Dunhuang documents; see IOL Tib J 677, available at http://idp.bl.uk/.

55. The translation's "but not said" reads with C, G: *ma gsungs she na*, against D: *gsungs she na*.

56. Regarding the translation's "a state of ethics pertaining to teaching," see the following note.

57. D, G, and C concur in reading *brtan pa'i tshul khrims* ("steadfast ethics") here, as they do in reading *bstan pa'i tshul khrims* ("ethics pertaining to teaching") earlier. N reverses the pattern, reading *bstan pa'i tshul khrims* here and *brtan pa'i tshul khrims* earlier. The author of the text is obviously intending to pick up on the earlier reference, but the underlying Sanskrit is not clear.

Bibliography

Pali

For citations from Pali, I have made use of a searchable romanized electronic edition of the canon (http://www.tipitaka.org/romn). Excerpts quoted in the book have been checked against the following Pali Text Society editions.

Aṅguttara Nikāya (AN). Edition in R. Morris (vols. 1–2) and E. Hardy (vols. 3–5), eds. 1961–1981 [1885–1900]. *The Aṅguttara Nikāya*. London: Pali Text Society.

Dhammapada (Dh). Edition in O. von Hinuuber and K. R. Norman, eds. 1994–1995. *Dhammapada*. London: Pali Text Society.

Dīgha Nikāya (DN). Edition in T. W. Rhys Davids and J. Estlin Carpenter, eds. 1983–1992 [1889–1910]. *The Dīgha Nikāya*. 3 vols. London: Pali Text Society.

Itivuttaka (It). Edition in E. Windisch, ed. 2000 [1889]. *Itivuttaka*. London: Pali Text Society.

Jātaka/Jātakātthakathā (J/JA). Edition in V. Fausbøll, ed. 1990–1991 [1877–1896]. *The Jātaka Together with Its Commentary, Being Tales of the Anterior Births of Gotama Buddha*. 6 vols. London: Pali Text Society.

Kathāvatthu (Kvu). Edition in A. C. Taylor, ed. 1979 [1894–1897]. *Kathāvatthu*. 2 vols. London: Pali Text Society.

Majjhima Nikāya (MN). Edition in V. Trenckner and R. Chalmers, eds. 1991–1994 [1888–1902]. *The Majjhima Nikāya*. 4 vols. London: Pali Text Society.

Milindapañha (Miln). Edition in V. Trenckner, ed. 1986 [1880]. *Milindapañha*. London: Pali Text Society.

Nettipakaraṇa (Nett). Edition in E. Hardy, ed. 1995 [1902]. *The Netti-pakaraṇa, with Extracts from Dhammapāla's Commentary*. London: Pali Text Society.

Peṭakopadesa (Pe). Edition in A. Barua, ed. 1982 [1949]. *The Peṭakopadesa*. London: Pali Text Society.

Saṃyutta Nikāya (SN). Edition in M. Leon Feer, ed. 1973–1980 [1884–1904]. *The Samyutta Nikāya of the Sutta-piṭaka*. 6 vols. London: Pali Text Society.
Sumaṅgalavilāsinī (Sv). Edition in T. W. Rhys Davids and J. Estlin Carpenter, eds. 1968–1971 [1929–1932]. *Dīgha-nikāya Commentary: Sumaṅgalavilāsinī*. 3 vols. London: Pali Text Society.
Suttanipāta (Sn). Edition in D. Andersen and H. Smith, eds. 1990 [1913]. *The Suttanipata*. London: Pali Text Society.
Vinayapiṭaka (Vin). Edition in H. Oldenberg, ed. 1969–1995 [1879–1883]. *The Vinaya-Piṭakaṃ: One of the Principal Buddhist Holy Scriptures in the Pāli Language*. 5 vols. London: Pali Text Society.
Visuddhimagga (Vism). Attributed to Buddhaghosa. Edition in C. A. F. Rhys-Davids, ed. 1975 [1920–1921]. *The Visuddhi-magga of Buddhaghosa*. London: Pali Text Society.

Sanskrit (and Tibetan Translations from Sanskrit)

Abhidharmadīpa. Author unknown. Sanskrit in Jaini 1977.
Abhidharmadīpavibhāṣāprabhāvṛtti. Author unknown. Sanskrit in Jaini 1977.
Abhidharmakośa. Vasubandhu. Sanskrit in Shastri 1998.
Abhidharmakośabhāṣya. Vasubandhu. Sanskrit in Shastri 1998.
Abhidharmasamuccaya. Asaṅga. Sanskrit fragments in Gokhale 1947. Sanskrit reconstruction in Pradhan 1950.
Abhidharmasamuccayabhāṣya. Variously attributed. Sanskrit in Tatia 1976.
Abhisamayālaṃkārāloka. Haribhadra. Sanskrit in Vaidya 1960c.
Abhisamayālaṃkāraprajñāpāramitopadeśaśāstra. Attributed to Maitreya. Sanskrit in Stcherbatsky and Obermiller 1977.
Adhyāśayasañcodanasūtra. Sanskrit lost; D 69.
**Adhyayanapustakapāṭhanapuraskriyāvidhi*. Atiśa. Sanskrit lost; D 3975.
Akṣayamatinirdeśasūtra. Sanskrit lost; Tibetan in Braarvig 1993a.
Akṣayamatinirdeśasūtraṭīkā. Attributed to Vasubandhu. Sanskrit lost; D 3994.
Amarakośa. Amarasiṃha. Sanskrit in Dādhimatha 1997.
Arthaviniścayasūtra. Sanskrit in Samtani 1971.
Arthaviniścayasūtranibandhana. Sanskrit in Samtani 1971.
Aṣṭadaśasāhasrikāprajñāpāramitā. Sanskrit excerpts in Conze 1962, 1974b.
Aṣṭasāhasrikāprajñāpāramitāpañjikāsārottamā. Ratnākaraśanti. Sanskrit lost; D 3803.
Aṣṭasāhasrikāprajñāpāramitāvṛttimarmakaumudī. Abhayākaragupta. Sanskrit lost; D 3805.
Bhadracaripraṇidhāṇarāja. Sanskrit in Vaidya 1960d:420–436.
Bhāvanākrama (I–III). Kamalaśīla. Sanskrit of *Bhāvanākrama I* in Tucci 1958; Sanskrit of *Bhāvanākrama II* lost (see D 3916); Sanskrit of *Bhāvanākrama III* in Tucci 1971.
Bodhicaryāvatāra. Śāntideva. Sanskrit in Vaidya 1960b.
Bodhicaryāvatārapañjikā. Prajñākaramati. Sanskrit in Vaidya 1960b.
Bodhimārgapradīpapañjikā. Atiśa. Sanskrit lost; D 3948.
Bodhisattvabhūmi. Attributed to Asaṅga. Sanskrit in Dutt 1966.
Bodhisattvabhūmivṛtti. Guṇaprabha. Sanskrit lost; D 4044.

Bodhisattvabhūmivyākhyā. *Sāgaramegha/*Samudramegha. Sanskrit lost; D 4047.
Bodhisattvasaṃvaraviṃśaka. Candragomin. Sanskrit lost; D 4081.
Bṛhadāraṇyaka upaniṣad. Sanskrit in Olivelle 1998.
Catuḥśataka (*Varṇārhavarṇastotra*). Attributed to Mātṛceta. Sanskrit fragments and Tibetan in Hartmann 1987. See also Bailey 1950, 1951a.
Chāndogya upaniṣad. Sanskrit in Olivelle 1998.
Daśabhūmikasūtra. Sanskrit in Rahder 1926; Rahder and Susa 1931, 1932; Vaidya 1967; Kondō 1936.
Dharmasaṅgītisūtra. Sanskrit lost; D 238.
Divyāvadāna. Sanskrit in Cowell and Neil 1886.
Kāraṇḍavyūhasūtra. Sanskrit in Vaidya 1961b:258 308.
Kriyāsaṃgraha. Sanskrit manuscript reproduced in Rani 1977.
Laṅkāvatārasūtra. Sanskrit in Vaidya 1963.
Madhyamakāloka. Kamalaśīla. Sanskrit lost; D 3887.
Mahābhārata. Sanskrit in Sukthankar et al. 1933-1966.
Mahābhāṣya. Patañjali. Sanskrit in Shastri 2001.
Mahāparinirvāṇasūtra. Sanskrit fragments in Yuyama 1981 and Bongard-Levin 1986; D 119–121.
Mahāvyutpatti. Tibetan and Sanskrit in Mitsuhara et al. 2002.
Mahāyānapathasādhanavarṇasaṃgraha. Atiśa. Sanskrit lost; D 3954.
Mahāyānasaṃgrahopanibandhana. Asvabhāva. Sanskrit lost; D 4051. Tibetan excerpts in Griffiths et al. 1989.
Mahāyānasūtrālaṃkāra. Attributed to Maitreya/Asaṅga. Sanskrit in Lévi 1907.
Mahāyānasūtrālaṃkārabhāṣya. Vasubandhu. Sanskrit in Lévi 1907.
Mānavadharmaśāstra. Sanskrit in Olivelle 2005; Jha 1999.
Manubhāṣya. Medāthiti. Sanskrit in Jha 1999.
Miśrakastotra. Dignāga. Sanskrit lost; D 1150. Tibetan in Bailey 1951b.
Mūlamadhyamakakārikā. Nāgārjuna. Sanskrit in de Jong 1977.
Mūlasarvāstivādavinayavastu. Sanskrit in Dutt, Bhattacharya, and Sarma 1984; Bagchi 1967–1970; Gnoli 1977–1978, 1978.
Nyāyabiṇḍu. Dharmakīrti. Sanskrit in Stcherbatsky 1918.
Nyāyabiṇḍuṭīkā. Dharmottara. Sanskrit in Stcherbatsky 1918.
Nyāyasūtra. Akṣapada. Sanskrit in Thakur 1967.
Nyāyasūtrabhāṣya. Vātsyāyana. Sanskrit in Thakur 1967.
Padārthadharmasaṃgraha. Praśastapāda. Sanskrit in Jetly and Parikh 1991.
Prajñāpāramitāvajraketu. Sanskrit lost; D 30.
Pramāṇasamuccaya. Dignāga. Sanskrit lost; D 4203.
Pramāṇavārttika. Dharmakīrti. Sanskrit in Shastri 1994.
Pramāṇavārttikasvopajñavṛtti. Dharmakīrti. Sanskrit in Gnoli 1960.
Pramāṇavārttikavṛtti. Manorathanandin. Sanskrit in Shastri 1994.
Prātimokṣasūtra. Sanskrit in Bannerjee 1977.
Prātimokṣasūtrapaddhati. Sanskrit lost; D 4104.
Prātimokṣasūtraṭīkāvinayasamuccaya. Sanskrit lost; D 4106.
Prātimokṣasūtravṛtti. Sanskrit lost; D 4107.
Pratyutpannabuddhasaṃmukhāvasthitasamādhisūtra. Sanskrit lost; D 133. Tibetan in Harrison 1978.

Rāṣṭrapālaparipṛcchā. Sanskrit in Finot 1901.
Ratnameghasūtra. Sanskrit lost; D 231.
Saddharmapuṇḍarīkasūtra. Sanskrit in Vaidya 1960a.
Śālistambasūtra. Sanskrit fragments in Reat 1993; Tibetan in Schoening 1995:vol. 2.
Śālistambasūtraṭīkā. Kamalaśīla. Sanskrit lost; D 4001. Tibetan in Schoening 1995: vol. 2.
Samādhirājasūtra. Sanskrit in Vaidya 1961a.
Saṃdhinirmocanasūtra. Tibetan in Lamotte 1935.
Sarvadharmāpravṛttinirdeśa. Sanskrit fragments in Braarvig 2000; D 180.
Śatapañcāśatka. Variously attributed. Sanskrit, Tibetan, and Chinese editions in Bailey 1951b.
Śatapañcāśatkaṭīkā. Attributed to *Nandapriya/*Nandipriya/*Rāmapriya. Sanskrit lost; D 1148. Tibetan in Bailey 1951b.
Śatapathabrahmaṇa. Sanskrit in Mishra 2004 (Mādhyandina); Pimplapure 2005 (Kāṇva)
Śikṣāsamuccaya. Śāntideva. Sanskrit in Bendall 1902; Vaidya 1961b.
Sphuṭārthavyākhyā. Yaśomitra. Sanskrit in Shastri 1998.
Śrāvakabhūmi. Attributed to Asaṅga. Sanskrit in Shukla 1973.
Suhṛllekha. Nāgārjuna. Sanskrit lost; D 4182, 4496.
Suvarṇa(pra)bhāsottamasūtra. Sanskrit in Nobel 1937; Bagchi 1967.
Taittirīyasaṃhitā. Sanskrit in Kashyap 2002.
Tattvasaṃgraha (alt. *Tattvasaṅgraha*). Śāntarakṣita. Sanskrit in Krishnamacarya 1926; Shastri 1997.
Tattvasaṃgrahapañjikā (alt. *Tattvasaṅgrahapañjikā*). Kamalaśīla. Sanskrit in Krishnamacarya 1926, Shastri 1997.
Triṃśikāvijñaptibhāṣya. Sthiramati. Sanskrit in Buescher 2007; Lévi 1925.
Udānavarga. Sanskrit in Bernhard 1965.
Vajracchedikā. Sanskrit in Müller 1881; Conze 1957. Cf. also Schopen 1989b; Harrison and Watanabe 2006.
Vākyapadīya. Bhartṛhari. Sanskrit in Iyer 1963.
Vimalakīrtinirdeśasūtra. Sanskrit in *Vimalakīrtinirdeśa: A Sanskrit Edition Based upon the Manuscript Newly Found at the Potala Palace*. 2006. Tokyo: Taishō daigaku sōgō bukkyō kenkyūjo bongo butten kenkyūkai.
Vinayavastu. Sanskrit in Dutt, Bhattacharya, and Sarma 1984; Bagchi 1967–1970; Gnoli 1977–1978, 1978.
**Vivaraṇasaṃgrahaṇī*. Attributed to Asaṅga. Sanskrit lost; D 4042.
Vyākhyāyukti. Vasubandhu. Sanskrit lost; D 4061. Tibetan in Lee 2001.
Vyākhyāyuktisūtrakhaṇḍaśata. Sanskrit lost; D 4060. Tibetan in Lee 2001.
Vyākhyāyuktiṭīkā. Guṇamati. Sanskrit lost; D 4069.
Yājñavalkyasmṛti. Sanskrit in Ganapati 1982.

Tibetan

Dkar chag 'phang thang ka ma. 2003. Beijing: Mi rigs dpe skrun khang.
Pho brang stod thang ldan dkar gyi chos 'gyur ro cog gi dkar chag. D 4364. Edition in Herrmann-Pfandt 2008; Lalou 1953.

Secondary Sources, Reference Works, and Translations

Abbott, T. 1985. "Vasubandhu's Commentary on the Lotus Sūtra: A Study of Its History and Significance." Ph.D. diss., University of California, Berkeley.

Adikaram, E. W. 1946. *Early History of Buddhism in Ceylon*. Colombo: M. D. Gunasena and Company.

Agócs, T. 2000. "The Diamondness of the Diamond Sūtra." *Acta Orientalia* 53.1–2:65–78.

Akanuma, C. 1958. *The Comparative Catalogue of Chinese Āgamas and Pāli Nikāyas*. Tokyo: Hajinkaku shobō.

Allon, M. 1997. "The Oral Composition and Transmission of Early Buddhist Texts." In Connolly and Hamilton 1997:39–61.

Anālayo. 2006. "The *Ekottara-āgama* Parallel to the *Saccavibhaṅga-sutta* and the Four (Noble) Truths." *Buddhist Studies Review* 23.2:145–153.

——. 2008. "The Conversion of Aṅgulimāla in the *Saṃyukta-Āgama*." *Buddhist Studies Review* 25.2:135–148.

Anesaki, M. 1908. "The Four Buddhist Āgamas in Chinese." *Transactions of the Asiatic Society of Japan* 35.3:1–67.

Apte, V. 1998. *The Practical Sanskrit-English Dictionary, Revised and Enlarged Edition*. Delhi: Motilal Banarsidass.

Arènes, P. 1998. "Herméneutique des Tantra: Étude de quelques usages du 'sens caché.'" *Journal of the International Association of Buddhist Studies* 21.2:173–226.

——. 2002. "Herméneutique des Tantra: Les 'Six extrêmes (ou possibilités alternatives)' (*saṭkoṭi, mtha' drug*). A propos d'un exemple de prégnance des modèles exégétiques des sūtra." *Revue d'études Tibétaines* 1.1:4–43.

Arnold, D. 2005. *Buddhists, Brahmins, and Belief: Epistemology in South Asian Philosophy of Religion*. New York: Columbia University Press.

——. 2006. "On Semantics and Saṃketa: Thoughts on a Neglected Problem with Buddhist Apoha Doctrine." *Journal of Indian Philosophy* 34:415–478.

Aung, S. Z., and C. A. F. Rhys-Davids, trans. 1960 [1915]. *Points of Controversy or Subjects of Discourse, Being a Translation of the* Kathā-vatthu *from the* Abhidhammapiṭaka. London: Pali Text Society.

Auroux, S., et al., eds. 2000–2001. *History of the Language Sciences: An International Handbook on the Evolution of the Study of Language from the Beginnings to the Present*. 2 vols. Berlin: Walter de Gruyter.

Bagchi, S., ed. 1967. *Suvarṇaprabhāsasūtram*. Darbhanga, India: Mithila Institute of Post-Graduate Studies and Research in Sanskrit Learning.

——, ed. 1967–1970. *Mūlasarvāstivādavinayavastu*. 2 vols. Darbhanga, India: Mithila Institute of Post-Graduate Studies and Research in Sanskrit Learning.

Bailey, D. R. S., ed. and trans. 1950. "The *Varṇārhavarṇastotra* of Mātṛceṭa (I)." *Bulletin of the School of Oriental and African Studies, University of London* 13.3:671–701.

——. 1951a. "The *Varṇārhavarṇastotra* of Mātṛceṭa (II)." *Bulletin of the School of Oriental and African Studies, University of London* 13.4:947–1003.

——. 1951b. *The* Śatapañcāśatka *of Mātṛceṭa*. Cambridge: Cambridge University Press.

Balasooriya, S., et al., eds. 1980. *Buddhist Studies in Honor of Walpola Rahula*. London: Gordon Fraser.

Balcerowicz, P., ed. 2003. *Journal of Indian Philosophy* 31: "Proceedings of the International Seminar 'Argument and Reason in Indian Logic,' 20–24 June 2001—Kazimierz Dolny, Poland" (special triple issue).

Bannerjee, A. 1977. *Two Buddhist Vinaya Texts in Sanskrit:* Prātimokṣa Sūtra *and* Bhikṣukarmavākya. Calcutta: World Press Private Limited.

Bareau, A. 1955. *Les Premiers Conciles Bouddhiques.* Paris: Presses Universitaires de France.

Basham, A. L. 1963. *The Wonder That Was India.* New York: Hawthorn Publishers.

Bazarov, A. 2008. *Catalogue of the Collection of Tibetan Manuscripts and Xylographs "Chos grwa" (Parts: Tshad ma, Grub Mtha') of the Institute of Mongolian, Buddhist, and Tibetan Studies of Russian Academy of Sciences (Siberian Branch).* Varanasi: Central Institute of Higher Tibetan Studies.

Beal, S. 1969 [1884]. *Si-Yu-Ki: Buddhist Records of the Western World.* Delhi: Oriental Books Reprint Corporation.

Bechert, H. 1980. *The Language of the Earliest Buddhist Tradition.* Göttingen: Vandenhoeck and Ruprecht.

Bendall, C. 1902. *Çikshāsamuucaya: A Compendium of Buddhist Teaching Compiled By Çāntideva, Chiefly from Earlier Mahāyāna-Sūtras.* St. Petersburg: Imperial Academy of Sciences.

Bendall, C., and W. H. D. Rouse, trans. 1981 [1922]. *Śikṣā-samuccaya: A Compendium of Buddhist Doctrine.* Delhi: Motilal Banarsidass.

Berkwitz, S., J. Schober and Claudia Brown, eds. 2009. *Buddhist Manuscript Cultures: Knowledge, Ritual, and Art.* London: Routledge.

Bernhard, F. 1965. *Udānavarga*, vol. 1, *Einleitung; Beschreibung der Handscriften; Textausgabe; Bibliographie.* Göttingen: Vandenhoeck and Ruprecht.

Bingenheimer, M. 2008. "The Suttas on Sakka in Āgama and Nikāya Literature—With Some Remarks on the Attribution of the Shorter Chinese Saṃyukta Āgama." *Buddhist Studies Review* 25.2:149–173.

——. 2009. "More Suttas on Sakka and Why the Shorter Chinese Saṃyukta-āgama Should Not Be Attributed to the Kāśyapīya School." *Buddhist Studies Review* 26.2:127–153.

Blackburn, A. 2001. *Buddhist Learning and Textual Practice in Eighteenth-Century Lankan Monastic Culture.* Princeton, NJ: Princeton University Press.

Bloch, J. 1950. *Les inscriptions d'Aśoka.* Paris: Société d'edition "Les Belles Lettres."

Blumenthal, J. 2004. *The Ornament of the Middle Way: A Study of the Madhyamaka Thought of Śāntarakṣita.* Ithaca, NY: Snow Lion.

Bodewitz, H. W., and M. Hara, eds. *Gedenkschrift J. W. de Jong.* Tokyo: International Institute for Buddhist Studies.

Bodhi, B., trans. 1978. *The Discourse on the All-Embracing Net of Views: The* Brahmajālasutta *and Its Commentaries.* Kandy: Buddhist Publication Society.

——. 1989. *The Discourse on the Fruits of Recluseship: The* Sāmaññaphala Sutta *and its Commentaries.* Kandy: Buddhist Publication Society.

——. 2000. *The Connected Discourses of the Buddha: A Translation of the Samyutta Nikāya.* Somerville, MA: Wisdom.

Bond, G. 1980. "The *Netti-Pakaraṇa*: A Theravāda Method of Interpretation." In Balasooriya et al. 1980:16–28.

——. 1982. *The Word of the Buddha: The Tipiṭaka and Its Interpretation in Theravada Buddhism*. Colombo: M. D. Gunasena and Company.

——. 1988. "Gradual Path as a Hermeneutical Approach." In Lopez 1988a:29–45.

Bongard-Levin, G. M. 1986. *New Sanskrit Fragments of the* Mahāyāna Mahāparinirvāṇasūtra *(Central Asian Manuscript Collection at Leningrad)*. Tokyo: International Institute for Buddhist Studies.

Braarvig, J. 1985. "Dhāraṇī and Pratibhāna: Memory and Eloquence of the Bodhisattvas." *Journal of the International Association of Buddhist Studies* 8.1:17–29.

——. 1993a. *Akṣayamatinirdeśasūtra*, vol. 1, *Edition of Extant Manuscripts with an Index*. Oslo: Solum Forlag.

——. 1993b. *Akṣayamatinirdeśasūtra*, vol. 2, *The Tradition of Imperishability in Buddhist Thought*. Oslo: Solum Forlag.

——, ed. 2000. *Buddhist Manuscripts*. Vol. 1. Oslo: Hermes Publishing.

——, ed. 2002. *Buddhist Manuscripts*. Vol. 2. Oslo: Hermes Publishing.

——, ed. 2006. *Buddhist Manuscripts*. Vol. 3. Oslo: Hermes Publishing.

Brandom, R. 2000. *Articulating Reasons: An Introduction to Inferentialism*. Cambridge, MA: Harvard University Press.

Brenneis, D., and Macaulay, R., eds. 1996. *The Matrix of Language: Contemporary Linguistic Anthropology*. Boulder, CO: Westview Press.

Bronkhorst, J. 2006. "Commentaries and the History of Science in India." *Asiatische Studien/Études Asiatiques* 60.4:773–788.

Broido, M. 1983. "A Note on *dgos-'brel*." *Journal of the Tibet Society* 3:5–19.

——. 1984. "Abhiprāya and Implication in Tibetan Linguistics." *Journal of Indian Philosophy* 12:1–33.

——. 1988. "Killing, Stealing, Lying, and Adultery: A Problem of Interpretation in the Tantras." In Lopez 1988a:71–118.

Brough, J. 1950. "'Thus Have I Heard . . .'" *Bulletin of the School of Oriental and African Studies, University of London* 13.2:416–426.

——. 1980. "Sakāya Niruttiyā: Cauld kale het." In Bechert 1980:35–42.

Buescher, H. 2007. *Sthiramati's* Triṃśikāvijñaptibhāṣya*: Critical Editions of the Sanskrit Text and Its Tibetan Translation*. Vienna: Verlag der Österreichischen Akademie der Wissenschaften.

Bühler, G. 1894a. "Votive Inscriptions from the Sānchi Stūpas." In Burgess 1894: 87–115.

——. 1894b. "Further Inscriptions from Sānchi." In Burgess 1894:366–408.

Burgess, J., ed. 1894. *Epigraphia Indica*. Vol. 2. Calcutta: Superintendent of Government Printing.

Burnouf, E. 1925 [1852]. *Le lotus de la bonne loi, traduit du sanscrit, accompagné d'un commentaire et de vingt et un mémoires relatifs au buddhisme*. 2 vols. Paris, Maisonneuve Frères.

Buswell, R., ed. 1990. *Chinese Buddhist Apocrypha*. Honolulu: University of Hawai'i Press.

—— and R. Gimello, eds. 1992. *Paths to Liberation: The Mārga and Its Transformations in Buddhist Thought*. Kuroda Institute Studies in East Asian Buddhism 7. Honolulu: University of Hawai'i Press.

Cabezón, J. 1992. "Vasubandhu's *Vyākhyāyukti* on the Authenticity of the Mahāyāna Sūtras." In Timm 1992:221–243.

——, ed. 1998. *Scholasticism: Cross-cultural and Comparative Perspectives*. Albany: State University of New York Press.

Cabezón, J., and R. Jackson, eds. 1996. *Tibetan Literature: Studies in Genre*. Ithaca, NY: Snow Lion.

Caillat, C. 1984. "Prohibited Speech and *Subhāṣita* in the Theravāda Tradition." *Indologica Taurinensia* 12:61–73.

Cardona, G. 1975. "Paraphrase and Sentence Analysis: Some Indian Views." *Journal of Indian Philosophy* 3:275–281.

——. 1990. "On Attitudes Towards Language in Ancient India." *Sino-Platonic Papers* 15. Philadelphia: University of Pennsylvania Press.

Cavell, S. 1979. *The Claim of Reason: Wittgenstein, Skepticism, Morality, and Tragedy*. Oxford: Oxford University Press.

——. 1985. "The Division of Talent." *Critical Inquiry* 11.4:519–538.

Chandra, L. 1960. "Unpublished Gilgit Fragment of the *Prātimokṣa-sūtra*." *Wiener Zeitschrift für die Kunde Süd- und Ostasiens* 4:1–13.

Chattopadhyaya, D., ed. 1980. *Tāranātha's History of Buddhism in India*. Atlantic Highlands, NJ: Humanities Press.

Chavannes, E. 1894. *Mémoire composé a l'époque de la grande dynastie T'ang sur les religieux eminents qui allèrent chercher la loi dans les pays d'occident par I-Tsing*. Paris: Ernest Leroux.

Childers, R. 1870. "Khuddaka Pāṭha: A Pāli Text, with a Translation and Notes." *Journal of the Royal Asiatic Society*:309–339.

——. 1976 [1874]. *A Dictionary of the Pali Language*. Kyoto: Rinsen Book Company.

Chojnacki, C., J.-U. Hartmann, and V. Tschannerl, eds. 2000. *Vividharatnakaraṇḍaka: Festgabe für Adelheid Mette*. Indica et Tibetica 37. Swisttal-Odendorf, Germany: Indica et Tibetica Verlag.

Chou, T. 1991. *The Chinese Madhyama Āgama and the Pāli Majjhima Nikāya: A Comparative Study*. Delhi: Motilal Banarsidass.

Clarke, S. 2009a. "Monks Who Have Sex: *Pārājika* Penance in Indian Buddhist Monasticisms." *Journal of Indian Philosophy* 37:1–43.

——. 2009b. "When and Where Is a Monk No Longer a Monk? On Communion and Communities in Indian Buddhist Monastic Law Codes." *Indo-Iranian Journal* 52.2–3:115–141.

Collier, N. 1998. "Ornamenting Intentions: Intention and Implication in Buddhist Hermeneutics." Ph.D. diss., University of Chicago.

Collins, S. 1990. "On the Very Idea of the Pali Canon." *Journal of the Pali Text Society* 15:89–126.

——. 1992. "Some Oral Aspects of Pali Literature." *Indo-Iranian Journal* 35.2–3: 121–135.

——. 1998. *Nirvāṇa and Other Buddhist Felicities: Utopias of the Pali Imaginaire*. Cambridge: Cambridge University Press.

Connolly, P., and S. Hamilton, eds. 1997. *Indian Insights: Buddhism, Brahmanism, and Bhakti: Papers from the Annual Spalding Symposium on Indian Religions*. London: Luzac Oriental.

Conze, E. 1960. *The Prajñāpāramitā Literature*. The Hague: Mouton and Company.

——. 1962. *The Gilgit Manuscript of the* Aṣṭadaśasāhasrikāprajñāpāramitā: *Chapters 55 to 70 Corresponding to the Fifth Abhisamaya*. Rome: Istituto italiano per il Medio ed Estremo Oriente.
——. 1974a. *The Short Prajñāpāramitā Texts*. London: Luzac and Company.
——. 1974b. *The Gilgit Manuscript of the* Aṣṭadaśasāhasrikāprajñāpāramitā: *Chapters 70 to 82 Corresponding to the Sixth, Seventh, and Eighth Abhisamayas*. Rome: Istituto italiano per il Medio ed Estremo Oriente.
——, ed. 1957. *Vajracchedikā Prajñāpāramitā*. Rome: Istituto Italiano per il Medio ed Estremo Oriente.
Coward, H., and Raja, K. 1990. *The Philosophy of the Grammarians*. Princeton, NJ: Princeton University Press.
Cou—sins, L. S. 1983. "Pali Oral Literature." In Denwood and Piatigorsky 1983:1–11.
——. 1992. "Notes on Some Oral Aspects of Pali Literature." *Indo-Iranian Journal* 35:121–135.
Cowell, E. B., and R. A. Neil, eds. 1886. *The* Divyāvadāna: *a Collection of Early Buddhist Legends*. Cambridge: Cambridge University Press.
D'Amato, M. 2009. "Why the Buddha Never Uttered a Word." In D'Amato, Garfield, and Tillemans 2009:41–55.
D'Amato, M., J. Garfield, and T. Tillemans, eds. 2009. *Pointing at the Moon: Buddhism, Logic, Analytic Philosophy*. Oxford: Oxford University Press.
Dādhimatha, S., ed. 1997 [1915]. Nāmaliṅgānuśāsana, *alias* Amarakośa *of Amarasiṃha, with the Commentary* Vyākhyāsudhā *or* Rāmāśramī *of Bhānuji Dīkṣita*. Delhi: Chaukhamba Sanskrit Pratishthan.
Dallapiccola, A., ed. 1989. *Shastric Traditions in Indian Arts*. 2 vols. Stuttgart: Steiner Verlag Wiesbaden GMBH.
Das, S. 1960. *A Tibetan-English Dictionary with Sanskrit Synonyms*. Alipore, India: West Bengal Government Press.
Davidson, R. 1990. "An Introduction to the Standards of Scriptural Authenticity in Indian Buddhism." In Buswell 1990:291–325.
——. 1999. "Masquerading as Pramāṇa: Esoteric Buddhism and Epistemological Nomenclature." In Katsura 1999:25–35.
——. 2003. *Indian Esoteric Buddhism: A Social History of the Tantric Movement*. New York: Columbia University Press.
——. 2005. *Tibetan Renaissance: Tantric Buddhism in the Rebirth of Tibetan Culture*. New York: Columbia University Press.
——. 2009. "Studies in Dhāraṇī Literature I: Revisiting the Meaning of the Term Dhāraṇī." *Journal of Indian Philosophy* 37:97–147.
Dayal, H. 1970 [1932]. *The Bodhisattva Doctrine in Buddhist Sanskrit Literature*. Delhi: Motilal Banarsidass.
DeCaroli, R. 2004. *Haunting the Buddha: Indian Popular Religions and the Formation of Buddhism*. Oxford: Oxford University Press.
Deegalle, M. 1997. "Buddhist Preaching and Sinhala Religious Rhetoric." *Numen* 44:180–210.
——. 1998. "Marathon Preachers." *Asiatische Studien* 52:15–56.
——. 2006. *Popularizing Buddhism: Preaching as Performance in Sri Lanka*. Albany: State University of New York Press.

Demiéville, P. 1952. *Le concile de Lhasa : Une controverse sur le quiétisme entre bouddhistes de l'Inde et de la Chine au VIII siècle de l'ère chrétienne*. Bibliothèque de l'Institut des hautes études chinoises 7. Paris: Imprimerie Nationale de France.
——. 1958. Review of Tucci 1958. *T'oung Pao* 46:402–408.
Denwood, P., and A. Piatigorsky, eds. 1983. *Buddhist Studies: Ancient and Modern*. London: Curzon.
Derrett, J. D. M. 2006. "Musāvāda-virati and 'privileged lies'" *Journal of Buddhist Ethics* 13. Accessed at http://blogs.dickinson.edu/buddhistethics/files/2010/04/derrett-article.pdf.
Deshpande, M., and P. Hook, eds. 2002. *Indian Linguistic Studies: Festschrift in Honor of George Cardona*. Delhi: Motilal Banarsidass
Dhruva, A. B. 1930. *The* Nyāyapraveśa *of Dignāga*. Baroda: Oriental Institute.
Drewes, D. 2009. "Early Indian Mahāyāna Buddhism II: New Perspectives." *Religion Compass* 3:1–9.
Dreyfus, G. 1997a. *Recognizing Reality: Dharmakīrti's Philosophy and Its Tibetan Interpretations*. Albany: State University of New York Press.
——. 1997b. "Tibetan Scholastic Education and the Role of Soteriology." *Journal of the International Association of Buddhist Studies* 20.1:31–62.
——. 2003. *The Sound of Two Hands Clapping: The Education of a Tibetan Buddhist Monk*. Berkeley: University of California Press.
—— and S. McClintock, eds. 2003. *The Svātantrika-Prāsaṅgika Distinction: What Difference Does a Difference Make?* Boston: Wisdom.
Dudjom Rinpoche, Jigdrel Yeshe Dorje (bDud 'joms rin po che 'Jigs bral ye shes rdo rje) with G. Dorje and M. Kapstein. 1991. *The Nyingma School of Tibetan Buddhism*. 2 vols. Boston: Wisdom.
Dundas, P. 1996. "Somnolent Sūtras: Scriptural Commentary in Śvetāmbara Jainism." *Journal of Indian Philosophy* 24:73–101.
Dunne, J. 1996. "Thoughtless Buddha, Passionate Buddha." *Journal of the American Academy of Religion* 64.3:525–556.
——. 2004. *Foundations of Dharmakīrti's Philosophy*. Boston: Wisdom.
Dutt, N. 1931. "Notes on the Nāgārjunikoṇḍa Inscriptions." *Indian Historical Quarterly* 7.3.: 633–653.
——. 1966. *Bodhisattvabhūmi: Being the XVth Section of Asaṅgapada's Yogacarabhumi* [*sic*]. Patna, India: Jayaswal Research Institute.
Dutt, N., D. M. Bhattacharya, and S. Sarma, eds. 1984 [1939–1959]. *Gilgit Manuscripts*. 9 vols. Delhi: Sri Satguru Publications.
Dutt, S. 1962. *Buddhist Monks and Monasteries of India*. London: George Allen and Unwin.
Eckel, M. 1987a. "Indian Commentaries on the Heart Sūtra: The Politics of Interpretation." *Journal of the Association of Buddhist Studies* 10.2:69–79.
——. 1987b. *Jñānagarbha's Commentary on the Distinction Between the Two Truths*. Albany: State University of New York Press.
——. 1992. *To See the Buddha: A Philosopher's Quest for the Meaning of Emptiness*. Princeton, NJ: Princeton University Press.
——. 2008. *Bhāviveka and His Buddhist Opponents*. Cambridge, MA: Department of Sanskrit and Indian Studies, Harvard University.

Edgerton, F. 1953. *Buddhist Hybrid Sanskrit Grammar and Dictionary*. 2 vols. New Haven, CT: Yale University Press.

Eimer, H., and D. Germano, eds. 2002. *The Many Canons of Tibetan Buddhism*. Leiden: Brill.

Eltschinger, V. 2007. "On Seventh and Eighth Century Buddhist Accounts of Human Action, Practical Rationality, and Soteriology." In Kellner et al. 2007:135–162.

Emmerick, R. 1970. *The Sūtra of Golden Light*. London: Luzac.

Enomoto, F. 2000. "'Mūlasarvāstivādin' and 'Sarvāstivādin.'" In Chojnacki, Hartmann, and Tschannerl 2000:239–250.

——, J.-U. Hartmann, and H. Matsumura. 1989. *Sanskrit-Texte aus dem buddhistischen Kanon: Neuentdeckungen und Neueditionen*. Göttingen: Vandenhoeck and Ruprecht.

Falk, H. 1990. "Goodies for India: Literacy, Orality, and Vedic Culture." In Raible 1990:103–120.

Finot, L., ed. 1901. Rāṣtrapālaparipṛcchā, *sūtra du Mahāyāna*. St. Petersburg: Imperial Academy of Sciences.

Foucault, M. 1972. *The Archaeology of Knowledge*. Trans. A. M. Sheridan Smith. London: Tavistock Publications.

——. 1988. "Technologies of the Self." In Martin, Gutman, and Hutton 1988:16–49.

——. 2001. *L'Herméneutique du sujet: Cours au Collège de France (1981–1982)*. Edited by Frédéric Gros. Paris: Hautes Études.

Frauwallner, E. 1956. *Die Philosophie des Buddhismus*. Berlin: Akademie-Verlag.

——. 1961. "Landmarks in the History of Indian Logic." *Wiener Zeitschrift für die Kunde Südasiens* 5:125–148. Reprinted in Frauwallner 1982:847–870.

——. 1982. *Kleine Schriften*. Wiesbaden: Franz Steiner Verlag GMBH.

——. 1995. *Studies in Abhidharma Literature and the Origins of Buddhist Philosophical Systems*. Trans. S. F. Kidd. Albany: State University of New York Press.

Freeman, C. 1992. "Samvṛti, Vyavahāra, and Paramārtha in the *Akṣayamatinirdeśa* and Its Commentary by Vasubandhu." In Skorupski 1992:97–114.

Freud, S. 1914 [1901]. *The Psychopathology of Everyday Life*. Trans. A. Brill. London: T. Fisher Unwin.

Fujishima, M. R. 1888. "Deux chapitres extraits des mémoires d'I-Tsing sur son voyage dans l'Inde." *Journal Asiatique*, series 8, tome 12:411–439.

Funayama, T. 1992. "A Study of *Kalpanāpoḍha*: A Translation of the *Tattvasaṃgraha* vv. 1212–1263 by Śāntarakṣita and the *Tattvasaṃgrahapañjikā* by Kamalaśīla on the Definition of Direct Perception." *Zinbun* 27:33–128.

——. 1995. "Arcaṭa, Śāntarakṣita, Jinendrabuddhi, and Kamalaśīla on the Aim of a Treatise." *Wiener Zeitschrift für die Kunde Südasiens* 39:181–201.

Fussman, G. 1980. Review of T. Damsteegt, *Epigraphical Hybrid Sanskrit*. *Journal Asiatique* 268:423–424.

Galloway, B. 1991. "Thus Have I Heard: At One Time . . ." *Indo-Iranian Journal* 34:87–104.

Ganapati, T. 1982. *The Yājñavalkyasmṛti with the commentary Bālakrīḍa of Viśvarūpācārya*. New Delhi: Munshiram Manoharlal.

Ganeri, J. 2001. *Philosophy in Classical India: The Proper Work of Reason*. London: Routledge.

——. 2007. *The Concealed Art of the Soul: Theories of Self and Practices of Truth in Indian Ethics and Epistemology*. Oxford: Oxford University Press.

Garfield, J. 1995. *The Fundamental Wisdom of the Middle Way: Nāgārjuna's* Mūlamadhyamakakārikā. Oxford: Oxford University Press.

——. 2002. *Empty Words: Buddhist Philosophy and Cross-Cultural Interpretation*. New York: Oxford University Press.

Gerow, E. 1977. *Indian Poetics*. History of Indian Literature 5.3. Stuttgart: Harassowitz.

Ghatage, A. M., ed. 1976. *An Encyclopaedic Dictionary of Sanskrit on Historical Principles*. Vol. 1. Pune: Deccan College Postgraduate and Research Institute.

Gillon, B., and R. Hayes. 2008. "Dharmakīrti on the Role of Causation in Inference as Presented in *Pramāṇavārttika Svopajñavṛtti* 11–38." *Journal of Indian Philosophy* 36:335–404.

Gnoli, R. 1960. *The* Pramāṇavārttikam *of Dharmakīrti: The First Chapter with the Autocommentary*. Rome: Istituto Italiano per il Medio ed Estremo Oriente.

——. 1977–1978. *The Gilgit Manuscript of the* Saṅghabhedavastu*: Being the Seventeenth and Last Section of the Vinaya of the Mūlasarvāstivādin*. 2 vols. Rome: Istituto Italiano per il Medio ed Estremo Oriente.

——. 1978. *The Gilgit Manuscript of the* Śayanāsanavastu *and the* Ādhikaraṇavastu*: Being the Fifteenth and Sixteenth Sections of the Vinaya of the Mūlasarvāstivādin*. Rome: Istituto Italiano per il Medio ed Estremo Oriente.

Gokhale, P. 1993. *Nyāyabiṇḍu of Dharmakīrti: The Logic of Debate*. Delhi: Sri Satguru.

——. 1997. Hetubindu *of Dharmakīrti: A Point on Probans*. Delhi: Sri Satguru.

Gokhale, V. V. 1947. "Fragments from the *Abhidharmasamuccaya* of Asaṅga." *Journal of the Royal Asiatic Society of Great Britain and Ireland, Bombay Branch* 23:13–38.

Gombrich, R. 1987. "Three Souls, One or None: The Vagaries of a Pāli Pericope." *Journal of the Pāli Text Society* 11:73–78.

——. 1990a. "Recovering the Buddha's Message" In Skorupski 1990:5–20.

——. 1990b. "How the Mahāyāna Began." In Skorupski 1990:21–30.

Gombrich, R., and G. Obeyesekere. 1988. *Buddhism Transformed: Religious Changes in Sri Lanka*. Princeton, NJ: Princeton University Press.

Gómez, L. 1993. "Indian Materials on the Doctrine of Sudden Enlightenment." In Lai and Lancaster 1983:393–434.

——. 2000. "Two Jars on Two Tables." In Silk 2000:95–136.

Gómez, L., and J. Silk, eds. 1989. *Studies in the Literature of the Great Vehicle: Three Mahāyāna Buddhist Texts*. Ann Arbor, MI: Collegiate Center for the Study of Buddhist Literature.

Gonda, J. 1963. *The Vision of the Vedic Poets*. The Hague: Mouton and Company.

Graham, W. 1987. *Beyond the Written Word*. Cambridge: Cambridge University Press.

Granoff, P. 1991. "Buddhaghoṣa's Penance and Siddhasena's Crime: Remarks on Some Buddhist and Jain Attitudes towards the Language of Religious Texts." In Shinohara and Schopen 1991:17–34.

Griffiths, P. J. 1994. *On Being Buddha*. Albany: State University of New York Press.

——. 1999. *Religious Reading: The Place of Reading in the Practice of Religion*. Oxford: Oxford University Press.

——. 2002. "Asaṅga, *Abhidharmasamuccaya* (Summary)." In Potter 2002:434–452.

Griffiths, P. J., N. Hakamaya, J. Keenan, and P. Swanson. 1989. *The Realm of Awakening: Chapter Ten of Asaṅga's* Mahāyānasaṃgraha. Oxford: Oxford University Press.

Gummer, N. 2000. "Articulating Potency: A Study of the *Suvarṇa(pra)bhāsottama-sūtra*." Ph.D. diss., Harvard University.

Gyatso, J., ed. 1992. *In the Mirror of Memory: Reflections on Mindfulness and Remembrance in Indian and Tibetan Buddhism*. Albany: State University of New York Press.

Hadot, P. 1995. *Philosophy as a Way of Life: Spiritual Exercises from Socrates to Foucault*. Ed. A. Davidson; trans. M. Chase. Oxford: Blackwell.

——. 2002. *What Is Ancient Philosophy?* Trans. M. Chase. Cambridge: Belknap Press.

Hahn, M. 1992. "Mātrceṭas Brief an den König Kaniṣka." *Asiatische Studien* 46.1:147–179.

——, trans. 2003. *Invitation to Enlightenment: Letter to the Great King Kaniṣka by Mātṛceṭa / Letter to a Disciple by Candragomin*. Berkeley, CA: Dharma Press.

Hahn, M., J. W. Hartmann, and R. Steiner, eds. 1996. *Suhṛllekhāḥ: Festgabe für Helmut Eimer*. Swisttal-Odendorf, Germany: Indica et Tibetica Verlag.

Hale, B., and C. Wright, eds. 1997. *A Companion to the Philosophy of Language*. Oxford: Blackwell.

Halkias, G. 2004. "Tibetan Buddhism Registered: A Catalogue from the Imperial Palace of 'Phang thang." *Eastern Buddhist* 36.1–2:46–105.

Hallisey, C. 1994. "In Defense of Rather Fragile and Local Achievement: Reflections on the Work of Gurulugumi" In Reynolds and Tracy 1994:121–160.

Hara, M. 1992. "A Note on Dhammapada 97." *Indo-Iranian Journal* 35.2/3:179–191.

Harrison, P. 1978. *The Tibetan Text of the* Pratyutpanna-Buddha-Saṃmukhāvasthita-Samādhi-Sūtra. Studia Philologica Buddhica 1. Tokyo: Reiyukai Library.

——. 1990. *The Samādhi of Direct Encounter with the Buddhas of the Present*. Studia Philologica Buddhica 5. Tokyo: International Institute for Buddhist Studies.

——. 2003. "Mediums and Messages: Reflections on the Production of Mahāyāna Sūtras." *Eastern Buddhist* 35.1–2:115–151.

——. 2007. "The Case of the Vanishing Poet: New Light on Śāntideva and the Śiksāsamuccaya." In Klaus and Hartmann 2007:215–248.

—— and G. Schopen, eds. 1998. *Sūryacandrāya: Essays in Honor of Akira Yuyama on the Occasion of His Sixty-fifth Birthday*. Swisttal-Odendorf, Germany: Indica and Tibetica Verlag.

—— and S. Watanabe, eds. 2006. "Vajracchedikā Prajñāpāramitā." In Braarvig 2006: 89–132.

Hartmann, J-U. 1987. *Das Varṇārhavarṇastotra des Mātṛceṭa*. Saskrittexte aus den Turfanfunden 12. Göttingen: Vandenhoeck and Ruprecht.

Hattori, M. 1968. *Dignāga, on Perception*. Cambridge, MA: Harvard University Press.

——. 1977. "The Sautrāntika Background of the Apoha Theory." In Kawamura and Scott 1977:47–58.

——. 2000. "Dignāga's Theory of Meaning: An Annotated Translation of the *Pramāṇasamuccayavṛtti* Chapter V: *Anyāpoha-parikṣā* (I)." In Silk 2000:137–146.

Hayes, R. 1984. "The Question of Doctrinalism in the Buddhist Epistemologists." *Journal of the American Academy of Religion* 52.5:645–670.

——. 1986. "An Interpretation of Anyāpoha in Dignāga's General Theory of Inference." In Matilal and Evans 1986:31–59.

——. 1987. "On the Reinterpretation of Dharmakīrti's Svabhāvahetu." *Journal of Indian Philosophy* 15:319–332.
——. 1988. *Dignāga on the Interpretation of Signs*. Studies in Classical India 9. Dordrecht, The Netherlands: Kluwer.
——. 1991. "Introduction to Dharmakīrti's Theory of Inference as Presented in *Pramāṇavārttikasvopajñavṛtti* 1–10." *Journal of Indian Philosophy* 19:1–73.
——. 1994. "Nāgārjuna's Appeal." *Journal of Indian Philosophy* 22:299–378.
——. 2003. "Pramāṇasamuccaya: Inference for Oneself (*svārthānumāna*): Summary." In Potter 2003:337–342.
Heirman, A. 2009. "Speech Is Silver, Silence is Golden? Speech and Silence in the Buddhist Saṃgha." *Eastern Buddhist* 40.1–2:63–92.
Herrmann-Pfandt, A. 2002. "The *Lhan Kar Ma* as a Source for the History of Tantric Buddhism." In Eimer and Germano 2002:129–150.
——. 2008. *Die Lhan kar ma: Ein früher Katalog der ins Tibetische übersetzen buddhistischen Texte*. Vienna: Verlag der Österreichischen Akademie der Wissenschaften.
Hirakawa, A. 1960. Introduction [in English] to *A Study of the* Vinaya-Piṭaka. Tokyo: Sankibo Busshorin.
——. 1990. *A History of Indian Buddhism from Śākyamuni to Early Mahāyāna*. Trans. Paul Groner. Asian Studies at Hawai'i 36. Honolulu: University of Hawai'i Press.
Hodge, S., trans. 2003. *The* Mahāvairocanābhisaṃbodhitantra *with Buddhaguhya's Commentary*. New York: Curzon.
Hoernle, A. F. R. 1916. *Manuscript Remains of Buddhist Literature Found in Eastern Turkestan*. Oxford: Clarendon Press.
Honda, M. 1968. "Annotated Translation of the *Daśabhūmikasūtra*." In Sinor 1968: 115–276.
Hopkins, J., trans. 2006. *Mountain Doctrine: Tibet's Fundamental Treatise on Other-Emptiness and the Buddha-Matrix*. Ithaca, NY: Snow Lion Publications.
Houben, J., ed. 1996. *Ideology and Status of Sanskrit: Contributions to the History of the Sanskrit Language*. Leiden: E. J. Brill.
Houston, G. W. 1980. *Sources for a History of the bSam yas Debate*. Sankt Augustin, Germany: VGH-Wissenschaftsverlag.
Hubbard, J. 1999. "A Tale of Two Times: Preaching in the Latter Age of the Dharma." *Numen* 46:186–210.
Huntington, C. 1989. *The Emptiness of Emptiness: An Introduction to Early Indian Madhyamaka*. Honolulu: University of Hawai'i Press
Huntington, S. 1984. *The "Pāla-Sena" Schools of Sculpture*. Leiden: E. J. Brill.
Ihara, S., and Z. Yamaguchi, eds. 1992. *Tibetan Studies: Proceedings of the Fifth Seminar of the International Association for Tibetan Studies, Narita 1989*. 2 vols. Narita, Japan: Naritasan Shinshoji.
Inagaki, H. 1999. Amida Dhāraṇī Sūtra *and Jñānagarbha's Commentary*. Tokyo:Ryukoku gakkai.
Inden, R. 1990. *Imagining India*. Bloomington: Indiana University Press.
Iwata, T. 2007. "Dharmakīrti's Interpretation of the Word *iṣṭa* in the Definition of the Thesis." In Klaus and Hartmann 2007:275–288.
Iyer, K. S., ed. 1963. Vākyapadīya *of Bhartṛhari, with the* Prakīrṇakaprakāśa *of Helārāja, Kaṇḍa III, Part ii*. Pune: Deccan College Postgraduate and Research Institute.

Jackson, D. 1991. "The Status of Pramāṇa Doctrine According to Sa skya Paṇḍita and Other Tibetan Masters: Theoretical Discipline or Doctrine of Liberation?" *Buddhist Forum* 3:85–129.

Jackson, R. 1988. "The Buddha as *Pramāṇabhūta*: Epithets and Arguments in the Buddhist 'Logical' Tradition." *Journal of Indian Philosophy* 16:335–365.

Jaini, P. 1977. *Abhidharmadīpa with Vibhāṣāprabhāvṛtti*. Patna, India: Kashi Prasad Jayaswal Research Institute.

Jäschke, H. 1934. *A Tibetan English Dictionary with Special Reference to the Prevailing Dialects*. London: Kegan Paul.

Jetly, J. S., and V. G. Parikh, eds. 1991. Nyāyakandalī, *being a commentary on* Praśastapadabhāṣya, *with three sub-commentaries*. Vadodara, India: Oriental Institute.

Jha, G., trans. 1937–1939. *Tattvasaṃgrahapañjikā: English Translation*. 2 vols. Baroda, India: Oriental Institute.

——. 1999 [1920–1939]. Manusmṛti *with the* Manubhāṣya *of Medhātithi*. 10 vols. Delhi: Motilal Banarsidass.

de Jong, J. W. 1968. "Les Sūtrapiṭaka des Sarvāstivādins et des Mūlasarvāstivādins." In *Melanges d'Indianisme a la mémoire de Louis Renou*, 395–402. Paris: Éditions E. de Boccard.

——. 1973. Review article of Rahula 1971. *T'oung Pao* 59:339–346.

——, ed. 1977. *Mūlamadhyamakakārikāḥ*. Madras: Adyar Library and Research Centre.

Joshi, S. D., and S. D. Laddu, eds. 1983. *Proceedings of the International Seminar on Studies in the* Aṣṭādhyāyī *of Pāṇini*. Pune: University of Poona.

Kajiyama, Y. 1977. "Thus Spoke the Blessed One." In Lancaster 1977:93–99.

——. 1978. "Late Madhyamakas on Epistemology and Meditation." In Kiyota and Jones 1978:114–143.

Kaminishi, Ikumi. 2006. *Explaining Pictures: Buddhist Propaganda and Etoki Storytelling in Japan*. Honolulu: University of Hawai'i Press.

Kapstein, M. 1988. "Mi-pham's Theory of Interpretation." In Lopez 1988a:149–174.

——. 2000. *The Tibetan Assimilation of Buddhism: Conversion, Contestation, and Memory*. Oxford: Oxford University Press.

——. 2001. *Reason's Traces*. Somerville, MA: Wisdom.

Kapstein, M., and B. Dotson, eds. 2007. *Contributions to the Cultural History of Early Tibet*. Leiden: Brill.

Karunadasa, Y. 1990. *Ānanda: Papers on Buddhism and Indology*. Colombo: Felicitation Volume Editorial Committee.

Kashyap, R., ed. 2002. *Krisṇayajurvedīya Taittirīyasamhitā*. Vol. 1. Bangalore: Sri Aurobindo Kapāli Sāstry Institute of Vedic Culture.

Katsura, S. 1986. "Jñānaśrīmitra on Apoha." In Matilal and Evans 1986:171–184.

——. 1999. *Dharmakīrti's Thought and Its Impact on Indian and Tibetan Philosophy: Proceedings of the Third International Conference on Dharmakīrti and Pramāṇa*. Vienna: Österreichischen Akademie der Wissenschaften.

Kawamura, L., and K. Scott, eds. 1977. *Buddhist Thought and Asian Civilization: Essays in Honor of Herbert V. Guenther on His Sixtieth Birthday*. Emeryville, CA: Dharma Publishing.

Kawara, K. 1972. *The* Dharma-saṃgraha*: An Ancient Collection of Buddhist Technical Terms*. Amsterdam: Oriental Press.

Keenan, J., trans. 2000. *The Scripture on the Explication of the Underlying Meaning.* Berkeley, CA: Numata Center for Buddhist Translation and Research.

Keith, A. B. 1928. "The Authorship of the *Nyāyapraveśa*." *Indian Historical Quarterly* 4.1:14–22.

Kellner, B. 1997. *Nichts bleibt Nichts.* Vienna: Arbeitskreis für Tibetische und Buddhistische Studien.

——— et al., eds. 2007. *Pramāṇakīrtiḥ: Papers Dedicated to Ernst Steinkellner on the Occasion of His Seventieth Birthday.* 2 vols. Vienna: Wiener Studien zur Tibetologie und Buddhismuskunde.

Kieckhefer, R., and G. Bond, eds. 1988. *Sainthood: Its Manifestation in World Religions.* Berkeley: University of California Press.

Kieffer-Pülz, P., and J.-U. Hartmann. 1997. *Bauddhavidyāsudhākaraḥ: Studies in Honor of Heinz Bechert on the Occasion of His Sixty-fifth Birthday*. Swisttal-Odendorf, Germany: India et Tibetica Verlag.

Kinnard, J. 2002. "On Buddhist 'Bibliolaters': Representing and Worshiping the Book in Medieval Indian Buddhism." *Eastern Buddhist* 34.2:94–116.

Kiyota, M., and E. Jones. 1978. *Mahāyāna Buddhist Meditation: Theory and Practice*. Honolulu: University of Hawai'i Press.

Klaus, K., and J.-U. Hartmann. 2007. *Indica et Tibetica: Festschrift für Michael Hahn*. Vienna: Arbeitskreis für Tibetische und Buddhistische Studien.

Kondō, R. 1936. *Daśabhūmīśvaro Nāma Mahāyānasūtraṃ*. Tokyo: Daijyō bukkyō kenyō-kai.

Krasser, H. 2001. "On Dharmakīrti's Understanding of *Pramāṇabhūta* and His Definition of *Pramāṇa*." *Wiener Zeitschrift für die Kunde Südasiens* 45:173–199.

Krishnamacarya, E. 1926. Tattvasaṅgraha *of Śāntarakṣita with the Commentary of Kamalaśīla*. Gaekwad Oriental Series 30–31. Baroda, India: Central Library.

Kritzer, R. 2002. "The 'Additional Leaf' of the *Abhidharmasamuccayabhāṣya* Manuscript: The Result of the Ten Bad Courses of Action." *Journal Asiatique* 290.2:465–484.

———. 2005. *Vasubandhu and the* Yogācārabhūmi*: Yogācāra Elements in the* Abhidharmakośa-bhāsya. Tokyo: International Institute for Buddhist Studies.

Kulke, H., and Rothermund, D. 1998. *A History of India*. London: Routledge.

Lai, W., and L. Lancaster, eds. 1983. *Early Ch'an in India and Tibet*. Berkeley Buddhist Studies Series 5. Berkeley: Institute of East Asian Studies, University of California, Berkeley.

Lalou, M. 1953. "Les textes bouddhiques au temps du roi Khri-sroṅ-lde-bcan." *Journal Asiatique* 241:313–353.

Lamotte, É. 1935. *Saṃdhinirmocana Sūtra: L'explication des mystères*. Louvain, Belgium: Université de Louvain.

———. 1970. *Le traité de la grand vertu de sagesse de Nāgārjuna (*Mahāprajñāpāramitāśāstra*)*. Vol. 3. Louvain-la-Neuve, Belgium: Institute Orientaliste, Université de Louvain.

———. 1976a. *The Teaching of Vimalakīrti (*Vimalakīrtinirdeśa*)*. Trans. Sara Boin. London: Pali Text Society.

———. 1976b. *Le traité de la grand vertu de sagesse de Nāgārjuna (*Mahāprajñāpāramitāśāstra*)*. Vol. 4. Louvain-la-Neuve, Belgium: Institute Orientaliste, Université de Louvain.

——. 1980. *Le traité de la grand vertu de sagesse de Nāgārjuna* (Mahāprajñāpāramitāśāstra). Vol. 5. Louvain-la-Neuve, Belgium: Institute Orientaliste, Université de Louvain.

——. 1981a. *Le traité de la grand vertu de sagesse de Nāgārjuna* (Mahāprajñāpāramitāśāstra). Vol. 1. Louvain-la-Neuve, Belgium: Institute Orientaliste, Université de Louvain.

——. 1981b. *Le traité de la grand vertu de sagesse de Nāgārjuna* (Mahāprajñāpāramitāśāstra). Vol. 2. Louvain-la-Neuve, Belgium: Institute Orientaliste, Université de Louvain.

——. 1988a. *History of Indian Buddhism: From the Origins to the Śaka Era*. Trans. Sara Boin-Webb. Louvain-la-Neuve, Belgium: Institut Orientaliste de Louvain.

——. 1988b. "Assessment of Textual Interpretation in Buddhism." Trans. Sara Boin-Webb. In Lopez 1988a:11–27.

Lancaster, L., ed. 1977. *Prajñāpāramitā and Related Systems: Studies in Honor of Edward Conze*. Berkeley Buddhist Studies Series 1. Berkeley: Institute of East Asian Studies, University of California, Berkeley.

——. 1998. "Narratives of Exemplars: Perspectives on Doctrine and Practice in Early Buddhism." In Harrison and Schopen 1998:107–124.

Lanman, C. R. 1967 [1884]. *A Sanskrit Reader: Text with Vocabulary and Notes*. Cambridge, MA: Harvard University Press.

La Vallée Poussin, L. de. 1911. "Fragments du *Śatapañcāśatkastotra* d' Aśvaghoṣa-Mātṛceṭa." *Journal of the Royal Asiatic Society*:762–769.

——. 1913. *Théorie des douze causes*. London: Luzac.

——. 1938. "Buddhica." *Harvard Journal of Asiatic Studies* 3.2:137–160.

Lee, J.-C.. 2001. *The Tibetan Text of the* Vyākhyāyukti *of Vasubandhu, Critically Edited from the Cone, Derge, Narthang, and Peking Editions*. Tokyo: Sankibo Press.

Levering, M., ed. 1989. *Rethinking Scripture: Essays from a Comparative Perspective*. Albany: State University of New York Press.

Lévi, S. 1907. *Mahāyānasūtrālaṃkāra: Exposé de la doctrine du grand véhicule selon le système Yogācāra*, vol. 1, *Texte*. Paris: Bibliothèque de l'Ecole des Hautes Études.

——. 1911. *Mahāyānasūtrālaṃkāra: Exposé de la doctrine du grand véhicule selon le système Yogācāra*, vol. 2, *Traduction—Introduction—Index*. Paris: Bibliothèque de l'Ecole des Hautes Études.

——. 1925. *Vijñaptimātratāsiddhi: Deux Traités de Vasubandhu—Viṃśatikā et Triṃśikā*. Paris: Bibliothèque de l'Ecole des Hautes Études.

Li, R. trans. 1995. *A Biography of the Tripiṭaka Master of the Great Ci'en Monastery of the Great Tang Dynasty*. Berkeley, CA: Numata Center for Buddhist Translation and Research.

——. 1996. *The Great Tang Dynasty Record of the Western Regions*. Berkeley, CA: Numata Center for Buddhist Translation and Research.

——. 2000. *Buddhist Monastic Traditions of Southern Asia: A Record of the Inner Law Sent Home from the South Seas*. Berkeley, CA: Numata Center for Buddhist Translation and Research.

Ligeti, L., ed. 1978. *Proceedings of the Csoma de Körös Memorial Symposium* (*Acta Orientalia Hungarica*). Budapest: Akademiai Kiado.

Lopez, D., ed. 1988a. *Buddhist Hermeneutics*. Honolulu: University of Hawai'i Press.

——. 1988b. "Sanctification on the Bodhisattva Path." In Kieckhefer and Bond 1988:172–217.

——. 1988c. *The Heart Sūtra Explained: Indian and Tibetan Commentaries.* Albany: State University of New York Press.
——, ed. 1995a. *Curators of the Buddha.* Chicago: University of Chicago Press.
——, ed. 1995b. *Buddhism in Practice.* Princeton, NJ: Princeton University Press.
——. 1996. *Elaborations on Emptiness.* Princeton, NJ: Princeton University Press.
——, ed. 2005. *Critical Terms for the Study of Buddhism.* Chicago: University of Chicago Press.
Lüders, H. 1909. "The Manikiala Inscription." *Journal of the Royal Asiatic Society of Great Britain and Ireland*:645–666.
——, E. Waldschmidt, and M. A. Mehendale, eds. 1963. *Bhārhut Inscriptions.* Corpus Inscriptionum Indicarum, vol. 2, part 2. Ootacamund: Government Epigraphist for India.
Lugli, L. 2010. "Meaning Without Words: The Contrast Between Artha and Ruta in Mahāyāna Sūtras." *Buddhist Studies Review* 27.2:139–176.
Macdonnell, A. 1969 [1929]. *A Practical Sanskrit Dictionary.* Oxford: Oxford University Press.
——. 1927. *A Sanskrit Grammar for Students.* Oxford: Oxford University Press.
MacQueen, G. 1981. "Inspired Speech in Early Mahāyāna I." *Religion* 11:303–319.
——. 1982. "Inspired Speech in Early Mahāyāna II." *Religion* 12:49–65.
Mair, V. 1988. *Painting and Performance: Chinese Picture Recitation and Its Indian Genesis.* Honolulu: University of Hawai'i Press.
Malalasekera, G. P. 1983 [1937]. *Dictionary of Pāli Proper Names.* 2 vols. New Delhi: Munshiram Manoharlal.
Martin, D. 1996. "Tables of Contents (*dkar chag*)." In Cabezón and Jackson 1996: 500–514.
——. 1997. *Tibetan Histories: A Bibliography of Tibetan-Language Historical Works.* London: Serindia.
Martin, L., H. Gutman, and P. Hutton, eds. 1988. *Technologies of the Self: A Seminar with Michel Foucault.* Amherst: University of Massachusetts Press.
Matilal, B. 1988. "Śābdabodha and the Problem of Knowledge-Representation in Sanskrit." *Journal of Indian Philosophy* 16:107–122.
——. 1990. *The Word and the World: India's Contribution to the Study of Language.* New York: Oxford University Press.
——. 1998. *The Character of Logic in India.* Albany: State University of New York Press.
—— and A. Chakrabarti, eds. 1994. *Knowing from Words: Western and Indian Philosophical Analysis of Understanding and Testimony.* Dordrecht, The Netherlands: Kluwer Academic Publishers.
—— and R. Evans, eds. 1986. *Buddhist Logic and Epistemology: Studies in the Buddhist Analysis of Inference and Language.* Dordrecht, The Netherlands: D. Reidel.
Matsuda, K. 1996. *Two Sanskrit Manuscripts of the* Daśabhūmikasūtra *Preserved at the National Archives, Kathmandu.* Tokyo: Centre for East Asian Cultural Studies for UNESCO, Toyo Bunko.
McClintock, S. 2000. "Knowing All Through Knowing One: Mystical Communion or Logical Trick in the *Tattvasaṃgraha* and *Tattvasaṃgrahapañjikā*." *Journal of the International Association of Buddhist Studies* 23.2:225–244.

——. 2003. "The Role of the 'Given' in the Classification of Śāntarakṣita and Kamalaśīla as Svātantrika-Madhyamikas." In Dreyfus and McClintock 2003:125–171.
——. 2010. *Omniscience and the Rhetoric of Reason: Śāntarakṣita and Kamalaśīla on Rationality, Argumentation, and Religious Authority*. Boston: Wisdom.
McCrea, L., and P. Patil. 2006. "Traditionalism and Innovation: Philosophy, Exegesis, and Intellectual History in Jñānaśrīmitra's *Apohaprakaraṇa*." *Journal of Indian Philosophy* 34.4:303–366.
McDaniel, J. 2008. *Gathering Leaves and Lifting Words: Histories of Buddhist Monastic Education in Laos and Thailand*. Seattle: University of Washington Press.
McMahan, D. 1998. "Orality, Writing, and Authority in South Asian Buddhism: Visionary Literature and the Struggle for Legitimacy in the Mahāyāna." *History of Religions* 37.3:249–274.
Meisig, K. 1987. *Das* Śrāmaṇyaphala-sūtra*: Synoptische Übersetzung und Glossar der chinesischen Fassungen verglichen mit dem Sanskrit und Pāli*. Freiburger Beiträge zur Indologie 19. Wiesbaden: O. Harrassowitz.
Mejor, M. 1991. *Vasubandhu's Abhidharmakośa and the Commentaries Preserved in the Tanjur*. Alt- und Neu- Indische Studien 42. Stuttgart: Franz Steiner Verlag.
Mills, M. 2003. *Identity, Ritual, and State in Tibetan Buddhism: The Foundations of Authority in Gelukpa Monasticism*. London: RoutledgeCurzon.
Mimaki, K. 1980. "Sur le rôle de l'*antaraśloka* ou du *saṃgrahaśloka*." In *Indianisme et Bouddhisme: Mélanges offerts à Mgr Étienne Lamotte*, 233–244. Louvain-la-Neuve: Institut Orientaliste de l'Université Catholique.
Mishra, Y., ed. 2004. *The Śatapathabrāhmana According to the Mādhyandina Recension with the Vedārthaprakāśa Bhāṣya of Sāyaṇācārya Supplemented by the Commentary of Harisvāmin*. Part 1. Varanasi: Sampurnanand Sanskrit University.
Mitsuhara, H., et al., eds. 2002. *Mahāvyutpatti*. Accessed at http://texa.human.is.tohoku.ac.jp/aiba/archive/mvyut/open/.
Mochizuki, K. 1995. "Die von Atiśa im Mahāsūtrasamuccaya zitieren *sūtren*." *Journal of Indian and Buddhist Studies* 44.1:479–476.
Monier-Williams, M. 1988. *A Sanskrit-English Dictionary*. Oxford: Clarendon.
Mori, S. 1990. "The Origin and the History of the Bhānaka Tradition." In Karunadasa 1990:123–129.
Müller, F. M. 1881. *Buddhist Texts from Japan*. Vol. 1, part 1. Oxford: Clarendon Press.
Nakamura, H. 1999 [1980]. *Indian Buddhism: A Survey with Bibliographical Notes*. Delhi: Motilal Banarsidass.
Ñāṇamoli, B., trans. 1962. *The Guide*. London: Pali Text Society.
——, trans. 1964. *The Piṭaka-Disclosure According to Kaccāna Thera*. London: Pali Text Society.
——, trans. 1999. *The Path of Purification*. Seattle: Pariyatti.
—— and B. Bodhi, trans. 1995. *The Middle Length Discourses of the Buddha: A New Translation of the Majjhima Nikāya*. Boston: Wisdom.
Nance, R. 2007. "On What Do We Rely When We Rely On Reasoning?" *Journal of Indian Philosophy* 35:149–167.
——. 2008. "Indian Buddhist Preachers Inside and Outside the Sūtras." *Religion Compass* 2.2:134–159.

——. Forthcoming. "Tall Tales, Tathāgatas, and Truth: On the 'Privileged Lie' in Indian Buddhist Literature." *Journal of the International Association of Buddhist Studies.*

——. In preparation a. "Reappraising the Reliances."

——. In preparation b. *The Logic of Explication: Vasubandhu's* Vyākhyāyukti.

Nattier, J. 1990. "Church Language and Vernacular Language in Central Asian Buddhism." *Numen* 37.2:195–219.

——. 1991. *Once Upon a Future Time: Studies in a Buddhist Prophecy of Decline.* Berkeley, CA: Asian Humanities Press.

——. 2003. *A Few Good Men.* Honolulu: University of Hawai'i Press

Nobel, J. 1937. *Suvarṇabhāsottamasūtra: Das Goldglanz-Sūtra. Ein Sanskrittext des Mahāyāna-Buddhismus.* Leipzig: Otto Harrassowitz.

Norman, K. R. 1979. "Dhammapada 97: A Misunderstood Paradox." *Indologica Taurinensia* 7:325–331.

——. 1983. *Pāli Literature.* Wiesbaden: Otto Harrassowitz.

Obermiller, E. 1931. *The History of Buddhism in India and Tibet (Chos-'byung) by Bu-ston.* Part 1. Heidelberg: Otto Harrassowitz.

——. 1932. *The History of Buddhism in India and Tibet (Chos-'byung) by Bu-ston.* Part 2. Heidelberg: Otto Harrassowitz.

Olivelle, P. 1998. *The Early Upaniṣads: Annotated Text and Translation.* Oxford: Oxford University Press.

——. 2005. *Manu's Code of Law: A Critical Edition and Translation of the* Mānavadharmaśāstra. Oxford: Oxford University Press.

Pachow, W. 2000. *A Comparative Study of the* Prātimokṣa*: On the Basis of Its Chinese, Tibetan, Sanskrit, and Pāli Versions.* Delhi: Motilal Banarsidass.

Pagel, U. 1994. "The *Bodhisattvapiṭaka* and the *Akṣayamatinirdeśa.*" In T. Skorupski, ed., *The Buddhist Forum* 3:333–373. London: School of Oriental and African Studies.

——. 1995. *The* Bodhisattvapiṭaka*: Its Doctrines, Practices, and Their Position in Mahāyāna Literature.* Tring, UK: Institute of Buddhist Studies.

——. 2008. "The Dhāraṇīs of Mahāvyutpatti #748: Origin and Formation." *Buddhist Studies Review* 24.2:151–191.

Panglung, J. 1981. *Die Erzählstoffe des Mūlasarvāstivāda-vinaya analysiert auf Grund der Tibetischen Übersetzung.* Studia Philologica Buddhica 3. Tokyo: Reiyukai Library.

Paranavitana, S., ed. 1970. *Inscriptions of Ceylon.* Vol. 1. Ceylon: Department of Archaeology.

—— and M. Dias. 2001. *Inscriptions of Ceylon.* Vol. 2, part 2. Ceylon: Department of Archaeology.

Patil, P. 2003. "On What It Is That Buddhists Think About—*Apoha* in the *Ratnakīrti-Nibandhāvalī.*" In Balcerowicz 2003:229–256.

——. 2009. *Against a Hindu God: Buddhist Philosophy of Religion in India.* New York: Columbia University Press.

——. 2010. "History, Philology, and the Philosophical Study of Sanskrit Texts: Jonardon Ganeri's *Philosophy in Classical India.*" *Journal of Indian Philosophy* 38:163–202.

Pimplapure, G., ed. *Kāṇva Śatapatha: A Critical Edition.* Bharatapuri: Nag Publishers.

Pollock, S. 1985. "The Theory of Practice and the Practice of Theory in Indian Intellectual History." *Journal of the American Oriental Society* 105.3:499–519.

——. 1989a. "The Idea of Śāstra in Traditional India." In Dallapiccola 1989:17–26.

——. 1989b. "Playing by the Rules: Śāstra and Sanskrit Literature." In Dallapiccola 1989:301–312.
——, ed. 2003. *Literary Cultures in History: Reconstructions from South Asia.* Berkeley and Los Angeles: University of California Press.
——. 2005. *The Language of the Gods in the World of Men: Sanskrit, Culture, and Power in Premodern India.* Berkeley: University of California Press.
Potter, K., ed. 1998. *Encyclopedia of Indian Philosophies*, vol. 7, *Abhidharma Buddhism to 150 A.D.* Delhi: Motilal Banarsidass.
——. 2002. *Encyclopedia of Indian Philosophies*, vol. 8, *Buddhist Philosophy from 100 to 350 A.D.* Delhi: Motilal Banarsidass.
——. 2003. *Encyclopedia of Indian Philosophies*, vol. 9, *Buddhist Philosophy from 350 to 600 A.D.* Delhi: Motilal Banarsidass.
Powers, J. 1992. *Two Commentaries on the* Saṃdhinirmocana-sūtra. Lewiston, NY: E. Mellen Press.
——. 1993. *Hermeneutics and Tradition in the* Saṃdhinirmocana-sūtra. Leiden: E. J. Brill.
——. 1995. *Wisdom of Buddha: The* Saṃdhinirmocanasūtra. Berkeley, CA: Dharma Publishing.
——. 2009. *A Bull of a Man: Images of Masculinity, Sex, and the Body in Indian Buddhism.* Cambridge, MA: Harvard University Press.
Pradhan, P., ed. 1950. *Abhidharma-samuccaya.* Santiniketan: Visva-Bharati.
Prapod, A., and P. Skilling. 1999. "Vasubandhu on Travel and Seclusion." *Manusya: Journal of Humanities* 2.1:13–24.
Prebish, C. 1975. *Buddhist Monastic Discipline: The Sanskrit Prātimokṣa Sūtras of the Mahāsaṃghikas and Mūlasarvāstivādins.* University Park: Pennsylvania State University Press.
Preisendanz, K. 2000. "Debate and Independent Reasoning vs. Tradition: On the Precarious Position of Early Nyāya." In Tsuchida and Wezler 2000:221–251.
——. 2008. "Text, Commentary, Annotation: Some Reflections on the Philosophical Genre." *Journal of Indian Philosophy* 36:599–618.
Przyluski, J. 1926–1927. *Le Concile de Rājagṛha.* 2 vols. Librairie Orientaliste Paul Geuthner.
Putnam, H. 1999. *The Threefold Cord: Mind, Body, and World.* New York: Columbia University Press.
Radicchi, A. 2002. "Two Buddhist Grammarians: Candragomin and Jayāditya." In Deshpande and Hook 2002:165–181.
Rahder, J. 1926. *Daśabhūmikasūtra.* Louvain, Belgium: J.-B. Istas.
——. 1928. *Glossary of the Sanskrit, Tibetan, Mongolian, and Chinese Versions of the* Daśabhūmikasūtra. Paris: P. Geuthner.
—— and S. Susa. 1931–1932. "The Gāthās of the *Daśabhūmikasūtra* (1) and (2)" *Eastern Buddhist* 5.4:335–359, 6.1:5–84.
Rahula, W. 1971. *Le compendium de super-doctrine (philosophie)* (Abhidharma-samuccaya) *d'Asaṅga, traduit et annoté.* Paris: Publications de L'Ecole Française d'Extrême-Orient.
Raible, W. 1990. *Erscheinungsformen kultureller Prozesse: Jahrbuch 1988 des Sonderforschungsbereichs "Übergänge und Spannungsfelder zwischen Mündlichkeit und Schriftlichkeit."* Tübingen: Gunter Narr Verlag.

Raja, K. K. 1986. "*Apoha* Theory and Pre-Dignāga Views on Sentence Meaning." In Matilal and Evans 1986:185–192.

Rani, S., ed. 1977. *Kriyā-saṃgraha—A Sanskrit Manuscript from Nepal Containing a Collection of Tantric Ritual by Kuladatta.* Śatapiṭaka Series 236. New Delhi: Sharada Rani.

Rappaport, R. 1999. *Ritual and Religion in the Making of Humanity.* Cambridge: Cambridge University Press.

Reat, N. R. 1993. *The Śālistamba Sūtra.* Delhi: Motilal Banarsidass.

Renou, L. 1963. "Sur le genre du sūtra dans la littérature sanskrite." *Journal Asiatique* 251:165–216.

Reynolds, F., and D. Tracy, eds. 1994. *Religion and Practical Reason.* Albany: State University of New York Press.

Rhys-Davids, C. A. F. 1907–1908. "Similes in the Nikāyas: A Classified Index." *Journal of the Pali Text Society* 5–6:52–251 (1907); 180–188 (1908).

Salomon, R. 1998. *Indian Epigraphy.* Oxford: Oxford University Press.

Salvini, M. 2011. "*Upādāyaprajñaptiḥ* and the Meaning of Absolutives: Grammar and Syntax in the Interpretation of Madhyamaka." *Journal of Indian Philosophy* 39.3:229–244.

Samtani, N. H. 1971. *The* Arthaviniścayasūtra *and Its Commentary* (Nibandhana*)*. Patna, India: K. P. Jayaswal Research Institute.

———. 2002. *Gathering the Meanings.* Berkeley, CA: Dharma Publishing.

Sankalia, H. D. 1934. *The University of Nālandā.* Madras: B. G. Paul and Company.

Sasaki, G. 1962. "Pariyāya und Nippariyāya." *Wiener Zeitschrift für die Kunde Süd- und Ostasiens* 6:47–59.

Sastri, H. 1929–1930. "Nālandā Stone Inscription of the Reign of Yaśovarmmadeva." *Epigraphia Indica* 20:37–46.

———. 1986. *Nālandā and Its Epigraphic Material.* Delhi: Sri Satguru Publications.

Sattar, A. 1994. *Tales from the* Kathāsaritsāgara. New York: Penguin USA.

Scharf, P. 1995. "Early Indian Grammarians on a Speaker's Intention." *Journal of the American Oriental Society* 115:66–76.

———. 2002. "Pāṇini, Vivakṣā, and Kāraka-rule-ordering." In Deshpande and Hook 2002:121–149.

Scherrer-Schaub, C. 1981. "Le terme yukti: Première etude." *Asiatische Studien* 35.2: 185–199.

Schoening, J. 1992. "The *Ārya-śālistambasya-ṭīkā*: Kamalaśīla's Commentary on the *Śālistamba-sūtra*." In Ihara and Yamaguchi 1992:221–236.

———. 1995. *The* Śālistamba Sūtra *and Its Indian Commentaries.* 2 vols. Vienna: Arbeitskreis für Tibetische und Buddhische Studien.

———. 1996. "Sūtra Commentaries in Tibetan Translation." In Cabezón and Jackson 1996:111–124.

Schopen, G. 1975. "The phrase '*sa pṛthivīpradeśaś caityabhūto bhavet*' in the *Vajracchedikā*: Notes on the Cult of the Book in Mahāyāna." *Indo-Iranian Journal* 17:147–181.

———. 1989a. "A Verse from the *Bhadracaripraṇidhāna* in a Tenth-Century Inscription Found at Nālandā." *Journal of the International Association of Buddhist Studies* 12.1:149–157; reprinted in Schopen 2005:299–305.

———. 1989b. "The Manuscript of the *Vajracchedikā* Found at Gilgit." In Gómez and Silk 1989:89–139.

——. 1994. "Doing Business for the Lord: Lending on Interest and Written Loan Contracts in the *Mūlasarvāstivāda-vinaya*." *Journal of the American Oriental Society* 114.4:527–554; reprinted in Schopen 2004:45–90.

——. 1996. "The Lay Ownership of Monasteries and the Role of the Monk in Mūlasarvāstivādin Monasticism." *Journal of the International Association of Buddhist Studies* 19.1:81–126; reprinted in Schopen 2004:219–259.

——. 1997a. *Bones, Stones, and Buddhist Monks*. Honolulu: University of Hawai'i Press.

——. 1997b. "If You Can't Remember, How to Make It Up: Some Monastic Rules for Redacting Canonical Texts." In Kieffer-Pülz and Hartmann 1997:571–582; reprinted in Schopen 2004:395–407.

——. 1998. "Marking Time in Buddhist Monasteries: On Calendars, Clocks, and Some Liturgical Practices." In Harrison and Schopen 1998:157–180; reprinted in Schopen 2004:260–284.

——. 2004. *Buddhist Monks and Business Matters: Still More Papers on Monastic Buddhism in India*. Honolulu: University of Hawai'i Press.

——. 2005. *Figments and Fragments of Mahāyāna Buddhism in India*. Honolulu: University of Hawai'i Press.

——. 2008. "Separate but Equal: Property Rights and the Legal Independence of Buddhist Nuns and Monks in Early North India." *Journal of the American Oriental Society* 128.4:625–640.

Seyfort Ruegg, D. 1981. *The Literature of the Madhyamaka School of Philosophy in India*. Wiesbaden: Otto Harrassowitz.

——. 1989. *Buddha-Nature, Mind, and the Problem of Gradualism in a Comparative Perspective: On the Transmission and Reception of Buddhism in India and Tibet*. Jordan Lectures in Comparative Religion 13. London: School of Oriental and African Studies.

——. 1992. "On the Tibetan Historiography and Doxography of the 'Great Debate of bSam yas.'" In Ihara and Yamaguchi 1992:237–244.

——. 1994. "*Pramāṇabhūta*, **Pramāṇa(bhūta)-puruṣa*, *Pratyakṣadharman*, and *Sākṣātkṛtadharman* as epithets of the Ṛṣi, Ācārya, and Tathāgata in Grammatical, Epistemological, and Madhyamaka Texts." *Bulletin of the School of Oriental and African Studies* 57.2:301–320.

——. 1995. *Ordre spirituel et ordre temporel dans la pensée bouddhique de l'Inde et du Tibet*. Paris: Institut de civilisation indienne, College de France.

Sharf, R. 1995. "Buddhist Modernism and the Rhetoric of Meditative Experience." *Numen* 42:228–283.

——. 2002. *Coming to Terms with Chinese Buddhism*. Honolulu: University of Hawai'i Press.

Shastri, B., ed. 2001. *Patañjali's* Vyākaraṇa Mahābhāṣya *with Kaiyaṭa's* Pradīpa *and Nāgojibhaṭṭa's* Uddyota *and Bhaṭṭoji Dīkṣita's* Śabdakaustubha. Delhi: Pratibha Prakashan.

Shastri, D., ed. 1994. Pramāṇavārttika *of Ācārya Dharmakīrti with the Commentary 'Vṛtti' of Ācārya Manorathanandin*. Series 3. Varanasi: Bauddha Bharati.

——, ed. 1997 [1968]. *Tattvasaṃgrahapañjikā*. 2 vols. Varanasi: Bauddha Bharati.

——, ed. 1998 [1973]. *Abhidharmakośabhāṣya*. 2 vols. Varanasi: Bauddha Bharati.

Sherburne, R. 2000. *The Complete Works of Atīśa Śrī Dīpaṃkara Jñāna, Jo-bo-rje*. New Delhi: Aditya Prakashan.

Shinohara, K., and G. Schopen, eds. 1991. *From Benares to Beijing: Essays on Buddhism and Chinese Religion in Honour of Jan Yün-Hua*. Oakville, Ontario: Mosaic Press.

Shukla, K. 1973. Śrāvakabhūmi *of Ācārya Asaṅga*. Patna, India: K. P. Jayaswal Research Institute.

Siderits, M. 1985. "Word Meaning, Sentence Meaning, and Apoha." *Journal of Indian Philosophy* 13:133–151.

Silk, J. 1989. "A Note on the Opening Formula of Buddhist Sūtras." *Journal of the International Association of Buddhist Studies* 12.1:158–163.

——, ed. 2000. *Wisdom, Compassion, and the Search for Understanding: The Buddhist Studies Legacy of Gadjin M. Nagao*. Honolulu: University of Hawai'i Press.

——. 2001. "Contributions to the Study of the Philosophical Vocabulary of Mahāyāna Buddhism." *Eastern Buddhist* 33.1:144–168.

——. 2002. "What, If Anything, Is Mahāyāna Buddhism? Problems of Definitions and Classifications." *Numen* 49:355–405.

——. 2008. *Managing Monks: Administrators and Administrative Roles in Indian Buddhist Monasticism*. Oxford: Oxford University Press.

Sinha, B. P. 1954. *The Decline of the Kingdom of Magadha, Circa 455–1000 A.D.* Bankipore, India: Motilal Banarsidass.

Sinor, D., ed. 1968. *Studies in South, East, and Central Asia*. New Delhi: International Academy of Indian Culture.

Sircar, D. 1967. *Inscriptions of Aśoka*, Rev. ed. Delhi: Government of India Publications Division.

Skilling, P. 1997a. *Mahāsūtras: Great Discourses of the Buddha*. Vol. 2, parts 1 and 2. Oxford: Pali Text Society.

——. 1997b. "From bKa' bstan bcos to bKa' 'gyur and bsTan 'gyur." In Steinkellner 1997:87–111.

——. 2000. "Vasubandhu and the *Vyākhyāyukti* Literature." *Journal of the International Association of Buddhist Studies* 23.2:297–350.

——. 2009. "Redaction, Recitation, and Writing: Transmission of the Buddha's Teaching in India in the Early Period." In Berkwitz et al. 2009:53–75.

Skilton, A. 2002. "State or Statement? Samādhi in Some Early Mahāyāna Sūtras." *Eastern Buddhist* 34.2:51–90.

Skorupski, T., ed. 1990. *The Buddhist Forum*, vol. 1, *Seminar Papers, 1987–1988*. New Delhi: Heritage.

——, ed. 1992. *The Buddhist Forum*, vol. 2, *Seminar Papers, 1988–1990*. New Delhi: Heritage.

——. 2002. *Kriyāsaṃgraha: Compendium of Buddhist Rituals (An Abridged Version)*. Tring, UK: Institute of Buddhist Studies.

Slaje, W., ed. 2008. *Śāstrārambha: Inquiries into the Preamble in Sanskrit*. Wiesbaden: Harrassowitz Verlag.

Snellgrove, D. 1987. *Indo-Tibetan Buddhism: Indian Buddhists and Their Tibetan Successors*. 2 vols. Boston: Shambhala.

Solomon, E. 1976. *Indian Dialectics: Methods of Philosophical Discussion*. 2 vols. Ahmedabad: B. J. Institute of Learning and Research.

Sparham, G., trans. 2006–2009. *Abhisamayālaṃkāra with Vṛtti and Āloka (I–IV)*. 3 vols. Fremont, CA: Jain Publishing.

Staal, F. 1972. *A Reader in the Sanskrit Grammarians*. Cambridge, MA: MIT Press.
Stcherbatsky, T. 1918. *Nyāyabiṇḍu*. Petrograd: Imperial Academy of Sciences.
—— and E. Obermiller, eds. 1977. *Abhisamayālaṅkāra-prajñāpāramitā-upadeśā-śāstra*. Fascicle 1. Tokyo: Meicho-Fukyū-Kai.
Steinkellner, E. 1978. "Remarks on Tantristic Hermeneutics." In Ligeti 1978:445–458.
——. 1989. "Who Is Byang chub rdzu 'phrul? Tibetan and Non-Tibetan Commentaries on the *Saṃdhinirmocanasūtra*—A Survey of the Literature." *Berliner Indologische Studien* 4/5:229–251.
——, ed. 1991. *Studies in the Buddhist Epistemological Tradition: Proceedings of the Second International Dharmakīrti Conference, Vienna, June 11-16, 1989*. Vienna: Österreichischen Akademie der Wissenschaften.
——, ed. 1997. *Tibetan Studies: Proceedings of the Seventh Seminar of the International Association for Tibetan Studies, Graz 1995*. Vienna: Verlag der Österreichischen Akademie der Wissenschaften.
——. 2003. "Once More on Circles." In Balcerowicz 2003:323–341.
——. 2004. "An Old Transmissional Mistake in Pātrasvāmin's Definition of the Logical Reason as Quoted by Śāntarakṣita and Jinendrabuddhi." In Bodewitz and Hara 2004:185–188.
—— and M. T. Much. 1995. *Texte der erkenntnistheoretischen Schule des Buddhismus*. Göttingen: Vandenhoeck and Ruprecht.
Stewart, M. 1989. *Nālandā Mahāvihāra: A Study of an Indian Pāla Period Buddhist Site and British Historical Archaeology, 1981-1938*. BAR International Series 529. Oxford: British Archaeological Reports.
Strong, J. 1992. *The Legend and Cult of Upagupta: Sanskrit Buddhism in North India and Southeast Asia*. Princeton, NJ: Princeton University Press.
Studholme, A. 2002. *The Origins of Oṃ Maṇipadme Hūṃ: A Study of the* Kāraṇḍavyūha Sūtra. Albany: State University of New York Press.
Sukthankar, V., et al., eds. 1933–1966. *The Mahābhārata for the First Time Critically Edited*. 19 vols. Pune: Bhandarkar Oriental Institute.
Suzuki, D. T., ed. 1960. *Catalogue and Index: The Tibetan Tripiṭaka, Peking Edition, Reprinted under the Supervision of the Otani University*. Vols. 165–168. Tokyo: Suzuki Research Foundation.
Taber, J. 1996. "Is Verbal Testimony a Form of Inference?" *Studies in Humanities and Social Sciences* 3.2:19–31.
Takakusu, J., trans. 1966 [1896]. *A Record of Buddhist Religion as Practiced in India and the Malay Archipelago*. Delhi: Munishram Manoharlal.
—— and M. Nakai, eds. 1934. *Samantapāsādikā: Buddhaghosa's Commentary on the Vinaya Piṭaka*. Vol. 4. London: Luzac and Company.
Tatia, N. 1976. *Abhidharmasamuccaya-bhāṣyam*. Patna, India: K. P. Jayaswal Research Institute.
Tatz, M. 1982. *Candragomin's Twenty Verses on the Bodhisattva Vow and Its Commentary by Sakya Dragpa Gyaltsen*. Dharamsala: Library of Tibetan Works and Archives.
——. 1986. *Asaṅga's Chapter on Ethics with the Commentary of Tsong-Kha-Pa, the Basic Path to Awakening, the Complete Bodhisattva*. Lewiston, NY: Edwin Mellen Press.
——. 1993. "Brief Communication." *Indo-Iranian Journal* 36:335–336.

Teiser, S. 2006. *Reinventing the Wheel: Paintings of Rebirth in Medieval Buddhist Temples.* Seattle: University of Washington Press.

Thakur, A., ed. 1967. Nyāyadarśana *of Gautama, with the* Bhāṣya *of Vātsyāyana, the* Vārttika *of Uddyotakara, the* Tātpāryaṭīkā *of Vācaspati, and the* Pariśuddhi *of Udayana.* Vol. 1, chap. 1. Darbhanga, India: Mithila Institute of Post-Graduate Studies and Research in Sanskrit Learning.

Thurman, R. 1988. "Vajra Hermeneutics." In Lopez 1988a:119–148.

Tillemans, T. 1993. *Persons of Authority.* Stuttgart: F. Steiner Verlag.

——. 1997. "On a Recent Translation of the *Saṃdhinirmocanasūtra.*" *Journal of the International Association of Buddhist Studies* 20.1:153–164.

——. 1999. *Scripture, Logic, Language: Essays on Dharmakīrti and His Tibetan Successors.* Boston: Wisdom.

——. 2000. *Dharmakīrti's Pramāṇavārttika: An Annotated Translation of the Fourth Chapter (Parārthānumāna), Vol. I (k. 1–148).* Vienna: Verlag der Österreichischen Akademie der Wissenschaften.

Timm, J., ed. 1992. *Texts in Context: Traditional Hermeneutics in South Asia.* Albany: State University of New York Press.

Travis, C. 1989. *The Uses of Sense: Wittgenstein's Philosophy of Language.* Oxford: Oxford University Press.

——.1996. "Meaning's Role in Truth." *Mind* 105:451–66.

——. 1997. "Pragmatics." In Hale and Wright 1997:87–107.

——. 2000. *Unshadowed Thought.* Cambridge, MA: Harvard University Press.

Tsuchida, R., and A. Wezler, eds. 2000. *Harānandalaharī: Volume in Honour of Professor Minoru Hara on His Seventieth Birthday.* Reinbek: Verlag für Orientalistische Fachpublikationen.

Tubb, G., and E. Boose. 2007. *Scholastic Sanskrit: A Manual for Students.* New York: American Institute of Buddhist Studies.

Tucci, G. 1928. "Is the *Nyāyapraveśa* by Dignāga?" *Journal of the Royal Asiatic Society*:7–15.

——. 1956. *Minor Buddhist Texts.* Part 1. Rome: Instituto Italiano per il Medio ed Estremo Oriente.

——. 1958. *Minor Buddhist Texts.* Part 2. Rome: Instituto Italiano per il Medio ed Estremo Oriente.

——. 1971. *Minor Buddhist Texts.* Part 3. Rome: Instituto Italiano per il Medio ed Estremo Oriente.

Ui, H., et al. 1934. *A Complete Catalogue of the Tibetan Buddhist Canons.* Tokyo: Tōhoku Imperial University.

Vaidya, P. L., ed. 1958. *Lalitavistaraḥ.* Darbhanga, India: Mithila Institute of Post-Graduate Studies and Research in Sanskrit Learning.

——. 1960a. *Saddharmapuṇḍarīkasūtra.* Darbhanga, India: Mithila Institute of Post-Graduate Studies and Research in Sanskrit Learning.

——. 1960b. Bodhicaryāvatāra *of Śāntideva, with the Commentary* Pañjikā *of Prajñākaramati.* Darbhanga, India: Mithila Institute of Post-Graduate Studies and Research in Sanskrit Learning.

——. 1960c. Aṣṭasāhasrikāprajñāpāramitā *with Haribhadra's Commentary Called* Āloka. Darbhanga, India: Mithila Institute of Post-Graduate Studies and Research in Sanskrit Learning.

——. 1960d. *Gaṇḍavyūhasūtra*. Darbhanga, India: Mithila Institute of Post-Graduate Studies and Research in Sanskrit Learning.
——. 1961a. *Samādhirājasūtra*. Darbhanga, India: Mithila Institute of Post-Graduate Studies and Research in Sanskrit Learning.
——. 1961b. Śikṣāsamuccaya *of Śāntideva*. Darbhanga, India: Mithila Institute of Post-Graduate Studies and Research in Sanskrit Learning.
——. 1961c. *Mahāyānasūtrasaṃgraha*. Vol. 1. Darbhanga, India: Mithila Institute of Post-Graduate Studies and Research in Sanskrit Learning.
——. 1963. *Saddharmalaṅkāvatārasūtram*. Darbhanga, India: Mithila Institute of Post-Graduate Studies and Research in Sanskrit Learning.
——. 1967. *Daśabhūmikasūtra*. Darbhanga, India: Mithila Institute of Post-Graduate Studies and Research in Sanskrit Learning.
Van Bijlert, V. 1989. *Epistemology and Spiritual Authority*. Vienna: Arbeitskreis für Tibetische und Buddhistische Studien Universität Wien.
Van der Kuijp, L. 1983. *Contributions to the Development of Tibetan Buddhist Epistemology*. Wiesbaden: Franz Steiner Verlag.
——. 1984. "Miscellanea to a Recent Contribution on/to the bSam-yas Debate" *Kailash* 11:149–184.
Van Nooten, B. 1983. "*Vivakṣā*, or Intention to Speak, as a Linguistic Principle." In Joshi and Laddu 1983:43–52.
Veidlinger, D. 2006. *Spreading the Dhamma: Writing, Orality, and Textual Transmission in Buddhist Northern Thailand*. Honolulu: University of Hawai'i Press.
Verhagen, P. 2005. "Studies in Indo-Tibetan Buddhist Hermeneutics (4): The *Vyākhyāyukti* by Vasubandhu." *Journal Asiatique* 293.2:559–602.
Vidyābhūṣana, S. C. 1990. *The Nyāya Sūtras of Gotama*. Delhi: Motilal Banarsidass.
Vogel, J. 1929. "Prakrit Inscriptions from a Buddhist Site at Nāgārjunikoṇḍa." *Epigraphia Indica* 20:11–12.
Vostrikov, A. I. 1970. *Tibetan Historical Literature*. Trans. H. C. Gupta. Calcutta: R. D. Press.
Walshe, M. 1995. *The Long Discourses of the Buddha: A Translation of the Dīgha Nikāya*. Somerville, MA: Wisdom.
Walter, M. 2009. *Buddhism and Empire: The Political and Religious Culture of Early Tibet*. Leiden: Brill.
Wangdu, P., and H. Diemberger, trans. 2000. *Dba' bzhed: The Royal Narrative Concerning the Bringing of the Buddha's Doctrine to Tibet*. Vienna: Verlag der Österreichischen Akademie der Wissenschaften.
Warder, A. K. 1974. *Indian Kāvya Literature*. Vol. 2. Delhi: Motilal Banarsidass.
Wezler, Albrecht. 1998. "Medhātithi on the Role of Manu, the Prayojana of the Manusmṛti, and the Incentive of the Brahmins to Study It." In Harrison and Schopen 1998:217–240.
Williams, P. 1989. *Mahāyāna Buddhism: The Doctrinal Foundations*. London: Routledge.
—— with A. Tribe. 2000. *Buddhist Thought: A Complete Introduction to the Indian Tradition*. London: Routledge.
Woodward, F. 2006 [1932]. *The Book of the Gradual Sayings (Aṅguttara-Nikāya), or, More-Numbered Suttas*, vol. 2, *The Book of the Fours*. Delhi: Motilal Banarsidass.

Wynne, A. 2004. "The Oral Transmission of Early Buddhist Literature." *Journal of the International Association of Buddhist Studies* 27.1:97–127.

Yuyama, A. 1981. *Sanskrit Fragments of the Mahāyāna Mahāparinirvāṇasūtra 1: Koyasan Manuscript*. Studia Philologica Buddhica, Occasional Paper Series 4. Tokyo: Reiyukai Library.

——. 1996. "A Critical Survey of Philological Studies of the *Daśabhūmika-sūtra*." In Hahn, Hartmann, and Steiner 1996:263–280.

Zhang Yisun, ed. 1999. *Bod kyi tshig mdzod chen mo*. 2 vols. Lhasa: Mi rigs dpe skrun khang.

Index of Texts

Index